Other Kaplan Books Related to Business School Admissions:

GMAT

GMAT with CD-ROM

GMAT Verbal Workbook

GRE & GMAT Exams Math Workbook

Get Your M.B.A. Part-Time: For the Part-Time Student with a Full-Time Life

Test Prep and Admissions

GMAT® 800
2005–2006 Edition

by Eric Goodman
and the Staff of Kaplan Test Prep and Admissions

Simon & Schuster

NEW YORK · LONDON · SYDNEY · TORONTO

Kaplan Publishing
Published by Simon & Schuster
1230 Avenue of the Americas
New York, NY 10020

For bulk sales to schools, colleges, and universities, please contact:
Order Department, Simon & Schuster, 100 Front Street, Riverside, N. J. 08075
Phone: (800) 223-2336, Fax: (800) 943-9831

Contributing Editor: Justin Serrano
Executive Editor: Jennifer Farthing
Project Editor: Ruth Baygell
Production Manager: Michael Shevlin
Interior Page Layout: Hugh Haggerty
Cover Design: Cheung Tai

Manufactured in the United States of America
Published simultaneously in Canada

March 2005
10 9 8 7 6 5 4 3
ISBN: 0-7432-6528-9

Table of Contents

Section Five: Problem Solving–Word Problems

Section Six: Data Sufficiency

About the Authors

Eric Goodman began teaching and writing for Kaplan two years after graduating from Cornell University. For over 12 years Eric has written courses, software, and books that have helped thousands of test takers master the GMAT, LSAT, and GRE. As an instructional designer, he has also authored online courses and computer-based simulations in the fields of economics, corporate training, and E-commerce. Eric lives in New York City with his wife Cathy and daughters Memphis and Dasha.

Michelle Karnes began teaching for Kaplan in 1996 and has since taught Kaplan's GMAT, LSAT, GRE, and SAT courses. She has also written online and Home Study instructional materials for Kaplan's GMAT and LSAT courses. Michelle is currently teaching at the Philadelphia Kaplan center and working toward a Ph.D in literature from the University of Pennsylvania.

Ed Downey is an instructional designer in New York City. Along with other projects, he has worked on standardized tests for much of the past 15 years. He graduated from New York University with an honors degree in philosophy.

kaptest.com/publishing

The material in this book is up-to-date at the time of publication. However, the Graduate Management Admission Council may have instituted changes in the test after this book was published. Be sure to carefully read the materials you receive when you register for the test.

If there are any important late-breaking developments—or any changes or corrections to the Kaplan test preparation materials in this book—we will post that information online at **kaptest.com/publishing**. Check to see if there is any information posted there regarding this book.

kaplansurveys.com/books

We'd love to hear your comments and suggestions about this book. We invite you to fill out our online survey form at **kaplansurveys.com/books**. Your feedback is extremely helpful as we continue to develop high-quality resources to meet your needs.

The Perfect Score

Ah, *perfection* . . . We humans are a demanding bunch. We don't bound out of bed in the morning aspiring to mediocrity, but rather striving for *perfection*. The *perfect* mate. The *perfect* job. The *perfect* shoes to go with the *perfect* outfit. We head to the beach on a *perfect* summer day to find the *perfect* spot to get the *perfect* tan.

Webster's defines perfection as "the quality or state of being complete and correct in every way, conforming to a standard or ideal with no omissions, errors, flaws or extraneous elements."

The GMAT test makers define perfection as a score of 800. If GMAT perfection is what you're after, then you've come to the right place. We at Kaplan have been training test takers to ace the GMAT for decades. We understand your desire for the highest possible score. For those of you shooting for the moon, we salute your quest for perfection. The *perfect* GMAT score. The *perfect* business school. The *perfect* career. Do we have the *perfect* book for you? You bet we do. You're holding it in your hands.

ABOUT THE GMAT

The GMAT is a standardized test that helps business schools assess the qualifications of students entering into their programs. Though many factors play a role in admissions decisions, the GMAT score is usually an important one. And, generally speaking, being average just won't cut it. While the median GMAT score is somewhere around 500, you need a score of at least 600 to be considered competitive by the top B-schools.

The first thing to know about the GMAT is that it is a computer-adaptive test (CAT); that is, a test taken on computer at a private workstation, scheduled at your convenience in a test-center near you. In a CAT, you see only one question at a time. Instead of having a predetermined mixture of basic, medium, and hard questions, the computer selects questions based on how well you are doing. You cannot skip a question, and you cannot move around within a section to check a previous answer.

The GMAT measures basic verbal, math, and analytical writing skills. You'll begin at the computer with the two **Analytical Writing Assessments**—essays on assigned topics—each 30 minutes. Then you'll move on to the two 75-minute multiple-choice sections: **Math (Quantitative)** and **Verbal**. The Math section—37 questions in all—contains two question types: Problem-Solving and Data Sufficiency. The Verbal section, with 41 questions, has three question types: Reading Comprehension, Sentence Correction, and Critical Reasoning.

Overall scaled scores range from 200–800. Because the test is graded on a preset curve, the scaled score will correspond to a certain percentile. So an overall score of 590, say, corresponds to the 80th percentile, meaning that 80 percent of test takers scored at or below that same level. The percentile helps business school admissions officers to see where you fall in a large pool of applicants.

For complete registration information about the GMAT, download the GMAT Information Bulletin from **mba.com/mba/TaketheGMAT**.

WHO SHOULD USE THIS BOOK

We should warn you up front: This book is not for the faint at heart. It is comprised exclusively of examples of the toughest material you're likely to see on the GMAT. No easy stuff, no run-of-the-mill strategies—just killer problems, passages, and questions, complete with Kaplan's proven techniques to help you transcend "above average" and enter the rarified arena of GMAT elite. If you're entertaining the notion of pulling off the perfect 800, then you're going to have to face down the most brutal material the GMAT test makers have to offer. Even if a perfect score is not your immediate goal, diligent practice with the difficult material in this book can help develop your skills and raise your score. If you're looking for a more fundamental introduction to the GMAT, or practice with questions ranging from easy to difficult, then we recommend working through the traditional Kaplan GMAT book as a prerequisite for the highly challenging material contained in this volume.

HOW TO USE THIS BOOK

This book is divided into sections corresponding to the scored question types contained on the GMAT: Critical Reasoning, Reading Comprehension, Sentence Correction, Problem Solving, and Data Sufficiency. *(Note: The Analytical Writing Assessment is not included in this book because it doesn't contribute to your 200-800 score, and no AWA prompt is written to be any more difficult than any other.)* Each section provides detailed guidelines on how to make the most of the material. Jump right to the section that gives you the most trouble, or work through the sections in the order presented—it's up to you.

No matter what you do, try not to overload; remember that this is dense, complicated material, and not representative of the range of difficulty you'll see on test day. One thing's for sure: If you can ace this stuff, the real thing will be a breeze. Good luck, and enjoy!

KAPLAN

A Special Note for International Students

The M.B.A. (Master of Business Administration) has become a degree of choice for businesspersons around the globe. Variations of U.S.-style M.B.A. programs exist in Asia, Europe, and the Americas. In recent years, hundreds of thousands of international students have studied business and management in the United States.

As the United States increases its participation in the global economy, U.S. business schools are reaching out to attract exceptional international candidates into their graduate programs. However, competition for admission to prestigious programs is heavy and international students need to plan carefully if they wish to enter a top U.S. graduate management program.

If you are not from the United States, but are considering attending a graduate management program at a university in the United States, here is what you'll need to get started.

- If English is not your first language, you'll probably need to take the Test of English as a Foreign Language (TOEFL®) or show some other evidence that you are proficient in English. Some graduate business schools now require a minimum TOEFL score of 550 (213 on the computer-based TOEFL), while others will require a 600 (250 on the computer-based TOEFL). The ability to communicate in English, both verbally and in writing, is extremely important to your success in an American M.B.A. program.

- You may also need to take the GMAT® (Graduate Management Admissions Test). Some graduate business programs may require you to take the GRE® (Graduate Record Examination) as well.

- Since admission to many graduate business programs is quite competitive, you may wish to select three or four programs you would like to attend.

- Select a program that meets your current or future employment needs, rather than simply a program with a big name. For example, if you hope to work in the hotel and tourism industry, make sure the program you choose specializes in that distinct area.

- You need to begin the application process at least a year in advance. Be aware that many programs only offer August or September start dates.

- Finally, you will need to obtain an 1-20 Certificate of Eligibility from the school you plan to attend if you intend to apply for an F-1 Student Visa to study in the United States.

Kaplan English Programs*

If you need more help with the complex process of business school admissions, assistance preparing for the TOEFL or GMAT, or help improving your English skills in general, you may be interested in Kaplan's programs for international students.

Kaplan International Programs were designed to help students and professionals from outside the United States meet their educational and career goals. At locations throughout the United States, international students take advantage of Kaplan's programs to help them improve their academic and conversational English skills, raise their scores on the TOEFL, GMAT, and other standardized exams, and gain admission to the schools of their choice. Here is a brief description of some of Kaplan's programs for International Students:

General Intensive English

Kaplan's General Intensive English classes are designed to help you improve your skills in all areas of English and to increase your fluency in spoken and written English. Classes are available for beginning to advanced students, and the average class size is 12 students.

TOEFL and Academic English

This course provides you with the skills you need to improve your TOEFL score and succeed in an American university or graduate program. It includes advanced reading, writing, listening, grammar, and conversational English. You will also receive training for the TOEFL using Kaplan's exclusive computer-based practice materials.

GMAT Test Preparation Course

The Graduate Management Admissions Test (GMAT) is required for admission to many graduate programs in business in the United States. Hundreds of thousands of American students have taken this course to prepare for the GMAT. This course includes the skills you need to succeed on each section of the GMAT, as well as access to Kaplan's exclusive computer-based practice materials.

Other Kaplan Programs

Since 1938, more than 3 million students have come to Kaplan to advance their studies, prepare for entry to American universities, and further their careers. In addition to the above programs, Kaplan offers courses to prepare for the SAT®, GRE®, LSAT®, MCAT®, DAT®, USMLE®, NCLEX®, and other standardized exams at locations throughout the United States.

Applying to Kaplan English Programs

To get more information, or to apply for admission to any of Kaplan's programs for international students and professionals, contact us at:

Kaplan International Programs
700 South Flower, Suite 2900
Los Angeles, CA 90017, USA
Phone: (213) 385-2358
Fax: (213) 383-1364
Website: www.kaplanenglish.com
Email: world@kaplan.com

FREE Services for International Students

Kaplan now offers international students many services online—*free of charge*! Students may assess their TOEFL skills and gain valuable feedback on their English language proficiency in just a few hours with Kaplan's TOEFL Skills Assessment. Log onto www.kaplanenglish.com today.

---

*Kaplan is authorized under federal law to enroll nonimmigrant alien students. Kaplan is accredited by ACCET (Accrediting Council for Continuing Education and Training).

section one

CRITICAL REASONING

CHAPTER ONE

The Critical Reasoning Challenge

Do you like to point out the assumptions in others' arguments? Do you like to home in on logical flaws like a detective, and analyze precisely how arguments could be made better, or worse? Then GMAT Critical Reasoning is for you. So start dissecting op-ed pieces and cutting the contestants on television debates down to size. When you see your GMAT score, you'll be glad you did!

Which of the following can be most properly inferred from the passage above?

(A) Mastering the Critical Reasoning question type will ensure an excellent GMAT score.

(B) No question type contained on the GMAT is represented in more sections of the GMAT than is Critical Reasoning.

(C) Op-ed pieces and television debates contain content that is related in some way to material tested in GMAT Critical Reasoning.

(D) Logical flaws and assumptions are question types that appear only on the GMAT.

(E) Thinking like a detective has no impact on one's GMAT score.

Explanation: Choice (C) is correct. The final two sentences strongly imply that dissecting op-eds and debates will lead to a higher score, which, in fact, it certainly can. There must therefore be some relation between GMAT content and the content of these forums. As for the others:

Mastering Critical Reasoning is *necessary* to achieve a top GMAT score, but is not *sufficient*; one must ace the other content areas of the test as well. So (A) is not inferable. There's no basis for (B) either—the number of sections on the test is outside the scope of the argument. (D) isn't inferable. For all we know, other tests such as the LSAT test these same areas. And (E) represents the opposite of what the passage suggests: The instructor strongly implies that the proclivity for playing detective is relevant to (hence, inferably bodes well for) one's Critical Reasoning performance.

So win arguments! Prove people wrong! Amaze your friends! Be the life of the party! Get an 800 on the GMAT! … Just a few of the many and varied uses of the ability to master the subtle art of Critical Reasoning.

Disclaimer: Hacking through the bogus arguments of others and/or demonstrating superior logical acumen in everyday conversation will NOT make you the most popular person in town.

However, the ability to do so *will* do wonders for your GMAT score. The purpose of this section is to help you hone your critical thinking skills through practice on some of the toughest Critical Reasoning material around.

USING THE CRITICAL REASONING QUESTIONS IN THIS BOOK

This section is broken up into chapters that detail various difficulties commonly encountered in GMAT Critical Reasoning. It is designed to allow you to learn as you go and to apply your learning to subsequent questions as you progress through the section.

- In chapter 2 you'll be introduced to *seven major categories* of difficult Critical Reasoning questions, each highlighted by an example.

- In chapter 3 you'll find *seven more questions* that test whether or not you can recognize the distinctions and logical elements introduced in the first group.

- Finally, chapter 4 offers *28 additional questions representative of all the elements and forms discussed* in the previous chapters.

STRATEGIES FOR CRITICAL REASONING

Here are a few general pointers to keep in mind when tackling all Critical Reasoning questions, but especially the challenging questions like the ones you're about to see:

Keep your eye out for the author's evidence, conclusion, and any assumptions relied upon in the argument. The wordiness and logical subtlety of the questions that follow often cause test-takers to lose sight of what's actually being said, and it's nearly impossible to answer questions like these correctly when one is foggy about the specifics. The conclusion is the "what" of the matter; the evidence is the reasons "why" the author feels entitled to make that particular claim; and assumptions are any missing premises that are nonetheless needed in order for the conclusion to stand.

Paraphrase the text. You can get a leg up on tough text by simplifying the passage's ideas and translating them into your own words. The same goes for the longer Reading Comprehension passages.

Familiarize yourself with the common Critical Reasoning concepts tested. Review the logical elements and structures discussed throughout the section, and look to recognize which of them are present in each Critical Reasoning question you encounter in this book as well as in any other questions you practice with during your GMAT preparation. While the specific subjects you'll encounter (names, places, scenarios, etc.) will naturally be different from those you'll see on your test, the underlying logical patterns remain incredibly consistent. Use the questions and explanations that follow to get to know them.

CHAPTER TWO

Seven Categories of Difficult Critical Reasoning Questions

1. NUMBERS AND STATISTICS

The GMAT test makers just *love* their statistics. Perhaps that's because statistics are used these days—often fallaciously—to supposedly "prove" or justify just about anything. That makes numbers and statistics a particularly fertile ground for Weaken the Argument questions, or, as in the present case, a plain old Inference question that requires us to simply interpret the stats.

1. The paintings of French painter Trianne Dejere sold best in the period following the production of La Triumph, now Dejere's most famous piece. In the twelve month period preceding the unveiling of this piece, Dejere sold 57% of the works she produced in this period, a far greater percentage than in previous years. In the twelve month period following a glowing review of La Triumph in a popular magazine, however, Dejere sold 85% of the paintings she produced. Interestingly, Dejere's revenue from painting sales was roughly the same in both periods, since she sold the same number of paintings in the twelve months before presenting La Triumph as she did in the twelve months following the favorable review.

   Which of the following statements can be properly concluded from the passage, if the information above is true?

   (A) Due to the positive review, Dejere was able to charge substantially more for the works produced after La Triumph than the works produced before it.

   (B) Dejere was more concerned with positive reviews than with increasing the prices of her paintings.

   (C) The positive review of La Triumph brought Dejere's work to the attention of more art collectors than were previously aware of her work.

   (D) Dejere painted fewer works in the twelve month period following the review of La Triumph than she had in the twelve month period preceding its unveiling.

   (E) Dejere paid more attention to marketing her paintings after La Triumph received such a positive reception.

Explanation: The Paintings of Trianne Dejere

1. Trianne Dejere's paintings sold best after she revealed her most famous piece. In the twelve months before that unveiling, she sold 57% of her works. In the twelve months following the unveiling, she sold 85% of her works. Nevertheless, in both periods, she sold the same number of paintings.

An 800 test taker zeroes in on percents and ratios, knowing that often the test makers are testing his ability to distinguish between rates and raw numbers.

We need to consider what conclusion this evidence would support. If 57% equals the same number of paintings before the unveiling as 85% equals after the unveiling, then Dejere must have produced more paintings in the period before the unveiling; that's the only way that the numbers could work out. (D) states this from the other angle: Dejere must have painted fewer paintings after the unveiling. (D) is the correct answer.

(A) The author tells us that revenue from both periods is equal since Dejere sells the same number of paintings in both. Therefore, if she had charged more in the second period, she would have made more money than she had in the first, which would contradict the stimulus. Because this is inconsistent with the passage, it certainly can't be inferred from it.

(B) The information given pertains solely to the hard facts of the matter: the number sold and revenues gained during different time periods. (B) is therefore outside of the scope of the argument, since the author never mentions Dejere's motivations for painting. We can't reasonably conclude anything about her "concerns" here.

(C), if anything, might suggest that Dejere sold more paintings in the second period, which the stimulus explicitly contradicts. Further, the stimulus provides no information about how art collectors might have responded to the review, giving us no basis to form a conclusion about those collectors.

(E) might also suggest that sales would be higher in the second period, but we know that the sales were the same. However, there's really no reason to look this deeply into it. The main reason for chopping (E) is because marketing is never discussed.

An 800 test taker does not read more into a stimulus than what's given.

---

2. SURVEYS AND STUDIES

This category is intimately related to the previous one. More often than not, the surveys, studies, and occasional experiments that show up in Critical Reasoning questions are backed by numbers and percentages, and we can almost consider these two types as one big category. However, it's worth breaking them up because 1) surveys and studies have their own predictable patterns on the GMAT, and 2) they don't always involve numbers or percentages, and sometimes, when they do, as is the case in question 2 here, the numerical info is secondary to the mechanisms of the study itself. You'll be seeing quite a few surveys and studies in the pages that follow.

An 800 test taker approaches a Critical Reasoning survey, study, or experiment with skepticism, knowing full well that it might be testing an understanding of how these presentations of information can go awry.

---

2. A social worker surveyed 200 women who recently had given birth to their first child. Half of these women had chosen to give birth in a hospital or obstetric clinic; the other half had chosen to give birth at home under the care of certified midwives. Of the 100 births that occurred at home, only five had presented any substantial complications, whereas 17 of the hospital births had required extra attention because of complications during delivery. The social worker concluded from this survey that the home is actually a safer environment in which to give birth than is a hospital or clinic.

    Which of the following, if true, most seriously calls the social worker's conclusion above into question?

    (A) All of the women in the study who were diagnosed as having a high possibility of delivery complications elected to give birth in a hospital.
    (B) Many obstetricians discourage their patients from giving birth in their own homes.
    (C) Women who give birth in their own homes tend to experience less stress during labor and delivery than do those who deliver in hospitals.
    (D) Women who give birth in hospitals and clinics often have shorter periods of labor than do those who give birth at home.
    (E) Pregnant doctors prefer giving birth in a hospital.

Explanation: Home Births

2. Here's a very typical example of how surveys appear in GMAT Critical Reasoning. A social worker surveys 100 women who chose to give birth in a hospital, and 100 who chose to have their babies at home. The social worker concludes that the home is the safer environment in which to give birth, based entirely on the fact that in the sample studied, there were more cases of complications in the hospital. She assumes that the environment was responsible for the number of complications, and overlooks any other possible reason for the survey results. (A) weakens the argument by providing such an alternate reason for the statistical disparity: Women who were at high risk for complications all decided to give birth in a hospital. In other words, the study was skewed; the women in the two groups (the 100 who gave birth in the home and the 100 who gave birth in the hospital) were not equally likely to have complications to begin with. (A) is correct.

> An 800 test taker scrutinizes the sample groups used in surveys presented in Critical Reasoning questions, looking for disparities in the data or characteristics of the groups involved that may invalidate the survey.

(B) and (E) both make inappropriate appeals to authority—the fact that many doctors prefer hospital births alters neither the results of the study nor the conclusion drawn from these results.

> An 800 test taker is not fooled by appeals to authority. She knows that conclusions must be backed up by solid evidence, not by the opinions or actions of experts.

(C) provides the opposite of what we're looking for—it strengthens the argument by providing a possible reason why home births are safer.

(D) The point at issue is where it's safer to give birth, not the respective labor times. Since there's no evidence that *shorter* labors are *safer* labors, (D) doesn't weaken the argument.

3. SCOPE SHIFTS

Have you ever been in an argument in which you just know that your opponent is pulling a fast one, but you can't quite put your finger on the flaw in his argument? Perhaps, somewhere along the way, he subtly changed the direction of the argument. This is a classic argumentative technique; in fact, one that the GMAT test makers are quite fond of. In some Critical Reasoning questions, the author introduces a subtle distinction that slightly alters or shifts the scope or focus of the argument, as in the following example:

> Educators have been complaining that salaries are not high enough to draw enough top applicants to teaching jobs at the high school level. This is clearly absurd; there is fierce competition for teaching jobs at all levels, with many candidates vying for each new job that opens up.

Do you see the scope shift? The claim that the author attempts to refute deals with *top* applicants, whereas the evidence that the author provides for her rebuttal involves applicants *in general*. It may seem like a minor difference, applicants vs. *top* applicants, but it opens up a logical chasm. This is exactly the type of subtle distinction the test makers like to exploit. Such distinctions provide great material, especially for Assumption, Weaken the Argument, and Logical Flaw questions. They show up both in passages and choices. Now give this question a try:

3. It is mistaken to attribute Zanco's failure to the publicity about the supposedly inhuman working conditions in the foreign factories that furnish Zanco with many of its parts. Zanco's failure has more to do with defects in its products than with any boycott on moral grounds. After all, plenty of other companies are supplied by factories with working conditions just as bad as those in Zanco's suppliers, and the public does not hesitate to buy their products.

    The argument in the passage is based on which of the following assumptions?

    (A) People are unlikely to let moral considerations affect what products they decide to purchase.
    (B) People who patronize companies supplied by factories where working conditions are as bad as those of Zanco's suppliers are aware of those conditions.
    (C) The working conditions in the factories that supply Zanco with parts are not as bad as has been claimed.
    (D) Zanco's sales did not dip sharply after the poor working conditions in its suppliers' factories became known.
    (E) The poor quality of Zanco's products is not a result of the working conditions in the foreign factories where its parts are manufactured.

Explanation: Zanco's Failure

3. The assertion that Zanco's failure is not due to publicity about poor working conditions in its suppliers' factories only makes sense if those who buy the products of those other companies are *aware* of the bad working conditions in their suppliers' factories. After all, if people bought products from the other companies without knowing that they too were supplied by sweatshop-style factories, the comparison would be moot and the logic of the argument would go down the drain. The scope shift centers around the word "publicity." The conclusion that Zanco's failure was not due to publicity about bad working conditions is backed up by evidence concerning companies with bad working conditions *that says nothing about publicity*. Publicity is a key feature of the conclusion, but drops off the map in the evidence, and therein lies the scope shift and the necessity of (B), the correct answer.

(A) Even if people are likely to base purchasing decisions on moral considerations, it doesn't weaken the conclusion that people didn't do this in the case of Zanco.

(C) The point isn't that the working conditions of Zanco's suppliers have been unfairly exaggerated, but that these conditions are not a factor in the company's failure. It wouldn't affect the argument if, contrary to (C), working conditions are just as bad as the negative publicity claims.

(D) Even if Zanco's sales did dip sharply after people found out about the poor working conditions, we couldn't conclude that the dip resulted from the public's refusal to buy Zanco's products on moral grounds—the sales dip could have easily resulted from something else and merely coincided with the public's learning of the factory conditions.

(E) It doesn't matter whether or not there's a connection between the poor quality of the products and the lousy working conditions—the existence or lack of such a connection doesn't affect the logic of the argument.

4. CAUSATION

The great German philosopher, Friedrich Nietzsche, put it perfectly in his 1888 book *Twilight of the Idols*:

"There is no more dangerous error than that of *mistaking the consequence for the cause*: I call it reason's intrinsic form of corruption." (italics Nietzsche's)

The GMAT test makers have apparently taken the philosopher's words to heart; GMAT test takers mistake cause and effect at their own risk. Some Critical Reasoning questions even contain precisely the same kind of reasoning as the example Nietzsche furnishes on the same page as the above quote:

"Everyone knows the book of the celebrated Cornaro in which he recommends his meager diet as a recipe for a long and happy life—a virtuous one, too… I do not doubt that hardly any book…has done so much harm, has shortened so many lives, as this curiosity, which was so well meant. The reason: mistaking the consequence for the cause. The worthy Italian saw in his diet the *cause* of his long life: while the prerequisite of long life, an extraordinarily slow metabolism, a small consumption, was the cause of his meager diet." (italics Nietzsche's)

What Nietzsche is saying is that a meager diet didn't cause Cornaro to live long; instead, a necessary condition of long life caused him to eat little.

The GMAT test makers are fond of all kinds of causation problems. In some, one causal element is mistaken for another. In others, correlation is mistaken for causation, or occasionally, vice versa. Later on you'll see an example, similar to the Cornaro case above, in which cause and effect are reversed—that's a popular one. Question 4 here illustrates another very common and basic way that causation is tested on the GMAT.

4. Reading skills among high school students in Gotham have been steadily declining, which can only be the result of overcrowding in the schools.

   Which of the following, if true, most seriously weakens the argument expressed above?

   (A) The high school system in Gotham succeeds in giving students a good education at considerably less cost than do most systems.

   (B) Several cities have found that overcrowding in the schools is not always associated with lower reading scores.

   (C) Gotham schools have a greater teacher-to-student ratio than most other school systems.

   (D) Students' reading skills have not declined in other cities where the high schools are just as crowded as those of Gotham.

   (E) Schools are not overcrowded in many cities where high school reading scores have declined more than they have in Gotham.

Explanation: Gotham Reading Skills

4. The important word in the author's conclusion is the word *only*. She states that the problem of declining reading skills can only have one cause: overcrowding. Anything that renders doubtful the causal connection between Gotham's overcrowding and Gotham's declining reading scores will seriously weaken the argument. (E) does this by pointing out a case in which skills have declined, yet there is no overcrowding. So something *other* than overcrowding *can* account for a decline in reading skills. (E) wins. (Note: This ties in perfectly with the logical element present in the next question.)

(A) just tries to make an excuse for Gotham schools by pointing out that they spend less money. While this may furnish a reason for the overcrowding, it does nothing to hurt the argument that the overcrowding causes declining scores.

(B) and (D) point to overcrowding without declining skills. Yet the author didn't say that overcrowding always leads to declines in skills, but rather that declines in skills are always a result of overcrowding. Be careful to keep the causal mechanism straight!

(C), if anything, strengthens the argument by pointing out that the decline in reading scores cannot be attributed to a low teacher-to-student ratio. It must, therefore, be attributed to some other cause (e.g., overcrowding).

5. ALTERNATIVE EXPLANATIONS

Perhaps, when arguing in real life, you've used the "Oh yeah? But what about…" defense. We look for alternative explanations for things all the time, to prove our own points or argue against others. This is another common feature of Critical Reasoning questions. Some arguments are flawed, or can be weakened, because their authors fail to see that a piece of evidence can lead to more than one possible conclusion, or that a situation or result can have more than one possible explanation. The latter is precisely the case in "Tennis Styles" below.

5. According to some sports historians, professional tennis players develop unique playing styles that result from a combination of the peculiarities of each player's physical attributes and the influence of coaches during their early adaptation to the game. But when the increase in strength and endurance of modern players is discounted, it becomes readily apparent that the playing styles of the current crop of professional tennis players are no different from the styles of players from previous generations. Clearly, there is a universally efficient tennis style to which all professional tennis players conform.

   The argument above is most weakened by which of the following statements?

   (A) The differences in physical attributes among tennis players are even more pronounced than the sports historians believe.
   (B) Few current professional tennis players are familiar with the professional tennis players of fifty years ago.
   (C) The increased strength of current tennis players contributes more to the development of individual playing styles than does increased endurance.
   (D) All of the early coaches of today's professional tennis players were professional tennis players themselves earlier in their lives.
   (E) Weight training and greater attention to diet are the primary factors in the increased strength and stamina of the current generation of professional tennis players.

Explanation: Tennis Styles

5. The author begins by describing the view of some sports historians, who subscribe to a basic formula: physical attributes + a coach's influence = a player's "unique" tennis style. After dismissing the relevance of modern players' greater strength and endurance, however, the author argues that current styles are really no different from previous styles, implying that the historians' claim of the existence of "unique" tennis styles is bogus. And this implication is stated outright in the last sentence, where the author posits the existence of a universally successful tennis style shared by all professionals. In other words, the author uses the fact that tennis styles haven't changed over the years to argue that there's simply one best way to play tennis; in contrast to the historians' theory of "unique," the author proposes the theory of "universality." But the author ignores a plausible alternative explanation; namely, the role of the tennis coach. If, as (D) has it, the early coaches of today's players were the professionals of yesteryear, then it's reasonable to believe that the style the author considers "universal" may simply be the style (one possible one among many) that was handed down from one generation to the next. Perhaps if the current crop of tennis stars don't go on to teach the next generation, whole new styles will develop. If the current style is *learned*, then it may not be universally inherent to the game. If (D) is true, the author's claim of "universality" is weakened. That makes (D) the winner.

(A) emphasizes the truth of the first part of the sports historians' view regarding the individuality of physical attributes. Since the author doesn't explicitly disagree that players vary in terms of some attributes, this choice doesn't weaken the argument.

(B) if anything, strengthens the argument: If most current players don't know of the players of previous generations, yet their styles are for the most part similar to that of those players, then we'd be more likely to believe that the author is on to something with the claim that a universally efficient style exists in the world of professional tennis.

(C) makes an irrelevant distinction between strength and endurance. Saying that one has a greater impact than the other has no effect on the argument, which never even begins to rank those two factors.

(E) The factors that contribute to the greater strength and weight of today's players are beyond the scope of this argument. The argument focuses on the similarity of styles that is evident once these factors are discounted. *Why* the current players are stronger and heartier than the previous bunch is not the issue.

KAPLAN

6. EXPLAIN/PARADOX

Often in Critical Reasoning the test makers will ask you to find a viable explanation for a phenomenon, and in certain cases, the event or finding in question is downright surprising or paradoxical. These present considerable challenges in that you first have to understand the paradoxical situation (or "apparent discrepancy," as it's sometimes referred to), and then you have to recognize a valid solution to it. Let's see how you make out with the puzzle of the Comaquogue tribe:

6. Before the advent of writing, each of the isolated clans of the Comaquogue tribe had master storytellers whose function was to orally transmit the clan's tradition from one generation to the next. When writing was developed within certain clans of the tribe, their master storytellers disappeared within a few generations. This stands to reason, since the availability of written records obviated the need for masterful oral communicators to keep the tradition of literate clans alive. What has puzzled anthropologists, however, is the total lack of masterful storytellers in modern illiterate Comaquogue clans.

    Which of the following, if true, best helps to explain the puzzling situation mentioned above?

    (A) Modern illiterate Comaquogue clan members display personality characteristics that resemble their ancestors more closely than they resemble the characteristics of modern literate Comaquogue clan members.

    (B) Modern illiterate Comaquogue clans participate in more ritual gatherings than most modern literate Comaquogue clans do, but they participate in fewer ritual gatherings than did their common ancestors.

    (C) Modern illiterate Comaquogue clans are recently descended from long-time literate clans that failed to pass on the skills of reading and writing due to a devastating 75-year war.

    (D) The celebrations of modern illiterate Comaquogue clans involve a great deal of singing and dancing, and children are taught clan songs and dances from a very young age.

    (E) The traditions of modern illiterate Comaquogue clans are an amalgamation of the cumulative experiences of previous generations plus innovations to the heritage added by the current generation of clan members.

Explanation: Comaquogue Storytellers

6. The author clearly identifies the source of the confusion when he mentions what puzzles anthropologists. They're perplexed by two facts which seem inconsistent with each other. First, the advent of writing in certain Comaquogue clans seems to have caused the disappearance of the master storytellers within those tribes. Nevertheless, the second fact is that modern illiterate Comaquogue clans also lack master storytellers. The basic question is: Why do these modern illiterate clans lack storytellers when earlier clans lost their storytellers only after they learned how to read? Let's look to the answer choices and find one that specifically answers this question.

> An 800 test taker rephrases the paradox as a question and finds the choice that best answers it.

(A) does nothing to explain why the modern illiterate clans lack storytellers. Personality similarities don't have any clear relationship to literacy and storytellers.

(B) A comparison of the frequency of clan gatherings also does not in any way explain why the current illiterate tribes lack storytellers.

(C) would explain the discrepancy. If it were true, then the storytellers did disappear when the clans became literate, but they subsequently lost that literacy. Thus the modern tribes could both be illiterate and lack storytellers, as is the case in the stimulus, and they could have lost their storytellers during an earlier literate period. The inconsistency is no longer an inconsistency—all of the pieces of the puzzle find a home in this explanation. (C) is correct.

(D) again touches on the issue of modern Comaquogue rituals without referring to literacy and storytelling, the central elements of the argument's paradox.

(E) is too broad to resolve this discrepancy. It might give you the room to start making assumptions, but it doesn't specifically address the issues of literacy and storytelling. Regardless of the sentiments in (E), the fact remains that the modern illiterate clans have no master storytellers when the evidence suggests that they should.

> An 800 test taker doesn't read too much into an answer choice in order to try to make it work. He knows a choice has to be right without any extra help.

7. THE "ODD-MAN-OUT"

Next up in our potpourri of tough questions are those that ask you to locate the one choice that *doesn't* satisfy a particular requirement; in other words, to find the "odd-man-out." These are difficult because the right answer may do the opposite of what's required, or may simply be irrelevant to the situation at hand. At the same time, the wrong choices are *all* relevant, and sometimes look and sound the same, lulling us into a state of mind in which every choice, including the bogus right answer, sounds reasonable. Finally, some test takers simply blow past the word "EXCEPT" or "NOT" in the question stem, and blow the question on that account. The next question is of the "which is *not* assumed" variety.

7. A political candidate committed to the principal tenets of a political party may not always explain the implications of his or her party commitment to the voters in full detail. Adele Richardson, for example, is a minor-party candidate in contention for a seat on the school board. She is not likely to inform conservative voters in her district that the national leadership of her party has recently recommended that school curricula be more closely monitored by agencies of the federal government.

    Each of the following is assumed in the argument above EXCEPT:

(A) A political candidate is likely to be more interested in winning an election than in proselytizing the electorate.

(B) The candidate of any party is likely to support the policy decisions made by the national leadership.

(C) All candidates for such community positions as membership on the school board must have commitments to national parties.

(D) Conservatives in Adele Richardson's district do not support federal intervention in decisions made by community school officials.

(E) Voters in Adele Richardson's district are not fully aware of the policy statements made by the national leadership of her party.

Explanation: School Board Candidate

7. Four assumptions means we must be dealing with a pretty shaky, or at least, incomplete, argument. The author states a general point in the first sentence: A candidate who has faith in the beliefs of a party may not find it in her interest to explain those beliefs to voters. Enter Ms. Richardson, school board hopeful. Her party would like to see tight government regulation of school curricula, but in accordance with the claim in the first sentence, the author thinks that she's not likely to explain this to conservative voters. Since there are four assumptions here, our best bet is to go right to the choices, looking for the odd-man-out.

(A) If (A) is *not* true, then the argument is weakened, which shows that (A) must be assumed. If a candidate is interested in proselytizing the electorate rather than winning an election, then, contrary to the author's assertion, the candidate would have no reason to conceal her opinions from voters likely to disagree with her.

(B) must be assumed because if a candidate is *not* likely to support the national leadership's policy decisions, then the author's assertion about Richardson makes no sense.

(C) is the only nonassumption here: The argument doesn't depend on candidates for community positions having commitments to national parties. The author addresses only those candidates who *are* committed to a political party's central tenets; he says nothing about what's required to run for community positions. Adele Richardson happens to be committed to a national party, but this needn't be true of all candidates for such positions. (C) is correct.

(D) is a fairly obvious assumption: Why would Richardson conceal her party's recommendation from conservatives if conservatives supported it? Instead, she'd be more likely to parade the party recommendation in order to garner conservative votes.

(E) is also assumed: The only way Richardson can conceal her party's recommendation from voters is if they're not fully aware of it already.

CHAPTER THREE

Now Try These...

Next, try your hand at the following seven questions. Each question represents one of the categories just discussed. See if you can pick out the logical element operative in each.

8. Movie pirating, the illegal videotaping of a new theater release and subsequent selling of the tape on the black market, is a major concern to the film studios that produce today's mainstream movies. When pirating sales are high, individual studios whose movies are being taped and sold illegally lose a large amount of revenue from black-market viewers who would otherwise pay the full theater price. A low level of pirating sales during a specific period, however, is a fairly reliable indicator of an economic downturn in the movie industry as a whole during that period.

   Which of the following, if true, most helps to reconcile the discrepancy noted above?

   (A) The film studios that produce today's mainstream movies occasionally serve as distribution outlets for smaller budget independent films that are also susceptible to pirating.

   (B) Movie piraters exclusively target blockbuster hits, the existence of which is inextricably tied to the financial success of the movie industry during any given period.

   (C) Most movie piraters use small, handheld video cameras that are specially designed to record images in the darkened environment of a movie theater.

   (D) The five largest film studios take in a disproportionate amount of movie revenue compared to hundreds of smaller and independent film studios, regardless of whether pirating activity during a specific period is high or low.

   (E) A movie pirater who is highly active in selling movies on the black market can sometimes make a full living doing so, while a less active pirater will usually have to supplement the income generated from pirated movies.

9. An economic or political crisis in a poor country can lead to a lack of faith in the country's leaders, which is often followed by violent behavior, dissent, and even revolt among specific segments of the population. In many cases, propaganda is immediately issued from media outlets that quells such reactions by downplaying the extent of the recent crisis, thereby helping to restore belief in the efficacy of the government. However, the habitual violence exhibited by certain groups of disaffected youths in such countries generally has nothing to do with a lack of faith in their leaders, but rather is the consequence of an endemic boredom and lack of any vision of a positive future for themselves.

   Which of the following statements follows most logically from the statements in the passage above?

   (A) It is easier to quell periodic revolts in poor countries than it is to solve the habitual problem of youth violence.

   (B) In all poor countries, propaganda alone cannot entirely diffuse dissent stemming from an economic or political crisis.

   (C) Economic and political crises do not lead to any instances of youth violence in poor countries.

   (D) The effect that propaganda has in putting down revolts in poor countries is primarily related to its ability to alter people's fundamental beliefs.

   (E) To the extent that propaganda may help to decrease youth violence in a poor country, it is probably not the result of restoring the youths' faith in their country's leadership.

10. Sarrin monks practice the Pran meditation technique only when extremely damaging weather conditions confront the farming villages surrounding Sarrin monasteries. Pran meditation is a more highly disciplined form of the ritual meditation that the monks practice daily, and involves unique practices such as isolation and fasting.

    Which of the statements below does NOT follow logically from the passage above?

    (A) Some meditation practices are less disciplined than Pran meditation.

    (B) Pran meditation among Sarrin monks does not take place according to a precisely regulated schedule.

    (C) The ritual meditation that a typical Sarrin monk practices daily does not take place in an atmosphere of isolation.

    (D) Monks practice some types of meditation in response to threats faced by the local population.

    (E) The ritual meditation that Sarrin monks practice daily is largely undisciplined.

11. A local department store hires college students for one month every spring to audit its unsold inventory. It costs the department store 20 percent less to pay wages to students than it would cost to hire outside auditors from a temporary service. Even after factoring in the costs of training and insuring the students against work-related injury, the department store spends less money by hiring the student auditors than it would by hiring auditors from the temporary service.

    The statements above, if true, best support which of the following assertions?

    (A) The amount spent on insurance for college-student auditors is more than 20 percent of the cost of paying the college students' basic wages.

    (B) It takes 20 percent less time for the college students to audit the unsold inventory than it does for the outside auditors.

    (C) The department store pays its college-student auditors 20 percent less than the temporary service pays its auditors.

    (D) By hiring college students, the department store will cause 20 percent of the auditors at the temporary service to lose their jobs.

    (E) The cost of training its own college-student auditors is less than 20 percent of the cost of hiring auditors from the temporary service.

12. The plastics commonly used in household garbage bags take, on average, 100 years to decompose in landfills. From an environmental standpoint, the plastic bag industry should be forced to switch to newly developed plastics, which begin to decompose after only 20 years.

    Which of the following pieces of information would be most helpful in evaluating the argument above?

    (A) the rate of growth or decline in sales of plastic garbage bags

    (B) the number of plastic garbage bags sold last year that eventually wound up in landfills

    (C) the feasibility of enforcing legislation that regulates the plastics used in garbage bags

    (D) the length of time it takes the newly developed plastic to fully decompose in landfills.

    (E) a comparison of the production cost of one bag made with the old plastics and of one bag made with the new plastics

13. Membership in the Theta Delta Psi fraternity is easily obtained by those who have previously had strong social connections with existing fraternity members before college. However, one must have attended high school with one or more of the members in order to forge such strong social connections. People who lack these social connections because they have not attended high school with one or more current fraternity members will therefore find it difficult to join the fraternity.

    This argument displays flawed reasoning because it neglects to consider the possibility that

    (A) many of those who went to high school with Theta Delta Psi fraternity members did not themselves become members of the fraternity

    (B) it is more important in the long run to socialize with non-fraternity members than to develop strong connections with fraternity members

    (C) it is more difficult to forge social connections with fraternity members than with non–fraternity members

    (D) one may easily obtain membership in the fraternity through means other than having strong social connections with existing fraternity members

    (E) some current members of the fraternity did not go to high school with other members

14. For years, scientists have believed that a certain hormone produced by the human liver was triggered by Enzyme U, which is released in the pancreas. Recently, however, researchers in Belgium discovered that Enzyme U is always preceded by the release of Enzyme W in the brain. Based on this, these researchers hypothesize that Enzyme W, not Enzyme U, triggers the production of the liver hormone.

    If a second research project were set up to verify the findings of the Belgian researchers, which of the following test results would most seriously weaken their hypothesis?

    (A) Enzyme W is released, but not followed by the release of Enzyme U, although the liver hormone is produced.

    (B) Enzyme U is released, but neither preceded by the release of Enzyme W, nor followed by the production of the liver hormone.

    (C) Neither Enzyme W nor Enzyme U is released and the liver hormone is not produced.

    (D) Enzyme W is released, followed by the release of Enzyme U and the production of the liver hormone.

    (E) Enzyme U is released and followed by the production of the liver hormone, although Enzyme W is not released.

ANSWERS AND EXPLANATIONS, QUESTIONS 8–14

Explanation: Movie Pirating

8. Here's a difficult **paradox** to resolve. Our first task is to understand the discrepancy. The author tells us that a high volume of pirating sales causes studios to lose a great deal of money. However (a "contrast" Keyword which signals the discrepancy in the stimulus), a low volume of pirating sales generally indicates a period of economic weakness in the movie industry.

> An 800 test taker keys in on structural signals that illuminate the author's purpose. Words such as *but* and *however* signify contrast and are especially important because they tell us that a twist is upcoming.

Why does a low level of pirating sales, which would seem to benefit the industry, actually signal a period of economic weakness in the industry? This is the question that we need to answer, so let's proceed to the answer choices.

(A) doesn't address the issues involved in the discrepancy, focusing as it does on whether these studios distribute smaller films.

(B) is correct because it creates a direct connection between pirating and the financial success of the entire industry. If pirating is related exclusively to big hits, then a low level of pirating signals a lack of blockbuster hits, in which case it's more understandable how a low level of pirating would correspond to periods of economic downturns in the industry.

(C) is off base, focusing as it does on the methods of pirated tape production and not on the connection between pirating and the economic health of the movie industry.

(D) is similarly off base, since it offers a comparative analysis between the largest and not so large studios, which isn't a comparison relevant to the original discrepancy.

(E) gives us information about the profitability of selling pirated movies, which may be interesting but doesn't explain why low pirating sales would signal an economic low point in the entire movie industry.

> An 800 test taker identifies the primary issues involved in complex discrepancy questions, and then searches for a choice that addresses those issues while eliminating choices that violate that scope.

Explanation: Teen Angst

9. This is the one featuring the element of **causation**; in fact, the argument begins with a full chain of causality: A crisis (step 1) can lead to a decrease in people's faith in their country's leaders (step 2), which can in turn lead to violence in unspecified segments of the population (step 3). Propaganda limits the perception of the crisis, thereby keeping the first domino from falling, and therefore favorably impacting at least the second step in the chain. This is the author's first explanation for violence, and the propaganda solution refers only to it. The author then gives an entirely different explanation for violence, this time more specifically explaining *youth* violence. Accordingly, youth violence is caused by boredom and lack of vision regarding a promising future. We have two paths explaining violence, and the answer to this Inference question will certainly test our ability to distinguish between them. Let's evaluate the answer choices, keeping the distinctions in mind.

(A) While the author offers us one potential antidote to the first type of violence without making any such reference in regards to the second, that doesn't mean that there is no solution for the second type. Because something isn't mentioned, that doesn't mean it doesn't exist, so we have no way of inferring which type of violence is easier to quell.

(B) For all we know, propaganda alone may be enough to entirely diffuse dissent in some poor countries, possibly those without disaffected youth, or even those with disaffected youth who are not driven to dissent by such crises.

(C) is too extreme and distorts the argument. The author writes that economic and political crises lead to violence among "specific segments of the population," which may include youth; the author certainly doesn't rule out that possibility. Further, because boredom and lack of vision lead to habitual youth violence, that doesn't mean that only boredom and lack of vision lead to youth violence. The two explanations aren't mutually exclusive.

(D) also goes too far out on a limb. The author mentions two effects of the propaganda; it downplays the extent of the crisis and restores faith in the government. However, we don't know that an alteration in people's "fundamental beliefs" is inherent in either one of these cases; we simply know that the propaganda has an effect on their immediate actions at the time of the crisis.

(E) does the trick: Since the author does not directly link habitual youth violence to economic or political crises, or to the decrease in faith which such crises create, propaganda probably doesn't decrease that violence by restoring faith in the country's leaders. The author specifically says that habitual youth violence is not caused by a loss of such faith, so restoring the faith probably wouldn't help matters any. If propaganda helps to quell habitual youth violence, then it probably does it in some other way.

An 800 test taker is wary of extreme answer choices that make over-eager claims such as those found in choices (A) through (D) here. He knows that the right choice in an Inference question won't intensify the argument.

Explanation: Pran Meditation

10. Here's our **"Odd-Man-Out"** example, and since we need to find the one statement that *isn't* inferred, we should keep careful track of the boundaries around the argument. That way we'll be better prepared to spot what *isn't* there. The author begins by noting that the Sarrin monks use Pran meditation only in cases of severe weather. The author then explains the differences between Pran meditation and ritual meditation. Understanding the differences will likely be key to getting this question right. Pran meditation is different from ritual meditation because it's more highly disciplined and uniquely involves isolation and fasting. Thus there are three specific ways in which Pran meditation is different from ritual meditation. Let's go to the choices.

(A) The author states that Pran meditation is more disciplined than ritual meditation, so (A) must be true. Since we have one example of a less disciplined form of meditation, we can rightfully infer that *some* practices are less disciplined.

An 800 test taker understands that on the GMAT, the word *some* strictly means "one or more."

(B) The monks practice Pran meditation only when there's severe weather and, since weather isn't precisely scheduled, then Pran meditation must not be precisely scheduled either. Sure, that's an inference.

(C) If Pran meditation involves the *unique* practice of isolation, then no other meditation, including ritual meditation, involves isolation. This is therefore also inferable from the passage.

(D) *Some* means "one or more," so since the monks practice Pran meditation in response to local weather threats, then some types of meditation do in fact exist as a response to local threats.

(E) is correct because, even though the author implies that ritual meditation is *less* disciplined than Pran meditation, that doesn't mean that it's UNdisciplined. (E) takes us beyond what the passage supports, so it's not a valid inference and is therefore the correct answer here.

An 800 test taker has a keen eye and ear for distortions of the passage text.

Explanation: Student Auditors

11. We don't have to look too deeply into this one to determine that it falls squarely into the **numbers and statistics** realm. All we have is evidence, and the first piece presents a statistical claim: The department store pays college students 20 percent less than it would pay employees from a temporary service. Next comes the numerical claim: Add the costs of training and insurance, and the store *still* pays less for college students. The correct answer must arise from the facts: college students cost the store up to 20 percent less than do employees from a temporary service—even after training and insurance. Prephrasing an answer would be tough, so we should move right to testing the choices.

An 800 test taker has an intuitive sense of when to try to prephrase answers and when to simply use a solid understanding of the given information to test the choices. In either case, he attacks the choices *aggressively*.

(A) attempts to relate the amount spent on insurance for student auditors to the total amount of their wages, but we have no basis for which to make this comparison. The amount spent on insurance for college-student auditors can be more, less, or equal to 20 percent of their basic wages without violating the numerical facts presented.

(B) and (D) should have been fairly easy kills. (B) involves time, a subject not included in the stimulus, while (D) mentions the loss of jobs at the temporary service, even though we know nothing about the overall demand for their auditors.

(C) is a little more subtle, but it involves how much the temporary service *pays* its auditors, not how much it charges the store for them. A classic "scope shift," in fact—and a pretty good premonition of things to come.

An 800 test taker always pays attention to the scope of the argument; this helps him to axe easy and more difficult choices alike.

(E) fits, and one way we can verify that it's correct is to see what happens it it's *not* true. If the cost of training college students is *more* than 20 percent of the cost of hiring auditors from the temporary service, the overall cost of college students must be higher than the cost of temporary-service auditors. That would contradict the stimulus, so (E) must be true.

An 800 test taker has many tricks up her sleeve. She knows that one way to verify an answer in an Assumption or Inference question is to see what happens when she denies or negates the choice. If doing so makes the argument fall apart, then she knows she's found the winner.

Explanation: Landfill Plastics

12. Some questions test nothing more than whether you've recognized a **scope shift**, and this one falls into that category. The question stem complicates matters, however, and requires a bit of translation. A piece of information that would help us evaluate the argument is essentially a piece of information that would strengthen or weaken the argument. The right choice will need to have one of those effects in order for us to be able to say that this argument is good or bad. In other words, the operative question the student has to ask himself to test each choice is: "Does this help me pass judgment on the argument?" Such evaluations are common in GMAT Critical Reasoning.

An 800 test taker interprets question stems in the light of how they instruct him to deal with the passage.

Now, if you picked up on the scope shift, then you would have known that the right choice will somehow address it. The shift is subtle, but definite, and perhaps if you didn't see it up front on your own, you would have recognized the shift when you came to correct choice (D). The author argues for the switch to the new plastics, but takes no account of the fact that there's a disparity in the information given. The newly developed plastic takes only 20 years to *begin* to decompose, but we need to know how long it takes for it to *fully* decompose in landfills before we can pass judgment on the argument. Only then would we be able to compare the new plastics to the current bags. (D) provides this information and is therefore correct.

(A) and (B) present irrelevant issues. We're trying to evaluate whether the change from one plastic to another is environmentally beneficial. Neither of these pieces of information helps us to differentiate between the environmental impact of the old vs. new bags.

(C) Whether or not the industry will be able to switch over to and legally maintain the new plastic bags is outside the scope. The question is whether or not it *should*.

An 800 test taker understands that when an argument is based around the notion that something "should" be done, whether or not it "can" be done is logically irrelevant.

(E) offers up an irrelevant distinction. The argument is made from an environmental standpoint; the cost per bag has no logical bearing on this.

Explanation: Fraternity Membership

13. In this one, getting the right answer depends on your ability to spot an **alternative possibility** not addressed by the author. In fact, the question stem tells us outright that this is the case. The alternative is fairly subtle, but is nonetheless the key to the question. The argument begins by offering one route through which a student can gain a coveted membership to the Theta Delta Psi fraternity. For those aspirants who attended high school with a current member of the house and developed a strong social connection with that member before college, entrance into the fraternity is easy. People who didn't attend high school with a current member can't easily attain membership through this route, but we were never told that this was the *only* way to easily get into the fraternity. The author concludes that the unconnected individuals will have difficulty joining the fraternity, but that's only valid if the route the author describes is the only possible easy route. But the author never says that. (D) thus gets at the major point the author fails to consider in issuing her hasty conclusion: the possibility that there might be other ways to easily get into the frat. The social connections described *will* get one into the frat easily, but nowhere does the author state or imply that such connections are actually *necessary*; maybe there are other means of easy entry.

(A) First of all, those who attended high school with fraternity members are not necessarily the same people who have forged strong social connections with them. So the "many"-referred to here may not even be relevant to the argument. Secondly, even assuming these guys *are* good high school buddies of the members, the author argues only about what conditions make for easy entry into the frat, and need not consider the possibility that many high school classmates of the members would choose not to join.

(B) Associations with non–fraternity members are not relevant to the argument and fall outside of its scope. Additionally, this choice discusses the long term benefits of such connections; we only care about entrance into the fraternity, not about life-long happiness.

(C) The relative difficulty of building these connections has nothing to do with their necessity for membership. This choice also shares with (B) an interest in non–fraternity members, whom the author never mentions.

(E) is perfectly consistent with the author's argument, as it totally avoids the issue of the ease with which these "current members" got in. This choice falls outside of the author's scope, which is about the possibility of getting into the fraternity *with ease*, and we therefore can't fault the author for neglecting the possibility raised here.

An 800 test taker always pays close attention to the author's topic and scope. Here, choice (D) is the only one to address the difficulties of obtaining membership; most of the others fall outside of that scope.

Explanation: Enzymes U and W

14. Here's an example of a typical GMAT-style **study.** We're asked to find a set of results that would weaken a particular hypothesis, so the first thing to do is to locate and understand the hypothesis. It's tough to know at this point whether the weakener will simply offer some kind of proof against the hypothesis, or whether it will call attention to an assumption necessary for the hypothesis to hold. The Belgian researchers maintain that, since Enzyme U is always preceded by the release of Enzyme W, it must be Enzyme W, as opposed to U, that triggers the release of the liver hormone. Since the researchers argue that Enzyme W triggers the release of the liver hormone, in order to weaken this argument we can look for evidence either of another cause or of a situation in which the liver hormone appears in the presence of Enzyme U without Enzyme W. Choice (E) directly counters the hypothesis by providing an example of the effect without the supposed cause. If the release of Enzyme U is followed by the production of the liver hormone, even though Enzyme W was not released, then that hammers the researchers' conclusion that Enzyme W is responsible for the hormone.

(A) strengthens, rather than weakens, the causal link between Enzyme W and production of the liver hormone. This choice provides an exact confirmation of what the researchers would predict.

(B) strengthens part of the hypothesis—the part that claims that Enzyme U does not trigger the production of the hormone—although it mentions nothing about W. It also contradicts the notion that U is always preceded by W, but does nothing to weaken the major hypothesis that W triggers the liver hormone.

(C) is perfectly consistent with the hypothesis: Without W, the researchers would not expect the liver hormone to be produced.

An 800 test taker can recognize statements that are perfectly consistent with a set of facts.

(D) represents exactly what we'd expect to happen if the hypothesis were true, so it's clearly not the weakener we seek.

No doubt you noticed the element of **causation** here—the study centers around a fairly textbook case of cause-and-effect. As you'll see, the logical elements presented thus far rarely occur in isolation. So let's take stock of where we are, and then move on to questions that combine the various features highlighted in the previous questions.

CHAPTER FOUR

Putting It All Together

By now, you should have a very definite idea of the many kinds of challenges presented in GMAT Critical Reasoning. While we've broken down these challenges into clearly defined, separate categories, the truth is that difficult questions are often combinations of the various logical elements you've just encountered. In other words, the logical elements presented so far may, and often do, overlap in a single question. As you would expect, the existence of multiple logical elements within questions complicates matters significantly.

In this chapter, you'll get practice with plenty of complex Critical Reasoning questions. Not every question contains more than one logical element, but most do, and the distinguishing logical or structural characteristics of each are cited in the explanations. The questions are arranged in groups of four so that you can learn as you go along and get practice recognizing the logical patterns that recur throughout the Critical Reasoning sections. Enjoy!

CRITICAL REASONING PRACTICE SET 1

1. Attention Deficit Disorder (ADD) is a condition characterized by an inability to focus on any topic for a prolonged period of time, and is especially common among children five to ten years old. A recent study has shown that 85 percent of seven-year-old children with ADD watch, on average, more than five hours of television a day. It is therefore very likely that Ed, age seven, has ADD, since he watches roughly six hours of television a day.

The argument above is flawed because it

(A) cites as a direct causal mechanism a factor that may only be a partial cause of the condition in question

(B) fails to indicate the chances of having ADD among seven-year-old children who watch more than five hours of television a day

(C) limits the description of the symptoms of ADD to an inability to focus for a prolonged period of time

(D) fails to consider the possibility that Ed may be among the 15 percent of children who do not watch more than five hours of television a day

(E) does not allow for other causes of ADD besides television watching

2. Choi: All other factors being equal, children whose parents earned doctorates are more likely to earn a doctorate than children whose parents did not earn doctorates.

Hart: But consider this: Over 70 percent of all doctorate holders do not have a parent that also holds a doctorate.

Which of the following is the most accurate evaluation of Hart's reply?

(A) It establishes that Choi's claim is an exaggeration.

(B) If true, it effectively demonstrates that Choi's claim cannot be accurate.

(C) It is consistent with Choi's claim.

(D) It provides alternative reasons for accepting Choi's claim.

(E) It mistakes what is necessary for an event with what is sufficient to determine that the event will occur.

3. The recent proliferation of newspaper articles in major publications that have been exposed as fabrications serves to bolster the contention that publishers are more interested in selling copy than in printing the truth. Even minor publications have staffs to check such obvious fraud.

The above argument assumes that

(A) newspaper stories of dubious authenticity are a new phenomenon

(B) minor publications do a better job of fact-checking than do major publications

(C) everything a newspaper prints must be factually verifiable

(D) only recently have newspapers admitted to publishing erroneous stories

(E) publishers are ultimately responsible for what is printed in their newspapers

4. A recent university study indicated that students who receive full scholarships tend to maintain higher grade point averages than do students who must take out loans or work to finance school. The study concluded that scholarships enable students to achieve high grade point averages by alleviating the stress related to financial concerns and freeing up students' time to study more.

The study's conclusion depends on which of the following assumptions?

(A) Students who take out loans maintain higher grade point averages than those who work to finance school.

(B) Finance-related stress affects student performance in a manner similar to that of restricted study time.

(C) Students who must work to pay for their studies cannot maintain high grade point averages.

(D) High grade point averages were not the primary criterion upon which the scholarship awards were based.

(E) Controlling stress level is less important to student performance than is intensive studying.

Explanation: Attention Deficit Disorder

Distinguishing Features: Study, Statistics, Scope Shift

1. The author's conclusion pops up at the end, where she states that Ed is likely to have ADD because he watches television a lot and is seven. The key piece of evidence is the recent study cited by the author that states that 85% of seven-year-olds with ADD watch more than five hours of television per day. The study thus discusses only the television-watching habits of seven-year-olds *who have ADD*. The author's conclusion is flawed because it makes a conclusion about a seven-year-old television watcher based on a study about seven-year-old television watchers *with ADD*. In other words, there's a scope shift between the evidence and the conclusion. The author errs in accepting the survey as relevant to Ed. (B) expresses this flaw most clearly: In order to make conclusions about Ed and whether he might have ADD, the author must come up with evidence that pertains to Ed, since the original evidence does not. She needs a statistic that states the likelihood that a seven-year-old who watches more than five hours of TV a day would have ADD. The evidence provided *sounds* like that, but isn't, and (B) captures the gist of the author's mistake. (B) wins.

(A) is confusing, but the argument isn't really about degrees of causation. The author doesn't suggest that age and television-watching *cause* a child to contract ADD, but that those factors generally appear with the disorder. (A) distorts the author's conclusion by suggesting that it says that Ed's television-watching has caused him to contract ADD, but the author never suggests this.

(C) Yes, the description of ADD symptoms *is* limited in the manner cited in (C), but that's not a problem. Perhaps some doctors might disagree with the author's definition, but its validity is not the issue at the heart of this argument. Rather, the argument's concerned with Ed's chances of having ADD based on a particular study.

(D) directly contradicts the stimulus, where we learn that Ed *does* actually watch more than five hours of television per day. You may have also noticed that the 15% figure is bogus—it's derived from the 85% figure in the stimulus, but that figure refers to the percentage of children with ADD who watch more than five hours of TV a day. Inferably, we can therefore say that 15% of children with ADD do not watch more than five hours of TV a day, but we can't turn this into 15% of children *in general* who don't watch more than five hours, as (D) attempts to do.

(E) again distorts the argument, which never suggests that television watching causes ADD. Since no causality is mentioned, we can only assume that the data represents a correlation.

Explanation: Doctorate Children

Distinguishing Features: Numbers and Statistics, Scope Shift

2. Hart's 70 percent figure pretty much tells us that numbers and statistics is the name of the game here. We're asked to evaluate Hart's response to Choi, so let's see what Choi has in mind. Choi's statement is a comparison among individuals: If my parents have earned doctorates and yours didn't, then Choi says that the odds are better that I will earn a doctorate than you will. Choi's claim goes no further. He doesn't claim that children of doctors are *guaranteed* to earn doctorates, and he doesn't even claim that they are *likely* to earn doctorates. He merely claims that these children are *more likely* to earn doctorates than their counterparts who do not have a parent that earned a doctorate. So even if only 5 percent of doctors' children earn doctorates themselves, Choi's claim is still correct as long as fewer than 5 percent of children whose parents didn't earn a doctorate went on to earn a doctorate themselves.

Thus the irrelevancy of Hart's 70 percent figure, which gives us information on a different group—*those who already earned their doctoral degree.* Because she has shifted the scope, the data Hart presents can be true and still have no bearing on Choi's claim. An example: Suppose that there are 10 people in the world with doctorates. Choi merely claims that children of these people are more likely to get doctorates than children of other people. Hart comes along and says that of the 10 people, say, 8 of them (over 70%) come from doctorate-less parents. Does that alter Choi's claim in any way? No. All other factors being equal, the children of those doctors could still be more likely to earn doctorates, even if most doctorate holders don't have that particular heritage. Because of this, Hart's consideration doesn't contradict Choi's claim in any way, and we can therefore say that Hart's statement is consistent with it. (C) is the answer.

An 800 test taker spots inconsistencies, but also recognizes statements that are consistent; that is, that do NOT contradict one another.

(A), (B), and (D) are all off the mark in that they require a connection between Hart and Choi that simply isn't there. Because the speakers' target groups are different, no positive or negative connection can be made between the two claims, and so we therefore cannot say that one shows the other to be exaggerated (A) or false (B), or that one helps the other (D).

(E) The concept of necessity versus sufficiency cannot be invoked against Hart because Hart's statement is merely the presentation of a statistic. As such, in this case there is no "event" to which this type of mistake could apply.

Explanation: Publishers and Fraud

Distinguishing Feature: Scope Shift

3. This next question is deceptively tough—it doesn't really appear to be a difficult argument to follow. The trouble comes from the subtle shift in scope that's introduced as the argument proceeds. If you caught it, then this is a fairly feasible question. If not, then you're likely to end up staring at the choices, wondering if there actually is one that's correct. The argument is based on a scope shift: The author concludes that publishers are more interested in selling copy than in printing the truth. The evidence is that many newspaper articles have recently been exposed as frauds. The assumption—that is, the necessary yet unstated premise here—is contained in (E): that publishers *know about*, or must take responsibility for, the truth of every article in their newspapers. If that's not the case, then the author cannot fairly blame publishers for the rash of bogus stories. So (E) is the answer because it must be assumed in order for this argument to stand.

Now, this assumption—and the scope shift that creates the need for it in the argument—is a bit subtle; you may say, "well, of course publishers are responsible for what is printed in their newspapers." However:

> An 800 test taker understands that the "reasonableness" of a piece of information doesn't disqualify it from being an assumption. Any fact that's required by the argument but is not explicitly stated by the author qualifies as an assumption.

Even top test takers can't be expected to prephrase every right answer, and it's quite possible that even they would not have come up with this answer on their own. No matter; that's what the choices are there for.

> An 800 test taker recognizes the validity of an answer choice when she sees it, even if the concept contained in the choice didn't occur to her up front. Top test takers know how to use the choices to help them succeed.

Eliminating the wrong choices here may have been more than half the battle. Many people are at least able to get it down to (C) and (E).

(A) and (D) are pretty much out of left field. The conclusion doesn't have anything to do with the relative novelty of inauthentic articles (or admissions thereof), despite the tangential reference in the stimulus to "recent" proliferation.

(B) contains a distortion. Minor publications' fact-checking apparatus is mentioned in order to emphasize that the big publications ought to check too; it's not there as the basis of a quality comparison.

(C) is a popular wrong choice, but is too extreme. "Everything a newspaper prints must be factually verifiable" encompasses the movie clock, the weather forecast, today's horoscope, and *Dilbert*. The author's not peeved because *Beetle Bailey* was inaccurate, but because false stories are appearing without adequate checking. The issue isn't lies, but *willful* lies. If you proved to this author that every one of those bogus stories was thoroughly checked and published in good faith, her complaints would fade away.

Explanation: Student Scholarships

Distinguishing Features: Study, Scope Shift, Causation, Alternative Explanation

4. Here's another study to ponder. The evidence of the study indicates that students on full scholarships maintain higher grade point averages (GPAs) than do students who work or take out loans. From this evidence, the study concluded that the scholarships "enable" those students to earn higher GPAs by alleviating financial stress and freeing up the students' time. Notice how the evidence links scholarships and higher GPAs, but the conclusion jumps into the realm of cause and effect—a common GMAT shift in scope. The word *enable* is your clue that the author is now speaking of a causal mechanism.

An 800 test taker understands the many ways that causation is suggested in GMAT arguments.

The author assumes that the only possible reason for the association is the causal mechanism cited in the conclusion, and the correct answer will very likely bolster this notion by eliminating an alternative explanation. Choice (D) hits on the right issue, and it should remind you of Nietzsche's Cornaro example presented earlier. It's possible that the author of this argument got the causal mechanism backwards. She argues that scholarships lead to high GPA's, but maybe the opposite is true: high GPA's lead to scholarships. The argument won't work if there's another reason for the correlation cited in the evidence. If high GPAs are the primary criterion for the scholarships in the first place, then it's not surprising that scholarship holders tend to earn higher GPAs than others. The students must generally be of otherwise equal ability before the conclusion can safely be drawn. (D) is the answer because it eliminates a very plausible alternative explanation for the correlation cited in the first sentence, and thus is the assumption on which this conclusion depends.

(A) offers an irrelevant comparison that does not make the study's conclusion any more likely. Even if students who take out loans do not maintain higher GPAs than those who work to finance school, students with scholarships can still maintain higher GPAs than both of the other groups.

(B) is irrelevant to the argument because it makes a comparison between the positive effects of scholarships. The argument concludes that more time and less financial worry together enable students to maintain higher GPAs. The conclusion does not rely on any particular distinction between these factors.

(C) is in no way required by the argument. Even if students who must work to pay for their studies can maintain high GPAs, the GPAs of scholarship students can still be higher.

(E), like choice (B), makes an irrelevant comparison. Stress and study time are two factors that may influence student performance, but there's no specific comparison of their relative importance that's necessary for this argument to work. Scholarships may still confer an advantage in the manner cited no matter what the relative importance of these factors may be.

CRITICAL REASONING PRACTICE SET 2

5. Rats are generally more active than mice. But since gerbils are generally more active than hamsters, it follows that rats are generally more active than hamsters.

    Any of the following, if introduced into the argument as an additional premise, makes the argument above logically correct EXCEPT:

    (A) Gerbils are generally more active than rats.
    (B) Mice are generally more active than hamsters.
    (C) Mice are generally more active than gerbils.
    (D) Mice and gerbils are generally equally active.
    (E) Rats and gerbils are generally equally active.

6. Studies of trauma victims suggest that shock brought on by violent or life-threatening situations causes damage to the hippocampi, structures in the brain that play a crucial role in learning and memory. Researchers found that in combat veterans suffering from post-traumatic stress symptoms, which include nightmares and vivid flashbacks, the hippocampi were eight percent smaller in volume than in combat veterans who suffered no such symptoms. The researchers concluded that the hippocampi had lost cell mass as a result of trauma.

    Which of the following, if true, would most seriously weaken the researchers' conclusion drawn above?

    (A) In another study, subjects who had experienced the death of a close relative were found to have no reduction in the volume of their hippocampi when compared to those whose close relatives were all still living.
    (B) In the study, the traumatized veterans were compared with other veterans of similar background, body size, and other characteristics that might have a bearing on brain size.
    (C) Some individuals are born with hippocampi whose volume is smaller than average, and this reduced volume makes them more susceptible to post-traumatic stress symptoms.
    (D) Combat veterans who experience post-traumatic stress symptoms perform significantly worse on tests of verbal memory compared with veterans who suffer no such symptoms.
    (E) Further study revealed that veterans who had seen more intense combat and had more severe post-traumatic symptoms exhibited even greater reduction in the volume of their hippocampi.

7. In order to promote off-season business, Mt. Dunmore Lodge made the following "Welcome Back" offer to their winter guests: guests who rent a room for at least a week during ski season can come back during the summer and get 25% off the standard summer price of any room they rent. After the summer passed, the owners of the lodge determined that the majority of their guests had taken advantage of the "Welcome Back" offer and paid the reduced rates. However, they were surprised to find they still managed to rent more rooms at full price than they did at the discount rate.

   Which of the following, if true, most helps to explain the apparent discrepancy in the passage?

   (A) Most of the guests who stayed at Mt. Dunmore Lodge during the winter did not stay for a full week.

   (B) Those guests taking advantage of the "Welcome Back" discount were more likely to bring their families with them than were those guests who were paying full price.

   (C) Some of the guests who received the "Welcome Back" discount also received a 10% rate reduction through their auto club.

   (D) In order to pay for the construction of a new gymnasium and a new pool, the owners of the lodge raised their summer prices considerably.

   (E) On average, guests who took advantage of the "Welcome Back" discount spent more money at the hotel on additional goods and services than guests who paid full price for their rooms.

8. Candidate: I am worried about the effects that the recent media coverage of my personal life will have on my chances of gaining office. Even though the reports are untrue, some voters interviewed on television, in response to these reports, have already expressed doubts regarding my ability to lead.

   Campaign manager: Your concern is unfounded. Of 1,000 people in this city randomly surveyed by e-mail, only 25 have responded that their perception of your ability to lead has been negatively impacted by the recent media coverage.

   The campaign manager's argument is most vulnerable to criticism on the ground that it fails to acknowledge the possibility that

   (A) future media reports that follow up on the story of the candidate's personal life will further damage the public's perception of the candidate's ability to lead

   (B) the candidate's main opponent will use the opportunity created by the recent media coverage to conduct her own survey to assess the damage done to her opponent's credibility

   (C) the voting public would understand that its reaction to the recent media coverage of the candidate's personal life was the intended primary focus of the survey

   (D) opinions expressed in television interviews are not always the most reliable indicator of how interviewees are likely to act in given situations

   (E) many of those surveyed who are skeptical of the candidate's ability to lead due to the recent reports did not respond to the survey

Explanation: Rats, Gerbils, Mice and Hamsters

Distinguishing Feature: Odd-Man-Out

5. We're told that four of the five answer choices make the argument correct, but that one will not, so we're dealing with another "odd-man-out" scenario. This implies that the argument contains a lot of ambiguity, since each of the four wrong choices is able to fill in a gap in the argument. Our best bet is to read the stimulus and get a sense of its possibilities, thinking about what else might be needed to make the argument work.

There are two pieces of evidence here: Rats are generally more active than mice, and gerbils are generally more active than hamsters. From these statements, the argument concludes that rats are generally more active than hamsters. (For the sake of brevity, we will eliminate the word *generally* from here on.). The key to making the argument work is to link the two pieces of evidence in a way that places rats above hamsters. The correct answer, however, will be the one that does not make this connection. It may be helpful here to jot down a quick sketch with R above M and G above H. This may help you to test the choices, eliminating the ones that force R above H as the argument contends. Let's try the choices.

(A) leaves the argument hanging: Gerbils may be more active than rats, but this still leaves the rats/hamsters relationship up for grabs—it would not necessarily follow that rats are more active than hamsters as the author maintains. That means (A) is our winner here. The rest of the choices, however, do validate the conclusion:

(B) If mice are more active than hamsters and rats are more active than mice, then rats are also more active than hamsters.

(C) If mice are more active than gerbils, then mice are also more active than hamsters—which are less active than gerbils. This means that rats, which are more active than mice, are also more active than gerbils and hamsters.

(D) If mice and gerbils are equally active, then rats, which are more active than mice, must be more active than hamsters, which are less active than gerbils.

(E) Same basic reasoning: Hamsters are less active than gerbils, so if rats and gerbils are equal, then rats would trump hamsters again.

Explanation: Trauma Victims

Distinguishing Features: Study, Causation, Alternative Possibility

6. Here we have a cause-and-effect argument presented in the context of a study. The trauma of the vets must have caused the loss of hippocampi cell mass, the doctors conclude, because those with stress symptoms had smaller hippocampi than those without the symptoms. We're looking for something that would weaken the argument, and a classic way of attacking cause-and-effect is illustrated by (C), which points out that the cause and effect could actually be working in reverse—it could be that the symptoms are the result of the small hippocampi, rather than vice versa. This should remind you of Nietzsche's Cornaro example presented a few pages back. (C) it is.

An 800 test taker knows all the potential weaknesses of a causal argument. When confronted with the proposition that X caused Y, he considers the possibility that Y may have in fact caused X; that some third factor Z caused both X and Y; or that the two things are merely correlated and thus not causally related at all.

(A) The argument concerns the effects of "violent or life-threatening" events. The death of a close relative is traumatic, of course, but it isn't "violent or life-threatening," as those terms are used here. So (A) is irrelevant.

(B) and (E) do the opposite of what we're looking for here. The very fact that (B) asserts the similarity among all the veterans studied tends to support, rather than weaken, the study's findings. And (E), if anything, strengthens the argument by cementing the connection between trauma and tiny hippocampi.

An 800 test taker keeps her eye on the ball at all times, and does not carelessly choose a strengthener when asked for a weakener, or vice versa.

(D) omits the main issue—the connection between trauma and hippocampi damage—and hence cannot have any effect on the reasoning.

Explanation: Mt. Dunmore Lodge

Distinguishing Features: Paradox, Numbers and Statistics, Scope Shift

7. One of the toughest things about this question is fully understanding the puzzling phenomenon described. Here's the discrepancy we're asked to resolve: How can it be that most winter guests availed themselves of discounted pricing, yet the lodge nevertheless rented more rooms at full price? Clearly it's a numerical mystery, which will require a numerical solution. (B) provides such an answer: If the discounted folks were comprised mainly of families, packing in more guests per room, while the full-price guests tended to come solo with fewer guests per room, then it's easier to explain how there could be lots of discounted guests wandering around the hotel but more rooms rented at full price. (B) wins.

Notice that the solution to the paradox hinges on the recognition that elements in the evidence and conclusion that appear to be similar are in fact totally different things (number of guests versus number of rooms). In other words, the paradox centers around a scope shift.

> An 800 test taker suspects that in Paradox questions, some sort of shift between the argument's evidence and conclusion may be at the heart of the seeming contradiction.

(A) These guests aren't even eligible for the summer discount, so they play no part in the argument or the confusing result.

(C) That some people got an added discount doesn't serve to explain the paradox. The relevant comparison is between discounted guests and nondiscounted guests, so the fact that some discounted guests are enjoying even greater savings doesn't change a thing.

(D) The argument centers on a full versus discounted rate. What that rate is is irrelevant; it does nothing to explain why more rooms were rented at full rate in light of the evidence.

(E) goes beyond the scope of the passage. Other charges above and beyond room rates are never discussed and are therefore not an issue.

> An 800 test taker doesn't hesitate to work out actual examples to clarify her understanding of a numerical concept. Here, imagine, for instance, that the hotel has 10 rooms, and rents three at a discount and seven at full price. Now suppose that the discounted rooms contain five people per room, while the full-price rooms each contain one person. Voila! More full-priced rooms than discounted, but more discounted guests than full-priced ones.

Explanation: Candidate and Media

Distinguishing Features: Survey, Alternative Possibility

8. With most elections being largely conducted via the media these days, it's no surprise that this candidate is worried that apparently negative media coverage will weaken his chances of getting elected. His manager tries to reassure him by providing the results of an e-mail survey of 1,000 people, only 25 of whom responded negatively to the candidate as a result of the media coverage. The question stem directs us to find a weakness in the manager's argument, and it lies in the survey. What if others who are skeptical about the candidate *simply didn't respond* to the survey? The fact that only 25 responded negatively does not necessarily mean that the other 975 are okay with the reports and have confidence in the candidate's ability to lead, although this is the interpretation the manager implies.

> An 800 test taker, when presented with a survey, asks whether the supposed results accurately represent the views of the whole group surveyed.

(E) picks up on this problem in the manager's argument: If the skeptics were disinclined to respond to the survey, then the conclusion that the candidate need not worry may be unfounded, and the candidate's concern may be legit. (E) is the correct answer.

An 800 test taker is expert at "putting two and two together"—in this case, the fact that we're looking for a vulnerability in the manager's argument and that her argument is based on a survey. That's no coincidence. To an 800 test taker, (E) jumps out as the most common logical flaw associated with surveys: the failure to accurately interpret the response.

(A) is beyond the argument's temporal scope. The candidate and his manager only discuss the impact of the recent media coverage; the possible effects of future coverage don't play a relevant role in that discussion.

(B) identifies a possible use to which the candidate's opponent might put the media coverage, but that too is outside the scope. Maybe the opponent's survey won't show any residual concerns based on the survey, or maybe it will. By itself, (B) doesn't point out a weakness in the argument.

(C) There's no indication that the survey was intended to hide its main focus; presumably, those surveyed knew that the survey was intended to measure the fallout from the media coverage. So (C) need not be something that the campaign manager's argument fails to acknowledge.

(D) deals with television interviews, which show up in the candidate's argument but not in his campaign manager's. Therefore, (D) doesn't identify a problem with the manager's argument.

CRITICAL REASONING PRACTICE SET 3

9. Tsumi bats are a rare breed of omnivorous bat found only in highly temperate climates. Most Tsumi bats living in captivity develop endocrine imbalances from their normal zoo diets, which consist mostly of fruits and berries. The healthiest way to feed the bats, therefore, is to provide them primarily with nuts, grubs, and vegetables and only minimal amounts of fruits and berries.

    Which of the statements below does NOT reflect an assumption upon which the argument depends?

    (A) Those who care for Tsumi bats in captivity should avoid feeding them diets that produce endocrine imbalances.

    (B) Tsumi bats living in captivity will not be malnourished on diets that contain minimal fruits and berries.

    (C) Tsumi bats living in captivity will consume diets that consist of nuts, grubs, and vegetables but no fruits or berries.

    (D) Tsumi bats living in captivity will be adequately nourished on a diet that consists primarily of nuts, grubs, and vegetables.

    (E) For Tsumi bats living in captivity, no health problem stemming from diets consisting mostly of nuts, grubs, and vegetables would surpass in severity the health problems associated with endocrine imbalances.

10. A wave of incidents of unusual violence, from murder to acts of self-destruction, plagued the small medieval town for a period of five years, nearly wiping out the population. At the same time, there was an unusual shift in the area's weather pattern. Rainfall was so heavy and continuous that the wheat crop probably fell prey to the ergot fungus. When eaten, grain thus affected can cause ergotism, a disease associated with hallucinations and other disturbing psychological side effects. In the end we can conclude that the violence was the result of freakish weather conditions.

    Which of the following is the most effective rebuttal to the contention made above?

    (A) It is based upon a series of plausible suppositions rather than upon contemporary evidence.

    (B) No clear distinction is drawn between cause and effect.

    (C) Explanations of historical events cannot be convincing when too great a role is assigned to chance or the irrational.

    (D) The author makes no distinction between probable occurrence and actual occurrence.

    (E) Such crucial terms as "unusual violence" are not adequately defined in regard to the specific historical event.

    Questions 11–12 are based on the following passage.

    A consumer survey of independent feature films revealed that the percentage of action films that received the survey's highest rating was greater than the percentage of romance films that received the highest rating. Yet, the survey organizers were probably erroneous in their conclusion that subject matter determines a feature film's popular appeal, since the action films were all directed by filmmakers with at least one hit film to their credit, while the romance films were directed by newer filmmakers, many of whom had not produced a previous film.

11. The statements above, if true, support which of the following inferences?

    (A) Fewer romance films than action films received the survey's highest rating.

    (B) There is no relationship between the popular appeal of the feature films evaluated in the survey and any previous successes of the directors of those films.

    (C) If consumers were surveyed regarding their impressions of big-budget mainstream films, the percentage of romance films that would receive the survey's highest rating would be lower than the percentage of action films that would receive the highest rating.

    (D) Experienced filmmakers are more likely to produce hit films than are new filmmakers.

    (E) Among directors with the same number of hit films to their credit, differences in the subject matter of their feature films may not affect the way the films are popularly rated.

12. Each of the following, if true, supports the author's contention that the organizers misinterpreted the survey data EXCEPT:

    (A) The fact that one has directed a previous hit film is a positive indicator of that director's filmmaking talent.

    (B) Consumer ratings of a new film are influenced by the previous history of success of the film's director.

    (C) Action films generally require larger budgets than romance films and are thus prohibitive for many first-time film directors.

    (D) It is rare for the films of first-time directors to attain the popular appeal of films directed by filmmakers with at least one hit film to their credit.

    (E) Directors who have produced a previous hit film generally obtain the largest budgets and attract the most talented and well-known actors for their subsequent films.

Explanation: Tsumi Bats

Distinguishing Feature: Odd-Man-Out

9. Four valid assumptions in the answer choices? The stem itself prepares us to expect a pretty weak argument. Our job is to locate the statement that's not assumed in the argument. The author concludes that, to achieve maximum health, Tsumi bats should be fed certain nuts and veggies and a minimum amount of fruits and berries. The evidence comes in the second sentence: These bats, who are now fed mostly fruits and berries, develop endocrine imbalances. It's not worth the effort to try to prephrase all the assumptions inherent in this argument, but if a few ideas jumped out at you, great. At the very least, you should proceed to the answer choices with a clear understanding of the evidence and conclusion.

(A) is a valid assumption. The author suggests that the bat's endocrine imbalance is a problem, and that a revised diet might fix that problem. Thus the argument does assume that bats should not be fed endocrine imbalance-producing foods.

(B) and (D) are valid assumptions too. If the proposed diet will make the bats "healthiest," then the argument assumes that it will adequately nourish them (D) and that it won't malnourish them (B). Negate these choices and the argument falls apart, confirming that these are necessary assumptions here.

An 800 test taker confirms whether a statement is a necessary assumption in an argument by seeing what happens to the argument when that statement is denied or negated. If the argument crumbles, that's proof positive that the statement is necessary and thus must be assumed.

(C) The conclusion states that the bats will be fed a minimal amount of fruits and berries, while this choice says that they will eat none. Must that be a necessary part of this argument? No, it's too extreme: The author says straight away that some fruits and berries is okay, so it need not be assumed that the bats are denied these foods altogether. (C) is therefore our winner—our "odd-man-out."

> An 800 test taker reads the answer choices extremely carefully and notices even very subtle inaccuracies. Here, (C) is correct because it discusses a diet with "no" fruits or berries instead of "minimal" fruits and berries.

(E) focuses again on the author's claim that the recommended diet will make the bats healthiest. If that is true, then the author must assume that it won't create any health problems that are more detrimental to the bats' health than the endocrine imbalances that inspired the proposed diet in the first place.

Explanation: The Case of the Poison Grain

Distinguishing Features: Causation, Scope Shift

10. This passage tells a story similar to the anonymous fable of the poison grain, in which all of a kingdom's grain crop is mysteriously poisoned, causing anyone who ate it to go insane. The author describes a wave of unusual violence that swept over a medieval town for a period of five years, characterized by acts ranging from self-destruction to murder. That's followed by a description of a chain of events, beginning with an unusual shift in weather patterns that coincided with the violent period. Due to unusually heavy rainfall, the wheat crop probably fell prey to the ergot fungus, which can cause ergotism, a disease characterized by hallucinations and other psychological abnormalities. The author then concludes that the violence was caused by ("was the result of") the freakish weather conditions. There's the element of causation alluded to above.

> An 800 test taker recognizes causation in all of the various ways in which it is suggested by the wording of arguments.

When presented with a causal argument—especially when looking for a rebuttal that argument—the first thing to do is check to see that the causal mechanism described is appropriate. The author blames the unusual acts of violence in the town on ergot fungus. However, he doesn't know for a fact that the ergot fungus was present in the town's wheat. He knows conditions were ripe for the formation of the fungus (i.e., lots of rain), and he knows fungus-infected wheat can cause psychological disturbances—but the crucial point, the actual presence of the fungus, is mere supposition. (Note how the author says that the wheat crop "probably" fell prey to the fungus.) As (D) points out, the conclusion treats the probable occurrence of the fungus as if it were a certain, actual occurrence. And therein lies the scope shift as well; the author argues from probability in the evidence to a clear-cut, definite statement of actual causation in the conclusion. In arguing against this reasoning, it would be perfectly appropriate to point out that the author misses the distinction described in (D), the correct answer.

(A) Contrary to (A), the argument does use contemporary evidence: the shift in the area's weather patterns at the time of the incidents of violence.

(B) Actually, the author *does* set up a clear chain of cause and effect—rain causes fungus which causes psychological abnormality. The causes and effects are perfectly distinct; the question is whether the causal mechanism described is *valid*.

(C) distorts the argument, since no role at all is assigned to the chance or irrational in causing the psychological disturbances.

(E) The term "unusual violence" is reasonably well defined as involving acts of murder and self-destruction so pervasive as to endanger the town's very survival. We really can't ask for a more comprehensive definition than that.

Explanation: Indie Films

Distinguishing Features: Survey, Alternative Explanation, Causation, Numbers and Statistics, Odd-Man-Out

11. Lots going on here, for sure. This one touches on many of the logical elements highlighted in this chapter. We get two opposing views presented in a single argument. A survey showed that as a group, action films were rated higher than romance films. Viewpoint number one comes from the survey organizers, who concluded from this that subject matter of popular movies must determine their appeal. Seems reasonable, but the author states that this conclusion is probably wrong and offers an alternative explanation. She notes that the producers of the action films were more experienced in successful film production. Notice that the author doesn't disagree that actions films receive better ratings, but rather supports a different explanation for that superiority; the effect is the same in both viewpoints, but the causes differ. We're looking for an inference based on this argument, so once you have a firm grasp of the content, it's time to move to the answer choices. In addition, note the author's use of the contrast Keyword *yet* in the second sentence.

An 800 test taker takes careful notice of "Keywords"—structural signals that authors employ in order to help convey their ideas. Contrast Keywords like *yet* or *however* are especially powerful, as their job is to signal that something new is about to follow.

(A) This answer choice confuses percents and numbers. The survey is based on the percentage of films in each category to receive the highest rating, not on the actual number of films to receive the top rating. For instance, according to the argument it could be possible that 50% of 10 action films receive the high rating, and 20% of 100 romance films receive the high rating, in which case fewer actions films receive the highest rating, despite the action films group receiving the higher percentage of top ratings. A lower percentage does not necessarily mean a lower number.

(B) On the contrary: The author *does* suggest a relationship between previous directorial successes and the popular appeal of the survey films, so this answer choice contradicts the author's argument.

(C) The argument is about independent feature films. Based on that argument, we cannot infer anything about what a survey of big-budget mainstream films would show.

(D) distorts the information in the stimulus. Sure, of the filmmakers whose work is represented in this particular survey, some have a hit film to their credit, while some have never even made a movie before. Does that allow us to conclude who's "more likely" to produce a hit? For all we know, the folks with previous hits were new filmmakers themselves when they produced those hits. The absolute statement in (D) is not inferable.

(E)'s all that's left. The author suggests that having a previous hit film to the director's credit is more important than subject matter in determining ratings, so it logically follows that subject matter may not be a significant factor in the popular ratings of films made by directors with an equal number of previous hits. By positing another factor besides subject matter that accounts for the survey results, the author's argument certainly does allow for the possibility that subject matter *may* have no effect on the ratings. (E) wins.

> An 800 test taker is intimately familiar with the kinds of wrong choices that appear again and again on the GMAT. The wrong choices here contain some fairly common wrong answer types: confusing numbers and percentages (A); a choice that suggests the opposite of what's in the passage (B); a choice that strays outside the scope (C); and a classic distortion (D).

12. The second question based on this stimulus asks us to locate the one answer choice that *doesn't* strengthen the author's argument, which means we need to locate the odd-man-out. We therefore want to eliminate the four choices that strengthen the connection between the popular appeal of a director's film and that director's having a past hit film; or that strengthen the connection between lack of a hit film and lesser popular appeal. The right answer will be the choice that *doesn't* support the author's causal link between previous directorial success and the popular appeal of that director's other films.

> An 800 test taker expects that some question stems will not be written in the clearest possible manner. Before proceeding to the answer choices in such questions, she pauses for a moment to consider what she's being asked and what *kind* of answer choice she's looking for, even when it's impossible to specifically prephrase an answer.

(A) If previous hits indicate talent, then the author's theory of the link between previous hit films and popular appeal of the survey films seems more plausible, and we're more likely to believe that the organizers *are* wrong, as the author maintains, about the effects of subject matter.

(B), (D), and (E) all strengthen the argument by tying past experience of success to present cinematic successes. (B) links previous experience to ratings directly. (D) takes it from another angle and explains that the films of first-timers do not often achieve the same popular appeal as that attained by previous hit-makers. It still strengthens the argument by offering a direct relationship between past success and appeal. (E) links prior experience of success to the ability to obtain the best actors, offering another benefit that accrues to experienced directors and makes them more likely to produce hit films. Like (A), all of these choices make it seem more reasonable to argue that the organizers have misunderstood the role of subject matter in the survey ratings. That is, they all support the author's alternative explanation.

(C) *Why* many first-time directors don't make action films has no impact on this argument. The fact remains that of the films in this particular survey, the action films were made by more experienced directors while the romances were made by novices, and the author uses this fact to counter a previous conclusion. (C) gives us one possible explanation for this fact, but has no effect on how this fact is *used* by the author, which, after all, constitutes the crux of her argument. This is the one choice that does not strengthen (or, for that matter, even affect) the author's argument, so it is the right answer here.

CRITICAL REASONING PRACTICE SET 4

13. A career in dermatology is still a safe bet for medical school graduates. In the U.S., the number of cases of skin cancer linked to ultraviolet (UV) radiation in sunlight has remained relatively constant every year even though far fewer adults are intentionally exposing themselves to UV sunlight now than were doing so at the height of the suntan craze 20 years ago.

Each of the following, if true, could explain the relative stability in the incidence of skin cancer each year despite the decrease in intentional exposure to UV sunlight EXCEPT:

(A) Because of decreasing levels of ozone in the upper atmosphere, more people are now exposed accidentally to excessive UV sunlight.

(B) People who continue to intentionally expose themselves to UV sunlight are absorbing larger doses of the harmful radiation than the average sun-tanner did in the past.

(C) Levels of UV radiation from sources other than sunlight are increasing every year.

(D) While fewer women are intentionally exposing themselves to UV sunlight, the number of men doing so has increased significantly.

(E) In most victims, skin cancer is linked to exposures to UV sunlight that occurred up to 30 years before the onset of the disease.

14. Over the past seven years, private college tuition rates have increased, resulting in a large decrease in private college attendance across the country. Private college revenues, however, have progressively increased in each of the seven years during this period, and researchers predict further increases in the years to come.

Which of the following, if true, offers the best explanation for the situation described above?

(A) Most private colleges increase tuition rates approximately once every two years.

(B) Attendance at vocational schools generally exceeds attendance at private colleges in most cities.

(C) The increase in tuition rates at private colleges has influenced many prospective students to seek a state scholarship to attend a public university.

(D) The decrease in students attending private colleges over the last seven years has been more than offset by the increases in tuition.

(E) Private colleges gain a larger percentage of their revenue from alumni contributions than do public universities.

15. A team of pediatricians recently announced that dogs are more likely to bite children under age 13 than any other age group. Their finding was based on a study showing that the majority of all dog bites requiring medical attention involved children under 13. The study also found that the dogs most likely to bite are German shepherds, males, and non-neutered dogs.

    Which of the following, if true, would most weaken the pediatricians' conclusion that dogs are more likely to bite children under age 13 than any other age group?

    (A) More than half of dog bites not requiring medical attention, which exceed the number requiring such attention, involve people aged 13 and older.

    (B) The majority of dog bites resulting in the death of the bitten person involve people aged 65 and older.

    (C) Many serious dog bites affecting children under age 13 are inflicted by female dogs, neutered dogs, and dogs that are not German shepherds.

    (D) Most dog bites of children under age 13 that require medical attention are far less serious than they initially appear.

    (E) Most parents can learn to treat dog bites effectively if they avail themselves of a small amount of medical information.

16. A certain laboratory is studying the incidence of fatal liver damage in rats. Sixty-five percent of all rats whose environments exposed them to low levels of the toxin sulfur dioxide died of liver disorder. Ninety percent of all rats who died of liver disorder, however, were not exposed to any environmental toxins.

    Which of the following would provide a feasible explanation for the statistics above?

    (A) Environmental and nonenvironmental causes of liver disease in rats are mutually exclusive.

    (B) There is only one cause of fatal liver disease in rats.

    (C) Environmental toxins are not particularly dangerous to the livers of rats.

    (D) Only a small portion of the entire group of rats studied was exposed to environmental sulfur dioxide.

    (E) Most rats will not suffer from exposure to low levels of sulfur dioxide.

Explanation: Incidence of Skin Cancer

Distinguishing Features: Numbers and Statistics, Paradox, Alternative Explanation, Odd-Man-Out

13. Here's another question that touches on a whole bunch of the logical elements we've been discussing. We're asked to find the choice that could *not* possibly explain a phenomenon. This tells us that four of the answer choices *could* possibly explain the paradoxical phenomenon. As always, read the stimulus carefully, paying close attention to the details and what they imply. Here's the story: Since far fewer adults are intentionally exposing themselves to UV sunlight today compared to 20 years ago, the number of cases of skin cancer linked to exposure to the UV radiation in sunlight should be decreasing. But the passage creates a seeming paradox, because the number of cases of skin cancer has actually remained constant every year. Four of the answer choices will resolve the paradox by providing alternative explanations for the phenomenon of skin cancer that are not related to the total number of adults today who are intentionally exposing themselves to sunlight. The correct answer will leave the paradox intact.

An 800 test taker has a sense for what the right and wrong choices will look like or do, even when, in an "odd-man-out" situation, she can't pre-phrase such choices precisely.

(D) is the one that does not help to resolve the paradox. Even if the number of men who are intentionally exposing themselves to UV sunlight has increased, we still know from the stimulus that far fewer adults altogether are intentionally exposing themselves. So the mystery remains: the rate of skin cancer among adults altogether should be decreasing, although we're told it's not. (D) is the answer. The other four choices, however, do provide acceptable solutions to the mystery:

(A) Accidental exposure to UV sunlight may be compensating for the decrease in intentional exposure, keeping the cancer rate the same.

(B) The cancer rate among people who intentionally expose themselves to UV sunlight may be higher because they are getting a larger dose of the harmful rays, thus keeping the overall cancer rate the same.

(C) If levels of UV radiation from sources other than sunlight are increasing, that could compensate for the decrease in intentional exposure to the sun.

(E) If skin cancer is linked to exposures to sunlight that occurred up to 30 years before the onset of the disease, then the decrease in intentional exposure to UV sunlight in recent years probably does not yet show up in the rate of skin cancer.

Explanation: Tuition Rates

Distinguishing Features: Numbers and Statistics, Explain

14. Here we have a specific, and common kind of number question: an increase/decrease problem. The author discusses two simultaneous trends that might seem to contradict one another. Tuition has increased at private universities, leading to a decrease in enrollment—so far that's logical. However, revenue at these universities has continued to increase despite the decreased enrollment. The correct answer must offer some source of revenue that more than compensates for the decrease in revenues created by the lower enrollment. That's where (D), the correct answer, fits in: If the tuition hikes have brought in more revenue than the loss of enrollment has taken away, then it's easy to see how both trends discussed in the stimulus can simultaneously exist.

(A) The frequency with which private schools increase tuition doesn't begin to explain the revenue situation in the stimulus. The relevant fact is that tuitions are increasing, which triggers the rest of argument. In what specific manner they're increasing is irrelevant.

(B) offers an irrelevant distinction between vocational schools and private colleges that doesn't contribute any new information to the stimulus. Vocational schools are outside the scope, which focuses only on the situation related to the decrease in enrollment at private colleges.

(C) tells us what happens to some students who can no longer afford private universities. Their fate, sorry to say, doesn't matter, and again it doesn't add any new information to the scenario. We already know that enrollment decreased; this choice just gives us a human-interest story when we really want to know how it's possible under these circumstances for revenues to actually increase.

(E) is similar to (B) in that it provides another irrelevant distinction. It compares the role of alumni contributions at public and private colleges, while the stimulus does not express any interest in public universities or in alumni contributions. Even if private colleges do get a larger percentage of money from alumni, decreasing enrollment shrinks the number of alumni and would, if anything, seem to decrease revenue even further—thereby deepening the mystery rather than explaining it.

> An 800 test taker knows that in an Explain question, the information provided in the stimulus remains true, and that the task is to reconcile, not to change, the presented facts.

Explanation: Dog Bites

Distinguishing Features: Scope Shift, Study, Numbers and Statistics

15. We don't have to look far for the conclusion in this one—it's restated right in the question stem: Dogs are more likely to bite children under age 13 than any other age group. The evidence is found in the second sentence dealing with the findings in the study. The last sentence expands on the study, but essentially adds nothing of value to the logic of the stimulus; it's basically "filler" material.

So what's the scope shift? The conclusion is about dogs biting children under 13, but the evidence is based on dog bites *requiring medical attention.* (A) weakens the argument by addressing this scope shift. It basically says that many dog bites that *don't* require medical attention (bites that are within the scope of the conclusion) happen to people *over* 13. Now, this doesn't *disprove* the argument; it merely weakens the link between the stated evidence and the stated conclusion. The pediatricians counted up all the people bitten by dogs who came in for medical attention, found most of them to be under age 13, and concluded *from this alone* that dogs are more likely to bite children under age 13. This general conclusion is based on evidence about a very specific group. If it's true, as (A) says, that many who don't seek treatment are over 13, then the argument is weakened. (A) it is.

An 800 test taker has a sure-fire method for spotting scope shifts.
She asks herself:
1) What's the focus, subject, or scope of the conclusion?
2) What's the focus, subject, or scope of the evidence?
3) Are they the same?

(B) We're not concerned with the results of the dog bites, only the frequency of bites by age group. Even if everyone over 65 dies as a result of being bitten, it could still be true that children under 13 are most likely to be bitten.

(C) is a takeoff on the filler sentence: Once again, it's the sheer number of bites that's important, not the kinds of dogs inflicting them.

(D) Same thing: The number of bites, not the seriousness of them, is the issue.

(E) is irrelevant; what *can* happen plays no role in the study and the conclusion based on it.

Explanation: Rats and Liver Damage

Distinguishing Features: Study, Numbers and Statistics, Paradox, Scope Shift

16. Here's another study to ponder, and the stem alerts us to the fact that we need to find a plausible explanation for the statistics cited. That alone suggests that the stats are puzzling, or at least a bit unusual, which is reinforced by the contrast Keyword *however* in the final sentence. So what's going on in this one? We have a significant number of rats dying of liver disorder after being exposed to sulfur dioxide, but most of the rats who died of liver disorder were not exposed to any environmental toxins. This is not unlike what we've seen previously: a situation in which what seems like the same groups are actually not. Specifically, you should have realized immediately that the 65% and the 90% figures refer to two different groups, and thus that there is no discrepancy in the statistics. The 65% figure represents all rats exposed to sulfur dioxide; 90% represents the percentage of all rats that died of liver disorder. (D) points this out. If only a small number of rats were exposed to sulfur dioxide, then it's not surprising that 90% of the rats that died of liver damage died of something other than sulfur dioxide exposure. After all, only a small number of them were exposed to sulfur dioxide in the first place. (D) wins.

(A) The exclusivity of causes of liver damage is irrelevant to this study. Any of the rats could have had both causes, but only one seriously enough to cause death.

(B) explains nothing. If there is only *one* cause of liver disease in rats, then what killed the rats that were *not* exposed?

(C) As for this one, why did 65% of the exposed rats die, if environmental toxins are not very dangerous? This seems counterintuitive, and so it can't possibly help to explain the statistics.

(E) says basically the same thing as (C), with different wording. It's wrong for the same reason—namely, that it contradicts the evidence. If 65% of the rats exposed to low levels of sulfur dioxide died, then most rats probably *will* suffer from such exposure.

CRITICAL REASONING PRACTICE SET 5

Questions 17–18 are based on the passage below.

> The proliferation of colloquialisms is degrading the English language. A phrase such as she was like, "no way!" you know?—a meaningless collection of English words just a few decades ago—is commonly understood by most today to mean she was doubtful. No language can admit imprecise word usage on a large scale without a corresponding decrease in quality.

17. The argument relies on which of the following assumptions?

    (A) Colloquialisms always evolve out of a meaningless collection of words.

    (B) The colloquialisms appearing in the English language introduce imprecision into the language on what would be considered a large scale.

    (C) The Russian, French, and German languages cannot admit imprecise word usage on a large scale without an inevitable decrease in the quality of those languages.

    (D) The English language would not be degraded if there did not exist an alternative informal way to express the sentiment "she was doubtful."

    (E) The widespread use of colloquialisms represents the most serious form of language degradation.

18. Which of the following, if true, most weakens the argument above?

    (A) Linguists have shown that the use of imprecise language on a small scale does not generally impair understanding.

    (B) Many colloquialisms that appeared in earlier forms of the English language disappeared over time as the people who used those particular phrasings were assimilated into larger groups with different language patterns.

    (C) Dissemination of a new word or phrase by the mass media is an important factor in whether or not the new word or phrase will become a colloquialism.

    (D) Colloquialisms are more likely to be coined by the youth in a culture than by any other segment of the population.

    (E) Languages of the highest quality often evolve over time out of a collection of colloquial usages woven into the formal dialect of a given people.

19. In the years 1971 to 1980, the population of the state prison system was on average about 82 percent of maximum occupancy. During those years, the average number of prisoners entering the system each year was equivalent to 9.1 percent of maximum occupancy. From the years 1981 to 1984, the average number of prisoners entering the system each year fell to 7.3 percent of maximum occupancy, yet the population of the state prison system rose to almost 89 percent of maximum occupancy.

    Which of the following, if true, helps to resolve the apparent discrepancy?

    (A) The average sentence of a prisoner in the state system increased from 1981 to 1984.

    (B) Beginning in 1981, many of those entering the state prison system had been transferred from prisons in other states.

    (C) Between 1981 and 1984, the percentage of prisoners incarcerated for violent crimes increased by 26 percent.

    (D) In 1981, a legislative fact-finding committee proposed a revision of the state's parole and work release programs.

    (E) Between 1971 and 1984, the proportion of active criminals actually caught and incarcerated in the state prison system has steadily increased.

20. An antique and curiosity shop is weighing the advantages of renewing its regular advertisement in a monthly trade publication. The shop originally placed the advertisement in order to increase business, but found that the majority of its sales are made to those who do not read the publication and have not seen the ad. The shop is considering canceling the advertisement in that publication in order to save money.

    The answer to which of the following questions would be LEAST relevant to the shop's decision?

    (A) How does the cost of the advertisement compare to the profit from purchases made by those who have responded to it?

    (B) Are there other trade publications that attract the shop's typical clientele in which an advertisement would be likely to reach prospective customers at the same cost?

    (C) Is a significant proportion of the shop's competitors satisfied with the effect of their advertisements in trade publications?

    (D) How many buyers who responded to the advertisement were professional antique dealers who generally make relatively expensive purchases?

    (E) Is any significant change expected in the pattern of the trade publication's circulation?

Explanation: "Like, No Way! You Know?"

Distinguishing Features: Scope Shift, Causation, Alternative Possibility

17. How's that for eloquence? The strange part is that most of us really have no problem understanding the meaning of this phrase. Which is, in fact, the author's beef in the stimulus. He gets right to the point: the conclusion that the increase in colloquialisms degrades the English language. For evidence, the author then (1) gives us an example of a colloquialism, the illustrious phrase in the title above, and (2) states that imprecise word usage on a large scale basically decreases the quality of the language, hence, the tie in with the conclusion in the first sentence. The assumption resides in the gaps between these pieces of information; we were never told that these colloquialisms were rampant or imprecise. Indeed, the author states that *imprecise* words admitted on a *large scale* decrease a language's quality, without showing that colloquialisms really fall into either category. That omission constitutes the shift in scope. For the author's conclusion to be valid based on this evidence, he must assume that the evidence is relevant to the conclusion, and that colloquialisms are both imprecise and prevalent in English. The right answer choice, (B), picks up on both. Without this, the evidence simply doesn't lead all the way to the conclusion.

(A) focuses on the source of colloquialisms, which the author addresses but which plays a central role in neither the evidence nor the conclusion. This could or could not be true without impacting the conclusion.

(C) basically restates the evidence. If "no language" can permit such laxity, then these three languages would logically follow along, but since the stimulus already tells us this much, (C) is not a necessary assumption here.

> An 800 test taker recognizes the difference between a stated piece of evidence and an unstated—yet required—part of an argument (i.e., its assumption).

(D), if anything, presents us with a flawed inference, which would only be accurate if the author assumed that the stated colloquialism were the *only* colloquialism in English, and that *only* colloquialisms degrade the English language. He assumes neither, so if this were an Inference question, (D) would be wrong on these counts. As far as being assumed—that is, being something that's *required* by the argument—(D) is even further off base.

(E) is too extreme. The author identifies one cause (proliferating colloquialisms) which leads to one effect (*like, um, degraded English*). To make this argument, he does not need to assume that this cause is more or less serious than any other. Even if colloquialisms were a minor part of this problem, the author's conclusion could still be valid.

18. *Okay, it's, like, um, time for the second question on this passage about degraded English, you know?* We're asked to weaken the same argument. To recap: The author concludes that the proliferation of colloquialisms degrades English. He then gives an example of a colloquialism and asserts as evidence that lots of imprecise word usage decreases the quality of a language. The right answer probably won't involve denying the argument's assumption, since the first question for this stimulus already focused on that element. Therefore, we can go through the choices one by one looking for a choice that will decrease the viability of the conclusion.

(A) discusses imprecise language "on a small scale" while the stimulus focuses on such language "on a large scale." Therefore, (A) is outside of the argument's scope.

(B) Since the author's argument relates colloquialisms to the quality of a language, information about their historical longevity does not impact the argument one way or the other. The real issue is the damage they do to the language while they're around.

(C) explains the media's role in determining the fate of a potential colloquialism. Since the argument itself does not concern itself with the media or with the mechanisms by which a colloquialism becomes a colloquialism, (C) has no effect on this argument.

(D) Like (C), (D) brings up the issue of the source of colloquialisms. The argument focuses on the *effect* of colloquialisms; their source plays no role in that focus.

(E) breaks apart the author's causal argument. The author asserts that colloquialisms lower the quality of a language, while (E) explains that they actually often contribute to the "highest quality" languages in the long run. (E) is the answer because it addresses a possibility which the author doesn't consider and which would weaken the author's argument.

An 800 test taker knows that the two most common ways to weaken an argument are by breaking down the argument's central assumption, and by asserting alternative possibilities relevant to the argument.

Explanation: Prison Paradox

Distinguishing Features: Numbers and Statistics, Paradox

19. Here we have a case in which an apparent paradox stems from a misunderstanding of statistics. Clear up the misunderstanding, and the paradox vanishes—that is, the rise described at the end no longer seems surprising.

An 800 test taker knows that numbers and statistics can be fertile ground for all sorts of questions. She knows these questions may ask her to find the choice that points out a flaw or weakness in an argument, or, as in this case, that resolves an apparent discrepancy. Either way, she recognizes that understanding the ways in which numbers and percentages are used—or misused—is the key to answering any question concocted out of a numerical or statistical situation.

Here are the facts: In the early years, the prisons were 82% full, and just over 9% of the total possible occupancy arrived each year in the form of new prisoners. Now that the latter figure is down to 7.3%, the author is surprised that the prisons are more full: 89% full. She evidently expects that as one figure drops, so should the other. The key is seeing that she is focusing on the trend in incoming prisoners only, when the totals take into account all prisoners. Consider the long-termers. If the average length of sentences of all prisoners is increasing, then it's small wonder that the prisons are more crowded now, even if a smaller percentage of the inmates are newcomers. That's what (A), the correct answer, is all about.

(B) Where the prisoners came from has no impact on how many are, or should be, here in this state.

(C) Nothing in the evidence concerns the nature of crime, so no information about what landed these people in jail in the first place can resolve the paradox.

(D) A "proposed revision" is way too weak. Was it instituted? And even if it was, what effect would it have? There's no way to know, so (D) is irrelevant and does nothing to clear up what the author considers to be a surprising result.

(E), even if true, begs the question of why the percentage of the prison total entering the system is lower than years ago, but the prisons are fuller. All (E) says is that fewer criminals are getting off scot free.

Explanation: Antique Shop

Distinguishing Feature: Odd-Man-Out

20. In this next one we're asked to find the choice that is least relevant to making a certain decision. Thus, answering the other four questions will provide evidence that will either strengthen or weaken the rationale for the decision. You should read the stimulus while thinking about the kinds of things you might want to know before making such a decision. Here's the situation: The ad was placed to increase business, but most sales are made to people who have not seen the ad. Based on this evidence, the shop owner concludes that perhaps the ad should not be renewed. The evidence here concerns the majority of the shop's sales, but the conclusion involves canceling the ad—the implication being that the ad is not paying for itself. We wish to eliminate the four answer choices that contain information relevant to the decision; that is, that may offer clues as to whether the ad indeed pays for itself or not. Imagine that you are a business consultant, and consider whether you would ask the shop owner the question contained in each choice.

An 800 test taker is able to creatively envision the kinds of situations that might help him to evaluate answer choices.

(C) contains information irrelevant to the decision. Nothing in the original argument concerns the satisfaction of the shop's competitors. Even if competitors are not satisfied with the effects of their ads in trade publications, this particular ad in this particular publication may make money for this store. It may be interesting information for other reasons, but the answer to the question in (C) would not be very helpful in making the decision at hand, which makes (C) the correct answer.

(A)'s question would yield information particularly useful in making the decision. Although the ad doesn't bring in most business, it might bring in some, and that business might be worth more than the cost of the ad.

(B) may very well also produce information useful in making the decision. The existence of other, more productive uses for the ad money is certainly a pertinent consideration.

(D)'s question would reveal useful information. Even though most of the sales are not generated by the ad, the value of the sales that are might be relatively high. Knowing the number of big spenders the ad attracts would certainly aid in making the decision.

(E) fits well into the arsenal of pertinent questions. The future audience of the publication is crucial to assessing the wisdom of renewing the ad.

CRITICAL REASONING PRACTICE SET 6

21. General: The commander of the Air Force has recommended that we deploy the G28 aircraft in the reconnaissance mission, because the G28 can fly lower to the ground without being detected and could therefore retrieve the necessary information more efficiently than the currently stationed D12. But the D12 is already in the area and poised for takeoff, and would have just enough time to accomplish the mission if deployed immediately, while the G28 would require four days just to arrive in the area and get outfitted for the mission. Since the mission's deadline is immovable, I am forced to overrule the commander's recommendation and order the deployment of the D12.

Which of the following is assumed in the general's argument?

(A) The quality of information retrieved from the mission would be higher if the D12 were deployed than if the G28 were deployed.

(B) By the time the G28 arrived in the area and was outfitted for the mission, the D12 would have already completed the mission if deployed immediately.

(C) The ability of an aircraft to fly low to the ground is not a significant consideration when choosing aircraft for a reconnaissance mission.

(D) It would take longer for any aircraft not currently in the area besides the G28 to arrive in the area and get outfitted for the mission.

(E) Any time saved during the mission due to the operation of the more efficient G28 would not offset the additional time required to deploy the G28.

22. History has shown that severe and sudden political instability strikes country Y roughly once every 50 years. The most recent example was the attempt on the president's life in 1992. The reaction of average investors in country Y to crisis situations in the country cannot be predicted in advance. The government's fiscal affairs department has introduced an electronic protection mechanism into the stock market of country Y in the hopes of avoiding a prolonged large-scale selloff. The mechanism is triggered in specific instances based on estimations of how average investors will react to changes in corporate data and economic indicators.

    If the statements above are true, which of the following conclusions can be drawn regarding the electronic protection mechanism?

    (A) Sometime within the next 50 years an attempt on the president's life will trigger the protection mechanism.

    (B) Whether the protection mechanism will function appropriately in response to a sudden political event depends on whether the event is seen by investors as positive or negative.

    (C) It is unclear how well the protection mechanism would work in the event of a sudden political coup if such an event is partially or wholly unrelated to changes in corporate data and economic indicators.

    (D) There would be no way for the protection mechanism to differentiate between market fluctuations resulting from economic factors and those that are caused by political instability.

    (E) The protection mechanism would be purposely destroyed by political insurgents if they were able to infiltrate the government's fiscal affairs department.

Questions 23–24 are based on the passage below.

The incidence of suicide in the country of Travonia has increased dramatically in recent years, as evidenced by the fact that since the introduction of several nonprescription brands of sleeping pills, the number of deaths from overdoses alone has nearly doubled. However, certain types of suicides have not increased in number during this period. It is true that elderly suicides have seen a greater than 70 percent increase, but teen suicides now account for only 30 percent of all suicides in the country. This is a significant decrease over 1985, when teen cases represented 65 percent of all country-wide suicides.

23. The argument above is most vulnerable to criticism on the grounds that it does which of the following?

    (A) It discounts the possibility of suicides occurring in groups other than the elderly and teenagers.

    (B) It takes for granted that the introduction of non-prescription sleeping pills has had the same effect on two different demographic groups.

    (C) It assumes that a decrease in the percentage of teen suicides necessarily signifies a decrease in the number of teen suicides.

    (D) It overlooks the possibility that the total number of deaths in Travonia has increased since 1985.

    (E) It relies on evidence that contradicts its conclusion.

24. The assertion that suicides are increasing in Travonia is most justified if which of the following is assumed?

(A) The elderly suffered the greatest number of overdoses from the non-prescription sleeping pills.

(B) Overdosing on sleeping pills was not the most pervasive method of suicide in Travonia ten years ago.

(C) The number of deaths from natural causes in Travonia has decreased in recent years.

(D) The majority of deaths resulting from overdosing on non-prescription sleeping pills were not accidental.

(E) Travonia's suicide rate is higher than the world-wide average suicide rate.

Explanation: D12 Versus G28

Distinguishing Features: Numbers, Scope Shift, Alternative Possibility

21. Next up we have "Critical Reasoning meets Top Gun." The general is trying to determine which of two types of aircraft would better fit the needs of the Air Force for an upcoming mission, and there are a number of logical elements present here. While the commander of the Air Force prefers the G28 because it could perform the necessary task more efficiently, the general orders that the D12 be used instead. He provides one piece of evidence to support this decision: Only the D12 can perform the task in time to meet the mission's deadline. When an author argues for one option over another, the author must assume that the benefit provided by the preferred option can only be found in that option. In other words, the author must assume that the G28 would not fulfill the mission in the allotted period of time. But perhaps there's an alternative? The general says that it would take four days for the G28 to be ready for the mission, but he never explicitly says that the G28 *couldn't* meet the deadline. Perhaps the plane's greater efficiency would enable it to still complete the mission in the allotted period of time, despite the later start. That's a plausible alternative that the general has overlooked. In order for the general's conclusion to be valid, he must assume that the G28 could not perform the mission by the immovable deadline. Thus he assumes that the G28's efficiency would not recoup the extra time that it would take for the G28 to begin the mission. (E) is the answer.

The number issue is a common one: The test makers like to create situations in which a decrease in one area is made up, in fact, even surpassed, by an increase in something else. And one could see this scenario in terms of a scope shift, as well: The general speaks of the efficiency of the G28 early on, but then makes his recommendation based solely on the time factor. Recognizing that shift is key to understanding the assumption here.

> An 800 test taker has the ability to see situations in Critical Reasoning questions from a number of angles, and to think through problems on a number of different levels. The more tools in your test-day arsenal, the better.

(A) The stimulus never states that one aircraft retrieves higher quality information than the other; one is simply *more efficient*. So (A) is not relevant to the general's decision.

(B) goes too far. The author never states how long the mission would take, so there's no basis for assuming that the D12 would be done before the G28 arrived.

(C) The ability to fly low to the ground *is* a significant consideration to the commander, and the general never contests the importance of this consideration. He just overrides it by making the deadline a *more* significant consideration, so he need not assume (C) in order to formulate his recommendation.

(D) focuses on aircraft other than the G28. Aren't two enough to deal with? The author seems to think so, because he discusses only the D12 and the G28. How long it would take *other* kinds of planes to get to the scene is irrelevant to the general's argument, which specifically deals with a choice between these two.

Explanation: Market Protection Mechanism

Distinguishing Feature: Causation

22. The president of country Y is sure having a hard time of it, being shot at and all. No matter. The real issue here is this electronic market regulation gizmo that's supposed to help the country avoid a major economic disaster. Our job is to draw a conclusion about it.

There's a lot going on here, so let's recap: Roughly every 50 years, country Y experiences political instability. The reaction of average investors to such crises cannot be predicted, so a crisis leads to, or causes, uncertainty. Country Y has created an electronic protection mechanism for its financial market that relies on estimates of how average investors will react to changes in corporate data and economic indicators. The purpose of the mechanism is to avoid a major market selloff. The correct answer will draw an inference that logically connects the different ideas stated in the evidence. It's difficult to prephrase the correct answer here, so your best bet is to test the choices rigorously, looking for the one that absolutely must be true.

(A) goes too far in its inference that an attempt on the president's life will happen within 50 years. The 1992 attempt was only an example of the political instability that occurs roughly every 50 years, and the 50-year period was an average, not an absolute limit. Furthermore, even if there is an attempt on the president's life, it is unclear how investors will react because their behavior in such situations cannot be predicted in advance. For all we know, the market will go up and the mechanism will not be needed.

(B) goes beyond the scope of the argument. Whether investors perceive sudden political events positively or negatively isn't mentioned in the stimulus, so we can't infer that that perception makes any difference to the accuracy of the mechanism.

(C) draws a reasonable conclusion based on the evidence. If political instability involves changes in corporate data and economic indicators, then the mechanism should work the way it is designed to work. But if the incident does not involve those elements, then the way the mechanism will work becomes unclear, because the behavior of investors will be unpredictable. (C) wins.

(D) This statement goes too far to be inferable. The mechanism might be able to differentiate between various types of market fluctuations, even though it might not be able to trigger appropriate responses to some of them.

(E) takes the argument far beyond its original scope. Nothing in the stimulus leads to a prediction of what might happen to the protection mechanism in the event of political instability.

Explanation: Suicide in Travonia

Distinguishing Feature: Numbers and Statistics

23. Where do the test makers find these depressing places? People in Travonia are killing themselves in record numbers. Let's see what's going on. The author states that Travonia's suicide rate has increased, citing an increase in the number of overdoses following the recent release of certain brands of sleeping pills. Getting to the heart of the argument, the author then asserts that certain types of suicides have not increased in number, conceding that the percentage of elderly suicides has increased but noting that the percentage of teen suicides has decreased. The latter fact sounds like good news on the face of it, but is tempered by the fact that the author blurs the distinction between numbers and percents. Just because the percentage represented by teen suicides has decreased, that doesn't mean that fewer teens are committing suicide. A decreased percentage needn't signify a decreased number of suicides, and the author's flaw comes in failing to recognize this, as (C) expresses. A common logical flaw, indeed.

(A) The argument doesn't explicitly discuss other groups, but it certainly doesn't discount the possibility that other groups might exist.

(B) Not really, since the author doesn't link the sleeping pill takers to either demographic group, as mentioned in the explanation for (A).

(D) The total number of deaths in general is outside the scope of the argument, which deals exclusively with deaths from suicides and overdoses. The author need not consider the overall death figures in Travonia in order to make this argument.

(E) is vague, and wrong. The evidence about percentages doesn't contradict the author's conclusion, it just doesn't necessarily support it in the way the author suggests.

An 800 test taker is crystal clear on the distinction between numbers and percentages.

---

24. Now for part 2 of "Suicide in Travonia." Re-evaluating the argument, we can see that the author presents one piece of evidence in support of her assertion: Deaths resulting from sleeping pill overdoses have almost doubled since new nonprescription sleeping pills have been released. In order to use these overdoses to support the assertion that suicides have increased dramatically, the author must assume that the overdoses were indeed deliberate and hence qualify as suicides. (D) clearly expresses this assumption.

(A) brings up the same problem that we saw in the previous question's answer choices: the author makes no links between the people overdosing on the sleeping pills and the teens and elderly folk discussed later in the stimulus. The author needn't assume such a connection in order to assert that suicides have increased dramatically.

An 800 test taker understands the relationship between groups represented in the stimulus, and specifically knows which connections are necessary, and *not* necessary, between them.

(B) Knowing what was the most pervasive suicide method ten years ago doesn't have any real bearing on the claim in the first sentence of the passage. Maybe the method was overdosing on sleeping pills, maybe not. Either way, this doesn't help justify the assertion that recent suicides are up.

(C) is far outside the scope. Deaths from natural causes have no necessary relation to this argument about suicide.

(E)'s relative comparison of Travonia's suicide rate to the world's is not relevant to the assertion in question. The author only asserts that suicides in Travonia have increased; there is no mention of their relative increase or of the suicide rate in other countries.

CRITICAL REASONING PRACTICE SET 7

25. A study found that last year roughly 6,700 homeless people in the United States were admitted to hospitals due to malnutrition. In the same year, a little more than 7,200 nonhomeless people were admitted to hospitals for the same reason. These findings clearly show that the nonhomeless are more likely to suffer from malnutrition than are the homeless.

    The answer to which of the following questions would be most likely to point out the illogical nature of the conclusion drawn above?

    (A) What is the relative level of severity of the malnutrition suffered by each group cited in the study?
    (B) To what extent, on average, are the nonhomeless better off financially than are the homeless?
    (C) To what extent are the causes of malnutrition in the nonhomeless related to ignorance of proper dietary habits?
    (D) What percentage of each group cited in the study suffered from malnutrition last year?
    (E) What effect would a large increase in the number of homeless shelters have on the incidence of malnutrition among the homeless?

26. Kopke: In the past ten years, most of the new clothes that I have purchased have fallen apart within a few short years. However, all of the clothes that I have purchased at vintage clothing shops are still in excellent condition, despite the fact that they were all over thirty years old at the time that I bought them. Clearly, clothes are not manufactured as well today as they were when those vintage clothes were made.

Which of the following is a weakness in the argument above?

(A) It fails to demonstrate that the clothes manufactured thirty years ago were of higher quality than clothes of all other eras.

(B) It neglects the possibility that the clothes of thirty years ago, when prices are adjusted for inflation, cost more than clothes manufactured today.

(C) It confuses the number of clothing items sold with the proportion of those items that are no longer useful.

(D) It does not explain why clothing manufacturing standards have fallen over time.

(E) It fails to take into account clothes made over thirty years ago that are no longer fit for sale.

27. Psychologists who wish to have one of their book reviews nominated for the prestigious Boatwright Psychology Review award should not submit book review articles that review more than three books at a time. This is because editors for the Boatwright Psychology Review will not publish a book review article if it is too lengthy and cumbersome to read. In their submission guidelines, the editors explicitly state that review articles that cover more than three books at a time are considered too lengthy and cumbersome to read.

Which of the following statements represents an assumption upon which the argument above depends?

(A) The books review article that covers the most books must be the lengthiest and most cumbersome article to read.

(B) If a book review article is published in the Boatwright Psychology Review, that article will receive the prestigious Boatwright Psychology Review award.

(C) All articles published in the Boatwright Psychology Review must be limited to a certain length specified by the editors.

(D) The Boatwright Psychology Review editors generally prefer book review articles that cover one book rather than two books.

(E) To be nominated for the Boatwright Psychology Review award, a psychologist's book review article must be published in the Boatwright Psychology Review.

28. An international study recently examined the effects of second-hand smoke on health. Surprisingly, although the dosages of harmful chemicals from second-hand smoke are so small that their effect should be negligible, the study found that nonsmoking spouses of smokers displayed an incidence of heart disease that was significantly greater than that of nonsmokers who were not as regularly exposed to second-hand smoke.

Each of the following, if true, could contribute to an explanation of the unexpectedly high incidence of heart disease in smokers' spouses EXCEPT:

(A) A disproportionately high number of people married to smokers are among the older segment of the married population, a group that inherently has a higher-than-average risk of heart disease.

(B) On average, more alcohol and coffee, both of which have been linked to heart disease, are consumed in the homes of smokers than in the homes of nonsmokers.

(C) A disproportionately high number of smokers are married to other smokers, and the risk of heart disease increases in proportion to the number of smokers living in a household.

(D) Smokers generally tend to live in higher-stress environments than do non-smokers, and stress is a factor associated with above average incidence of heart disease.

(E) A disproportionately high number of smokers live in areas with a high level of industrial pollutants, which have been shown to be a factor in increased risk of heart disease.

Explanation: Homeless, Nonhomeless, and Malnutrition

Distinguishing Features: Numbers and Statistics, Study

25. The GMAT test makers have an incredible knack for writing short, unassuming arguments that nonetheless pack a major wallop. This one's a good example. It's one of the shortest arguments you'll see, and it doesn't even contain any difficult words, but it sure gives people fits—and that's because of the statistics involved. It goes to show that it really doesn't take much more than a few well-placed statistics to, shall we say, *liven things up*. The first thing you might have noticed is that the argument contains both numbers and statistics. The 6,700 and 7,200 figures represent actual numbers of people, while the conclusion states what's "more likely" to happen—a clear reference to an element of probability. Knowing from the stem that the argument is fatally flawed, this should have already raised a red flag. Here's the specific lowdown: Since only 6,700 homeless people suffering from malnutrition were admitted to U.S. hospitals last year, compared to 7,200 nonhomeless people, the nonhomeless must be more likely to suffer from malnutrition. Perhaps the argument immediately struck you as a little wacky, as it well should have given the clues in the question stem.

An 800 test taker is suspicious whenever she sees raw numbers side by side in an argument with rates, percentages, or probabilities—especially in a Logical Flaw question.

We're asked to find a question whose answer would most effectively illuminate the problem with the argument, and, as strongly suggested above, this boils down to a numbers versus percentages game: We cannot figure the odds of suffering from malnutrition solely from the number of malnourished people in each group. We must also know the overall total of people in each group before we can create ratios and thus figure out the "likelihood" of suffering from this condition. The only way for this conclusion to be valid is if the total number of homeless people in the U.S. equals the total number of nonhomeless people—then the 7,200 hospitalized nonhomeless, as opposed to the 6,700 hospitalized homeless, would suggests that the nonhomeless are more likely to suffer from malnutrition. But this is clearly a ludicrous assumption (at least at the present time)—there's no way the number of homeless equals the number of nonhomeless people in the U.S. The answer to the question in the correct choice will somehow point this out, thus making the flaw in the reasoning (using raw numbers as the basis for a conclusion about likelihood) plain to see. Choice (D) provides the question whose answer would provide the information we need to correctly understand the odds. Since the U.S. has far fewer homeless people than it has people with homes, the 6,700 figure would form a far higher percentage of homeless people who suffer from malnutrition than the percentage of nonhomeless people based on the 7,200 cases of malnutrition among this group. The answer to this question would allow us to see how the raw numbers cited do not support the author's counterintuitive conclusion that the nonhomeless are more susceptible to malnutrition than are the homeless. Go with (D).

(A) goes beyond the scope of the argument. The argument involves the likelihood of suffering from malnutrition, not the relative levels of severity.

(B) also introduces a new issue—finances. No matter how much people with homes are better off financially than are the homeless, the fact remains that more nonhomeless were hospitalized for malnutrition than homeless, and the answer to this question would do nothing to reveal the illogical conclusion that's drawn from this data.

(C) introduces another new issue. The argument draws no conclusion about the causes of malnutrition within these groups, only about the likelihood of malnutrition. Nailing down the precise causes of malnutrition in one of the groups wouldn't change the numbers in the evidence nor point out the problem with the logic.

(E) is irrelevant to the argument as presented. The future possibility of remedying homelessness to some degree does not impact upon these numbers and this particular conclusion drawn from them. The reasoning still seems off, but the answer to the question in (E) will not show how the logic goes astray.

Explanation: Kopke's Vintage Clothing

Distinguishing Features: Alternative Explanation, Scope Shift

26. The stem alerts us to the fact that there's a flaw afoot, so we should expect something in Kopke's speech to get all fouled up. In more official GMAT lingo, that simply means that the evidence won't adequately support the conclusion. And what is that conclusion? Kopke's maintains that clothes manufactured 30 years ago were constructed better than clothes manufactured today. His evidence is that clothes he's purchased within the last ten years have fallen apart, while the clothes he bought in vintage shops are all in excellent shape despite their age. This might sound persuasive so far, but we know from the stem that this is a flawed argument. Think about where Kopke's logic goes astray. For one thing, he compares all the clothes he's bought within the last ten years to only the clothes that have *survived* 30 years before he purchased them. That's a subtle shift, but a shift nonetheless. The correct answer should point out the dubious nature of this comparison, and indeed, choice (E) points out the inappropriateness of this kind of comparison. The only "vintage" clothes he takes into account are those that have proven to be extremely durable. So it isn't much of a surprise that they're still functional. Kopke doesn't consider the clothes made long ago that have fallen apart, so he can't evaluate the overall standards of that era. Comparing only the extremely durable vintage clothes to all modern clothes is like comparing apples and oranges, so choice (E) gets to the heart of the flaw here. It suggests an alternative explanation for the "favorable" comparison that Kopke relies on in forming his conclusion.

(A) The argument doesn't address all eras, so Kopke doesn't have to compare the clothes made 30 years ago with those of every other era.

> An 800 test taker doesn't fault an author for failing to do something he's not logically obligated to do.

(B) Kopke's argument does not address cost at all—just quality. Considering cost would not affect the validity of the argument.

(C) Kopke doesn't take into account vintage clothes that are no longer fit for sale (see the explanation for choice (E) above), but he never equates the proportion of tattered clothes with the total number of clothing items sold. So choice (C) doesn't describe a weakness in the argument.

(D) The argument doesn't hinge on explaining why standards have fallen, just that they have.

> An 800 test taker notes the scope of the argument from the get-go, and immediately discounts choices that violate it.

Explanation: Boatwright Award

Distinguishing Feature: Scope Shift

27. author concludes that psychologists who want their work to be nominated for the Boatwright Psychology Review award should only submit articles containing reviews on three or fewer books. The evidence follows: the Boatwright Psychology Review basically will not publish any book review article that reviews more than three books. Look back over the conclusion and evidence, and you'll realize that they aren't really talking about the same thing. The conclusion is about what one should do in order to get his work nominated for the award, and the evidence is about what one should do in order to get his work *published*. That's a classic scope shift. The only way to make these two different subjects relate to one another is to assume that one must have a review article published in the Review in order to be eligible for the award. Otherwise the evidence about publication requirements would have no relevance to the conclusion about nomination requirements. (E) expresses this central assumption faithfully, tying the evidence concerning publishing to the conclusion concerning nominations.

An 800 test taker knows that the logical gap that results from a scope shift can often be bridged by an assumption.

(A) While the stimulus suggests that articles covering more books are longer, it nowhere suggests that this proportional relationship carries out to the extremes. What makes for the longest articles isn't central to the evidence and conclusion, and hence need not be assumed in order for this argument to work.

(B) overstates the link between the two subjects. The argument in the stimulus assumes that publication is necessary for a book to be *nominated*, while (B) says that publication guarantees that a book will *win* the award. The argument doesn't concern itself with which book might win the award, so (B) isn't directly relevant to it.

(C) is too broad to be necessary here. The argument concerns book review articles, which do come with certain length restrictions. But (C) deals with *all* articles, and we don't know nor do we really care anything about articles besides book reviews that Boatwright may contain (editorials, feature articles, etc.). These may or may not have length restrictions, but this particular argument doesn't depend on this issue.

(D) makes an irrelevant distinction that doesn't directly pertain to the central issue: what must be done with an article before it can be nominated for the prestigious award. One book and two books are both on the acceptable side of the length restriction—no distinction between them need be assumed here.

Explanation: Second-Hand Smoke

Distinguishing Features: Study, Causation, Odd-Man-Out, Alternative Explanation, Scope Shift

28. Perusing the list of distinguishing features, you're likely to ask "what's *not* in this one?"—and the answer is "not much." This one nearly has it all, and we can take the features in order to describe what's going on. First of all, we're dealing with another study, and you should be fairly familiar by now with the kinds of mishaps, misconceptions, and downright mistakes that can arise when researchers get their hands on things. The study involves the nonsmoking spouses of smokers; that is, people who are presumably in contact with a decent amount of second-hand smoke. While the author contends that second-hand smoke shouldn't really have any effect, the study found that the incidence of heart disease in nonsmokers married to smokers is actually much higher than that of nonsmokers not exposed to second-hand smoke. So while there shouldn't be any causal mechanism at work here, the author implies that the study's finding suggests that there is. Now, we're asked to evaluate possible explanations of the unexpectedly high incidence of heart disease in smokers' nonsmoking spouses, and to choose the one that *wouldn't* contribute to an explanation. So there are the odd-man-out and alternative explanation features—four of the choices will provide plausible alternative explanations for the surprising results, while the right answer will not. And let's jump right to our odd-man-out, since it relates to the final feature mentioned above—scope shift. As difficult as this question may be for a number of reasons, the right answer is actually quite simple if you noticed the shift that takes place between the scope of the study and the scope of choice (C): The study focuses entirely on nonsmokers married to smokers. Cases in which *smokers* are married to other smokers fall outside of this scope, so (C) has no power to clear up the mystery at hand.

As for the wrong choices—that is, the valid explanations—they all hinge on the causation issue; or, more specifically, breaking down the notion of causality in order to show that the study's finding is not so surprising after all. Remember, the author is surprised at the finding because supposedly, second-hand smoke shouldn't cause a higher incidence of heart disease. Each wrong choice lessens the surprise by suggesting that second-hand smoke is in fact *not* to blame here, but that some other factor *correlated* with smoking is actually responsible for the higher incidence of spousal heart disease.

An 800 test taker recognizes the difference between causation and correlation, and is intimately familiar with the ways in which the GMAT tests this distinction.

(A) If the spouses of smokers tend to be older, and older people are more prone to heart disease, this helps explain the findings in a way that would satisfy the author—a way that's consistent with her belief that second-hand smoke, by itself, shouldn't cause the increased incidence of heart disease noted in the study.

(B) Same thing: If smoking homes are generally homes with increased alcohol and coffee intake, and these things are associated with heart disease, then we'd be less surprised by the findings in light of the fact that the effects of second-hand smoke should be negligible.

(D) and (E) Same thing: If smoking is correlated with higher stress and higher pollution levels, both of which are related to heart disease, the mystery would be lessened.

section two

READING COMPREHENSION

CHAPTER FIVE

The Reading Comprehension Challenge

Roses are red. Violets are blue.

The passage suggests that which of the following is a distinctive feature of a flower?

(A) size

(B) aroma

(C) beauty

(D) color

(E) petals

Ever since you learned to read, you've been tested on your comprehension of written material, so it's no surprise that Reading Comprehension is the most familiar section in all of standardized testing. Medicine, law, archaeology, psychology, dentistry, teaching, business—the exams that stand at the entrance to study in these and other fields have one thing in common: Reading Comprehension passages. No matter what academic area you pursue, you have to make sense of dense, even unfamiliar prose, and business school is no exception.

If you're looking to score an 800 on the GMAT, then you shouldn't expect to see too many easy Reading Comp passages. For the purposes of this book, we've compiled for your test-taking pleasure a group of the densest, nastiest passages we could find. If you can ace these in a reasonable amount of time, it's safe to say that you have absolutely nothing to fear from Reading Comp questions come test day.

Oh, and as for that gem of modern poetry above, the correct choice is (D)—but you already knew that.

USING THE READING COMPREHENSION PASSAGES IN THIS BOOK

The Reading Comp passages in this book are broken up into two categories:

The Art of Social Science Maintenance

and

Blinded by Science

GMAT Reading Comp passages deal with three topics with basically equal frequency: business, social science, and natural science. You'll see business and social science passages in the first category, but since natural science passages are often the most daunting to test takers, you'll find them in a section all their own.

STRATEGIES FOR READING COMPREHENSION

Here are a few general pointers to help guide your attack:

- **Read for the author's purpose and main idea.** It's easy to get bogged down in details, especially in difficult passages like the ones that follow. But if you keep the author's purpose—that is, the reason he or she wrote the passage—and main idea in mind, you'll be able to answer many general types of questions immediately.

- **Paraphrase the text.** You'll be able to process and apply the information in any passage, including these toughies, if you simplify the passage's ideas and translate them into your own words.

- **Create an outline, or "roadmap," of the passage.** The fact that the GMAT is now a computerized exam makes it more, not less, important for you to write down notes as you read the passage. If you chart out the structure of the passage and main idea of each paragraph, you'll better understand the passage and be able to find the information that the questions require more easily.

- **Don't overinvest.** Since GMAT Reading Comp passages vary in length from 150–300 words and since a passage can have 2–5 questions (usually 3–4), it's impossible to give a general rule about how much time to spend on any given passage. Still, aim to spend no more than four minutes reading even the most difficult passage and spend an average of one minute per question. By the way, for purposes of practice, most of the passages in this section will be on the longer side, but your approach to shorter and longer passages should be the same. Remember that Reading Comp questions constitute one third of the questions in the Verbal section of the exam. Do not spend so much time on them that you neglect the other two-thirds of the section.

An 800 test taker considers where she is in the Verbal section when she decides how much time to invest in any given Reading Comp passage.

- **Read the explanations.** Review the key points of each passage, comparing your own synopsis of the passage to ours. Notice whether you are consistently identifying the main idea and focusing on the relevant parts of the passages. As in the other sections of this book, the thought processes and habits of 800 test takers are highlighted throughout the explanations. Study them as you go along, and try to make those habits your own.

CHAPTER SIX

The Art of Social Science Maintenance

Even if business and political science or history are familiar fields to you, you've likely encountered Reading Comprehension passages that quickly take you past your comfort level. The subject of the passage doesn't independently determine its difficulty; a Reading Comp passage on opportunity costs can be much harder than one on the migrating patterns of the water-shrew. The following four passages are challenging because of their treatment of business or social science subjects and because of their particularly demanding questions. Use all of your skills to cut them down to size.

Every day the mailboxes of America are filled with solicitations provided by the direct marketing industry. America's response to this deluge has been strangely mixed. On the
(5) negative side, poorly executed direct marketing produces unwanted, annoying and wasteful solicitations, also known as "junk mail." Also, aggressive direct marketing techniques, aided by new tools in technology, represent a serious
(10) threat to informational privacy. Sophisticated computer matching programs can produce intrusive personal profiles from information which, standing alone, does not threaten individual privacy.

(15) The 1991 Harris-Equifax Consumer Privacy Survey addressed popular attitudes towards direct mailing practices and their impact on informational privacy. When asked how they viewed direct mail offers in general, 46 percent
(20) of the respondents said they were a "nuisance," 9 percent considered them to be "invasions of privacy," and only 6 percent said they were "useful." But if Americans have such a negative opinion of the direct marketing
(25) industry, they have a strange way of showing it. Direct mail advertising expenditures rose from $7.6 billion in 1980 to $23.4 billion in 1990. The laws of the market dictate that companies would not have made these efforts without
(30) prospects of success. Moreover, almost half of the citizens surveyed who considered direct mail offers to be "invasions of privacy" had themselves bought something in response to a direct mail ad in the past year.

(35) Analysis of this seeming contradiction reveals the central problem of regulation in this industry: everyone hates receiving "junk mail," and everyone ought to be concerned about informational privacy. Still, direct marketing
(40) offers real advantages over other means of shopping. Even those who believe that the direct mailing industry has a generally negative societal impact probably would prefer to remain on some mailing lists. We like shopping by
(45) mail, and we don't want to throw out the good with the bad.

1. Which one of the following, if true, would best strengthen the author's explanation of the "seeming contradiction" expressed in line 35?

(A) Awareness of commercial infringements on the rights of citizens has never been higher.

(B) The number of people on more than one mailing list has increased in direct proportion to the increase in direct marketing expenditures.

(C) Consumers do not perceive a connection between their individual purchasing behavior and infringements on their personal rights.

(D) Some people believe that the benefits associated with the recent success of the direct marketing industry will filter down to consumers over time.

(E) Some opinion polls on other topics indicate a similar discrepancy between what people say about an issue and how they act in relation to that issue.

Every day the mailboxes of America are filled with solicitations provided by the direct marketing industry. America's response to this deluge has been strangely mixed. On the
(5) negative side, poorly executed direct marketing produces unwanted, annoying and wasteful solicitations, also known as "junk mail." Also, aggressive direct marketing techniques, aided by new tools in technology, represent a serious
(10) threat to informational privacy. Sophisticated computer matching programs can produce intrusive personal profiles from information which, standing alone, does not threaten individual privacy.
(15) The 1991 Harris-Equifax Consumer Privacy Survey addressed popular attitudes towards direct mailing practices and their impact on informational privacy. When asked how they viewed direct mail offers in general, 46 percent
(20) of the respondents said they were a "nuisance," 9 percent considered them to be "invasions of privacy," and only 6 percent said they were "useful." But if Americans have such a negative opinion of the direct marketing
(25) industry, they have a strange way of showing it. Direct mail advertising expenditures rose from $7.6 billion in 1980 to $23.4 billion in 1990. The laws of the market dictate that companies would not have made these efforts without
(30) prospects of success. Moreover, almost half of the citizens surveyed who considered direct mail offers to be "invasions of privacy" had themselves bought something in response to a direct mail ad in the past year.
(35) Analysis of this seeming contradiction reveals the central problem of regulation in this industry: everyone hates receiving "junk mail," and everyone ought to be concerned about informational privacy. Still, direct marketing
(40) offers real advantages over other means of shopping. Even those who believe that the direct mailing industry has a generally negative societal impact probably would prefer to remain on some mailing lists. We like shopping by
(45) mail, and we don't want to throw out the good with the bad.

2. Which one of the following critiques most approximates the logic underlying the author's concern regarding the effects of the computer matching programs mentioned in lines 10–14?

(A) An ecologist who states that since each of three species individually would not damage an ecosystem, it is safe to introduce all three into the ecosystem overlooks the possibility that the dominance of one species may lead to the extinction of one or both of the other two species.

(B) An ecologist who states that since each of three species individually would not damage an ecosystem, it is safe to introduce all three into the ecosystem overlooks the possibility that the three species taken together may very well pose a serious threat to the ecosystem.

(C) An ecologist who states that since each of three species individually would not damage an ecosystem, it is safe to introduce all three into the ecosystem overlooks the possibility that the addition of the three species to the ecosystem may preclude the addition of any further species.

(D) An ecologist who states that since each of three species individually would not damage an ecosystem, it is safe to introduce all three into the ecosystem overlooks the possibility that the ecosystem may not be the optimal environment for the species in question.

(E) An ecologist who states that since each of three species individually would not damage an ecosystem, it is safe to introduce all three into the ecosystem overlooks the possibility that any one of three species may have posed a risk to the previous ecosystem in which it lived.

Every day the mailboxes of America are filled with solicitations provided by the direct marketing industry. America's response to this deluge has been strangely mixed. On the
(5) negative side, poorly executed direct marketing produces unwanted, annoying and wasteful solicitations, also known as "junk mail." Also, aggressive direct marketing techniques, aided by new tools in technology, represent a serious
(10) threat to informational privacy. Sophisticated computer matching programs can produce intrusive personal profiles from information which, standing alone, does not threaten individual privacy.
(15) The 1991 Harris-Equifax Consumer Privacy Survey addressed popular attitudes towards direct mailing practices and their impact on informational privacy. When asked how they viewed direct mail offers in general, 46 percent
(20) of the respondents said they were a "nuisance," 9 percent considered them to be "invasions of privacy," and only 6 percent said they were "useful." But if Americans have such a negative opinion of the direct marketing
(25) industry, they have a strange way of showing it. Direct mail advertising expenditures rose from $7.6 billion in 1980 to $23.4 billion in 1990. The laws of the market dictate that companies would not have made these efforts without
(30) prospects of success. Moreover, almost half of the citizens surveyed who considered direct mail offers to be "invasions of privacy" had themselves bought something in response to a direct mail ad in the past year.
(35) Analysis of this seeming contradiction reveals the central problem of regulation in this industry: everyone hates receiving "junk mail," and everyone ought to be concerned about informational privacy. Still, direct marketing
(40) offers real advantages over other means of shopping. Even those who believe that the direct mailing industry has a generally negative societal impact probably would prefer to remain on some mailing lists. We like shopping by
(45) mail, and we don't want to throw out the good with the bad.

3. Which one of the following can be inferred from the passage about direct mail advertising expenditures in the years between 1980 and 1990?

   (A) The rise in expenditures during this period is suggestive of the expectations of companies engaged in direct marketing at the time.

   (B) The profit derived from sales linked to these expenditures in 1990 was more than double the profit derived from such sales in 1980.

   (C) The lowest yearly expenditure on direct mail advertising during this period occurred in 1980.

   (D) Direct marketing companies expect the pattern of expenditures during this period to continue in the decades to come.

   (E) The rise in expenditures during this period closely parallel the laws of the market.

Every day the mailboxes of America are filled with solicitations provided by the direct marketing industry. America's response to this deluge has been strangely mixed. On the
(5) negative side, poorly executed direct marketing produces unwanted, annoying and wasteful solicitations, also known as "junk mail." Also, aggressive direct marketing techniques, aided by new tools in technology, represent a serious
(10) threat to informational privacy. Sophisticated computer matching programs can produce intrusive personal profiles from information which, standing alone, does not threaten individual privacy.
(15) The 1991 Harris-Equifax Consumer Privacy Survey addressed popular attitudes towards direct mailing practices and their impact on informational privacy. When asked how they viewed direct mail offers in general, 46 percent
(20) of the respondents said they were a "nuisance," 9 percent considered them to be "invasions of privacy," and only 6 percent said they were "useful." But if Americans have such a negative opinion of the direct marketing
(25) industry, they have a strange way of showing it. Direct mail advertising expenditures rose from $7.6 billion in 1980 to $23.4 billion in 1990. The laws of the market dictate that companies would not have made these efforts without
(30) prospects of success. Moreover, almost half of the citizens surveyed who considered direct mail offers to be "invasions of privacy" had themselves bought something in response to a direct mail ad in the past year.
(35) Analysis of this seeming contradiction reveals the central problem of regulation in this industry: everyone hates receiving "junk mail," and everyone ought to be concerned about informational privacy. Still, direct marketing
(40) offers real advantages over other means of shopping. Even those who believe that the direct mailing industry has a generally negative societal impact probably would prefer to remain on some mailing lists. We like shopping by
(45) mail, and we don't want to throw out the good with the bad.

4. The author would most likely agree with which one of the following statements?

(A) Despite its drawbacks, direct marketing has had an overall positive effect on American society.

(B) The attitudes revealed in opinion polls can provide insight into actual behavior.

(C) Regarding the effects of commercial enterprises, presenting a nuisance is a more serious offense to society than is invasion of privacy.

(D) Everyone who would prefer to remain on at least one mailing list thinks that direct marketing negatively affects society in some way.

(E) The growth in direct marketing would be even more significant in the future if the percentage of people who found direct mail offers to be a nuisance were to decrease.

Junk Mail

What Makes It Difficult

We've all been the victims of junk mail at some point or another, so the concept behind this one is not intimidating in the same manner as, say, the anomalous character of the Soviet Union, a topic you'll run into sooner than you'd like. And the writing itself isn't too difficult to understand, either. The real problem lies in the questions. Question 1 is a "Strengthen the Argument" challenge, common in Critical Reasoning questions, but more rare and cumbersome in Reading Composition. Question 2 is a real monster: we're asked to go outside the passage in search of a situation that mirrors the underlying logic of a critique. Not fun. The other questions present formidable challenges as well. Here's the lowdown on the passage.

Key Points of the Passage

Purpose and Main Idea: The author's purpose is to explain why direct mail marketing has been so successful despite Americans' seemingly negative attitudes towards direct mail techniques. The main idea is that even though Americans dislike receiving "junk mail," they value the advantages of shopping by mail and continue to respond positively to direct mail marketing, increasing the industry's success.

An 800 test taker persistently searches for the overriding main idea, and hangs in there even when the author's full point isn't revealed until late in the passage.

Paragraph Structure: Paragraph 1 introduces us to the notion that Americans' response to direct mail marketing has been "strangely mixed." We get the "negative side" of the American response in the first paragraph, as the author explains why Americans view direct mail marketing as annoying and invasive.

Paragraph 2 then helps us to see why the American response can be considered "mixed." It starts out by providing evidence from an opinion survey that supports the author's claim that Americans view direct mail negatively. It then shows that despite their attitudes, Americans' behaviors in response to direct mail have been positive: direct mail has become a highly successful marketing industry. Evidence from the same opinion survey cited earlier is given to show that Americans buy items through direct mail even though they dislike its techniques.

This "seeming contradiction" is explained in paragraph 3, where the author tells us that Americans shop by direct mail even though they dislike it because it is convenient and offers distinct advantages over other types of shopping. In essence, Americans like shopping by mail—so they put up with the drawbacks of direct mail techniques.

An 800 test taker boils down the ideas in a passage to their simplest form.

ANSWERS AND EXPLANATIONS

1. C **2. B** **3. A** **4. B**

1. (C)

This "strengthen the argument" question requires that we first understand how the author explains the "seeming contradiction" in paragraph 3. He argues that Americans respond to direct marketing because of its conveniences, even though Americans don't like the annoyance or the invasion of privacy. This evidence assumes that Americans are willing to maintain certain shopping habits despite the drawbacks associated with them. Choice (C) bolsters this assumption and therefore strengthens the argument. If consumers don't perceive a connection between their shopping behaviors and infringements on their rights, they are more likely to react as the author says they do: to continue shopping by mail despite its disadvantages.

(A), (B) These choices focus on one portion of the author's argument but do not help strengthen it as a whole. The fact that awareness of infringement is high, choice (A), would strengthen only one part of the author's claim: that people don't like direct mail. It doesn't bolster the full argument that direct mail marketing is successful despite these infringements due to the fact that Americans like to shop by mail. Similarly, with (B), the increased number of people on multiple mailing lists does not necessarily strengthen the argument that people use direct mail despite its drawbacks because they like its conveniences. These individuals may be on multiple lists simply because their names were sold to direct mail companies.

(D) This choice can be seen as contradicting the author's explanation of why direct mail marketing is successful. (D) states that direct marketing may eventually benefit consumers—its success will filter down to consumers over time. But the author tells us that people respond to direct mail marketing because they like its advantages—in other words, they benefit from it now, as they are using it. That's why they put up with its annoyance and invasion of privacy. If (D) is true, perhaps there's more to the story than the author perceives, but that's not your problem.

(E) The only thing that (E) may strengthen (and it's tenuous at best) is the notion that the "seeming contradiction" that the author describes exists. Even that's a stretch. Either way, the implications of the opinion polls in (E) have no bearing whatsoever on our author's explanation for the discrepancy at hand.

> An 800 test taker understands that just like in Critical Reasoning, strengtheners and weakeners in Reading Comp often work by bolstering or damaging the assumptions in an author's argument.

2. (B)

Ouch. We're asked to identify the criticism that most closely approximates the logic of the author's concern over the use of computer matching programs. Well, why is the author concerned about these? The line reference brings us right to the crux of the matter: "Sophisticated computer matching programs can produce intrusive personal profiles from information which, standing alone, does not threaten individual privacy." Extracting the general logical structure of this, we have a situation in which harmless individual elements, when combined, become harmful in some way. That's the situation we need to find among the choices, and (B) best approximates this situation: the species alone aren't dangerous to the ecosystem, but put them together and look out! The mechanism at work in (B) mirrors the mechanism the author describes in paragraph 1—namely, the way that computer matching systems can combine non-intrusive independent bits of information into a profile that threatens individual privacy.

It's helpful to restate exactly what we're looking for in order to eliminate the wrong choices: the logic of the original example in the passage states that things (bits of information) that individually don't have a certain effect (i.e., threaten privacy) DO have that effect when put together.

(A) Here, we have species that individually don't harm the ecosystem (so far so good), but when put together may harm each other. Not the same thing.

(C), like all of the wrong choices, starts out okay with individual species that by themselves don't harm the ecosystem, so we have to look to the end of the choice to see where it goes awry. In this case, the ecologist is chastised for objecting to the joint introduction of all three species into the ecosystem on the grounds that doing so may not allow other species to join later. This result would not necessarily cause damage to the ecosystem, which is the result that we're looking for in order for this critique to match the logic of the passage's computer matching example.

(D) This time the ecologist's assertion is based on the grounds that the species in question may be happier somewhere else. Again, the "overlooked possibility" is not one that necessarily causes harm: The ecosystem might not be an optimal environment for the species, but that doesn't necessarily mean that the ecosystem itself will be damaged.

(E) Their *previous* ecosystems? What does that have to do with putting them together here in the ecosystem in question? This is far from the logic underlying the example in the passage.

An 800 test taker is able to apply what she learns in the passage to other issues in different contexts.

---

3.   (A)

The mention of expenditures from 1980–1990 brings us squarely to paragraph 2, where the author informs us that expenditures rose significantly during that stretch, and that "companies would not have made these efforts without prospects of success." Inference questions are not great candidates for prephrasing, so you probably moved directly to the choices. Hopefully you saw that (A) is a reasonable inference based on this information. It stands to reason that companies spent more money on advertising because they expected to benefit from it (in accordance with the "laws of the market"). Therefore, the rise in direct marketing expenditures can reasonably be said to reflect their expectations regarding success.

(B), (C), and (D) The passage implies that companies benefited from direct marketing—meaning, they made greater profits—but we have no idea how much they benefited. Thus, a specific claim like (B)'s assertion that they made "more than double" the profit at the end than at the beginning of the period is not warranted. Similarly, we are told that expenditures rose from 1980 to 1990, but we don't know how much they rose in any given year. In fact, we can't be sure that expenditures rose every single year—we're told only that the 1990 figure was greater than the 1980 figure. For all we know, expenditures could have decreased in 1981, thus making this the lowest expenditure year. So we don't have enough information to infer choice (C). The same is true of choice (D). We're told only that expenditures rose from 1980-90. We cannot infer anything about what companies might expect expenditures to be in the future.

(E) distorts information in the passage. The author tells us that "the laws of the market dictate" that companies would not have invested in direct marketing unless they expected it to be successful. But to say that the rise in expenditures "parallels" the laws of the market is a distortion of this concept. The rise in expenditures may be explained with reference to the laws of the economic market, but that's about it. (E)'s manner of combining these two elements of the passage is unwarranted.

4. (B)

This Inference question requires us to determine which statement could most likely be attributed to the author, based on the information presented in the passage. Again, our grasp of the author's purpose in writing the passage comes into play. This passage looks at the difference between Americans' attitudes about direct mail and their behaviors in response to it. Evidence for the public's attitudes is provided through opinion surveys, which suggests that the author believes that the attitudes revealed in surveys can help us understand public behavior—choice (B). Think of it this way: If the author didn't agree with (B), then there would be no contradiction to resolve, because the data from the opinion polls would be meaningless. The passage as is can exist only if the author believes that polls can provide insight as stated in choice (B).

(A) exaggerates the author's conclusion. We are told that Americans respond to direct mail because they perceive its benefits, but it would be going too far to conclude from this that the author believes that direct mail has "an overall positive effect on American society."

(C) presents an unwarranted comparison that in no way can be attributed to the author. Nuisance and privacy invasion are two categories of responses from the poll of paragraph 2, with the former outranking the latter in the public's mind, but we can't infer from this that the author believes that presenting a nuisance is a greater offense than invading privacy when it comes to direct marketing, no less in the context of "commercial enterprises" as a whole.

An 800 test taker zeroes in on comparisons presented in choices to determine whether they are warranted or unwarranted.

(D) switches the terms of the second-to-last sentence of the passage, which reads "Even those who believe that the direct mailing industry has a generally negative societal impact probably would prefer to remain on some mailing lists." Not only does (D) get this backwards, but it also fails to take into account the qualified nature of the author's assertion indicated by the word *probably*.

(E) Again, we are not given enough information to draw this inference. The author does not discuss the future growth of direct marketing, so it's too much of a stretch to infer how the author thinks the industry might increase or decrease. In addition, the passage states that the direct marketing industry has grown despite people's negative attitudes about it. Growth in the industry does not therefore seem directly proportional to negative attitudes, which is another reason why it is unwarranted to ascribe the belief in (E) to the author.

So far, so good? For your information, this first passage was a full 300 words, pretty much as long as they get. Now that you're warmed up, see what you can make of the rest of the Reading Comp questions.

The debt crisis affecting many developing countries has had three causes: imprudent management and borrowing by debtor countries; imprudent lending by banks; and
(5) rising interest rates. The unprecedented rise in real interest rates to about 6 percent by 1982 increased the burden on borrowers and completely changed the nature of the debt problem. In past debt crises, when loans were
(10) made at fixed rates, real interest rates rose with deflation. But once price levels stabilized, the interest burden would be higher only to the extent of the proportional decline in price levels, and it remained quite possible that
(15) inflation would eventually reduce the burden. In this crisis, though, the real interest rate has risen and stayed high, and inflation has brought no relief.

During the 1980s, fear of financial loss led
(20) U.S. commercial banks to sharply curtail their lending activity in debtor countries. In 1982, nine large banks had over 250 percent of their capital in loans to developing countries; by mid-1986, the nine banks had reduced their
(25) activities to the point where they had sufficient equity and reserves to withstand potential losses. Although banks have stabilized their positions, many continue to carry developing-country debt at face value.

(30) Present bank strategies deal with the debt crisis by extending the effective maturity of loans. Although any method that reduces the flow of resources from debtor countries will help in the short run, further lending promises
(35) little relief to the debt problem. So long as real interest rates remain high, developing countries will remain in debt.

1. The primary purpose of this passage is to discuss

(A) the factors that have led to the current levels of debt carried by developing countries

(B) the deleterious effects of rising interest rates

(C) American banking in the 1980s and its impact on debtor nations

(D) the future of U.S. banking with respect to its interest rates and loan policies

(E) economic conditions in developing countries that might prevent them from or enable them to repay U.S. loans

The debt crisis affecting many developing countries has had three causes: imprudent management and borrowing by debtor countries; imprudent lending by banks; and

(5) rising interest rates. The unprecedented rise in real interest rates to about 6 percent by 1982 increased the burden on borrowers and completely changed the nature of the debt problem. In past debt crises, when loans were

(10) made at fixed rates, real interest rates rose with deflation. But once price levels stabilized, the interest burden would be higher only to the extent of the proportional decline in price levels, and it remained quite possible that

(15) inflation would eventually reduce the burden. In this crisis, though, the real interest rate has risen and stayed high, and inflation has brought no relief.

During the 1980s, fear of financial loss led

(20) U.S. commercial banks to sharply curtail their lending activity in debtor countries. In 1982, nine large banks had over 250 percent of their capital in loans to developing countries; by mid-1986, the nine banks had reduced their

(25) activities to the point where they had sufficient equity and reserves to withstand potential losses. Although banks have stabilized their positions, many continue to carry developing-country debt at face value.

(30) Present bank strategies deal with the debt crisis by extending the effective maturity of loans. Although any method that reduces the flow of resources from debtor countries will help in the short run, further lending promises

(35) little relief to the debt problem. So long as real interest rates remain high, developing countries will remain in debt.

2. Which of the following characterizes responses to the debt crisis in the 1980s?

(A) increased pressure on debtor countries to pay interest due on loans

(B) an increase in the percentage of their total capital large banks devoted to foreign loans

(C) a decrease in the funds designated by banks to cover potential losses

(D) reliance by banks on inflationary pressure to reduce debt levels

(E) a decline in bank lending and an increase in capital reserves

The debt crisis affecting many developing countries has had three causes: imprudent management and borrowing by debtor countries; imprudent lending by banks; and
(5) rising interest rates. The unprecedented rise in real interest rates to about 6 percent by 1982 increased the burden on borrowers and completely changed the nature of the debt problem. In past debt crises, when loans were
(10) made at fixed rates, real interest rates rose with deflation. But once price levels stabilized, the interest burden would be higher only to the extent of the proportional decline in price levels, and it remained quite possible that
(15) inflation would eventually reduce the burden. In this crisis, though, the real interest rate has risen and stayed high, and inflation has brought no relief.

During the 1980s, fear of financial loss led
(20) U.S. commercial banks to sharply curtail their lending activity in debtor countries. In 1982, nine large banks had over 250 percent of their capital in loans to developing countries; by mid-1986, the nine banks had reduced their
(25) activities to the point where they had sufficient equity and reserves to withstand potential losses. Although banks have stabilized their positions, many continue to carry developing-country debt at face value.
(30)   Present bank strategies deal with the debt crisis by extending the effective maturity of loans. Although any method that reduces the flow of resources from debtor countries will help in the short run, further lending promises
(35) little relief to the debt problem. So long as real interest rates remain high, developing countries will remain in debt.

3. The author suggests that methods currently in place for dealing with the debt crisis are inadequate because they

(A) increase the upward pressure on real interest rates without allowing any opportunity for reduction

(B) allow real wages to rise at the expense of economic growth in debtor countries

(C) fail to address problems of mismanagement in debtor and creditor countries

(D) do not promote long-term growth

(E) sacrifice a reduction of real interest rates for a short-term increase in loan maturity

The debt crisis affecting many developing countries has had three causes: imprudent management and borrowing by debtor countries; imprudent lending by banks; and
(5) rising interest rates. The unprecedented rise in real interest rates to about 6 percent by 1982 increased the burden on borrowers and completely changed the nature of the debt problem. In past debt crises, when loans were
(10) made at fixed rates, real interest rates rose with deflation. But once price levels stabilized, the interest burden would be higher only to the extent of the proportional decline in price levels, and it remained quite possible that
(15) inflation would eventually reduce the burden. In this crisis, though, the real interest rate has risen and stayed high, and inflation has brought no relief.

During the 1980s, fear of financial loss led
(20) U.S. commercial banks to sharply curtail their lending activity in debtor countries. In 1982, nine large banks had over 250 percent of their capital in loans to developing countries; by mid-1986, the nine banks had reduced their
(25) activities to the point where they had sufficient equity and reserves to withstand potential losses. Although banks have stabilized their positions, many continue to carry developing-country debt at face value.

(30)   Present bank strategies deal with the debt crisis by extending the effective maturity of loans. Although any method that reduces the flow of resources from debtor countries will help in the short run, further lending promises
(35) little relief to the debt problem. So long as real interest rates remain high, developing countries will remain in debt.

4. In the passage, the author identifies all of the following as contributing to the current debt crisis EXCEPT

(A) careless borrowing by developing countries

(B) sustained high real interest rates

(C) unwillingness of banks to transfer the burden of loans to other countries

(D) unwise decisions made by commercial lending institutions

(E) failure of inflation to reduce the interest burden

The Debt Crisis

What Makes It Difficult

The concept of a debt crisis is not in and of itself too off-putting, but the passage gets quite dense, especially in paragraph 2, and the questions tend to focus on the most complicated pieces of the passage. What is most challenging about this passage is its use of financial terms such as "capital reserves" and "developing-country debt" without explaining them in any real detail. Also, it throws a lot of numbers and percents at you. The real danger posed by a passage like this is that it will lead unwary test takers to spend an unreasonable amount of time sorting out the details. The writing in the passage itself is not too bad, so it shouldn't take too long to get what you need from the passage and proceed to the questions.

An 800 test taker doesn't try to memorize all the details in a passage. He only wades into the details when a question requires him to do so.

Key Points of the Passage

Purpose and Main Idea: The author's purpose is to describe the causes of the debt crisis. Her main idea is that the rise in real interest rates has prolonged the debt crisis, limiting the effectiveness of measures to diminish it.

Paragraph Structure: Paragraph 1 outlines three causes of the current debt crisis. It blames debtor countries, U.S. banks, and the increased interest rate. It also explains why this debt crisis has been more difficult to resolve than those before it.

Paragraph 2 outlines bank strategies for dealing with the debt crisis in the 1980s. Initially, banks scaled back on their loans to debtor countries and, although they are no longer cutting back on loans, the banks haven't increased them either. The banks still do not lend out more than they can cover with their own capital.

The criticism of banking strategies continues into paragraph 3. The paragraph describes one potential solution attempted by the banks (extending the maturity date on the loans) but notes its long-term limitations.

An 800 test taker jots down a roadmap for every passage, knowing that it's difficult and unnecessary to keep all of the key information in her head.

ANSWERS AND EXPLANATIONS

1. A **2. E** **3. D** **4. C**

1. (A)

This is a standard "primary purpose" question so you should already have a sense of what the right answer should say.

An 800 test taker uses his roadmap to answer "global" (primary purpose or main idea) questions.

As we noted in the roadmap, the author's purpose is to describe the causes of the debt crisis, and that's what answer choice (A) says. Notice that this answer choice throws in a curve: instead of using the familiar term (by this point, at least) "debt crisis," (A) defines the debt crisis. Hopefully you saw through this minor effort to confuse you.

(B) focuses only on a detail in the passage: while the passage does mention the harmful effects of rising interest rates, it does so only in the first paragraph. The author did not write this passage with the primary intent to describe those effects, so (B) is not the passage's primary purpose.

(C) is another detail, this time contained in paragraph 2. Again, it is factually correct to say that the author describes American banking in the 1980s and its impact on debtor nations, but the passage does not primarily intend to describe such facts.

An 800 test taker always keeps track of the question that was asked.

(D) was not mentioned at all. While paragraph 3 contains a prediction that the problem will continue, it doesn't mention what U.S. banks will do in response.

(E) is touched on indirectly in the passage, but even if it were discussed directly that still wouldn't make (E) the right choice. You're not looking for something that's merely true according to the passage, but rather for the passage's main idea. (E) isn't it.

2. (E)

This question asks you to look for general patterns: based on the information in the passage, which of the answer choices fairly summarizes the responses to the debt crisis in the 1980s? You know from your roadmap or from a quick skim that the events of the 1980s are discussed in paragraph 2. Reread that paragraph, focusing on the responses to the debt crisis, and you'll see that banks primarily responded by cutting back on their loans. (E) is closest to this prephrase; while the passage doesn't directly say that banks increase their capital reserves, you can safely infer that they did so based on the information in paragraph 2.

(A) is plausible (if banks shrank their loans then it is certainly possible that they pressured debtor countries to pay back some of those loans), but plausible is useless here. The passage doesn't describe pressure for repayment as characteristic of the 1980s, so (A) doesn't cut it.

(B) is exactly the opposite of what we're looking for. Just because (B) deals with the right subject matter, don't overlook the fact that its content is severely off track.

> An 800 test taker is not fooled by wrong answer choices that use the same words or phrases as the passage. He focuses on what the answer choices *mean*, not on the individual words they use.

(C) is the opposite of the inference contained in choice (E). Banks appear to have increased, not decreased, the funds they've made available to cover potential losses.

(D) is not mentioned, well, anywhere in the passage, and certainly not in paragraph 2, so we can safely rule it out.

3. (D)

This Inference question asks what the author sees as the problems with the current "solutions" to the debt crisis and is therefore quite specific. We've read about only two solutions: the first is that banks have decreased their loans to debtor nations, and the second is that banks have extended the maturity of the loans to those nations. If you didn't consider the first as a solution, you have a point; it doesn't really solve anything. Still, banks did limit loans in order to decrease the severity of their problem. Regardless, the author doesn't critique the first solution but does comment on the second: extended maturity periods offer only short-term benefits, or answer choice (D).

> An 800 test taker prephrases answers to questions whenever possible. While Inference questions are not generally friendly to prephrasing, she takes advantage of those very specific ones that are.

(A) gives banks too much responsibility for the problems that have befallen debtor countries. While the author does say that real interest rates have risen and that inflation hasn't decreased them, she does not blame the banks' attempted solutions for such problems. Indeed, the author says that the interest rates rose because of deflation.

(B) We didn't read anything about the real wages in debtor countries so we certainly can't infer anything about them.

(C) While the skeptical reader may have wondered why the "imprudent management and borrowing by debtor countries" mentioned in paragraph 1 wasn't addressed again in the passage, the fact remains that such problems are not mentioned again, regardless of the reason. The author does not suggest that the debtor and lender countries' solutions have failed; she only specifically blames the attempted solutions of the lender country, or the United States.

(E) is contradicted by the passage. It may be tempting at first because it uses the term "short-term," familiar from the passage. Also, it's confusing, particularly at the beginning, but if you took the time to unravel it then you saw that it is inaccurate. Banks have extended, not restricted, loan maturity.

4.   (C)

"EXCEPT" detail questions can be cumbersome to answer, but this one is pretty focused. Go back to the passage, especially paragraph 1, and find the causes of the debt crisis (rise in real interest rates, debtor nations' financial mismanagement, U.S. banks' excessive loans, etc.) and then move to the answer choices.

(A) is suggested by the first sentence: debtor countries have had imprudent management and borrowing practices. The implication is surely that they have borrowed more money than they should have.

(B) is clearly stated in the first paragraph, and it's even mentioned a few times later on.

(C) is the correct answer because it's not mentioned in the passage. Aside from the fact that this choice is illogical (other countries would undoubtedly not appreciate the opportunity to carry the loans of debtor countries), it's also unsupported by the passage.

(D) paraphrases one of the problems discussed in paragraph 1, specifically the "imprudent lending by banks." If the loans were imprudent, then it's fair to say that the banks (or "commercial lending institutions"—hopefully you picked up on the rephrasing without much effort) have made "unwise decisions."

(E) is directly expressed at the end of the first paragraph. Inflation normally helps the interest rate to lower, but this time inflation hasn't worked.

An 800 test taker reads through all of the answer choices in the Verbal section before making his final choice.

Both Alexander Gerschenkron and Jerry Hough view the former Soviet Union as an "anomalous" nation in certain fundamental respects. Gerschenkron sees the Soviet Union
(5) as deviating from the expected European pattern of industrialization, while Hough emphasizes how the Soviet Union differed from the standard type of bureaucratic organization. Despite this difference in orientation, both
(10) authors share a similar theoretical approach.

First, both authors react in their works to specific explanations already existing in their fields. Gerschenkron responds to the prevailing belief that all countries pass through stages of
(15) industrialization similar to that of England's industrial growth and that states must possess certain specific prerequisites before they can industrialize. Hough reacts to the notion that only a bureaucracy that embodies the
(20) conventional American image of organization can operate efficiently. This idealized American image, known as monism, sees efficiency as maximized when bureaucrats perform only those duties passed down to them from a
(25) central authority.

Second, both Gerschenkron and Hough also attempt to use their work to supplement the existing explanations prevailing in their fields. Gerschenkron expands W. W. Rostow's
(30) industrialization model by defining a causal factor, the "degree of economic backwardness," that he believes impacts, among other things, the speed and structure of a country's industrialization. In a similar vein, Hough
(35) concludes that the centralized, monistic model of organization must be expanded if it is to enable efficient administration. He uses the Soviet experience to show that overlapping bureaucratic duties can sometimes promote
(40) organizational efficiency.

Ultimately, Gerschenkron and Hough succeed at their similar tasks; not only do both authors provide enough evidence to document the anomalous nature of the cases they
(45) investigate, but they use their anomalous cases to increase the explanatory range of the existing theories without altering those theories beyond recognition.

1. The author's main point in the passage is reflected most accurately in which one of the following statements?

(A) Gerschenkron and Hough share a similar theoretical enterprise in their works, and both manage this enterprise successfully.

(B) In their research, both Gerschenkron and Hough react to prevailing theories within their fields.

(C) Gerschenkron and Hough both use evidence from the Soviet case to highlight the anomalous features of the former Soviet experience.

(D) The works of Gerschenkron and Hough are expansive because both authors attempt to refute existing theories within their fields and to replace these theories with better explanations.

(E) The works of Gerschenkron and Hough are similar with respect to the specific central tenets of their research.

Both Alexander Gerschenkron and Jerry Hough view the former Soviet Union as an "anomalous" nation in certain fundamental respects. Gerschenkron sees the Soviet Union
(5) as deviating from the expected European pattern of industrialization, while Hough emphasizes how the Soviet Union differed from the standard type of bureaucratic organization. Despite this difference in orientation, both
(10) authors share a similar theoretical approach.

First, both authors react in their works to specific explanations already existing in their fields. Gerschenkron responds to the prevailing belief that all countries pass through stages of
(15) industrialization similar to that of England's industrial growth and that states must possess certain specific prerequisites before they can industrialize. Hough reacts to the notion that only a bureaucracy that embodies the
(20) conventional American image of organization can operate efficiently. This idealized American image, known as monism, sees efficiency as maximized when bureaucrats perform only those duties passed down to them from a
(25) central authority.

Second, both Gerschenkron and Hough also attempt to use their work to supplement the existing explanations prevailing in their fields. Gerschenkron expands W. W. Rostow's
(30) industrialization model by defining a causal factor, the "degree of economic backwardness," that he believes impacts, among other things, the speed and structure of a country's industrialization. In a similar vein, Hough
(35) concludes that the centralized, monistic model of organization must be expanded if it is to enable efficient administration. He uses the Soviet experience to show that overlapping bureaucratic duties can sometimes promote
(40) organizational efficiency.

Ultimately, Gerschenkron and Hough succeed at their similar tasks; not only do both authors provide enough evidence to document the anomalous nature of the cases they
(45) investigate, but they use their anomalous cases to increase the explanatory range of the existing theories without altering those theories beyond recognition.

2. The passage suggests that both Gerschenkron and Hough would be most likely to agree with which one of the following statements?

(A) Scientific studies of the former Soviet Union should be limited to an emphasis on industrialization patterns or methods of bureaucratic organization.

(B) W. W. Rostow's industrialization model can be expanded by incorporating the variable of economic backwardness.

(C) All countries pass through stages of industrialization similar to those experienced by England during its early growth.

(D) Empirical research into anomalous cases can broaden the explanatory range of current theories.

(E) Empirical research should focus on attempting to falsify theories through emphasis on disconfirming cases.

Both Alexander Gerschenkron and Jerry Hough view the former Soviet Union as an "anomalous" nation in certain fundamental respects. Gerschenkron sees the Soviet Union
(5) as deviating from the expected European pattern of industrialization, while Hough emphasizes how the Soviet Union differed from the standard type of bureaucratic organization. Despite this difference in orientation, both
(10) authors share a similar theoretical approach.

First, both authors react in their works to specific explanations already existing in their fields. Gerschenkron responds to the prevailing belief that all countries pass through stages of
(15) industrialization similar to that of England's industrial growth and that states must possess certain specific prerequisites before they can industrialize. Hough reacts to the notion that only a bureaucracy that embodies the
(20) conventional American image of organization can operate efficiently. This idealized American image, known as monism, sees efficiency as maximized when bureaucrats perform only those duties passed down to them from a
(25) central authority.

Second, both Gerschenkron and Hough also attempt to use their work to supplement the existing explanations prevailing in their fields. Gerschenkron expands W. W. Rostow's
(30) industrialization model by defining a causal factor, the "degree of economic backwardness," that he believes impacts, among other things, the speed and structure of a country's industrialization. In a similar vein, Hough
(35) concludes that the centralized, monistic model of organization must be expanded if it is to enable efficient administration. He uses the Soviet experience to show that overlapping bureaucratic duties can sometimes promote
(40) organizational efficiency.

Ultimately, Gerschenkron and Hough succeed at their similar tasks; not only do both authors provide enough evidence to document the anomalous nature of the cases they
(45) investigate, but they use their anomalous cases to increase the explanatory range of the existing theories without altering those theories beyond recognition.

3. Which one of the following is explicitly cited as evidence to demonstrate a specific use to which Gerschenkron put his work?

(A) Gerschenkron reacted to the accepted notion that industrialization does not require states to possess any prerequisite characteristics.

(B) Gerschenkron and Hough differed regarding the specific orientation of their respective works.

(C) Gerschenkron described the monistic image of bureaucratic organization in order to show how centralized authority helps to promote bureaucratic efficiency.

(D) Gerschenkron demonstrated that the speed of a country's industrialization affects the country's degree of economic backwardness.

(E) Gerschenkron incorporated a new factor into the model of industrialization put forth by a previous theorist.

Both Alexander Gerschenkron and Jerry Hough view the former Soviet Union as an "anomalous" nation in certain fundamental respects. Gerschenkron sees the Soviet Union
(5) as deviating from the expected European pattern of industrialization, while Hough emphasizes how the Soviet Union differed from the standard type of bureaucratic organization. Despite this difference in orientation, both
(10) authors share a similar theoretical approach.

First, both authors react in their works to specific explanations already existing in their fields. Gerschenkron responds to the prevailing belief that all countries pass through stages of
(15) industrialization similar to that of England's industrial growth and that states must possess certain specific prerequisites before they can industrialize. Hough reacts to the notion that only a bureaucracy that embodies the
(20) conventional American image of organization can operate efficiently. This idealized American image, known as monism, sees efficiency as maximized when bureaucrats perform only those duties passed down to them from a
(25) central authority.

Second, both Gerschenkron and Hough also attempt to use their work to supplement the existing explanations prevailing in their fields. Gerschenkron expands W. W. Rostow's
(30) industrialization model by defining a causal factor, the "degree of economic backwardness," that he believes impacts, among other things, the speed and structure of a country's industrialization. In a similar vein, Hough
(35) concludes that the centralized, monistic model of organization must be expanded if it is to enable efficient administration. He uses the Soviet experience to show that overlapping bureaucratic duties can sometimes promote
(40) organizational efficiency.

Ultimately, Gerschenkon and Hough succeed at their similar tasks; not only do both authors provide enough evidence to document the anomalous nature of the cases they
(45) investigate, but they use their anomalous cases to increase the explanatory range of the existing theories without altering those theories beyond recognition.

4. The author refers to the concept of monism in the second paragraph in order to

(A) support the claim that the former Soviet Union deviated in its development from the normal European pattern of industrialization

(B) refute the notion that Hough provides an alternative conception of bureaucratic efficiency

(C) demonstrate that Hough's work takes issue with the conventional view that efficient bureaucratic organization must conform to the American idealized image

(D) support the claim that Hough portrays the former Soviet Union as similar to most industrialized nations in its bureaucratic structure

(E) provide evidence for the conclusion that the former Soviet case displayed many elements of the idealized American model of bureaucratic organization

Gerschenkron and Hough

What Makes It Difficult

The names alone are a pain, so maybe keeping track of them as simply G and H is the way to go. As for serious considerations, the subject matter is fairly dry and it's fairly difficult to visualize what these guys are talking about, though "book review" passages are common in Reading Comprehension. The concept of the Soviet Union as an "anomalous" nation is a tough one to assimilate, and the various repetitions of "anomalous" throughout the final paragraph magnify this complexity. The "compare and contrast" passage structure, while common to GMAT Reading Comp, is blurred a bit by the presentation of similarities in the work of Gerschenkron and Hough. Keeping the two theorists' views straight in your mind is no easy task, and the questions continually test your ability to distinguish one from the other. The choices are long and complex. Overall, a very tough passage. Let's break it down to its key points.

Key Points of the Passage

Purpose and Main Idea: The author's purpose is to compare how Gerschenkron and Hough approach the case of the former Soviet Union in their scholarly works. The main idea is that both authors share a similar theoretical approach in their works, and both are successful in their theoretical endeavors.

Paragraph Structure: Paragraph 1 introduces the passage by noting that both Gerschenkron and Hough view the former Soviet Union as an anomalous nation. Although they focus on different aspects of the former Soviet anomaly, they nonetheless share a similar approach in their research.

Paragraph 2 explains one aspect of similarity between the authors' approaches: both develop ideas in reaction to existing theories in their fields. We are told first what Gerschenkron reacts to and then what Hough reacts to in his work.

Paragraph 3 provides a second aspect of similarity between the authors' approaches: both attempt to supplement existing theories in their fields. Again, we are given a description of Gerschenkron's attempt, and then a description of Hough's.

The final paragraph summarizes the points made in paragraphs 2 and 3. It also draws a final conclusion: not only are the authors' tasks similar, but they both succeed in these tasks.

An 800 test taker knows that a good roadmap doesn't include every detail of a passage, but recaps the points of each paragraph and reminds him where the evidence to support these points can be found.

ANSWERS AND EXPLANATIONS

1. A   2. D   3. E   4. C

1. (A)

This question asks for the author's main point, or the main idea of the passage. This question would be a good one to prephrase, since a careful focus on purpose and structure should make the main idea clear. In this case, the main idea has two parts and is summed up in paragraph 4: the theorists share similar tasks, and they succeed at these tasks as well. This is well stated in choice (A).

(B), (C) These choices describe only parts of the author's claim; they are not broad enough to reflect the main idea. Choice (B) summarizes the point of paragraph 2, while choice (C) discusses a point raised in paragraph 1 about the anomalies of the former Soviet case.

(D) contradicts the author's argument as laid out in paragraph 4. The author specifically states that the theorists use their anomalous cases to "increase the explanatory range of the existing theories." In other words, their works supplement the existing theories. This is a far cry from replacing the theories, as choice (D) suggests.

(E) Again, the opposite is suggested: the author tells us in paragraph 1 that Gerschenkron and Hough focus on different aspects of the Soviet experience—Gerschenkron on industrialization and Hough on bureaucratic organization. Their specific central tenets differ, but their overall theoretical approach is the same.

2. (D)

Next we're asked to choose a statement about which both Gerschenkron and Hough would likely agree. Rather than attempt to prephrase the answer (the possibilities could be very broad), we should scan the choices to determine the correct one. (D) provides the best summary of a statement that would align with both theorists' views, since paragraph 4 tells us that both men use research into anomalous cases to broaden the explanatory value of existing theories. Presumably, since both theorists use such cases to broaden such explanations, they would agree that using such research in this way is possible.

(A) The author doesn't suggest that studies of the former Soviet Union should be limited to any subjects, and neither does she imply that Gerschenkron and Hough believe this. All we know is that industrialization and bureaucracy are their respective areas of concern. We can't infer that they think that Soviet studies should be limited to their subjects.

(B) Gerschenkron would agree with this, but the passage does not indicate Hough's views on Rostow's model.

(C) Not even Gerschenkron would buy this one; the author states in paragraph 2 that Gerschenkron reacts against this notion. And of course, we don't know what Hough's views would be on the subject.

(E) Again, on the contrary: Gerschenkron and Hough do not attempt to falsify the existing theories they deal with—they attempt to supplement them. They would therefore, if anything, probably disagree with the notion that empirical research should focus on falsification.

An 800 test taker is extremely sensitive to distortions of the text.

3. (E)

This question asks for a detail from the passage. We know this because we're asked for a statement that is "explicitly cited" in the text. Can't get much clearer than that! (E) generalizes the author's point in paragraph 3 regarding Gerschenkron, the references being to the discussion of Gerschenkron's incorporation of the "economic backwardness" factor into Rostow's industrialization model.

(A) On the contrary: Paragraph 2 tells us that Gerschenkron reacted to the notion that states must possess specific characteristics in order to industrialize.

(B) True, Gerschenkron may differ from Hough in the specific orientation of his work, but this statement is not explicitly cited as evidence of how Gerschenkron put his work to use.

(C) This description applies to neither Gerschenkron nor Hough's work. Gerschenkron addressed industrialization, not bureaucratic organization, and Hough's work showed that monism is not the only efficient method of bureaucratic organization.

(D) reverses the evidence in the text. Paragraph 3 tells us that Gerschenkron showed that economic backwardness affects the speed of industrialization, not vice versa.

4. (C)

This question asks us to determine what function is served by the introduction of the concept of monism in paragraph 2. This paragraph demonstrates that both authors react in their works to existing theories. Without looking at the answer choices, we can prephrase that "monism is introduced to show that Hough's work reacted to an existing theory." Do we find such an answer with a scan of the choices? In fact, (C) conveys just this idea—albeit a bit more specifically than our prephrase.

An 800 test taker attempts to prephrase answers to Critical Reasoning and Reading Comprehension questions and is adept at spotting the choice in each question that conveys the gist of her prephrase.

(A) This choice refers to the subject discussed by Gerschenkron, not Hough.

(B) and (D) present yet two more notions that go against the grain of the passage. Hough reacts against the American system known as monism, and according to paragraph 3, Hough's examination of the former Soviet case results in an alternative conception of bureaucratic efficiency. In addition, the author tells us in paragraph 1 that Hough portrayed the former Soviet Union as anomalous, or different, in its bureaucratic structure. The mention of monism in paragraph 2 is in no way included to show otherwise.

(E) Again, the author states that Hough portrayed the former Soviet Union as *different* from the American monistic model.

An 800 test taker realizes that with passages including a number of theorists and theories, the test makers are simply testing his ability to keep the various elements of the passage straight.

We must question the assumption that for-profit health care institutions carry the obligation to provide free care for people who lack the means to pay for it themselves. There (5) are several reasons to believe that the obligation to provide adequate health care for those without it rests with the federal government. First, the obligation to secure a just distribution of benefits and burdens across (10) society is a general societal necessity. Second, the federal government is the institution employed by society to meet society-wide distributive requirements. It has the capacities to finance an exceptionally expensive program (15) for guaranteed adequate health care. The government's taxing power also allows that the burden of financing health care be spread across different segments of society, not depending on the vagaries of how wealthy or (20) poor a state or local area may be. The government additionally has the power to coordinate health care programs across local and state boundaries. This would reduce inefficiencies that allow people to fall between (25) the cracks of the patchwork of local and state programs, and ensure that there are not great differences in the minimum of health care guaranteed to all in different locales.

If we are one society, then political and (30) economic contingencies in different areas should not determine the level of health care that all citizens should receive. The federal government could provide guaranteed access to health care itself or by supplying vouchers to (35) be used in the health care marketplace. How access should be secured—and to what extent market mechanisms ought to be utilized—is a separate question.

1. According to the passage, the federal government possesses all the following powers in regard to health care EXCEPT the power to

   (A) raise the revenue to finance health care expenditures

   (B) distribute the costs of health care equitably among different demographics in the country

   (C) ensure that people be able to access health care despite the presence of state and local boundaries

   (D) require for-profit corporations to assume a greater role in providing health care to those without it

   (E) set comparable and reasonable standards for minimum acceptable levels of health care

We must question the assumption that for-profit health care institutions carry the obligation to provide free care for people who lack the means to pay for it themselves. There
(5) are several reasons to believe that the obligation to provide adequate health care for those without it rests with the federal government. First, the obligation to secure a just distribution of benefits and burdens across
(10) society is a general societal necessity. Second, the federal government is the institution employed by society to meet society-wide distributive requirements. It has the capacities to finance an exceptionally expensive program
(15) for guaranteed adequate health care. The government's taxing power also allows that the burden of financing health care be spread across different segments of society, not depending on the vagaries of how wealthy or
(20) poor a state or local area may be. The government additionally has the power to coordinate health care programs across local and state boundaries. This would reduce inefficiencies that allow people to fall between
(25) the cracks of the patchwork of local and state programs, and ensure that there are not great differences in the minimum of health care guaranteed to all in different locales.

If we are one society, then political and
(30) economic contingencies in different areas should not determine the level of health care that all citizens should receive. The federal government could provide guaranteed access to health care itself or by supplying vouchers to
(35) be used in the health care marketplace. How access should be secured—and to what extent market mechanisms ought to be utilized—is a separate question.

2. Which of the following would be most consistent with the "society-wide distributive requirements" mentioned in lines 12–13?

(A) The revenue from a federal tax increase is used in part to raise standards of health care in less affluent regions and communities

(B) The federal government consents to more stringent health care standards for less affluent communities

(C) The federal government disavows legislation designating elementary health care as a public responsibility

(D) A revenue shortfall caused by a federal tax cut is compensated for by an increase in state taxes

(E) The federal government transfers allocated funds from its food stamp program to a program which guarantees health care

We must question the assumption that for-profit health care institutions carry the obligation to provide free care for people who lack the means to pay for it themselves. There

(5) are several reasons to believe that the obligation to provide adequate health care for those without it rests with the federal government. First, the obligation to secure a just distribution of benefits and burdens across

(10) society is a general societal necessity. Second, the federal government is the institution employed by society to meet society-wide distributive requirements. It has the capacities to finance an exceptionally expensive program

(15) for guaranteed adequate health care. The government's taxing power also allows that the burden of financing health care be spread across different segments of society, not depending on the vagaries of how wealthy or

(20) poor a state or local area may be. The government additionally has the power to coordinate health care programs across local and state boundaries. This would reduce inefficiencies that allow people to fall between

(25) the cracks of the patchwork of local and state programs, and ensure that there are not great differences in the minimum of health care guaranteed to all in different locales.

If we are one society, then political and

(30) economic contingencies in different areas should not determine the level of health care that all citizens should receive. The federal government could provide guaranteed access to health care itself or by supplying vouchers to

(35) be used in the health care marketplace. How access should be secured—and to what extent market mechanisms ought to be utilized—is a separate question.

3. It can be inferred from the passage that the author considers the method by which health care is guaranteed to people to be

(A) an issue that may prevent agreement on the principle of securing health care for all

(B) a responsibility primarily of state and local governments

(C) an issue that is distinct from the guarantee of health care itself

(D) dependent on variations in market mechanisms among different locales

(E) a practical problem that may never be satisfactorily resolved

Funding Health Care

What Makes It Difficult

The author of this passage wants to let for-profit health care institutions off the hook by saddling the federal government with the responsibility to pay for health care for the needy. It is pretty clearly structured and the concepts it discusses are probably not too alienating. Still, the sentences are often cluttered (it's passages like this one that make you wonder if the writers know about the grammatical concepts covered in Sentence Correction questions). Notice, for instance, that the author describes those who can't afford health care as "people who lack the means to pay for it" rather than stating his idea more directly. If you cut past the unnecessary wordiness and focus on the structure, you should be able to grasp the content of the passage itself without too much discomfort. The questions do what they can to challenge you as much as possible by testing details and inferences. There's no rule requiring the test makers to give you global questions for every passage. Here, we get detail, inference, and application questions to ponder.

Key Points of the Passage

Purpose and Main Idea: The author's purpose is to argue that the federal government, rather than for-profit health care institutions, should pay for the health care of those who can't afford it. The main idea is that the federal government is best equipped to provide health care for those without it.

Paragraph Structure: Paragraph 1 states the argument and provides two reasons why the federal government should provide health care to those who don't have it. The author starts with a general principle: benefits and burdens should be distributed across society. Next, he claims that the federal government is best able to distribute fairly the benefit of health care and the burden of its cost.

Paragraph 2 briefly considers two ways that the government might be able to provide health care for those in need: it could either directly pay for the health care of those who can't afford it, or provide vouchers. This final paragraph merely considers general ways that the government might fulfill the responsibility that the author assigns to it.

ANSWERS AND EXPLANATIONS

1.D   2. A   3. C

1. (D)

Since this question asks which power the government does *not* possess according to the passage, it is our job to review the passage and identify the powers that the government *does* possess.

> An 800 test taker answers "all...but" and "EXCEPT" questions by eliminating the four choices supported by the text and choosing the one that remains.

Your roadmap should indicate that paragraph 1 is the best place to look for a list of such powers. We see that the government can finance and coordinate the distribution of health care. Review the paragraph and then move on to the answer choices. (D) might be tricky because, by arguing that the government rather than for-profit institutions should shoulder the cost of health care, the passage might perhaps imply that the government *could* force for-profit companies to cover the cost if it wanted to. Nevertheless, the passage never makes such a claim: nowhere does it state that the government has the power to force for-profit health care companies to foot the bill for health care. Remember, the right answer choice will contain information that the passage did not directly provide; shaky, unsupported inferences are certainly not stated in the passage.

(A) Paragraph 1 mentions the government's taxing power, a power that clearly enables it to raise money in order to finance health care, as (A) states.

(B) might seem a bit suspicious since *equitably* is not a word or concept we ever encounter in the passage. Still, by saying that the government spreads the burden of financing health care across society, the author does suggest that such a distribution is fair. Remember, you're looking for the power that the author does not mention at all. Choice (B) is too well-supported by the passage to be the right answer.

(C) is stated toward the end of the first paragraph: the government can "coordinate health care programs across local and state boundaries." Answer choice (C) is a fair paraphrase.

(E) is clearly stated at the end of the first paragraph. The government can establish a "minimum of health care" to be provided to everyone.

A passage like this one illustrates that if you read the first question before reading the passage, you'd focus on only the question, looking for the details listed in the answer choices as you read. You'd probably get the question right, but you'd have to reread the passage in order to answer the remaining questions. That would be a huge waste of time.

> An 800 test taker does not read the first question before reading the passage.

2. (A)

This Application question basically asks you to make sense of the rather confusing phrase *society-wide distributive requirements*. Looking back at the passage, you can see that the author implicitly defines the phrase like this: The government can distribute the costs and benefits of health care. Now, you need to look for an answer choice that describes the government actually distributing such costs and/or benefits or accepting the obligation to do so. (A) is perfect: The government takes the money it raises and uses that money to expand the distribution of health care. (A) is entirely consistent with the discussion of "society-wide distributive requirements" in paragraph 1.

(B) is directly contradicted by the passage. The author states that the government shouldn't make standards higher or lower in different areas but should make sure that the standards are the same everywhere.

(C) is also inconsistent with paragraph 1; in order for the government to distribute benefits and costs across society, the author suggests that the government needs to distribute health care, a key benefit, to all. The government should therefore embrace, not disavow, legislation that makes it responsible for providing elementary health care.

(D) doesn't reflect what the author had in mind. The government should burden and reward state and local governments equally. To compensate for a federal deficit with increased revenues from the states wouldn't necessarily be faithful to that principle. Are the states being taxed equally? Are they receiving fairly distributed benefits as a result? Without more information, we can't know whether (D) is consistent with the author's views.

(E) also lacks support from the passage. Nowhere does the author suggest that one program of benefits should be used to fund another. And, what does this have to do with the equal distribution of costs and benefits anyway? This choice doesn't answer the question that was asked.

> An 800 test taker does not get sidetracked by the answer choices. Once she knows what she's looking for, she doesn't let the answer choices confuse her.

3. (C)

Great—another inference to make. On the plus side, we do know that the inference will deal with the methods of providing health care, something that's only really discussed in paragraph 2. (C) is inferred by the last sentence of the passage. The way in which health care might be provided "is a separate question," so *how* the government should provide such care is a different issue than *whether* the government should provide it. In other words, the author distinguishes the general principle (health care for all) from the specific mechanisms of its distribution (vouchers, etc.).

(A) takes us places that the passage never did. The author describes two possible methods of providing health care to the needy but never suggests that disagreement about those methods might prevent the government from providing health care to all. In fact, he never discusses disagreement on the issue at all.

An 800 test taker knows that an inference on the GMAT is something that is directly supported by the Reading Comp passage or Critical Reasoning stimulus. An inference is not just possible; it's necessarily true based on the passage.

(B) contradicts the passage's main idea. The federal government, not the state and local governments, should be responsible for providing health care.

(D) might be tricky because the author does suggest that different areas have different health care needs. Nevertheless, he never suggests that the methods of distributing health care need to vary depending on the area. Be careful not to confuse paragraphs 1 and 2; this question pertains only to paragraph 2.

(E) is too pessimistic to be consistent with the passage. While the author suggests that people will have different opinions on how best to provide health care, he never implies that they will not be able to reach a decision on how to do so. If anything, he takes it for granted that they will.

Had enough of business and the social sciences? Good, because it's now time to switch gears and explore the wonderful world of natural science. Remember not to worry too much about the details on your first reading; you're not expected to become a science whiz, but you are expected to understand the general structure and overall purpose of each passage.

CHAPTER SEVEN

Blinded by Science

As you certainly know, the writers of the GMAT don't try to create passages that speak to your everyday experiences. In fact, they like to take you out of your comfort zone, often with the aid of off-putting, scientific Reading Comprehension passages. Because the subject matter of a passage, no matter how alienating, doesn't let you off the hook from having to answer the questions about it, we've compiled four passages on such esoteric, mind-numbingly technical topics as lake stratification, mitochondria, symbiotic stars, and plate tectonics.

These are designated as "hard" science passages, not in the sense of being difficult (although they certainly are), but rather to distinguish these technical science passages from "soft" science passages, which view scientific topics from other angles such as the history or social repercussions of scientific findings. When "hard" science passages appear on the test, they often give test takers fits—especially those coming to business school from a nontechnical background such as humanities or social science. The key to successfully tackling science passages is to not allow yourself to be overwhelmed by the technical terms and processes described.

An 800 test taker notes the location and purpose of intricate details, but doesn't attempt to memorize or even fully understand those details unless a question specifically asks about them.

Focus on the author's purpose and main idea, using the mass of details to fill in the big picture. You should dig deeper only when a question demands it. Follow these tips, and when someone asks you how hard the science passages are on the GMAT, you'll be able to proudly state, "hey, *it's not rocket science*"—even when it is.

A freshwater lake's summertime ecology is significantly affected by a phenomenon known as the thermocline. In a typical deep-water impoundment in the southern United States,
(5) the water temperature measures a uniform 38–42 degrees in late winter after any surface ice has melted. Wave action stirs oxygen into the water at the lake's surface, and the temperature uniformity allows distribution of
(10) this dissolved oxygen to all depths. With oxygen plentiful, many of the reservoir's fish species, both predator and forager, are found throughout the water column.

As the lake's surface temperature increases
(15) in early spring, that water expands. A layer of warmer water builds at the surface of the lake, resting like a pillow on the mass of colder water below. The pillow of warm surface water slowly increases in thickness, as heat is transferred
(20) into the depths by the limited stirring of wave action.

By early summer, a sharp boundary separates two independent bodies of water within the lake. The boundary is a temperature
(25) gradient called the thermocline, and it acts as a barricade to prevent any further mixing of oxygen into the chilly depths. The temperature barrier prevents oxygen from circulating downward from the surface, as it does in the
(30) winter, to replace the oxygen consumed by fish and dying zooplankton. In order to survive, fish are forced upward into the relatively narrow zone between the thermocline and the surface.

The cold nights of autumn cool the surface
(35) to the point that it is heavier than the water below the thermocline. In a process known as the turnover, a current of richly oxygenated water plunges to the bottom of the reservoir, forcing stagnant water back to the surface. The
(40) lake reaches equilibrium by early winter and remains there until the process repeats itself the following spring.

1. The passage suggests that which one of the following can be inferred about dissolved oxygen in a lake?

   (A) The colder the water, the less dissolved oxygen it can hold.

   (B) There is always more dissolved oxygen within six feet of the surface than at 60 feet beneath the surface.

   (C) The formation of ice can completely block the supply of dissolved oxygen.

   (D) Dissolved oxygen is not necessary for organisms other than fish and zooplankton.

   (E) Wave action at the surface increases dissolved oxygen levels in the lake.

A freshwater lake's summertime ecology is significantly affected by a phenomenon known as the thermocline. In a typical deep-water impoundment in the southern United States,
(5) the water temperature measures a uniform 38-42 degrees in late winter after any surface ice has melted. Wave action stirs oxygen into the water at the lake's surface, and the temperature uniformity allows distribution of
(10) this dissolved oxygen to all depths. With oxygen plentiful, many of the reservoir's fish species, both predator and forager, are found throughout the water column.

As the lake's surface temperature increases
(15) in early spring, that water expands. A layer of warmer water builds at the surface of the lake, resting like a pillow on the mass of colder water below. The pillow of warm surface water slowly increases in thickness, as heat is transferred
(20) into the depths by the limited stirring of wave action.

By early summer, a sharp boundary separates two independent bodies of water within the lake. The boundary is a temperature
(25) gradient called the thermocline, and it acts as a barricade to prevent any further mixing of oxygen into the chilly depths. The temperature barrier prevents oxygen from circulating downward from the surface, as it does in the
(30) winter, to replace the oxygen consumed by fish and dying zooplankton. In order to survive, fish are forced upward into the relatively narrow zone between the thermocline and the surface.

The cold nights of autumn cool the surface
(35) to the point that it is heavier than the water below the thermocline. In a process known as the turnover, a current of richly oxygenated water plunges to the bottom of the reservoir, forcing stagnant water back to the surface. The
(40) lake reaches equilibrium by early winter and remains there until the process repeats itself the following spring.

2. The passage suggests that the effects of temperature stratification

(A) would be relevant to the interests of fisheries managers

(B) on an individual lake cannot be predicted

(C) represent the most important factor influencing a lake's ecology

(D) become more pronounced as a lake gets older

(E) are most severe in the lakes of the southern United States

A freshwater lake's summertime ecology is significantly affected by a phenomenon known as the thermocline. In a typical deep-water impoundment in the southern United States,
(5) the water temperature measures a uniform 38-42 degrees in late winter after any surface ice has melted. Wave action stirs oxygen into the water at the lake's surface, and the temperature uniformity allows distribution of
(10) this dissolved oxygen to all depths. With oxygen plentiful, many of the reservoir's fish species, both predator and forager, are found throughout the water column.

As the lake's surface temperature increases
(15) in early spring, that water expands. A layer of warmer water builds at the surface of the lake, resting like a pillow on the mass of colder water below. The pillow of warm surface water slowly increases in thickness, as heat is transferred
(20) into the depths by the limited stirring of wave action.

By early summer, a sharp boundary separates two independent bodies of water within the lake. The boundary is a temperature
(25) gradient called the thermocline, and it acts as a barricade to prevent any further mixing of oxygen into the chilly depths. The temperature barrier prevents oxygen from circulating downward from the surface, as it does in the
(30) winter, to replace the oxygen consumed by fish and dying zooplankton. In order to survive, fish are forced upward into the relatively narrow zone between the thermocline and the surface.

The cold nights of autumn cool the surface
(35) to the point that it is heavier than the water below the thermocline. In a process known as the turnover, a current of richly oxygenated water plunges to the bottom of the reservoir, forcing stagnant water back to the surface. The
(40) lake reaches equilibrium by early winter and remains there until the process repeats itself the following spring.

3. Which one of the following is not mentioned in the passage as a step in the yearly lake stratification process?

(A) Fish congregate in the water layer above the thermocline in the summer.

(B) Water temperatures achieve a general uniformity by late winter.

(C) The thermocline reaches its maximum depth by early summer.

(D) Oxygen levels decline in the layer beneath the thermocline.

(E) The fall turnover replaces stagnant water in the depths with oxygen-rich water.

A freshwater lake's summertime ecology is significantly affected by a phenomenon known as the thermocline. In a typical deep-water impoundment in the southern United States,
(5) the water temperature measures a uniform 38-42 degrees in late winter after any surface ice has melted. Wave action stirs oxygen into the water at the lake's surface, and the temperature uniformity allows distribution of
(10) this dissolved oxygen to all depths. With oxygen plentiful, many of the reservoir's fish species, both predator and forager, are found throughout the water column.

As the lake's surface temperature increases
(15) in early spring, that water expands. A layer of warmer water builds at the surface of the lake, resting like a pillow on the mass of colder water below. The pillow of warm surface water slowly increases in thickness, as heat is transferred
(20) into the depths by the limited stirring of wave action.

By early summer, a sharp boundary separates two independent bodies of water within the lake. The boundary is a temperature
(25) gradient called the thermocline, and it acts as a barricade to prevent any further mixing of oxygen into the chilly depths. The temperature barrier prevents oxygen from circulating downward from the surface, as it does in the
(30) winter, to replace the oxygen consumed by fish and dying zooplankton. In order to survive, fish are forced upward into the relatively narrow zone between the thermocline and the surface.

The cold nights of autumn cool the surface
(35) to the point that it is heavier than the water below the thermocline. In a process known as the turnover, a current of richly oxygenated water plunges to the bottom of the reservoir, forcing stagnant water back to the surface. The
(40) lake reaches equilibrium by early winter and remains there until the process repeats itself the following spring.

4. The author is primarily interested in discussing

(A) the effect of fish and other aquatic organisms on a phenomenon known as the thermocline

(B) the relationship between a lake's ecology and water purity

(C) the contribution of the thermocline to overfishing in Southern lakes

(D) an effect of the seasonal warming and cooling of water in freshwater lakes

(E) the changes in a lake's water temperature caused by fluctuating oxygen levels

Lake Stratification

What Makes It Difficult

A common thread to most science passages is the employment of jargon—technical terms and phrases peppered throughout the passage that serve to scare off, or at least befuddle, the unsophisticated test taker.

An 800 test taker cuts past jargon, returning to cumbersome technical details only when a question demands it.

This passage is no exception, introducing us to things such as the "thermocline" and a process called "the turnover"—heck, they even throw in *deep-water impoundment* as a synonym for the simple term *lake*. You have to ask: is that really necessary? But the jargon here isn't even as thick as in some of the others that follow. The problem in this passage is keeping track of the various processes at work. Lots of details, lots of mechanisms, lots of numbers to keep on top of—that's the challenge here. But if you break each part of the process down into simple ideas, it's not so hard to handle. The passage is, after all, mostly descriptive, so we simply need to follow the cycle described from winter through the rest of the seasons and back to winter again, bearing in mind that the author is interested, as stated early on, in the role this process plays in a lake's summertime ecology.

Key Points of the Passage

Purpose and Main Idea: The author's purpose is to explore the cyclical process of lake stratification and its effects on lake ecology. The main idea is that seasonal temperature differences within lake water cause the cyclical formation of water layers of various temperatures separated by the thermocline, which prevents oxygen from reaching the colder, deeper lake waters and periodically causes redistribution of fish within the lake.

Paragraph Structure: Paragraph 1 introduces the thermocline phenomenon and describes its development using the example of freshwater lakes in the southern United States. The description of the cycle that the author will offer throughout the passage begins at the end of the paragraph with info about late winter, when lake water temperatures are uniform and fish species thrive at all depths of the lake.

Paragraph 2 describes the changes that occur in early spring: the water on the surface of the lake becomes warmer and lighter than the water below it. This warm water expands and forms a layer over the water below.

Paragraph 3 describes the development and results of the thermocline. In summer, the warm water on top of the lake becomes distinctly separated from the colder water below it by the thermocline, a temperature gradient that acts as a boundary between the two parts of the lake. The thermocline boundary prevents oxygen from reaching the lower depths of the lake, and this causes fish to swim up to the warmer surface of the lake to survive.

The final paragraph describes the reversal of the cycle. In fall, the water at the surface above the thermocline cools and becomes heavier than the water below the thermocline. This allows oxygen to plunge to the depths of the lake, and the lake reaches equilibrium again by early winter.

ANSWERS AND EXPLANATIONS

1. E   2. A   3. C   4. D

1. (E)

This Inference question asks about the subject of dissolved oxygen, which is raised many times in the passage. It's not easy here to pinpoint exactly which part of the passage we should review to answer this question, so the best tactic is to evaluate the answer choices, returning to the passage for verification when necessary.

An 800 test taker knows when and how to allow the answer choices to guide her to the relevant portions of the text when a question is fairly open-ended.

We're told in paragraph 1 that wave action stirs oxygen into the water, making (E) the best inference in this set.

(A) We aren't given information relating water temperature to oxygen capacity. True, during certain months the thermocline prevents oxygen from *reaching* the cooler depths, but for all we know, cold water can hold just as much dissolved oxygen as warm water given the chance.

(B) On the contrary: the passage tells us in paragraph 1 that during late winter, oxygen is found plentifully throughout all of a lake's water levels.

(C) The only thing we're told about ice formation is that ice melts in late winter, which is not nearly enough information to allow us to infer the statement in (C).

(D) This choice misrepresents the author's claim in paragraph 3. We're told that fish and zooplankton consume oxygen below the surface, but not that they're the *only* organisms that do so.

2. (A)

Here we have another Inference question, denoted by the word *suggests*. What does the author suggest about the effects of temperature stratification? The most significant effect he discusses is how temperature stratification causes fish to move to the top layer of lakes during the summer. This might certainly be pertinent for fisheries, as choice (A) indicates.

(B) No, the passage shows that the effects of temperature stratification can be predicted to some degree, at least in terms of the general effect on lake ecology. It also shows that the general timing of these effects can be predicted as well.

(C) and (E) exaggerate the author's claims in the passage. Paragraph 1 states that the lake's ecology is "significantly affected" by the thermocline, but we don't know if the thermocline is the *most* important factor (C). It is also clear that temperature stratification affects southern U.S. lakes, but these effects aren't compared to those of other lakes, so we can't determine the relative severity of the effects (E).

> An 800 test taker recognizes extreme wording that damages the plausibility of certain answer choices, and instinctively stays away from choices that include exaggerated or extreme ideas.

(D) is outside the scope of the argument. The age of lakes is never brought up in the author's discussion, nor is anything implied regarding the way lake age might affect the stratification process described.

3. (C)

Here's a detail question asking us to look for something that was NOT mentioned in the passage, a bit harder than the traditional detail question. Fortunately, the wrong answers are all stated in the passage fairly clearly. (C) is the only choice that's not mentioned. In fact, it even tends to contradict the passage: Paragraph 3 tells us that the depth of the thermocline fluctuates with temperature and winds, so we can't be sure when the depth is at its maximum.

All of the other answer choices repeat information from the passage. Paragraph 3 tells us that fish move above the thermocline in the summer, so this eliminates (A). We're told in paragraph 1 that water temperatures are uniform in late winter, eliminating (B). Paragraph 3 helps us eliminate (D), because it states that the thermocline shuts off the supply of oxygen to the lower depths. Finally, choice (E) can be eliminated by paragraph 4, which describes how the turnover brings oxygen to deeper, stagnant water.

4. (D)

The stem itself gives away the fact that the author's purpose is "to discuss" something, so there's no need to choose among various verbs (discuss, argue, refute, etc.)—but what is he interested in discussing? The author's main concern should be firmly planted in your mind by now; he's simply interested in discussing the process and effects of lake stratification. Choice (D) comes very close to this prephrase, merely substituting "seasonal warming and cooling of water. . ." for the process described.

(A) and (E) both reverse the direction of causality in the author's discussion. The author is interested in how the thermocline affects lake ecology, not vice versa as in (A). Similarly, he shows how changing water temperatures, by means of the thermocline, affect oxygen levels—not the other way around, as (E) would have it.

> An 800 test taker is ultra sensitive to cause-and-effect relationships, and is not likely to mistake one for the other.

(B) and (C) go beyond the argument's scope. The author mentions "stagnant" water in paragraph 4, but does not focus on water purity throughout the passage. And the phenomenon of overfishing, if it exists, is not discussed at all.

Not so bad, huh? Well, of course, we're just getting started, and not surprisingly, things do get a bit worse. "Mitochondria," the next passage in our little group of nightmares, raises the bar, both in the density of the material and in technical jargon.

Some one and a half or two billion years ago, when the earth was still poor in oxygen, a primitive bacterium that made a precarious living from the anaerobic fermentation of
(5) organic molecules engulfed a smaller cell that had somehow evolved the ability to respire. Respiration liberates far more energy than fermentation, and the growing abundance of oxygen in the atmosphere must have been the
(10) driving force behind a symbiotic relation that developed between the two cells, with the aerobic cell generating energy in return for shelter and nutrients from its larger host.

In time the engulfed cell and others like it
(15) were to become subcellular organelles, passed on by host cells to their progeny. Eventually the host cells themselves changed, developing other subcellular structures and internal membranes and segregating their genetic
(20) material in chromosomes within a nucleus. These cells were the ancestors of all modern eukaryotic (nucleated) cells. The present-day descendants of those ancient symbiotic respiring bacteria are the mitochondria, the
(25) power plants of the eukaryotic cell.

Mitochondria are oval organelles, about half a micrometer in diameter and from two to five micrometers long. The mitochondrion has an outer membrane and an extensively folded
(30) inner membrane that encloses a fluid matrix. The organelle is the site of oxidative phosphorylation, the primary source of cellular energy. In the fluid matrix, organic molecules derived from the breakdown of foodstuffs are
(35) oxidized in a series of chemical reactions known as the citric acid cycle. Electrons removed in the course of oxidation are passed along a chain of respiratory-enzyme complexes arrayed in the inner membrane, driving the
(40) phosphorylation of adenosine diphosphate to form adenosine triphosphate (ATP), the universal energy carrier of cells. The cytoplasm (the region outside the nucleus) of eukaryotic cells contains a few mitochondria to many
(45) hundreds, depending on the energy demands placed on the cell.

1. The author of the passage would most likely agree with which one of the following statements about the "symbiotic relation" in line 10?

(A) The new cell that developed out of the symbiotic relation between anaerobic and aerobic cells has not changed over the last one-and-a-half billion years.

(B) Neither anaerobic nor aerobic cells had a specific function to perform in the new cell.

(C) Anaerobic and aerobic cells combined to create a new cell because neither type of cell was capable of surviving for long on its own.

(D) Anaerobic and aerobic cells could not have joined to form a new cell in the absence of the proper atmospheric conditions.

(E) The chromosomes of eukaryotic cells were originally located in aerobic cells before aerobic cells combined with anaerobic cells to form a new cell.

Some one and a half or two billion years ago, when the earth was still poor in oxygen, a primitive bacterium that made a precarious living from the anaerobic fermentation of
(5) organic molecules engulfed a smaller cell that had somehow evolved the ability to respire. Respiration liberates far more energy than fermentation, and the growing abundance of oxygen in the atmosphere must have been the
(10) driving force behind a symbiotic relation that developed between the two cells, with the aerobic cell generating energy in return for shelter and nutrients from its larger host.

In time the engulfed cell and others like it
(15) were to become subcellular organelles, passed on by host cells to their progeny. Eventually the host cells themselves changed, developing other subcellular structures and internal membranes and segregating their genetic
(20) material in chromosomes within a nucleus. These cells were the ancestors of all modern eukaryotic (nucleated) cells. The present-day descendants of those ancient symbiotic respiring bacteria are the mitochondria, the
(25) power plants of the eukaryotic cell.

Mitochondria are oval organelles, about half a micrometer in diameter and from two to five micrometers long. The mitochondrion has an outer membrane and an extensively folded
(30) inner membrane that encloses a fluid matrix. The organelle is the site of oxidative phosphorylation, the primary source of cellular energy. In the fluid matrix, organic molecules derived from the breakdown of foodstuffs are
(35) oxidized in a series of chemical reactions known as the citric acid cycle. Electrons removed in the course of oxidation are passed along a chain of respiratory-enzyme complexes arrayed in the inner membrane, driving the
(40) phosphorylation of adenosine diphosphate to form adenosine triphosphate (ATP), the universal energy carrier of cells. The cytoplasm (the region outside the nucleus) of eukaryotic cells contains a few mitochondria to many
(45) hundreds, depending on the energy demands placed on the cell.

2. The passage suggests which one of the following about "anaerobic fermentation" (line 4)?

(A) It occurs in the mitochondria located in cells' cytoplasm.

(B) It causes the breakdown of organic molecules during the citric acid cycle.

(C) It is the basis of energy production in modern eukaryotic cells.

(D) It can only be carried on by primitive bacterium in an oxygen-poor environment.

(E) It is not the most efficient way for cells to produce energy.

Some one and a half or two billion years ago, when the earth was still poor in oxygen, a primitive bacterium that made a precarious living from the anaerobic fermentation of
(5) organic molecules engulfed a smaller cell that had somehow evolved the ability to respire. Respiration liberates far more energy than fermentation, and the growing abundance of oxygen in the atmosphere must have been the
(10) driving force behind a symbiotic relation that developed between the two cells, with the aerobic cell generating energy in return for shelter and nutrients from its larger host.

In time the engulfed cell and others like it
(15) were to become subcellular organelles, passed on by host cells to their progeny. Eventually the host cells themselves changed, developing other subcellular structures and internal membranes and segregating their genetic
(20) material in chromosomes within a nucleus. These cells were the ancestors of all modern eukaryotic (nucleated) cells. The present-day descendants of those ancient symbiotic respiring bacteria are the mitochondria, the
(25) power plants of the eukaryotic cell.

Mitochondria are oval organelles, about half a micrometer in diameter and from two to five micrometers long. The mitochondrion has an outer membrane and an extensively folded
(30) inner membrane that encloses a fluid matrix. The organelle is the site of oxidative phosphorylation, the primary source of cellular energy. In the fluid matrix, organic molecules derived from the breakdown of foodstuffs are
(35) oxidized in a series of chemical reactions known as the citric acid cycle. Electrons removed in the course of oxidation are passed along a chain of respiratory-enzyme complexes arrayed in the inner membrane, driving the
(40) phosphorylation of adenosine diphosphate to form adenosine triphosphate (ATP), the universal energy carrier of cells. The cytoplasm (the region outside the nucleus) of eukaryotic cells contains a few mitochondria to many
(45) hundreds, depending on the energy demands placed on the cell.

3. According to the passage, the energy released by a eukaryotic cell is

(A) generated by the mitochondria contained in its cytoplasm

(B) dependent on the transformation of adenosine triphosphate into adenosine diphosphate

(C) caused by chemical reactions that take place outside of the mitochondrion's inner membrane

(D) related to the number of chromosomes in the cell nucleus

(E) incorporated into the mitochondrion's genetic material

Some one and a half or two billion years ago, when the earth was still poor in oxygen, a primitive bacterium that made a precarious living from the anaerobic fermentation of
(5) organic molecules engulfed a smaller cell that had somehow evolved the ability to respire. Respiration liberates far more energy than fermentation, and the growing abundance of oxygen in the atmosphere must have been the
(10) driving force behind a symbiotic relation that developed between the two cells, with the aerobic cell generating energy in return for shelter and nutrients from its larger host.

In time the engulfed cell and others like it
(15) were to become subcellular organelles, passed on by host cells to their progeny. Eventually the host cells themselves changed, developing other subcellular structures and internal membranes and segregating their genetic
(20) material in chromosomes within a nucleus. These cells were the ancestors of all modern eukaryotic (nucleated) cells. The present-day descendants of those ancient symbiotic respiring bacteria are the mitochondria, the
(25) power plants of the eukaryotic cell.

Mitochondria are oval organelles, about half a micrometer in diameter and from two to five micrometers long. The mitochondrion has an outer membrane and an extensively folded
(30) inner membrane that encloses a fluid matrix. The organelle is the site of oxidative phosphorylation, the primary source of cellular energy. In the fluid matrix, organic molecules derived from the breakdown of foodstuffs are
(35) oxidized in a series of chemical reactions known as the citric acid cycle. Electrons removed in the course of oxidation are passed along a chain of respiratory-enzyme complexes arrayed in the inner membrane, driving the
(40) phosphorylation of adenosine diphosphate to form adenosine triphosphate (ATP), the universal energy carrier of cells. The cytoplasm (the region outside the nucleus) of eukaryotic cells contains a few mitochondria to many
(45) hundreds, depending on the energy demands placed on the cell.

4. According to the passage, which one of the following occurs during the citric acid cycle?

(A) Organic molecules that are derived from food penetrate the mitochondrion's outer membrane

(B) Electrons help to transform adenosine diphosphate into adenosine triphosphate.

(C) Mitochondria from a eukaryotic cell's cytoplasm are transported to the cell's nucleus.

(D) Eukaryotic cells develop subcellular structures, internal membranes and nuclei.

(E) The fluid matrix enclosed by the mitochondrion's inner membrane is transformed into organic molecules that are later broken down in a series of chemical reactions.

Mitochondria

What Makes It Difficult

Well, we were just talking about jargon in the previous passage, and this one is chock full of it. It's quite a chore to simply chop through the heavy biology in the beginning to get a sense of where this author is going. In fact, it takes a good long while before the main character, mitochondria, even hits the stage. By the time that we recognize that the details in the beginning are presented to shed light on the evolution of mitochondria, the focus shifts to a complex discussion of the characteristics and function of mitochondria, laden of course with complicated terms and descriptions of heavy-duty processes.

Now, sometimes dense complicated passages are followed by easy questions, and these really aren't as bad as they could be. However, every question plays in some way with the technical terms and complex mechanisms described in the passage. Recognizing the following key passage points will help, but you'll also have to go back to the passage at points to pick up a few of the details.

Key Points of the Passage

Purpose and Main Idea: The author's purpose is to describe the evolution of mitochondria and its function in present-day organisms. The passage is purely descriptive, and so there is no main idea, per se. It's simply about mitochondria.

Paragraph Structure: Paragraph 1 describes a turning point in organic evolution, the coming together of a host cell with a smaller respiring cell. The author speculates on how this may have occurred (increase in atmospheric oxygen), and describes the benefit to each of the participating cells. The passage is still pretty wide open at this point; there's no telling where it might go.

An 800 test taker constantly interrogates the passage and the author until he's satisfied that he's nailed down both the author's main area of concern and purpose in writing the passage.

Paragraph 2 continues the saga of "the little cells that could": the engulfed cell evolved into specialized subcellular organelles, and the host evolved other structures within a nucleus. The hosts are the forebears of modern eukaryotic cells, and the present-day version of the respiring symbiotic duo are the mitochondria.

Is the author going to settle down to one concept here, or what? Thankfully, yes. Paragraph 3 describes mitochondria in great detail—its size, its structure, its function. The latter is the key, although you don't have to (and shouldn't!) try to take in the mess of technical details just yet; we'll return to those when necessary (and unfortunately, it does become necessary). The main thing is to see is that mitochondria supply cells with energy. *How* exactly it does that is not worth getting into just yet.

ANSWERS AND EXPLANATIONS

1. D   2. E   3. A   4. B

1. (D)

We're asked to infer something about the symbiotic relationship mentioned in paragraph 1, and there's a bunch of material relating to that early on, so we have no idea specifically what the test makers are after here. In other words, as is common in Inference questions, prephrasing an answer is not a good option. We should go right to the answer choices, looking to confirm or negate each one based on the information in the passage.

(A) and (B) are both flatly contradicted by the passage: the new cell *did* evolve quite a bit, and each partner cell in the original symbiotic relation *did* have a specific function.

(C)   Presumably, the cells managed pretty well on their own before the atmosphere became oxygen-rich, so there's no way we can infer that the combination occurred because the cells were in danger of dying out.

(D) is the winner: the reasonable implication of oxygen being the "driving force" is that, absent all of that oxygen, the symbiotic relation that led to the formation of the new cell would have been difficult if not impossible.

(E) not only distorts information in the passage—information in paragraph 2—but the information it plays on is located far from the cited line.

> An 800 test taker knows that the information needed to find the correct answer to questions containing a line reference usually won't be located very far from the cited line.

2. (E)

The line reference brings us right to the concept in question, so it's best to quickly review what's said about anaerobic fermentation. And it's what comes a bit later that's really the key to the question; we're told that "respiration liberates far more energy than fermentation," which is just another way of saying that anaerobic fermentation isn't the most efficient way for cells to produce energy. (E) is therefore inferable here.

(A), (B), and (C) are all far removed from the detail in question and misrepresent matters anyway.

(D) might be tempting—after all, we're told that primitive bacterium in an oxygen-poor environment did employ anaerobic fermentation. But it's not valid to deduce from this that *only* primitive bacterium in an oxygen-poor environment can carry on anaerobic fermentation. Perhaps you put (D) on hold until you reached (E)—but we really have to work much harder to justify (D) than (E).

> An 800 test taker doesn't bend over backwards to justify an answer choice, knowing that if a choice takes that much work to rationalize, it's almost certainly wrong.

3. (A)

"According to the passage" signifies a detail question, and you have to expect at least a few of those to make your life somewhat miserable. But it's not that bad, really, as long as you find the subject in question and focus on what's said about it. The striking term that appears in this question is "eukaryotic cell," which we find in paragraphs 2 and 3. These references tell us a few major things: mitochondria are located in the cytoplasm of eukaryotic cells, and they power these cells. And that's really all we need to know to answer the question—(A) paraphrases that very closely.

> An 800 test taker does not overestimate the amount of "comprehension" that Reading Comprehension requires; she seeks to understand only as much as she needs to pick up points.

(B) and (C) both contradict the passage: ADP is transformed into ATP, and the chemical reactions, according to information in paragraph 3, take place in the fluid matrix, which is *enclosed* by the mitochondrion's inner membrane.

(D) and (E) distort details taken from the wrong paragraphs, (D) a detail in paragraph 2 and (E) a detail in paragraph 4. Of the two, (D) is likely to be more tempting, since paragraph 4 makes no mention of eukaryotic cells. But neither is directly related to the energy released by a eukaryotic cell.

4. (B)

The detail "citric acid cycle" is even easier to skim for than the detail from the previous question—it shows up only in the middle of paragraph 3. There we see that the citrus acid cycle is a set of chemical reactions that oxidize molecules derived from food. If we keep reading, we sees that the oxidation moves the electrons along to turn ADP into ATP, just as (B) says. (B)'s wording is no mystery and no real challenge. The challenge lies in figuring out where the answer is going to come from, and translating the relevant text once found into simpler words.

> An 800 test taker often asks himself, "where is the answer likely to come from?"

(A), like a few choices in the previous question, gets it backwards. The citric acid cycle takes place in the fluid matrix, which is part of the mitochondrion's *inner* membrane

(C) and (E) distort information in the passage. The citric acid cycle is a process that takes place within the mitochondrion; it has nothing to do with the movement of a mitochondrion from one part of the cell to another (C). Nor does the citric acid cycle result in the transformation of the fluid matrix (E); rather, a transformation (of organic molecules) occurs *within* the fluid matrix during the citric acid cycle.

(D) plays on an irrelevant detail from paragraph 2. There's no reason why we should look at paragraph 2 in a question about the citric acid cycle.

A tiny fraction of binary systems belong to a curious subclass whose radiation has a wavelength distribution so peculiar that it long defied explanation. Such systems radiate
(5) strongly in the visible region of the spectrum, but some of them do so even more strongly at both shorter and longer wavelengths: in the ultraviolet region and in the infrared and radio regions.

(10) This odd distribution of radiation is best explained by the pairing of a cool red-giant star and an intensely hot small star, known as symbiotic stars, that travel around a common center. Recently two symbiotic-star systems,
(15) the first to be detected outside our galaxy, have been observed in the Large Cloud of Magellan.

The spectra of symbiotic stars indicate that the cool red giant is surrounded by a very hot ionized gas which satellite observations finally
(20) identified as radiating from an invisible hot companion. It is possible that symbiotic stars represent a transitory phase in the evolution of certain types of binary systems in which a substantial amount of matter transfers from the
(25) larger partner to the smaller.

The exact evolutionary course that turns a binary system into a symbiotic one is unknown. The comparative scarcity of known symbiotics in our galaxy suggests that if all binaries of
(30) modest mass pass through a symbiotic phase in their evolution, the phase must be extremely brief, perhaps as short as a million years. It is suspected that the evolutionary course of binary stars is predetermined by the initial
(35) mass and angular momentum of their gas clouds. Since red giants and Mira variables are thought to be stars with a mass of one or two suns, it seems plausible that the original cloud from which a symbiotic system is formed can
(40) consist of no more than a few solar masses of gas.

1. The passage implies that symbiotic star systems differ from other binary systems in which one of the following ways?

    (A) Symbiotically paired stars emit a radiation pattern different from that of most binary stars.

    (B) In symbiotic star systems, one star is the center of the other's orbit.

    (C) Symbiotically paired stars are the only binary stars which are capable of exchanging matter.

    (D) Symbiotic star systems are more common than other binary systems.

    (E) Symbiotic star systems are the only binary systems that can be detected by satellite-borne instruments.

A tiny fraction of binary systems belong to a curious subclass whose radiation has a wavelength distribution so peculiar that it long defied explanation. Such systems radiate
(5) strongly in the visible region of the spectrum, but some of them do so even more strongly at both shorter and longer wavelengths: in the ultraviolet region and in the infrared and radio regions.
(10) This odd distribution of radiation is best explained by the pairing of a cool red-giant star and an intensely hot small star, known as symbiotic stars, that travel around a common center. Recently two symbiotic-star systems,
(15) the first to be detected outside our galaxy, have been observed in the Large Cloud of Magellan.
The spectra of symbiotic stars indicate that the cool red giant is surrounded by a very hot ionized gas which satellite observations finally
(20) identified as radiating from an invisible hot companion. It is possible that symbiotic stars represent a transitory phase in the evolution of certain types of binary systems in which a substantial amount of matter transfers from the
(25) larger partner to the smaller.
The exact evolutionary course that turns a binary system into a symbiotic one is unknown. The comparative scarcity of known symbiotics in our galaxy suggests that if all binaries of
(30) modest mass pass through a symbiotic phase in their evolution, the phase must be extremely brief, perhaps as short as a million years. It is suspected that the evolutionary course of binary stars is predetermined by the initial
(35) mass and angular momentum of their gas clouds. Since red giants and Mira variables are thought to be stars with a mass of one or two suns, it seems plausible that the original cloud from which a symbiotic system is formed can
(40) consist of no more than a few solar masses of gas.

2. The primary purpose of the passage is to

(A) argue that a great percentage of binary star systems are symbiotic

(B) criticize the theory of symbiotic stars as overly speculative

(C) describe symbiotic stars as a distinct type of binary system

(D) present evidence that binary star systems have evolved from gas clouds

(E) compare symbiotic stars to red giants and Mira variables

A tiny fraction of binary systems belong to a curious subclass whose radiation has a wavelength distribution so peculiar that it long defied explanation. Such systems radiate
(5) strongly in the visible region of the spectrum, but some of them do so even more strongly at both shorter and longer wavelengths: in the ultraviolet region and in the infrared and radio regions.

(10) This odd distribution of radiation is best explained by the pairing of a cool red-giant star and an intensely hot small star, known as symbiotic stars, that travel around a common center. Recently two symbiotic-star systems,
(15) the first to be detected outside our galaxy, have been observed in the Large Cloud of Magellan.

The spectra of symbiotic stars indicate that the cool red giant is surrounded by a very hot ionized gas which satellite observations finally
(20) identified as radiating from an invisible hot companion. It is possible that symbiotic stars represent a transitory phase in the evolution of certain types of binary systems in which a substantial amount of matter transfers from the
(25) larger partner to the smaller.

The exact evolutionary course that turns a binary system into a symbiotic one is unknown. The comparative scarcity of known symbiotics in our galaxy suggests that if all binaries of
(30) modest mass pass through a symbiotic phase in their evolution, the phase must be extremely brief, perhaps as short as a million years. It is suspected that the evolutionary course of binary stars is predetermined by the initial
(35) mass and angular momentum of their gas clouds. Since red giants and Mira variables are thought to be stars with a mass of one or two suns, it seems plausible that the original cloud from which a symbiotic system is formed can
(40) consist of no more than a few solar masses of gas.

3. According to the passage, the radiation emitted by

symbiotic stars is distinctive in that it

(A) generates standard wavelengths

(B) consists partly of visible waves

(C) is transferred from one star to its partner

(D) is strongest at the extreme ends of the spectrum

(E) emanates primarily from the larger star

A tiny fraction of binary systems belong to a curious subclass whose radiation has a wavelength distribution so peculiar that it long defied explanation. Such systems radiate
(5) strongly in the visible region of the spectrum, but some of them do so even more strongly at both shorter and longer wavelengths: in the ultraviolet region and in the infrared and radio regions.
(10)   This odd distribution of radiation is best explained by the pairing of a cool red-giant star and an intensely hot small star, known as symbiotic stars, that travel around a common center. Recently two symbiotic-star systems,
(15) the first to be detected outside our galaxy, have been observed in the Large Cloud of Magellan.
    The spectra of symbiotic stars indicate that the cool red giant is surrounded by a very hot ionized gas which satellite observations finally
(20) identified as radiating from an invisible hot companion. It is possible that symbiotic stars represent a transitory phase in the evolution of certain types of binary systems in which a substantial amount of matter transfers from the
(25) larger partner to the smaller.
    The exact evolutionary course that turns a binary system into a symbiotic one is unknown. The comparative scarcity of known symbiotics in our galaxy suggests that if all binaries of
(30) modest mass pass through a symbiotic phase in their evolution, the phase must be extremely brief, perhaps as short as a million years. It is suspected that the evolutionary course of binary stars is predetermined by the initial
(35) mass and angular momentum of their gas clouds. Since red giants and Mira variables are thought to be stars with a mass of one or two suns, it seems plausible that the original cloud from which a symbiotic system is formed can
(40) consist of no more than a few solar masses of gas.

4. The author suggests that

   (A)   the detection of radiation from an invisible hot companion star prompted scientists to investigate the peculiar ionized gas surrounding cool red giants

   (B)   small hot stars attach to cool red giants because red giants have a mass of one or two suns

   (C)   a million years is a brief period of time for the occurrence of many solar events

   (D)   the only symbiotic star systems to be detected outside of our galaxy are in the Large Cloud of Magellan

   (E)   if binary stars of modest mass passed through symbiotic phases lasting much more than a million years, it is likely that more of them would have been detected

Symbiotic Stars

What Makes It Difficult

This one has a structure common to many GMAT science passages: it introduces a mystery that has puzzled scientists for some time, and then proceeds to document various findings that support a theory meant to explain the mystery. This passage holds together a little better than does "Mitochondria"; the structure is a bit more coherent. The author states the mystery up front, and then methodically presents the theory of symbiotic stars as a possible solution. But the theory contains a ton of details, which, of course, the test makers exploit in the questions. In passages where the details are so technical and abstract, so difficult to connect to everyday experience, you have to pay extra careful attention to the reason *why* the author includes the details. As always, it behooves you to break the passage down into its key elements.

Key Points of the Passage

Purpose and Main Idea: The author's purpose is to describe the phenomenon of symbiotic star systems; namely, their characteristics and possible origin. The passage is mainly descriptive, but if we had to settle on a main idea, it would sound something like this: The nature of symbiotic stars helps explain certain strange radiation distribution patterns that have long puzzled scientists.

Paragraph Structure: Paragraph 1 introduces a mystery that had "long defied explanation": certain binary star systems exhibiting quirky radiation patterns stronger on the extreme sides of the spectrum.

Paragraph 2 gets right to the explanation. Evidently, this pattern can be explained by the pairing of a cool big star and a hot little star. These two types of stars are attached to one another through a common center; hence, the notion of symbiosis. The paragraph goes on to explain how the big and small stars are detected, and where a few of these things have been found.

An 800 test taker paraphrases the author's ideas into the simplest terms possible.

Paragraph 3 throws in some more details about this partnership, and suggests that symbiotic stars represent a phase in the evolution of certain binary systems. There's no need to assimilate every detail just yet. You should simply mark this paragraph as the place where some of the mechanisms of these star systems are laid out.

In the last paragraph, the author continues this speculation as to the evolution of symbiotic stars, employing a good deal of scientific terminology in the process. Again, not to panic—get the gist and you'll know where to return to reread, if a question demands it.

An 800 test taker knows that all the information she needs to answer the questions is right there in the passage. She therefore jots down the paragraph topics in her roadmap to help her hunt for answers later.

ANSWERS AND EXPLANATIONS

1. A   2. C   3. D   4. E

1. (A)

Paragraph 1 states that symbiotic stars are distinctive from other binary star systems in the pattern of radiation that they emit. In fact, this is the basis of the whole mystery, right? So (A) must be true. Sometimes the first question on even a difficult passage is very straightforward.

(B) is wrong because the second paragraph specifically mentions that *both* stars in a symbiotic system travel around a common center.

(C) and (E) are way too broad; neither one is implied by anything in the passage, which doesn't speculate on what's the case out there in the universe in general.

(D) contradicts the first paragraph, where we're told that symbiotic stars make up a tiny fraction of binary systems.

2. (C)

Since the gist of the passage is that symbiotic stars represent a special type of binary star system— one with a bizarre radiation pattern—choice (C) is correct. And the neutral verb "describe" fits the author's method to a T. The same, however, can't be said of choices (A) and (B), which we can dismiss on the basis of their verbs alone. The author doesn't "argue" or "criticize" anything in this passage; he simply describes a phenomenon.

An 800 test taker pays very careful attention to the verbs in answer choices, especially in "primary purpose" questions.

(D) The theory that binary stars are born in gas clouds is a detail from the last paragraph, certainly not the passage's main point, so (D) cannot describe the primary purpose of this passage. Notice how it doesn't even mention the main concept of the passage, symbiotic stars. It's very hard to describe the author's purpose without a reference to the passage's central character.

(E)'s out because the author doesn't even tell us what Mira variables are, let alone compare them to symbiotic stars.

3. (D)

Next up is a detail question that relates to the main idea. The last sentence of the first paragraph states that the type of binary system later defined as symbiotic radiates "even more strongly at both shorter and longer wavelengths" than in the middle of the spectrum. Choice (D) is a near perfect paraphrase of this.

(A) We know from paragraph 1 that the radiation emitted is remarkable because it is *not* standard, at least within the context of binary systems more generally.

(B) cannot be correct. Although some of the radiation from symbiotic systems is visible, that's not what makes these systems' radiation patterns "distinctive."

(C) picks up on some of the language in the third paragraph by discussing a transfer from one star to the other. The problem with this answer choice is that *matter*, not *radiation*, is what transfers between the stars. While paragraph 3 says that the "invisible hot companion" radiates gas, it does not suggest that such radiation is transferred to the cool red giant. Clearly this choice requires you to be very careful.

(E) The passage never suggests that the radiation primarily emanates from the larger star, and even if we somehow made this leap, it would still be incorrect to say that this is what makes their radiation distinctive. None of this is hinted at in the passage.

4. (E)

Next up is an open-ended Inference question with no clues as to what the test makers are after, so we have no choice but to wade into the choices, looking for the one that's supported by the hard facts of the passage.

(A) bollixes up the order of things; in fact, it pretty much gets it backwards. In paragraph 3 we learn that the ionized gas surrounding the cool red giant looked weird to scientists for decades before radiation from the invisible hot companion was discovered, so it can't be the detection of radiation that prompted scientists to look into the matter.

(B) tries to fashion a causal relationship out of two facts in the passage. True, the small hot stars attach to the big cool ones, and yes, we're told in paragraph 4 that red giants have a mass of one or two suns. But what has one thing to do with the other? Nothing, as far as the passage suggests, so (B) is out.

An 800 test taker is suspicious of choices that attempt to link two or more elements from different parts of the passage.

(C) A million years may not seem so "brief" to us, but according to the passage that's a relatively short period of time for a symbiotic phase. Regardless, other solar events are outside the scope of the passage, so there's no way we can judge from the material at hand the time it takes for these to occur. For all we know, a million years is a long time for most solar events; all we know about is symbiotic stars.

(D) erroneously plays off the Magellan detail in paragraph 2. Just because a few symbiotics *were* found over there doesn't in any way suggest that the *only* symbiotic stars outside our galaxy are in the Large Cloud of Magellan.

(E) That leaves (E), which must be correct. In paragraph 4, the author says that the small number of symbiotics detected in our galaxy suggests that the symbiotic phase is brief—"perhaps as short as a million years." Evidently, the author sees a link between the length of the phase and our ability to detect symbiotic stars. Therefore, it's reasonable to infer that if these phases were much longer, we'd probably detect more of them.

The basic theory of plate tectonics recognizes two ways continental margins can grow seaward. Where two plates move away from a midocean rift that separates them, the
(5) continental margins on those plates are said to be passive. Such continental margins grow slowly from the accumulation of riverborne sediments and of the carbonate skeletons of marine organisms. Since most sequences of
(10) such accretions, or miogeoclinal deposits, are undeformed, passive margins are not associated with mountain building.

Along active margins continents tend to grow much faster. At an active margin an
(15) oceanic plate plunges under a continental plate, fragments of which then adhere to the continental margin. The process is met with extensive volcanism and mountain-building. A classic example is the Andes of the west coast
(20) of South America.

In the original plate-tectonic model western North America was described as being initially passive and then active. It was assumed that the continent grew to a limited extent along this
(25) margin as oceanic rocks accreted in places such as the Coast Ranges of California. The model was successful in explaining such disparate features as the Franciscan rocks of the California Coast Ranges, created by
(30) subduction, and the granite rocks of the Sierra Nevada that originated in volcanoes.

The basic plate-tectonic reconstruction of the geologic history of western North America remains unchanged in the light of microplate
(35) tectonics, but the details are radically changed. It is now clear that much more crust was added to North America in the Mesozoic era than can be accounted for by volcanism and by the simple accretion of sediments. Further, some
(40) adjacent terranes are not genetically related, as would be expected from simple plate tectonics, but have almost certainly traveled great distances from entirely different parts of the world.

1. Which one of the following best expresses the main idea of the passage?

(A) The margin of the west coast of North America developed through a combination of active and passive mechanisms.

(B) The growth of continental margins is only partially explained by the basic theory of plate tectonics.

(C) Continental margins can grow seaward in two ways, through sedimentation or volcanism.

(D) The introduction of microplate tectonics poses a fundamental challenge to the existing theory of how continental margins are formed.

(E) Continental margins grow more rapidly along active margins than along passive margins.

The basic theory of plate tectonics recognizes two ways continental margins can grow seaward. Where two plates move away from a midocean rift that separates them, the
(5) continental margins on those plates are said to be passive. Such continental margins grow slowly from the accumulation of riverborne sediments and of the carbonate skeletons of marine organisms. Since most sequences of
(10) such accretions, or miogeoclinal deposits, are undeformed, passive margins are not associated with mountain building.

Along active margins continents tend to grow much faster. At an active margin an
(15) oceanic plate plunges under a continental plate, fragments of which then adhere to the continental margin. The process is met with extensive volcanism and mountain-building. A classic example is the Andes of the west coast
(20) of South America.

In the original plate-tectonic model western North America was described as being initially passive and then active. It was assumed that the continent grew to a limited extent along this
(25) margin as oceanic rocks accreted in places such as the Coast Ranges of California. The model was successful in explaining such disparate features as the Franciscan rocks of the California Coast Ranges, created by
(30) subduction, and the granite rocks of the Sierra Nevada that originated in volcanoes.

The basic plate-tectonic reconstruction of the geologic history of western North America remains unchanged in the light of microplate
(35) tectonics, but the details are radically changed. It is now clear that much more crust was added to North America in the Mesozoic era than can be accounted for by volcanism and by the simple accretion of sediments. Further, some
(40) adjacent terranes are not genetically related, as would be expected from simple plate tectonics, but have almost certainly traveled great distances from entirely different parts of the world.

2. The passage supplies information for answering all of the following questions regarding continental margins EXCEPT:

(A) How have marine organisms contributed to the formation of passive continental margins?

(B) What were some of the processes by which the continental margin of the west coast of North America was formed?

(C) Are miogeoclinal deposits associated with mountain building along continental margins?

(D) How was the continental margin of the west coast of South America formed?

(E) How much crust added to North America in the Mesozoic era can be accounted for by the accretion of sediments from the ocean floor?

The basic theory of plate tectonics recognizes two ways continental margins can grow seaward. Where two plates move away from a midocean rift that separates them, the
(5) continental margins on those plates are said to be passive. Such continental margins grow slowly from the accumulation of riverborne sediments and of the carbonate skeletons of marine organisms. Since most sequences of
(10) such accretions, or miogeoclinal deposits, are undeformed, passive margins are not associated with mountain building.

Along active margins continents tend to grow much faster. At an active margin an
(15) oceanic plate plunges under a continental plate, fragments of which then adhere to the continental margin. The process is met with extensive volcanism and mountain-building. A classic example is the Andes of the west coast
(20) of South America.

In the original plate-tectonic model western North America was described as being initially passive and then active. It was assumed that the continent grew to a limited extent along this
(25) margin as oceanic rocks accreted in places such as the Coast Ranges of California. The model was successful in explaining such disparate features as the Franciscan rocks of the California Coast Ranges, created by
(30) subduction, and the granite rocks of the Sierra Nevada that originated in volcanoes.

The basic plate-tectonic reconstruction of the geologic history of western North America remains unchanged in the light of microplate
(35) tectonics, but the details are radically changed. It is now clear that much more crust was added to North America in the Mesozoic era than can be accounted for by volcanism and by the simple accretion of sediments. Further, some
(40) adjacent terranes are not genetically related, as would be expected from simple plate tectonics, but have almost certainly traveled great distances from entirely different parts of the world.

3. The author mentions the Franciscan rocks of the California Coast Ranges in order to make which one of the following points?

(A) The basic theory of plate tectonics accounts for a wide variety of geologic features.

(B) The original plate tectonic model falls short of explaining such features.

(C) Subduction processes are responsible for the majority of the geologic features found along the west coast of North America.

(D) Passive margins can take on many geologic forms.

(E) The concept of microplate tectonics was first introduced to account for such phenomena.

The basic theory of plate tectonics recognizes two ways continental margins can grow seaward. Where two plates move away from a midocean rift that separates them, the
(5) continental margins on those plates are said to be passive. Such continental margins grow slowly from the accumulation of riverborne sediments and of the carbonate skeletons of marine organisms. Since most sequences of
(10) such accretions, or miogeoclinal deposits, are undeformed, passive margins are not associated with mountain building.

Along active margins continents tend to grow much faster. At an active margin an
(15) oceanic plate plunges under a continental plate, fragments of which then adhere to the continental margin. The process is met with extensive volcanism and mountain-building. A classic example is the Andes of the west coast
(20) of South America.

In the original plate-tectonic model western North America was described as being initially passive and then active. It was assumed that the continent grew to a limited extent along this
(25) margin as oceanic rocks accreted in places such as the Coast Ranges of California. The model was successful in explaining such disparate features as the Franciscan rocks of the California Coast Ranges, created by
(30) subduction, and the granite rocks of the Sierra Nevada that originated in volcanoes.

The basic plate-tectonic reconstruction of the geologic history of western North America remains unchanged in the light of microplate
(35) tectonics, but the details are radically changed. It is now clear that much more crust was added to North America in the Mesozoic era than can be accounted for by volcanism and by the simple accretion of sediments. Further, some
(40) adjacent terrances are not genetically related, as would be expected from simple plate tectonics, but have almost certainly traveled great distances from entirely different parts of the world.

4. Which one of the following does the author mention as evidence for the inadequacy of the original plate tectonic model to describe the formation of continental margins?

(A) Nearly flat, undeformed crystal blocks have been found along some continental margins where there are mountains further inland.

(B) Sediments and fragments from the depths of the ocean accumulate along continental margins.

(C) Large pieces of the Earth's crust that appear to be completely unrelated are found in the same area today.

(D) Undeformed miogeoclinal deposits are usually not linked to mountain building.

(E) Oceanic plates drop beneath continental plates along active margins.

Plate Tectonics

What Makes It Difficult

There's not much to say about the difficulty of this final science passage that hasn't already been said about the others preceding it. We're faced with the same challenges: an esoteric, difficult topic containing its own unique lingo, a mass of technical details, and questions to test your understanding of them. As always, you're best served by getting the basic gist of the passage, noting where specific details occur so you can return to them as needed.

Key Points of the Passage

Purpose and Main Idea: The author's purpose is to describe the basic theory of plate tectonics. The main idea is that the theory ultimately falls short of explaining all the phenomena of growing continental margins.

Paragraph Structure: Paragraph1 introduces the basic theory of plate tectonics, which posits that there are two ways in which continental margins can grow seaward. The paragraph goes on to describe one of those ways, a mechanism known as passive margins. Details regarding passive margins abound, but it's best to let those pass for now and see where the author's going with all this. As always, we'll return to this material if a question demands it.

Paragraph 2 describes the other way continental margins can grow, and that's along active margins. A simple distinction is presented which is worth noting; continents grow faster along active margins.

> An 800 test taker pays careful attention to distinctions in passages that compare two or more people, theories, or phenomena.

Again, details are plentiful, as we'd expect in a science passage. We're told what actually happens at active margins, the results of such activity (volcanoes and mountains), and an example of these results (the Andes). Take in what you can, but again, there's no need to obsess over the particulars. All you really need to note is that this paragraph contains a process, some results, and an example.

> An 800 test taker first and foremost picks up on what *generally* occurs in each paragraph.

Paragraph 3 applies the model to a concrete example (western North America), illustrating how the concepts of passive and active margins, taken together, can accurately describe the growth of a continental margin and successfully explain various specific continental features.

Things are humming along quite well until we get to paragraph 4, which introduces something new—the concept of microplate tectonics. Here, with the aid of specific examples, the author shows how this new theory helps to explain certain phenomena that "simple" or "basic" plate tectonics cannot account for. While remaining in general accordance with the story told by basic plate tectonics, microplate tectonics "radically" changes some of the details. Much of the paragraph is given over to examples of how this is so.

ANSWERS AND EXPLANATIONS

1. B   2. E   3. A   4. C

1. (B)

First up is a main idea question. While the basic theory of plate tectonics explains much about the growth of continental margins, the fourth paragraph suggests that it cannot fully explain certain geologic details. (B) captures this, and is the correct answer.

An 800 test taker stays alert throughout the entire passage since the author's full main idea may not emerge until the end.

(A) and (E) both represent true statements, but they're details from the passage, not the passage's main idea.

An 800 test taker can distinguish between the main idea of a passage and facts that are merely reflected in the passage.

(C) distorts the notion of the two ways that continental margins can grow. Though the first paragraph mentions sedimentation as an example of passive margins, and paragraph 2 states that volcanism often results from active margin growth, the author never goes so far as to say that sedimentation and volcanism are the two ways that continental margins grow. And even if this could be inferred, it's still not big enough to be the main point of the passage.

(D) is incorrect because the first sentence of paragraph 4 states that the basic plate tectonic theory remains unchanged in the light of microplate tectonics; it's the details that are radically changed, not the basic theory.

2. (E)

This is an unusually worded detail question, but it does force us to focus on the details nonetheless. The question in each wrong choice is one that can be answered by the information in the passage, while the right answer is one that goes unanswered by the author. Let's check the choices.

(A) is covered in the first paragraph, which describes the growth of passive margins. There, the author says that passive margins grow, in part, through the accumulation of the carbonate skeletons of marine organisms.

(B) is the subject of the paragraph 3—the continental margin of the west coast of North America grew at first as a passive margin, and then as an active margin.

(C) is answered in the last sentence of paragraph 1: miogeoclinal deposits are associated with passive margins and are "generally not associated with mountain building."

(D) We have to search a bit for the answer to the question posed in choice (D): the last sentence of the second paragraph says that the west coast of South America is an active margin.

(E) That leaves (E), which must be correct. In fact, if you had full confidence eliminating the other four choices, you could choose (E) without much fanfare and move on.

An 800 test taker has confidence in her work, and uses that confidence to save time whenever possible.

Indeed, the question in (E) cannot be answered by information contained in the passage. Microplate tectonics has revealed that much more crust was added to North America in the Mesozoic period than was added from volcanism and the accretion of sediments, but that doesn't tell us precisely how much crust the accretion of sediments accounts for in the grand scheme of things.

3. (A)

The Coast Ranges of California are introduced in paragraph 3 to provide an example of the variety of geologic features that the original plate-tectonic model could successfully explain: the Franciscan Rocks, formed by local subduction, and the granite rocks of the Sierra Nevada, formed by volcanic action. (A) therefore represents the best account of why this detail was mentioned.

(B) is wrong because the problems with the basic plate tectonic model are discussed in paragraph 4, a paragraph in which the California Coast Ranges are never mentioned.

An 800 test taker remains conscious of where in the passage certain ideas are presented, and uses that knowledge to help eliminate choices that deal with material far from the issue in question.

(C) is a distortion of the facts. We don't know if subduction processes are responsible for the *majority* of the west coast's geologic features—we're told only that they are responsible for some, such as the Coast Ranges.

(D) is wrong because the Coast Ranges were formed by local subduction processes, according to paragraph 3, not by the actions of passive margins.

(E) The concept of microplate tectonics was introduced to account for phenomena that the basic, or original, plate-tectonic model could not adequately explain. But the Coast Ranges are features that the basic model *can* account for, so (E) is incorrect.

4. (C)

The inadequacy of the plate tectonic model is introduced in the final paragraph of the passage. There we're told that genetically distinct pieces of the Earth's crust are found in the same area, a fact which the original plate tectonic model cannot explain. (C) gets at this issue.

(A) The original plate tectonic model can account for (A)—see the third and fourth paragraphs.

(B), (D), and (E) are true statements—see the first and second paragraphs—but none of these statements has a direct bearing on the issue of the inadequacy of the original plate tectonic model.

An 800 test taker is not tempted by a choice simply because it contains a true statement. It must, first and foremost, answer the question that was asked.

section three

SENTENCE CORRECTION

CHAPTER EIGHT

The Sentence Correction Challenge

1. As of this morning, <u>none of my friends have been able to solve</u> the puzzle contained in last week's newspaper.

   (A) none of my friends have been able to solve

   (B) none of my friends was able to solve

   (C) not one of my friends has yet been able to solve

   (D) none of my friends has been able to solve

   (E) nobody among my friends have solved

You surely feel that it's hard to top the excitement that challenging grammar can elicit. Is *none* or *not one* correct? *Was* or *were*? *Has been* or *have been*? The answers to questions such as these clearly form the backbone of our society, the machinery that enables it to run effectively, the meaning of life even.

Well, that may not be true, but there is a certain joy to be found in Sentence Correction questions. They're short, they're designed to be answered quickly, they generally test a few, well-defined rules, and yet they still constitute one third of the verbal questions on the GMAT. Nevertheless, as you surely know from experience, not all Sentence Correction questions are created equal; some can only be described as very difficult. In this section, you'll see examples of the hardest questions, the ones that push the boundaries of the "well-defined rules" to determine whether you really, *really* know them, including their occasional exceptions. Once you master the principles discussed and tested in this section, you'll be able to conquer the GMAT's Sentence Correction questions and, as an added bonus, you'll also be able to correct the grammar of your friends and scoff in disgust when you read "between associates" rather than "among associates" in the newspaper. We'll come back to that.

Explanation: So what's the answer to the question above? It's (D), and here's why:

None is singular (like *every* or *everyone*) and *have been* is plural. Singular subjects need singular verbs, so we can immediately eliminate (A) and (E). As for (B), *Has been* beats *was*. Even though they're both singular, there is no valid reason to replace the original verb. *Has been* is in the perfect tense and, as such, describes an action that began in the past and continues into the present. The beginning of the sentence (*As of this morning*) indicates that we're dealing with this sort of situation: the friends have been working on the puzzle, still seem to be working on the puzzle, and are not able to solve it. *Was* describes an action that took place entirely in the past and therefore is inappropriate considering the beginning of the sentence. So much for (B). As for (C), there's nothing wrong with *None* that would require its substitution with *Not one* (and *none* is an elision of *not one* anyway). That leaves (D).

An 800 test taker knows that unnecessary changes are incorrect changes when it comes to Sentence Correction questions. He doesn't fix any part of the sentence unless it's broken.

Here are some guidelines on how to make the best use of the following Sentence Correction chapters.

USING THE SENTENCE CORRECTION QUESTIONS IN THIS BOOK

This section is designed to enable you to master the most difficult Sentence Correction questions. It divides the commonly tested errors into categories, and provides practice questions to help you gain mastery of each. Keep in mind that many, even most, Sentence Correction questions test more than one error at a time; our categories will reflect the sentence's primary challenge or the one that we want to highlight. Here's the specific breakdown of the section:

- In chapter 9 you will learn about the *eight most commonly tested grammatical errors* present in Sentence Correction questions.

- You will then find *practice questions* that present particularly challenging demonstrations of each type of error.

- In chapter 10 you'll find another *eight especially difficult errors* that are less commonly tested but must be mastered by anyone aiming for GMAT greatness.

- Finally, chapter 11 consists of *forty practice questions* that will enable you to reinforce all that you have learned in this section.

STRATEGIES FOR SENTENCE CORRECTION QUESTIONS

As you make your way through this material, keep the following principles in mind:

Read the original sentence carefully and try to spot grammatical errors by identifying whether something "sounds" wrong. Whenever possible, don't wait for the answer choices to reveal the sentence's error(s). When you find no flaws in the original sentence, use the differences among the answer choices to understand what grammatical or stylistic concepts are being tested and whether the original sentence presents the best option.

Be systematic. As you locate each error, eliminate all of the choices that contain that error. Do not read each answer choice back into the sentence individually; that wastes time and invites inaccuracy. Instead, identify the differences among the choices and eliminate those that offer less effective or grammatically incorrect alternatives.

Always look at every choice. Even when the original sentence seems fine, pay attention to the grammar that it tests and look through the choices systematically to see if any provides a better option. Remember that these questions test grammatical correctness *and* effectiveness of expression. Just because a sentence is grammatically correct, it won't be the correct option if another choice expresses the same idea more clearly.

Pay attention to the meaning of the sentence. Often the most difficult questions and answer choices will test your understanding of the original sentence and your ability to eliminate those choices that unnecessarily distort the original meaning.

Keep track of time. With approximately 14 Sentence Correction questions, 14 Critical Reasoning questions, and 14 Reading Comprehension questions in 75 minutes, you should aim to spend a minute and a quarter on each Sentence Correction question. Since the questions in this book are particularly difficult, you may need more time, but try to spend no more than an average of a minute and a half per question.

CHAPTER NINE

Eight Most Commonly Tested Errors in Sentence Correction

1. MODIFIERS

The hardest thing about correcting modifiers is recognizing them; they're usually easy to fix. The GMAT generally deals with modifying phrases. Usually set off by a comma, modifying phrases provide more information about the subject or object in the main clause of the sentence without naming it directly (so, in this sentence, *Usually set off by a comma* modifies *modifying phrases*). In order for a modifying phrase to be used correctly, it must be as close as possible to the thing or person it modifies. That's it; there's no other trick. Nevertheless, modifiers are so frequently misplaced and so commonly misused in everyday speech and writing that they can be hard to spot, which is why they constitute one of the primary and most frequent challenges in Sentence Correction questions.

SENTENCE CORRECTION PRACTICE SET 1

1. Of all the countries contiguous to China, the <u>Soviet Union's borders were the most strongly defended</u>.

    (A) the Soviet Union's borders were the most strongly defended

    (B) the borders of the Soviet Union were defended more strongly than any of the others

    (C) the Soviet Union's borders stood out for the strength of their defensive capabilities

    (D) the Soviet Union had the most strongly defended borders

    (E) the Soviet Union's were the borders most strongly defended

2. In addition to providing more course offerings than Willow High School, <u>the teachers at Menlo High School are better trained than those at</u> Willow, having received more information on instructing a multilingual and culturally diverse student body.

    (A) the teachers at Menlo High School are better trained than those at

    (B) Menlo High School has teachers who are better trained than those at

    (C) Menlo High School teachers are better trained than they are at

    (D) the teachers at Menlo High School are better in training than those at

    (E) Menlo High School has teachers who are better trained than at

Explanation: The Soviet Union's Borders

1. The introductory phrase, "Of all the countries contiguous to China," is the modifier. Clearly it describes a country contiguous to China that the author wants to comment on further. The country being modified, here the Soviet Union, must be named directly after the modifying phrase in order for the modifier to be used correctly, but in the original sentence we see not *the Soviet Union* but *the Soviet Union's borders*. Don't be fooled by the fact that (A) and (C) seem to begin by naming *the Soviet Union*. The possessive apostrophe makes the phrase *the Soviet Union's borders* equivalent to *the borders of the Soviet Union*, making the borders, not the country, the subject of the choices. Since the country, not its borders, should be modified by the original phrase, eliminate (A), (B), (C), and (E). (D) may not sound particularly eloquent, but it is the only grammatically correct, and therefore the only viable, option. (D) wins.

Explanation: Willow versus Menlo

2. Again we have an introductory modifying phrase. Here, it describes something with better course offerings than those of Willow High School, so clearly it modifies another school, later named as Menlo High School. Because the modifier describes Menlo High, Menlo must be named directly after the comma. Eliminate (A) and (D). Scanning for differences among the remaining choices, we see that they end differently: does *than those at*, *than they are at*, or *than at* work best with the rest of the sentence? The first works fine; we're dealing with teachers, so the pronoun (here *those*) should be plural, and it is; *at* is parallel with the *at* earlier in the choice, so that's fine; and *than* is necessary in a comparison begun with *better*. The second option is not grammatically incorrect but it's wordier than the first, so eliminate (C). The final is grammatically incorrect since *those* is necessary in order for the sentence to compare (as it must) teachers to teachers. We'll return to pronouns and word pairs later. (B) is correct.

An 800 test taker can identify modifiers effortlessly. In order to become perfectly familiar with them, practice identifying them in the articles or books you read and apply your skill to the GMAT.

SENTENCE CORRECTION PRACTICE SET 2

3. In 1905, The House of Mirth, Edith Wharton's novel about the blighted aspirations of <u>Lily Bart was published by Scribner's and it was</u> a reputable press in the early twentieth century.

    (A) Lily Bart was published by Scribner's and it was

    (B) Lily Bart, published by Scribner's, and was

    (C) Lily Bart was published by Scribner's, being

    (D) Lily Bart, which was published by Scribner's, was

    (E) Lily Bart, was published by Scribner's,

4. Declining revenues resulting from a decrease in business travel, <u>a source of income without which most commercial airlines could not survive, are</u> going to force many commercial airlines to increase prices and decrease services in the coming months.

    (A) a source of income without which most commercial airlines could not survive, are

    (B) a source of income without which most commercial airlines could not survive, is

    (C) and most commercial airlines use it as a source of income to survive with, are

    (D) which is a source of income which is needed by most commercial airlines who could not survive without it, are

    (E) which most commercial airlines use as a source of income without which they are unable to survive, is

5. Dreading another trip to the cat clinic, <u>her veterinarian was persuaded to treat her cat at her home, a rather combative two-year-old black male</u>.

    (A) her veterinarian was persuaded to treat her cat at her home, a rather combative two-year-old black male

    (B) she persuaded her veterinarian to treat her cat at her home, the cat being a rather combative two-year-old black male

    (C) Jessica persuaded her veterinarian to treat her cat, a rather combative two-year-old black male, at her home

    (D) Jessica persuaded her veterinarian that her rather combative two-year-old black male cat would best be treated at her home

    (E) she persuaded her veterinarian that her home should be the place that her rather combative two-year-old black male cat was treated at

Explanation: The House of Little Mirth

3. Here the modifier comes at the end; *a reputable press in the early twentieth century* modifies *Scribner's*. Once you spot the modifier, you know that it must directly follow *Scribner's* and you can eliminate every choice except (E). Since the modifier directly describes Scribner's, it should remain a modifier and not be separated from *Scribner's* by *and [it] was*. The addition of *and* suggests that what follows *and* and what precedes it are different ideas, that Scribner's and its reputation are equally and distinctly important to the sentence. For the purposes of this sentence, the two ideas are intimately related since the final phrase exists only to provide more information about Scribner's, not to be stressed in its own right. Therefore, the final phrase should modify *Scribner's* and you can eliminate (A) and (B). As for (C), *being* is unnecessary and therefore creates an error in expression. Finally, (D) suggests that Lily Bart was the reputable press. Only (E) uses the modifier correctly.

> An 800 test taker knows that Sentence Correction questions containing modifier errors can be answered quickly and accurately by one who knows how they work. Since there's often only one choice that uses the modifier correctly, mastering modifiers can result in fast points.

Explanation: Struggling Airlines

4. No, this isn't the most eloquent sentence that one could write, but it is grammatically correct and uses modifiers correctly. In the original sentence, the clause beginning *a source* modifies *business travel*, and follows it immediately, as any well placed modifier should. Answer choices (C) and (D) create an error by altering that clause so that it no longer acts as a modifier, though it must for the same reasons that *Scribner's* needed its modifier above. The remaining choices differ with respect to the final verb: is *is* or *are* correct? Since the subject of the sentence is *declining revenues*, itself plural, then the verb should be *are*. Eliminate (B) and (E). Only (A) remains.

Explanation: The Combative Cat

5. This sentence contains two modifier challenges: the introductory clause marks one modifier and the final clause (*a rather combative…*) marks another. As the sentence stands, the initial modifier is what's known as a dangling modifier; there is no subject in the sentence that it can modify. Knowing that you need the name of whoever dreads this trip to follow the modifier, you can eliminate (A), (B), and (E). *She* in (B) is unacceptable because the sentence doesn't tell you who "she" is. Both (C) and (D) correctly place the second unflattering modifier next to *cat*, but (D) is certainly wordier (*would best be treated* loses when compared to *to treat*). That leaves (C).

2. IDIOMS

The GMAT test makers love to test idioms, which we can define as speech forms that follow no general rules. For instance, there's no particular reason we say "I prefer rice to pasta" rather than "I prefer rice over pasta," but the first includes the correct idiom. You'll see many idioms like the one in the previous sentence that test your ability to match the verb (here *prefer*) with the correct preposition (*to*), and many that test common word pairs (*not only* must be followed by *but* or *but also*, for instance). Since there is no larger grammatical rule at play here, your ability to master Sentence Correction questions containing idioms depends on your ability to isolate the idiom and determine which option sounds best based on your knowledge of them.

SENTENCE CORRECTION PRACTICE SET 3

6. In the past few months, there has been extensive dispute <u>over if fare hikes should be a first or last recourse</u> in improving the transit system.

    (A) over if fare hikes should be a first or last recourse

    (B) about if fare hikes are a first or last recourse

    (C) about hiking fares as being a first or last recourse

    (D) over whether fare hikes should be a first or last recourse

    (E) concerning fare hikes and whether to raise them as a first or last recourse

7. <u>More adeptly handling responsibility than his predecessors were able to do</u>, the new owner of the property rapidly increased the production rate of the land.

    (A) More adeptly handling responsibility than his predecessors were able to do

    (B) As he was more adept at handling responsibility than were his predecessors

    (C) Handling more responsibilities adeptly than his predecessors

    (D) More adept than his predecessors at handling responsibility

    (E) Since he handled responsibility in a manner more adept than that of his predecessors

Explanation: Transit Fare Hike

6. The key idiom in the sentence is *dispute*; the sentence asks you to determine which is the correct preposition that should follow it. Skimming through the answer choices, you see that you have several options. Excerpt the idiom and ask yourself, assuming that one has to discuss such things, does one talk about a dispute "over" an issue, "about" an issue, or "concerning" an issue? The first is the correct idiom, so eliminate (B), (C), and (E). The only difference between (A) and (D) is the use of *if* or *whether*. Memorize this fact if you don't know it already: *whether* is the correct choice when the sentence describes alternatives; *if* is correct when it describes a hypothetical situation (*whether to participate* versus *if he participated, he would…*). Since this sentence presents two alternative options (*first or last recourse*), *whether* is correct. That leaves (D).

An 800 test taker knows that idioms can't be explained by stable rules; idioms are what they are and there's often no more to say about them. He identifies the idioms he doesn't know and memorizes them, knowing that idioms will show up frequently on the exam.

Explanation: Adept Management

7. One way to begin to correct this sentence is to recognize that word order itself can be idiomatic or unidiomatic. The initial phrase *more adeptly handling* sees several alterations in the choices, so let's start there. The options are: *more adept at handling, handling more…adeptly,* and *handled…in a manner more adept.* The word order in (C) and (E) is unidiomatic; (C) wrongly splits up *more* and *adeptly* and (E) should read *in a more adept manner.* The remaining options are idiomatically correct, but (A) and (B) are unnecessarily wordy, especially when compared to (D). In (A), *were able to do* is unnecessary, and *as he was* and *were* are both unnecessary in (B). We'll come back to wordiness in the section on expression. (D) it is.

KAPLAN

SENTENCE CORRECTION PRACTICE SET 4

8. In commercial garment construction, one advantage of serging over single-needle sewing is that the seam allowance is overcast as the seam is sewn <u>instead of with</u> a separate process requiring deeper seam allowances.

    (A) instead of with
    (B) rather than in
    (C) in contrast with
    (D) as opposed to
    (E) instead of

9. American executives, unlike their Japanese counterparts, <u>have pressure to show</u> high profits in each quarterly report, with little thought given to long-term goals.

    (A) have pressure to show
    (B) are under pressure to show
    (C) are under the pressure of showing
    (D) are pressured toward showing
    (E) have pressure that they should show

10. <u>However much parents in Johannson's district may agree that</u> the instruction of moral values should take place in the elementary school classroom, it is difficult for them to arrive at consensus concerning what those values are and how they should be taught.

    (A) However much parents in Johannson's district may agree that
    (B) Despite the fact that parents in Johannson's district may agree that
    (C) There is general agreement among the parents in Johannson's district that
    (D) Although the parents in Johannson's district agree for
    (E) Even though the parents in Johannson's district agree

Explanation: To Serge or Not to Serge

8. Beware of the short ones: their difficulty often compensates for their brevity. Here you're asked for the proper terms to express a fascinating comparison between serging and single-needle sewing. All of the options describe alternatives, but only one gets the idiom right: *with* is wrong in the original; *instead of* is okay, but the seam allowance isn't sewn *with* a separate process but *in* a separate process. Eliminate (A) and (C). (D) and (E) are wrong because they don't express the parallel in the sentence. The sentence describes two options: overcasting *as* the seam is sewn or *in* a separate process. The correct answer choice needs to include *in* at the end so that the two options can be grammatically parallel. We'll be talking about parallelism in just a bit. Only choice (B) remains.

> An 800 test taker doesn't forget to read her final choice back into the sentence. She knows that it's only possible to spot certain errors when the choice is viewed in the context of the sentence.

Explanation: The Pressure for Profits

9. Often the explanations for idiom questions aren't very satisfying because, well, an idiom is just right or wrong and doesn't follow larger rules. So, in this question, *have pressure to show* just isn't idiomatically correct. Compare it to the choices: even though *are under pressure to show* is wordier, it's a familiar and correct idiom. (C) is a wordier rendition of (B) so eliminate it. (E) is a wordier and equally incorrect version of (A) so take it out too. (D) has the wrong idiom: *toward* isn't the correct preposition. (B) remains.

Explanation: Morals and Elementary School

10. The options for this sentence present you with a list of different idioms from which to choose. Start with the end: is *agree that*, *agree for*, or *agree* correct? The first is fine, the second is unidiomatic because *for* doesn't go with *agree*, and the third is out because *that* is necessary in order for the sentence to make sense. That leaves (A), (B), and (C). (A) isn't particularly eloquent, but it's not grammatically flawed. (B) is out because *Despite the fact* doesn't fit with *may agree* (it can be a fact that they agree, but if we don't know whether they agree, then there's no fact to discuss). (C) is wordy, passive (more on this later), and it doesn't agree with the rest of the sentence; if you're skeptical, try reading it in. Only (A) survives.

> An 800 test taker doesn't worry about correcting the nonunderlined portion of the sentence. Even if it's awkwardly phrased, that's not your problem to solve.

---

3. PARALLELISM

Whenever a sentence creates a parallel, either by listing a series of things or comparing or contrasting different things, it needs to express the pieces of the parallel in the same grammatical form. That means that starting with a noun in the first piece requires you to start with a noun in the second, etc. As long as you identify the elements of the parallel and look for similar structure, you're primed for greatness.

SENTENCE CORRECTION PRACTICE SET 5

11. Declining enrollments are forcing smaller private colleges to choose <u>between raising tuition and the reduction of the staff</u>.

   (A) between raising tuition and the reduction of the staff

   (B) between rising tuition and staff reduction

   (C) between raising tuition or reducing staff

   (D) between raising tuition and reducing staff

   (E) between the rise of tuition and the reduction of the staff

12. The bylaws of a corporation specify how the directors of the corporation are to be elected, whether the existing stockholders will have first right to buy any new stock issued by the firm, <u>as well as duties of management committees</u>.

   (A) as well as duties of management committees

   (B) as well as the duties that the management committees have

   (C) and that the management committees have duties

   (D) outlining the duties of management committees

   (E) and what the duties of management committees will be

Explanation: Poor Private Colleges

11. Private colleges seem to be in a bit of a bind and this sentence describes two possible solutions to their financial woes. *Between* marks the comparison and lets you know that the options need to have the same grammatical structure, and since *raising tuition* does not have the same structure as *the reduction of the staff*, eliminate (A). (B) shares the same error so take it out as well. The remaining options are parallel (*raising* and *reducing* or *the rise* and *the reduction*) so look for other errors. (C) has *between...or* and (D) has *between...and*. The second uses the correct word pair since *between* must always be followed by *and* so eliminate (C). (E) is trickier, but it's wrong because *rise* distorts the meaning of the original sentence; *the raising* would, however unappealing, be correct. Go with (D).

Explanation: According to the Bylaws

12. The bylaws have three stipulations in this sentence, and whenever you see a list, you know to look out for flaws in parallelism. Think of the original sentence this way:

"The bylaws of a corporation specify: 1. how the directors…are to be elected

2. whether the existing stockholders…firm
   and/as well as

3. duties of management committees."

Each piece of the list needs to follow grammatically from the first part of the sentence, and each needs to have the same structure as the others. Item 3 is clearly not like the others, so eliminate (A), and go ahead and take out (B), (C), and (D) for breaking the parallel as well. (E) is a bit clumsy, but it's the only grammatically correct option.

An 800 test taker thinks of parallelism whenever she sees lists or word pairs like *between…and* and *fewer…than*.

SENTENCE CORRECTION PRACTICE SET 6

13. There is no agreement at present on what function, if any, certain herbs like gingko bilboa have <u>in slowing the deterioration or improving</u> memory.

    (A) in slowing the deterioration or improving

    (B) in the improvement or slowing of the deterioration of

    (C) in slowed or improved deterioration of

    (D) in the improvement to or the slowing of the deterioration of

    (E) in slowing the deterioration of or improving

14. To tackle the issue of Congressional campaign spending is <u>becoming embroiled in a war which is raging between those who support public financing with</u> those who would lift the limits on the amount political parties and individuals may donate.

    (A) becoming embroiled in a war which is raging between those who support public financing with

    (B) becoming embroiled in a war raging among those who support public financing with

    (C) to become embroiled in a war raging between those who support public financing and

    (D) to become embroiled in a war which is raging among those who support public financing and

    (E) becoming embroiled in a war raging between those who support public financing and

15. Often credited as the founder of English literature, Geoffrey Chaucer both contributed to a growing canon of English <u>literature, extended the capabilities of the language, and using it</u> to invent a new poetic meter.

    (A) literature, extended the capabilities of the language, and using it

    (B) literature, extended the capabilities of the language, and used it

    (C) literature and extended the capabilities of the language, using it

    (D) literature, extending the capabilities of the language and using it

    (E) literature and, extending the capabilities of the language, using it

Explanation: Herbal Remedies

13. *Slowing the deterioration* and *improving* are already parallel in the original sentence, but they're not in (B), so eliminate that option. (C) gives you a parallel structure, but it distorts the meaning of the original sentence and makes no sense in the context of the rest of the sentence. (D) is unidiomatic since it describes the *improvement to* rather than the *improvement of* memory. The only difference between (A) and (E) is the *of* following *deterioration. Of* is necessary because it completes the first phrase (*slowing the deterioration of…memory*). (E) it is.

An 800 test taker realizes that she may need to make a sentence wordier in order to make it correct. The shortest option is not always the best option.

Explanation: Campaign Financing

14. *To tackle…is* sets up a parallel; to tackle is to become embroiled. (A), (B), and (E) don't create the parallel so eliminate them. The only difference between (C) and (D) is the use of *between* or *among*, respectively. Here's another rule to memorize: *Between* is the correct preposition when two options are presented, and *among* is correct when there are more than two. Since there are two sides in this dispute, *between* is correct. Eliminate (D) and (C) remains.

Explanation: Chaucer's Poetry

15. *Both* tells you from the beginning that Chaucer did two things but the original sentence gives you three and, as if that weren't bad enough, the three aren't even expressed in parallel structures. Eliminate (A), and (B) as well for mimicking that error. (D) is out too because it doesn't offer a second accomplishment to parallel *contributed*. (C) and (E) give you the right number of elements, but (E) isn't parallel (*extending* doesn't match *contributed*) so take (C).

When an 800 test taker finds the original sentence confusing, he uses the nonunderlined portion to tell him what the underlined portion must include.

---

4. COMPARISONS

Comparisons usually involve terms such as *like*, *unlike*, *similar to*, and *in contrast to*. Basically, they mark a particular type of parallelism and, as such, require parallel structures in the objects, people, or whatever that are being compared. They deserve special consideration because comparisons demand more precise parallels, even with respect to content, and because they're tested so frequently that you should be familiar with their oddities. You'll notice that the terms of comparisons often begin modifying phrases; all the grammar that you'll review in this section ultimately works together.

SENTENCE CORRECTION PRACTICE SET 7

16. <u>In contrast to the symphonies of Haydn, a much freer use of dissonance is evident in the symphonies of Mahler.</u>

    (A) In contrast to the symphonies of Haydn, a much freer use of dissonance is evident in the symphonies of Mahler.

    (B) In contrast with Haydn's symphonies, Mahler uses dissonance much more freely.

    (C) In contrast to those of Haydn, the symphonies of Mahler demonstrate a much more free use of dissonance.

    (D) In contrast to Haydn's symphonies, Mahler's demonstrate a much freer use of dissonance.

    (E) In contrast with Haydn's symphonies, those of Mahler use dissonance much more freely.

17. The recent amendments to the rules governing professional baseball, like <u>those governing professional gymnastics, were motivated</u> by a desire to make the sport more interesting to watch.

    (A) those governing professional gymnastics, were motivated

    (B) those to the rules governing professional gymnastics, were motivated

    (C) those to the rules which govern professional gymnastics, were motivated

    (D) the amendments to the rules governing professional gymnastics, have been motivated

    (E) the amendments governing professional gymnastics, were being motivated

Explanation: Mahler and Haydn

16. This sentence compares the use of dissonance in the symphonies of Mahler and Haydn. The original sentence compares Haydn's symphonies to a freer use of dissonance, but comparisons must compare like objects (symphonies to symphonies, dissonance to dissonance). Eliminate (A) and (B) for breaking that rule. Focus on the different endings in the three remaining choices: Is *a much more free use of dissonance, a much freer use of dissonance,* or using *dissonance much more freely* correct? The first wrongly replaces *freer* with *more free,* so eliminate it, but the remaining options are both acceptable. (D) and (E) differ with respect to the initial phrase, so should it be *in contrast to* or *in contrast with*? The first is the correct idiom, so (D) is the right answer. Notice that the object of the comparison can be implied as long as the structure is parallel (*Mahler's* in (D) equals *Mahler's symphonies*).

Explanation: Spicing Up Baseball

17. *Like* marks the comparisons, this time between the amendments to the rules governing baseball and those to the rules governing gymnastics. The trick in the sentence is that there are three pieces to the comparison: the first is the amendments, the second is the rules, and the third is the sport. The first sentence parallels only two: "those governing gymnastics" parallels the sports and the rules (implied by "those") but not the amendments. Eliminate (E) as well because it parallels the first and third pieces but drops the second, the rules. You can look at the final verb in the choices to eliminate (D); *were* is better than *have been* since the action has been completed and *have been* suggests that it's still happening. The only difference between (B) and (C) is *rules governing* or *rules which govern*. The options seem more or less equal, but since the initial piece of the comparison mentions *rules governing,* the second piece needs to parallel that structure. (B) wins.

An 800 test taker is careful not to exclude or add items when working with comparisons. She knows that the objects of the comparison must always have grammatical structures that are perfectly consistent with each other.

SENTENCE CORRECTION PRACTICE SET 8

18. <u>Unlike German shepherds or Doberman pinchers, there is an unwillingness on the part of many people to believe that pit bulls might be fully domesticated.</u>

    (A) Unlike German shepherds or Doberman pinchers, there is an unwillingness on the part of many people to believe that pit bulls might be fully domesticated.

    (B) Many people, willing to believe that German shepherds and Doberman pinchers might be fully domesticated, are unwilling to believe the same of pit bulls.

    (C) Unlike German shepherds or Doberman pinchers, pit bulls bring out an unwillingness in many people to believe that they might be fully domesticated.

    (D) Many people are unwilling to believe that pit bulls might be fully domesticated even while they are willing to believe that German shepherds and Doberman pinchers might be.

    (E) Unlike German shepherds and Doberman pinchers, which many people are willing to believe can be fully domesticated, such belief does not extend to pit bulls.

19. In contrast to accredited universities that can grant degrees and whose students can be eligible for federal aid, <u>nonaccredited colleges, while still able to enroll students and to provide instruction, cannot provide their students with the same types of services</u>.

    (A) nonaccredited colleges, while still able to enroll students and to provide instruction, cannot provide their students with the same types of services

    (B) nonaccredited colleges cannot provide their students with the same types of services, though still able to enroll students and provide instruction

    (C) enrolling students and providing instruction, while unable to provide their students with the same types of services, are nonaccredited colleges

    (D) the services of nonaccredited colleges, while including the ability to enroll students and provide instruction, do not include the same types of services

    (E) those of nonaccredited colleges include enrolling students and providing instruction, but not the same types of services

20. Early medieval monasteries, <u>while clearly less accessible to outsiders, often served as repositories for texts like modern libraries</u>.

    (A) while clearly less accessible to outsiders, often served as repositories for texts like modern libraries

    (B) like modern libraries, often served as text repositories, though they were clearly less accessible to outsiders

    (C) while clearly less accessible to outsiders, often served as repositories for texts as does the modern library

    (D) like modern libraries, while clearly less accessible to outsiders, often served as repositories for texts

    (E) while clearly less accessible to outsiders, acted like modern libraries act by serving as repositories for texts

Explanation: Pit Bull Prejudice

18. The sentence sets up a comparison between Dobermans and German shepherds on one hand and pit bulls on the other. The beginnings of the choices give you a standard 3-2 split, so start with the choices beginning *Unlike* since there are three of them. (A) and (E) don't compare dogs to dogs so eliminate them. The remaining three choices create grammatically correct parallels, but (C) and (D) are wordier and less active than (B), so (B) is the best bet. We'll discuss active and passive voices later on.

Explanation: The Value of Accreditation

19. This sentence contrasts accredited universities with non-accredited colleges, and recognizing that the correct choice needs to begin by mentioning non-accredited colleges allows you to eliminate choices (C), (D), and (E). (B) is wrong because it misplaces the final modifier; *though still able…* modifies *nonaccredited colleges* and therefore needs to be placed directly next to it. That leaves (A), the original sentence.

An 800 test taker knows he must be able to eliminate four of the answer choices for specific and valid reasons before he can safely choose choice (A)—the original sentence.

Explanation: Monasteries and Libraries

20. This sentence is challenging because of all the things it's trying to do: You have to make a comparison between *early medieval monasteries* and *modern libraries*, while also taking into account a modifier for those early medieval monasteries. The modifier, "while clearly less accessible to outsiders," must come directly next to *early medieval monasteries*, so (B) and (D) are out. Additionally, in (B), it's not clear what *they* refers to. Now, of the remaining options, (A), (C), and (E), which phrasing works best—*like modern libraries* or *as does the modern library*? The second option is incorrect, as in choice (C); *libraries* needs to be plural in order to parallel *monasteries*. And finally, eliminate (E) because *acted like modern libraries act* is wordier and clumsier than *like modern libraries*. (A) is the correct answer.

An 800 test taker knows that while some sentences will take longer to unravel than others, rushing only dramatically increases the likelihood that he'll miss something important and choose the wrong answer.

---

5. VERB TENSE

Anybody who has studied a second language knows that there are dozens of rules that determine which verb tense to use in different situations. Rather than memorizing all those rules if you don't know them already, isolate the different verbs and determine whether they make sense together in their particular context. In other words, let the meaning of the sentence and the "sound" of the verb tenses guide you to the correct choice.

SENTENCE CORRECTION PRACTICE SET 9

21. Although the invention of the printing press led to a significant reconceptualization of textual production in the fifteenth century, <u>what has been equally significant in the twentieth century is</u> the invention of the computer.

    (A) what has been equally significant in the twentieth century is

    (B) equally significant in the twentieth century has been

    (C) no less significant in the twentieth century is

    (D) what was equally significant in the twentieth century were

    (E) no less significant in the twentieth century was

22. Some analysts warn that, if the projected expenditures for the Social Security Administration over the next ten years prove to be accurate, the entire social security system <u>will have been and will continue to be</u> in danger of failing.

    (A) will have been and will continue to be

    (B) has been and will continue to be

    (C) will continue, as it already has begun to be

    (D) would continue to be

    (E) will continue to be

Explanation: Word Processing Through the Ages

21. This sentence compares the invention of the printing press to that of the computer, and since the initial, nonunderlined portion of the sentence uses the simple past tense (*led*), the remainder of the sentence, continuing as it does to discuss a past event, must also use the simple past tense. Therefore, eliminate (A), (B), and (C) for including incorrect verb tenses. (D) and (E) give you different options for the final verb. Since *the invention of the computer* is the subject of this part of the sentence and is singular, the verb must be singular as well. Eliminate (D), and (E) remains.

An 800 test taker is aware that the subject of a sentence can come after the verb, particularly in constructions beginning with *there are* or *there is*.

Explanation: Social Security Not So Secure

22. The sentence includes a conditional clause (if/then, even though the *then* is implied) so focus on the verb tenses in that construction. Without needing to memorize the relevant rule, you probably know that if something happens, then something else will happen; the second verb will be in the future tense. Eliminate (D). Choices (A), (B), and (C) give you a verb in the future tense and an additional verb in the future perfect (*will have been*) or perfect tense (*has been* or *has begun*). These additions are unnecessary because *continue to be* already suggests that the social security system is in danger of failing. Therefore, (E) is the correct choice.

When you see conditional sentences or multiple verb tenses within a single sentence, pay particular attention to the tenses and determine whether they're correct.

SENTENCE CORRECTION PRACTICE SET 10

23. <u>When Veronica had purchased the Victorian mirror for her bedroom, she had</u> some concern that the style of the mirror would not suit that of her other furniture, a concern that dissipated once she hung the mirror.

    (A) When Veronica had purchased the Victorian mirror for her bedroom, she had

    (B) When Veronica purchased the Victorian mirror for her bedroom, she had

    (C) When Veronica has purchased the Victorian mirror for her bedroom, she will have

    (D) With the Victorian mirror for her bedroom having been purchased, Veronica has

    (E) Veronica had purchased the Victorian mirror for her bedroom when she came to have

24. Never before had the e-business industry <u>faced as many financial losses and employee cutbacks as they had</u> in the late 1990s.

    (A) faced as many financial losses and employee cutbacks as they had

    (B) had to face as many financial losses and employee cutbacks as it has to

    (C) faced the financial losses and employee cutbacks that they had faced

    (D) had to face as many financial losses and employee cutbacks as

    (E) faced as many financial losses and employee cutbacks as it faced

25. Scientists are currently trying to determine the extent <u>to which tectonic plates have been shifted</u> from their previous positions by earthquakes and other similar phenomena.

    (A) to which tectonic plates have been shifted

    (B) to which tectonic plates have shifted

    (C) of the shift of tectonic places

    (D) of tectonic plate shifting

    (E) that tectonic plates have been shifted

Explanation: Veronica's Victorian Mirror

23. You can start with the final verbs in the choices: since you know from the nonunderlined portion that the concern dissipated (past tense) once Veronica got home, you know that Veronica's concern has already passed and you can eliminate (C) and (D) because they're not in the past tense. Also, when choosing between *she had* and *she came to have*, you should favor the first because it's less wordy, leaving choices (A) and (B). The only remaining decision is whether the sentence should read *had purchased* or *purchased*. The second is correct because *had purchased* would suggest that this purchase occurred before Veronica felt concern (the past perfect *had purchased* would describe a time prior to the simple past *had some concern*), a situation that doesn't make sense in the context of the sentence. Veronica must have felt the concern *when* she purchased the mirror, not before, so choice (B) is right.

Explanation: The E-Business Industry

24. This one is particularly challenging because the phrase *Never before had* creates a peculiar sentence structure. If you started by focusing on the first verb in the choices—whether it should be *faced* or *had to face*—you had to realize that either one could be right depending on the rest of the choice. So, start with the final verb. (B) and (D) are out because the present tense in (B) doesn't make sense and the elimination of the verb in (D) doesn't work any better. As for the remaining choices, you can see by the structure of the sentence that the final verb in each choice parallels the first, that *faced* is the correct verb for both, but in different tenses. Pay attention to the meaning of the sentence: what happened in the 1990s had never happened before, so the first part of the sentence discusses the period of time before the 1990s. Therefore, the verb tense has to indicate a time *before* the 1990s, an option not possible if the second verb is *had (faced)*. The second verb has to be in the simple past tense (*faced*) so that the first one can describe an earlier time (*had faced*). That leaves (E).

> An 800 test takers knows the difference between the perfect tense and past perfect. The perfect tense (*has played*) describes either a very recent event or one that began in the past and has continued into the present. The past perfect (*had played*) describes an event both started and completed in the past.

Explanation: Shifting Tectonic Plates

25. Start with verb options: should the verb be *have been shifted* or *have shifted*? Normally one would want to avoid the passive *have been shifted*, but here it's necessary because the rest of the sentence tells you what did the shifting, i.e., the earthquakes. Therefore, the plates "have been shifted...by earthquakes"; eliminate (B). You can also eliminate (C) because *of the shift...by earthquakes* is incomplete without a verb. (E) is unidiomatic because *that* shouldn't follow *extent*. (D) makes no sense in the context of the sentence, so (A) stands.

6. SUBJECT/VERB AGREEMENT

It may seem rather obvious that subjects and verbs need to agree with each other in any given sentence, that you should say *the flower is* and *the flowers are*, but sometimes the subject of a sentence is harder to find and its agreement with the verb harder to determine than that. There's really only one way to effectively overcome this challenge: Find your subject, even when it's trying to hide, and see if it agrees with the verb.

SENTENCE CORRECTION PRACTICE SET 11

26. When presented with only circumstantial evidence, a juror tends to decide a case according to his or her gut instinct, <u>which are not formally</u> sanctioned or prohibited means of reaching a verdict.

    (A) which are not formally
    (B) which are not a formally
    (C) which is not a formally
    (D) which is formally not a
    (E) which is not formally

27. Out of the public's interest in the details of and conflicts in <u>other people's lives have grown a booming market for "reality" television shows that are bringing</u> "regular" people onto the television screen with increasing frequency.

    (A) other people's lives have grown a booming market for "reality" television shows that are bringing
    (B) other people's lives has grown a booming market for "reality" television shows that are bringing
    (C) another person's life has grown a booming market for a "reality" television show that is bringing
    (D) other people's lives has grown a booming market for "reality" television shows that is bringing
    (E) other people's lives has grown a booming market for "reality" television shows that bring

Explanation: Jury Procedures

26. *Gut instinct* is the subject of the second clause. (Think of it this way: What is not formally sanctioned or prohibited? Gut instinct. The "which" clause modifies gut instinct.) The verb needs to agree with the singular *instinct*. Choices (A) and (B) are incorrect, since they use *instinct are*. (C) and (D) include the word *a*, while (E) does not: Does *which is not* or *which is not a* work better? Reading the options into the sentence, you'll see that the final *a* is necessary to modify *means*. Finally, choice (D) changes the meaning of the sentence. In the end, (C) is your best choice.

An 800 test taker knows that not only do subjects need to agree with their verbs, but they need to agree with their objects as well. So, it's incorrect to say *the cats have a flea collar*, the object must be plural as in *the cats have flea collars*.

Explanation: Commercial Voyeurism

27. Get rid of all the stuff that separates subjects and verbs in this sentence and see what you're left with: *Out of the...interest...has grown a...market...that is bringing*. If you don't get distracted by the modifiers and extra phrases, you'll see that both subjects in the sentence (*interest* and *market*) are singular. Eliminate (A) and (B) for including obviously plural verbs, and (E) as well since *that bring* is plural. (C) distorts the meaning of the original sentence by describing only one television show, and you're left with (D).

An 800 test taker expects to see sentences in which the subject and verb are separated by intervening phrases or modifiers and remembers to keep track of the subject(s) throughout the sentence.

SENTENCE CORRECTION PRACTICE SET 12

28. Recent studies have shown that <u>there are now one teacher for every thirty-one students in California's elementary schools, not nearly as many than there were</u> even five years ago.

   (A) there are now one teacher for every thirty-one students in California's elementary schools, not nearly as many than there were

   (B) there are now one teacher for every thirty-one students in California's elementary schools, not nearly as many as there were

   (C) there is now one teacher for every thirty-one students in California's elementary schools, not nearly as many than there was

   (D) there is now one teacher for every thirty-one students in California's elementary schools, but that ratio is much lower than

   (E) there is now one teacher for every thirty-one students in California's elementary schools, not nearly as many as there were

29. Although the government's <u>expenditures on law suits involving tobacco companies amounts to a sum dramatically lower than</u> that spent by tobacco companies, many believe that the government should allocate no more funds to a battle they perceive as pointless.

   (A) expenditures on law suits involving tobacco companies amounts to a sum dramatically lower than

   (B) expenditures on law suits involving tobacco companies amount to a sum dramatically less than

   (C) expenditures on law suits involving tobacco companies amount to a sum dramatically lower than

   (D) law suit expenditures regarding tobacco companies amount to a dramatically lower sum than

   (E) law suit expenditures against tobacco companies amounts to a sum dramatically lower than

30. While an extensive <u>amount of research into the cause of acoustic neuromas have proven unsuccessful</u>, doctors have developed new surgical options that have dramatically increased patients' survival rates.

   (A) amount of research into the cause of acoustic neuromas have proven unsuccessful

   (B) amount of research into the cause of acoustic neuromas has proven unsuccessful

   (C) quantity of research into the cause of acoustic neuromas have proven to be unsuccessful

   (D) cause research into acoustic neuromas has proven unsuccessful

   (E) amount of research has proven unsuccessful into the cause of acoustic neuromas

Explanation: Teacher/Student Ratios

28. As you saw before, you need to be careful with sentences involving *there are* or *there is* since they place the subject after the verb. Here the subject is *one teacher* so the original verb needs to be *is*. Eliminate (A) and (B). Nevertheless, the subject for *there were* later in the sentence is an implied *teachers*, so it does indeed need to be plural; eliminate (C). Eliminate (D) because it changes the emphasis of the original sentence, placing it on the comparison with the previous ratio rather than on the present ratio, and because it would need to end with *that* or *the ratio* in order for the subject of the sentence to remain clear. (E) remains.

> An 800 test taker is systematic and knows that GMAT Sentence Correction success depends on a combination of knowing what to look for and knowing how to fix it.

Explanation: Law Suits and Tobacco Companies

29. *Expenditures* is plural so its verb (originally *amounts*) needs to be plural as well. Eliminate (A) and (E). Scan for differences among the remaining choices: should the sum be *less than* or *lower than*? *Lower than* is right; *less* is only correct when it refers to something that can't be counted (less legislation but lower sums). That leaves (C) and (D). Should the choice begin *expenditures on law suits* or *law suit expenditures*? The second is unclear and unidiomatic in this context so axe it and you're left with (C).

Explanation: Medical Research

30. Once again we deal with the noun *amount*, but here it's the subject of the first part of the sentence. Since *amount* is singular, the verb needs to be *has been*, so you can eliminate (A) and (C). *Amount of research* is better than *cause research* (which makes no sense at any rate), leaving you with (B) and (E). (E) creates a misplaced modifier, so (B) is the correct choice.

> An 800 test taker is aware that each wrong choice is usually wrong for more than one reason. If she doesn't know how to spot or correct one error, she looks for another one.

7. PRONOUNS

Pronouns are words such as *she*, *it*, and *who* that stand in for nouns, allowing us to say "Deborah purchased her piano with her savings" instead of something as clumsy as "Deborah purchased Deborah's piano with Deborah's savings." While pronouns are very frequently tested on the GMAT, there are really only two ways to mess them up: A pronoun is used incorrectly when the sentence doesn't make clear what or who the pronoun refers to, or when the sentence uses the wrong pronoun for the situation. You can fix each error by clarifying what the pronoun refers to (generally by removing or resituating it) or changing the pronoun, respectively.

SENTENCE CORRECTION PRACTICE SET 13

31. Each of the factory <u>owners that felt that pollution was a severe problem</u> wanted a drastically reformed system of industrial waste disposal in the area.

    (A) owners that felt that pollution was a severe problem

    (B) owners which felt that pollution was a severe problem

    (C) owners who felt that pollution was a severe problem

    (D) owners who felt that pollution to be a severe problem

    (E) owners, feeling that pollution was a problem quite severe,

32. Although the losing party <u>disapproves of every aspect of the opponent's platform, they later conceded that there must be a basis</u> for a cooperative government and agreed to compromise.

    (A) disapproves of every aspect of the opponent's platform, they later conceded that there must be a basis

    (B) disapproves of every aspect of the opponent's platform, it later conceded that there must be a basis

    (C) disapproved of every aspect of the opponent's platform, they later conceded that there had to be some basis

    (D) had disapproved of every aspect of the opponent's platform, it later conceded that there must be a basis

    (E) had disapproved of every aspect of the opponent's platform, they later conceded that there were grounds

Explanation: Factory Owners Unite

31. The pronoun in question is *that* and it refers to the factory owners, but the problem is that *that* is a pronoun to be used only for things; people must be referred to by the pronoun *who*. You can eliminate (A) and (B). The remaining choices differ at the end. (D) clearly grates on the ear and can be removed. *A problem quite severe* in (E) is rather too cute, and the choice also distorts the meaning of the sentence (it gives the impression that *all* of the owners are worried about pollution, which is not the meaning of the original sentence). Go with (C).

Explanation: Politicians Disagree

32. Always be suspicious of the pronoun *they*. In the original sentence, it should refer to the losing party, but it fails to do so correctly because *losing party* is singular and *they* is plural. Eliminate (A), (C), and (E). Pause to briefly congratulate yourself for eliminating three choices so quickly, and scan for differences among (B) and (D). They offer different options for the first verb, and since the party *later conceded* that a cooperative government was necessary, the first verb needs to describe a time *before* that concession. The present tense is out; *had disapproved* has to be the correct choice, and that leaves (D).

> An 800 test taker realizes that *it* and *they*, even though they are commonly misused, are still pronouns and still need to refer to particular nouns. He is suspicious whenever he sees either underlined in a Sentence Correction question.

SENTENCE CORRECTION PRACTICE SET 14

33. The symptoms of the participants in a recent decongestant effectiveness study, including a required "stuffy nose," parallel that of the multitudes of Americans with the common cold each winter.

    (A) parallel that of the multitudes of Americans with
    (B) parallel those of the multitudes of Americans afflicted with
    (C) parallel the multitudes of Americans afflicted with
    (D) parallels those of the multitudes of Americans afflicted from
    (E) parallels that of the multitudes of Americans afflicted from

34. Archaeologists have shown that ingesting lead in drinking water was a significant health hazard for the ancient Romans, like that of modern Americans.

    (A) like that of modern Americans
    (B) as that for modern Americans
    (C) just as modern Americans do
    (D) as do modern Americans
    (E) as it is for modern Americans

35. Those who have visited the Grand Canyon have typically seen layers of sediment in the gaping canyon, with different colors that mark the passage of time like the rings in a tree trunk.

    (A) seen layers of sediment in the gaping canyon, with different colors that mark
    (B) seen layers of sediment in the gaping canyon, whose different colors mark
    (C) been seeing layers of sediment in the gaping canyon, whose different colors are markers of
    (D) been able to see layers of sediment in the gaping canyon, with different colors marking
    (E) seen layers of sediment in the gaping canyon, marking by different colors

Explanation: Parallel Conditions

33. The pronoun under investigation here is *that* and it refers, if you looked carefully, to *symptoms* in the first part of the sentence. Basically, using a pronoun instead of repeating *symptoms* allows the sentence to be a bit more concise, but the gesture fails in this sentence because *that* is the wrong pronoun. Since *symptoms* is plural, it needs a plural pronoun and *that* needs to be *those*. Eliminate (A) and (E). (C) eliminates the pronoun altogether, not a valid option if we want to maintain parallelism so take (C) out of consideration. (B) and (D) give you different verb options, but since, as we've noted, *symptoms* is plural, it takes a plural verb and (B) wins.

Explanation: We, the Ancient Romans

34. Again we are presented with the need to choose the correct pronouns in order to allow for a parallel sentence structure. Here, the pronoun *that* tries to stand in for the entire phrase *ingesting lead in drinking water was a significant health hazard*, but it fails. *That* tries to do too much; a single pronoun can only refer to a noun, not a noun *and* a verb. A correct option needs a pronoun that refers back to the subject of the phrase ("ingesting lead") and a verb to recall *was*. Take out (A) and (B). You can eliminate (C) and (D) as well because *do*, like *that* in (A) and (B), doesn't refer accurately to the first part of the sentence; nobody was *doing* anything to begin with. (E) is right because *it* refers to *ingesting lead* and *is* refers to *was a significant health hazard*, creating a grammatically correct parallel.

Explanation: All the Canyon's Colors

35. The key to getting the right answer for this question is recognizing that the underlined portion of the sentence *should not* contain a pronoun. The answer choices give you the option of replacing *with different colors* with *whose different colors* but the second option is wrong because, if you added *whose*, it could refer to the layers or the Canon, and whenever a pronoun has more than one possible antecedent (the thing it refers to), it's used incorrectly. Eliminate (B) and (C). (A) is correct.

Eliminate (E) as well because the subject of "marking" is similarly unclear; is it the layers or the Canyon that is marking the passage of time? And (A) is better than (D) because, once again, *seen* is better than the wordier alternative *been able to see*. (A) is correct.

Whenever an 800 test taker sees that a pronoun can logically refer to more than one noun in a sentence, or that there's no noun for it to refer to, she knows that the pronoun is being used incorrectly and needs to be fixed.

---

8. EXPRESSION

As the Sentence Correction instructions will tell you, these questions test both grammatical correctness *and* effectiveness of expression. For the test makers, effective expression means succinct, active expression; whenever possible, eliminate unnecessary wordiness and passive constructions (more on those later). While you're not always given the option to make a sentence more eloquent, and you certainly wouldn't choose a grammatically flawed choice just because it's shorter or in some ways clearer, you'll still be asked quite frequently to improve the style or structure of a sentence.

SENTENCE CORRECTION PRACTICE SET 15

36. <u>As a result of having</u> nostrils, called nares, connected to olfactory bulbs that go back to the brain, sharks are capable of smelling even a few molecules of blood in the water.

    (A) As a result of having
    (B) As a result of their having
    (C) Because they have
    (D) Because of having
    (E) Because of their having

37. <u>It was anomalies in the orbit of Uranus that</u> led to the discovery of Neptune.

    (A) It was anomalies in the orbit of Uranus that
    (B) It was the orbit of Uranus showing anomalies that
    (C) They were anomalies in the orbit of Uranus that
    (D) The orbit of Uranus being anomalous was what
    (E) The anomalies in the orbit of Uranus was what

Explanation: A Shark's Sense of Smell

36. This is an example of a Sentence Correction question that explicitly and almost exclusively tests expression. *As a result of having* is not grammatically offensive, and it works fine with the rest of the sentence, but it is rather wordy and indirect. (B), (D), and (E) share the same basic structure with the imprecise *of having* expression. An active sentence or phrase starts with the subject (*they*) and then moves to the verb (*have*) and object (*nostrils*). Active expression is generally the most effective expression on the GMAT; always choose it when presented with a grammatically correct option as well. (C) is the best option because it is the most active and the most clear.

Explanation: Uranus' Orbit

37. While the previous sentence required you to improve expression, this question doesn't give you a viable opportunity to correct the rather clumsy phrase at the beginning of the sentence. The original sentence is, perhaps surprisingly, grammatically correct because this is a special type of construction. The entire underlined portion of the sentence operates as the singular subject for *led*. Since you would never want to choose this option without carefully reviewing the remaining choices, you would probably arrive at the answer by eliminating the others. (B) is a wordier version of (A), so eliminate it. *They were anomalies* in (C) is just not idiomatic. (D) and (E) seem promising at the start since they seem to provide active alternatives, but *being anomalous* is ugly enough to disqualify (D) and the subject and verb don't agree in (E). Go with (A).

An 800 test taker realizes that while he must always correct grammatical errors, he will not always have the opportunity to correct flaws in expression. He takes those opportunities only when they present themselves.

SENTENCE CORRECTION PRACTICE SET 16

38. While the immune system helps the human <u>body's trying to defend itself from a virus or disease that is harming it</u>, certain immunodeficiency disorders like AIDS attack the immune system itself and disable its healing mechanisms.

    (A) body's trying to defend itself from a virus or disease that is harming it

    (B) body's tries to defend itself from a virus or disease harming it

    (C) body to try to defend itself from a virus or disease that harm it

    (D) body to attempt to try to defend itself from a virus or disease that is harming it

    (E) body to try to defend itself from a virus or disease that is harming it

39. In a seminar paper delivered at the annual American Psychological Association conference, Dr. Spagnoli distinguished <u>pronounced alterations in mood, which may be frequent and occasionally severe without their constituting a clinical illness, from bipolar disorders</u>.

    (A) pronounced alterations in mood, which may be frequent and occasionally severe without their constituting a clinical illness, from bipolar disorders

    (B) bipolar disorders and pronounced alterations in mood, occurring frequently and occasionally severely, without constituting a clinical illness

    (C) pronounced alterations in mood, perhaps frequent and occasionally severe without constituting a clinical illness, and bipolar disorders

    (D) between pronounced alterations in mood, which may be frequent and occasionally severe without constituting a clinical illness, from bipolar disorders

    (E) between pronounced alterations in mood, which may be frequent and occasionally severe without constituting a clinical illness, and bipolar disorders

40. <u>After the company recalled one of its best-selling products, it would be forced to accept a one billion dollar loss, an expense that would have forced its main competitor to declare bankruptcy if it had suffered such a loss.</u>

    (A) After the company recalled one of its best-selling products, it would be forced to accept a one billion dollar loss, an expense that would have forced its main competitor to declare bankruptcy if it had suffered such a loss.

    (B) As the company recalled one of its best-selling products, it accepted a one billion dollar loss; forcing its main competitor to declare bankruptcy if it had suffered such a loss.

    (C) After the company recalled one of its best-selling products, its one billion dollar loss would have to be accepted; such a loss would have forced its main competitor to declare bankruptcy.

    (D) After the company recalled one of its best-selling products, it was forced to accept a one billion dollar loss; its main competitor would have been forced to declare bankruptcy if it had suffered such a loss.

    (E) When the company recalled one of its best-selling products, a one billion dollar loss it was forced to accept, an expense that would have forced its main competitor into bankruptcy.

Explanation: Immunodeficiency Disorders

38. From the outset, you can focus on fixing *the human body's trying*, an unattractive phrase on all counts. Eliminate (A), and you can take out (B) as well for making the phrase no better. Focusing on the final verb, you have *that is harming* or *that harm*. Since the subject is singular, eliminate (C) for containing the plural *harm*. When comparing (D) and (E), you can see that (D) adds an extra verb. The addition of *to attempt* is wordy and redundant; there's nothing expressed by *to attempt* that isn't already expressed by *to try*. That leaves (E).

Explanation: Moods and Disorders

39. Before moving to the question of expression, start with grammar. The answer choices provide you with some different idioms so let's start there. The verb *distinguished* needs to be followed by *from* unless it's followed by *between*, so eliminate (B) and (C). *Between* appears in (D) and (E) and, as you know from earlier examples, *between* must always be followed by *and*. Eliminate (D) for pairing *between* and *from*. Finally on the question of expression, (E) is superior to (A) because (A) contains an unnecessary *their*. (E) is the winner.

Explanation: Recalling Profits

40. There's no doubt about it: This is an ugly sentence and a very difficult question. Nevertheless, find some differences among the choices that will help you to tackle it. You can start with the verbs. We begin with *After the company recalled* and then move to *it would be forced*, but since the sentence is talking about something that already happened, the second verb should be *it was forced*. Eliminate (A) and (C). You can also eliminate (E) for offering the strange variation *a one billion dollar loss it was forced to accept*. (B) is wrong because it creates a sentence fragment. Make sure you know this fact: a semicolon is correct only when it joins two pieces that could stand as independent and complete sentences. In other words, you can use a semicolon only if you could use a period at the same place and still have complete sentences. (B) doesn't do that, so (D) remains.

> An 800 test taker knows that even though the GMAT does not explicitly test punctuation, it's important to know how semicolons and commas work.

CHAPTER TEN

Other Sentence Correction Challenges

While the categories you've seen so far describe the types of errors that you'll probably see most frequently, the test makers don't confine themselves to these eight errors. The following eight categories explain additional errors, either presented as subcategories of the original eight categories or as separate challenges, that show up with considerable frequency and can be particularly difficult. You've been introduced to some of them in the preceding questions, but here we'll look at each explicitly.

1. MEANING

It's always absolutely necessary that you pay attention to the meaning of the sentence that you're asked to correct, but we've placed "meaning" in its own category because certain sentences overtly and even primarily test whether you understand the sentence's meaning. They do this by giving you different options that significantly impact the meaning of the sentence and asking you to figure out which is right based on what you know the meaning must logically be given the different pieces of the original sentence. In the same way that GMAT math questions often require you to pause and understand the problem before you start to solve it, certain Sentence Correction questions demand particularly that you think about the meaning of the different parts of the sentence so that you can join them together correctly. While it is true that Sentence Correction questions are designed to be answered quickly, don't go so fast that you fail to process the meaning of the sentences.

SENTENCE CORRECTION PRACTICE SET 17

41. <u>Some of the wild dogs that were distributed to local pet sanctuaries by city health officials and exterminated last year were</u> collected as part of the city's initiative to protect local residents from dog attacks.

    (A) Some of the wild dogs that were distributed to local pet sanctuaries by city health officials and exterminated last year were

    (B) Some of the wild dogs that the local pet sanctuaries received and city health officials exterminated have been

    (C) Some of the wild dogs that were distributed to local pet sanctuaries or exterminated by city health officials last year had been

    (D) Last year some of the wild dogs that were distributed to local pet sanctuaries or exterminated by city health officials made

    (E) Last year city health officials distributed to local pet sanctuaries as well as exterminated some of the wild dogs that had been

42. The company claimed to have created a backpack so capacious that it could simultaneously hold four textbooks, a laptop computer, and necessary school <u>supplies and so light</u> and well-designed that even a seventh-grader could wear it comfortably.

    (A) supplies and so light

    (B) supplies so light

    (C) supplies, and it was so light

    (D) supplies, yet being so light

    (E) supplies, yet so light

43. Commercial pilots receive their training from regional airlines with increasing frequency, often preferring to avoid the expense of <u>the requirements of training offered by private companies</u> and the service required by the Navy or Air Force.

    (A) the requirements of training offered by private companies

    (B) requirements offered for training by private companies

    (C) the training requirements of private companies

    (D) the training offered by private companies

    (E) private companies' training

44. Doctors in the early twentieth century commonly mistook <u>endometriosis as simple menstrual cramps</u> and informed women that there was no medical cure for their condition.

    (A) endometriosis as simple menstrual cramps

    (B) endometriosis for simple menstrual cramps

    (C) simple menstrual cramps for endometriosis

    (D) endometriosis to be simple menstrual cramping

    (E) endometriosis and simple menstrual cramps

Explanation: The Living and Dead Dogs

41. You may notice a problem with this sentence right off the bat: It doesn't make sense for the officials to have given the dogs to pet sanctuaries *and* to have exterminated them as part of the same gesture. A sanctuary doesn't kill dogs, at least not if it really deserves to be called a sanctuary, so the sentence needs to describe the two actions (distributing the dogs to shelters and killing them) as alternatives. Choices (C) and (D) make that correction by substituting the original *and* with the much more logical *or*. Try reading the remaining options into the sentence and you'll see that (D) makes no sense in context; *made collected* is not anyone's idea of correct grammar. (C) remains.

> An 800 test taker understands that meaning is an inevitable part of grammar and an inevitable part of Sentence Correction questions. The purpose of grammar and its many rules is to facilitate communication, to make one person's meaning clear to someone else.

Explanation: The Perfect Backpack

42. What makes this backpack so apparently wonderful is its surprising combination of qualities: it can carry all this stuff without becoming too heavy and unwieldy to use. The original sentence does not express the contrast that creates the beauty of this object because it connects information about the backpack's abilities and its ergonomics with the word *and*. Choices (D) and (E) provide better options by including *yet*, a word that, as you surely know from your Reading Comprehension practice, describes a contrast. (E) is better than (D) since *being* is unnecessary. Go with (E).

Explanation: Pilot Training

43. The original problem, at least as far as meaning is concerned, comes in the "expense of the requirements." It's not the requirements that are expensive but the training. Eliminate (A) and (B). (C) contains the same error because, even though it adds *training* before *requirements*, the object is still *requirements* (*training* only modifies it). (D) and (E) both offer *training* as the object and to that extent are both correct, but (E) isn't parallel with *the service required* later in the sentence. So (D) it is.

Explanation: Medical Misdiagnosis

44. The sentence describes the misdiagnosis by doctors who thought that one condition (simple menstrual cramps) was really a more serious condition (endometriosis). Since the correct idiom should be *mistook … for*, (C) is the answer.

An 800 test taker recognizes that many answer choices will be wrong because they distort the meaning of the original sentence. Sometimes necessary grammatical changes will alter the meaning and that's fine, but an unnecessary alteration is always wrong.

2. IMPERFECT OPTIONS

You've probably noticed that the directions for the GMAT instruct you to choose the best choice rather than the right answer, and you've surely noticed that many "best choices" aren't exactly the best that you could hope for from an answer choice. Because the test makers do not always strive for perfection in their answer choices, you will often need to locate the least offensive of your options, particularly in the verbal sections. While no correct Sentence Correction answer choice will contain a grammatical error, some will contain rather questionable or cluttered phrasing. Therefore, do not be too quick to eliminate answer choices just because they sound rather awkward; eliminate an answer choice for good only after you find a better alternative.

SENTENCE CORRECTION PRACTICE SET 18

45. The public library allocated the revenues it received from the recently passed tax initiative <u>to the purchasing of more than two thousand books, fifty journal subscriptions, and fifteen computers</u>.

    (A) to the purchasing of more than two thousand books, fifty journal subscriptions, and fifteen computers

    (B) in order to purchase more than two thousand books, fifty journal subscriptions, and fifteen computers

    (C) so as to purchase more than two thousand books, fifty journal subscriptions, and fifteen computers

    (D) so that more than two thousand books, fifty journal subscriptions, and fifteen computers could be purchased

    (E) for the purchase of more than two thousand books, fifty journal subscriptions, and fifteen computers

46. The network determined that <u>seventeen commercials should be shown during a half-hour sitcom</u>, while a one-hour drama can be expected to contain twenty-nine.

    (A) seventeen commercials should be shown during a half-hour sitcom

    (B) in a half-hour sitcom seventeen commercials will be shown

    (C) in a half-hour sitcom, seventeen commercials should be shown

    (D) seventeen commercials should be shown in a half-hour sitcom

    (E) seventeen commercials will be shown by a half-hour sitcom

47. <u>Unlike the use of headset telephones, which allow drivers to keep their hands on the wheel</u>, all drivers are prohibited from using portable phones while driving.

    (A) Unlike the use of headset telephones, which allow drivers to keep their hands on the wheel

    (B) Besides using headset telephones, which allow drivers to keep their hands on the wheel

    (C) Unless headset telephones, which allow drivers to keep their hands on the wheel, are used

    (D) Other than the use of headset telephones, which allows drivers to keep their hands on the wheel

    (E) Aside from using headset telephones which allow drivers to keep their hands on the wheel

48. <u>The product was so secretly researched and tested in corporate headquarters that</u> consumers were unaware of its existence until it reached the stores and created a flurry of interest.

    (A) The product was so secretly researched and tested in corporate headquarters that

    (B) So secretly was the product researched and tested in corporate headquarters that

    (C) Researched and tested in corporate headquarters so secretly that

    (D) The research and testing of the product in corporate headquarters has been so secret that

    (E) A product was so secretly researched and tested in corporate headquarters as to make

Explanation: Library Allocations

45. The original sentence is less than poetic, but it makes no grammatical errors that would require its elimination. The sentence describes the allocation of funds to new purchases and you're looking for the correct expression of those purchases. The answer choices most clearly differ at the beginning so you can start there: is it acceptable to begin the underlined portion with any of these options? No, because the verb *allocated* needs to be followed by *to* in order to be used correctly and only answer choice (A) creates that proper idiom. Be careful not to get lost in the sentence or the answer choices and overlook the requirements created by the nonunderlined portion of the sentence. Even though (A) isn't a perfect choice, it's the only correct one.

An 800 test taker always identifies the grammatically correct choices before considering the effectiveness of expression. The correct choice will always contain correct grammar, if not stellar style.

Explanation: Commercial Allotments

46. The main grammatical problem in the sentence as it originally stands is *should be shown*. Looking at the rest of the sentence, you can see that *should be shown* contrasts with *can be expected to contain*. *Should* is wrong because it indicates that the number of commercials per sitcom is hypothetical; it needs to be changed to *will be shown* or an equally declarative construction in order for the sentence to be grammatically correct. Only choices (B) and (E) make that correction. You can then eliminate (E) for changing *during a half-hour sitcom* to *by a half-hour sitcom*. The alteration changes the meaning of the original sentence and makes no sense in its own right: the sitcom can't show commercials. (B) remains.

Explanation: Distracting Drivers

47. The sentence creates a comparison between headset and all other portable telephones. While one would normally look to create a parallel structure and, starting with the fact that the nonunderlined portion begins with *all drivers*, start the underlined portion with a parallel reference to drivers, no answer choice gives you that option. Therefore, look for a choice that lets you off the hook and doesn't require the two parts of the sentence to be parallel. The initial sentence is flawed because it compares the use of headset telephones to all drivers, and you know by now that "comparison" constructions must compare or contrast like objects (telephones to telephones, drivers to drivers). (B), (D), and (E) repeat the same error; each creates a comparison between using headsets and drivers. (C), while it doesn't create a correct comparison, gives you an option where a grammatical parallel isn't necessary. Choice (C) creates a complete clause on its own, with its own subject and verb (*Unless headset telephones…are used*), so it can stand apart from the rest of the sentence. Complicated, yes, but apply what you know about comparisons to get rid of the other four choices and you'll only be left with (C).

Explanation: Covert Research and Development

48. The initial sentence is a bit indirect but it's not grammatically flawed so keep it for now. (B) and (C) give you more awkward variations of (A) so eliminate both. (D) is out because the plural subject (*research and testing*) doesn't agree with the singular verb (*has been*). Also, the verb's in the wrong tense. Finally, (E) doesn't make sense in the context of the sentence. (A) it is.

> An 800 test taker lets the differences among the answer choices guide him when he's stumped, remembering that the point isn't to create a perfect sentence but to choose the best choice from the ones given.

3. THE PASSIVE VOICE [EXPRESSION II]

Though using the passive voice is not always grammatically wrong, unnecessary or awkward uses of it almost always require correction in Sentence Correction questions. While the active voice presents you with a subject, then a verb, then an object, as in *Rita purchased a house*, the passive voice flips the order: it starts with the object, then gives you the verb, and may or may not end with the subject (*The house was purchased by Rita* or *The house was purchased*). The passive voice, because it is usually wordier and less clear than the active voice, generally hinders effective expression. The test makers will test your ability to choose active over passive constructions, so learn to spot—and avoid—the passive voice whenever possible.

An 800 test taker looks for the most concise, grammatically correct answer choice.

SENTENCE CORRECTION PRACTICE SET 19

49. Although new farm subsidy legislation is presently being considered in the House of Representatives, <u>significant revision is to be expected if it is to be passed</u>.

    (A) significant revision is to be expected if it is to be passed
    (B) they do not expect it to pass without significant revision
    (C) the farmers expect significant revision if the legislation will be passed
    (D) it is not expected to be passed without being significantly revised
    (E) it is not expected to pass without significant revision

50. Having forfeited her severance package in order to keep the rights to her intellectual property, <u>it was believed by the employee that she had won a moral victory</u>.

    (A) it was believed by the employee that she had won a moral victory
    (B) she believed that she had won a moral victory
    (C) the employee believed that she had won a moral victory
    (D) the employee believed her moral victory to have been won
    (E) the employee believed that the moral victory was won

51. It has become apparent in recent Supreme Court rulings that <u>the rights of an individual to privacy are considerable but not absolute, and that such rights are particularly weakened when exigent circumstances are present</u>.

    (A) the rights of an individual to privacy are considerable but not absolute, and that such rights are particularly weakened when exigent circumstances are present

    (B) an individual's right to privacy is considerable but not absolute, and that such a right is particularly weakened when exigent circumstances are present

    (C) individuals' rights to privacy are considerable but not absolute, and that, when exigent circumstances are present, they make such rights particularly weaken

    (D) considerable but not absolute rights to privacy are given to an individual, and that exigent circumstances particularly weaken such rights

    (E) the Court considers individual rights as considerable if not absolute, and that such rights are particularly weakened when exigent circumstances are present

52. An individual will find it difficult to campaign successfully for public office <u>if there is an absence of support from political action committees</u>.

    (A) if there is an absence of support from political action committees

    (B) if the support of political action committees is absent

    (C) there being an absence of support from political action committees

    (D) when political action committee support is absent

    (E) without the support of political action committees

Explanation: Farm Legislation

49. The underlined portion of the sentence contains two passive constructions: *is to be expected* and *is to be passed*. Since we don't know who expects significant revision to be necessary, we can't eliminate the passive voice entirely unless we add a subject. (C) tries to do this but there's no indication in the original sentence that "farmers" are doing the expecting, and the final *will be passed* is the wrong tense for a phrase beginning with *if* in this context. (B) also adds a subject, but *they* is grammatically incorrect here since we have no idea who *they* might be. Of the remaining choices, none is grammatically incorrect, but (A) and (D) have two passive constructions while (E) only has one. The stylistic superiority of (E), plus the fact that it is grammatically correct, makes (E) the right answer.

Explanation: The Moral Victory

50. The initial sentence is not only wordy and passive but it also misuses modifiers. Since the initial, nonunderlined portion of the sentence modifies *the employee, the employee* needs to begin the underlined portion of the sentence. Eliminate (A), and you can take out (B) as well because, while it gives you a subject, it creates a pronoun error: nowhere in this sentence do we learn who *she* or *her* refers to. Of the remaining choices, (E) is grammatically incorrect because *was* is the wrong tense. Since the modifier begins with *Having*, the verb needs to be *had been*. Or, eliminate (E) and (D) because they include passive constructions while (C) is active and otherwise grammatically correct. (C) wins.

Explanation: The Protection of Privacy

51. The original sentence is certainly wordy but it's not grammatically incorrect. Therefore, scan the other choices for grammatical errors: *they make such rights particularly weaken* is not idiomatically correct word order or correct use of the verb *to weaken,* so eliminate (C). (E) changes the meaning of the original sentence; *if not absolute* suggests that the rights *are* possibly absolute. The remaining choices lack grammatical errors, but (A) and (D) are stylistically flawed. *The rights of an individual to privacy* in (A) and *rights to privacy are given* in (D) are wordier and less direct than *an individual's right to privacy* in (B). While (B) still contains the passive *is weakened* construction, it presents the most direct option, and is therefore our winner.

Understanding that the passive voice does not itself constitute a grammatical error, an 800 test taker only eliminates such a choice when there is a grammatically correct alternative in the active voice.

Explanation: Powerful PAC Support

52. The phrase *if there is an absence of support* is indirect enough to make you very suspicious of it, but make sure that you have a better option before you eliminate it. (B) is no better, and perhaps no worse. (C) doesn't make sense in the context of the sentence, so take it out. (D) tries to be more active by changing the original to *political action committee support,* but the change creates an unidiomatic phrase; in this case, *the support of political action committees* is better. (E) is the best choice because it is grammatically correct and avoids the passive and/or wordy constructions in the other options. Now you can eliminate (A) and (B) and click the bubble next to (E).

4. ELLIPSIS [PARALLELISM II]

Ellipsis is the omission from a sentence of words that are clearly understood or implied. It allows us to avoid a sentence such as *Holly has more CDs than Sean has CDs* and instead say *Holly has more CDs than Sean*. In the second sentence, *has CDs* is implied at the end. While ellipses are perfectly acceptable and grammatically correct, the makers of the GMAT often take it too far and eliminate essential parts from a sentence. If the meaning of the sentence has become at all unclear, then you'll need to bring some of those parts back into the sentence, making sure that you include them in such a way as to make the sentence clear and grammatically parallel. It is the parallelism that allows the abbreviated part of the sentence to imply the part that is missing.

SENTENCE CORRECTION PRACTICE SET 20

53. The analyst suggested that traders pay more attention to a broader measure of the money supply, known as M2, <u>but still not to ignore</u> standard indicators.

(A) but still not to ignore

(B) and not to ignore any longer

(C) but that they still not ignore

(D) and that they continue not to ignore

(E) but they should still not ignore

54. Before they will consider a settlement, the striking teachers demand that the school board fire the substitute teachers <u>and establishes payment scales guaranteeing cost of living increases</u>.

(A) and establishes payment scales guaranteeing cost of living increases

(B) and to establish payment scales that would guarantee cost of living increases

(C) and establishes payment scales to guarantee cost of living increases

(D) and establish payment scales to guarantee cost of living increases

(E) for establishing payment scales to guarantee cost of living increases

55. <u>Commissioner Wallace claims that he always has been and always will be a member of the American Civil Liberties Union.</u>

    (A) Commissioner Wallace claims that he always has been and always will be a member of the American Civil Liberties Union.

    (B) Commissioner Wallace claims that he always has and always will be a member of the American Civil Liberties Union.

    (C) Commissioner Wallace claims that he will always be a member of the American Civil Liberties Union.

    (D) Always having been a member of the American Civil Liberties Union, Commissioner Wallace claims that he will always continue to be so.

    (E) Commissioner Wallace has always been a member of the American Civil Liberties Union, and claims that he will always be.

56. While for years several scientists <u>attempted but could not</u> prove that so-called Planet X was a tenth planet in our solar system, later scientists convincingly disproved the possibility.

    (A) attempted but could not

    (B) attempted but were unable

    (C) attempted to prove but could not

    (D) having attempted to prove, could not

    (E) attempted to but could not

Explanation: Suggestions to Traders

53. Without ellipsis, the final part of the sentence would read *but the analyst suggested that traders not ignore standard indicators*. That's surely more than we need, but the abbreviated version in the original sentence swings too far in the other direction. In the original sentence, it's not perfectly clear who should avoid ignoring indicators and the structure of the final section isn't parallel with the first. In order for it to be parallel, "not to ignore" needs to parallel *that traders pay more attention* since both phrases are supposed to follow from *The analyst suggested*. Therefore, eliminate (A) and (B) for breaking rules of parallelism; neither creates a grammatically correct conclusion to *The analyst suggested*. (E) creates a similar problem. Try taking out the middle of the sentence and see if it would be okay to say *The analyst suggested that traders pay attention but they should still not ignore*. The problem is that *that traders pay attention* is not parallel to *they should not ignore*. Of the remaining options, you can eliminate (D) for altering the meaning of the original sentence by replacing *but* with *and*. (C) remains.

> An 800 test taker knows that ellipsis only works when the pieces that the abbreviated portion keeps imply the pieces it doesn't. In order for that to happen, the essential pieces must remain and must parallel the structure of the rest of the sentence.

Explanation: Teachers on Strike

54. The striking teachers demand two things that need to be expressed in grammatically parallel structures. The first, not underlined, is *that the school board fire substitute teachers*. Since this demand is not underlined, and since the second demand will have to parallel it, you know in advance what the structure of the second demand absolutely has to be: that the school board establish payment scales or *and [that the school board] establish payment scales*. Once you understand the principle of ellipsis you can proceed with confidence: only answer choice (D) uses it correctly. (E) alters the meaning of the original sentence quite dramatically and choices (A), (B), and (C) are not parallel. In order to see that more clearly, try placing *that the school board* between *and* and the first verb in each of these choices and you'll see the problem.

Explanation: Membership Has its Privileges

55. In this sentence, the complete phrase comes at the end and the ellipses precede it: *Commissioner Wallace claims that he always has been [a member of the ACLU] and [that he] always will be a member of the ACLU*. The brackets mark the ellipses, and the fact that the sentence is grammatically correct even with the omitted material indicates that the ellipses are used correctly. Choices (B) and (C) take out too much. (B) fails because *always has [a member of the ACLU] and always will be a member* doesn't work; the first verb needs to be complete and read *always has been*. (C) takes out the first verb completely but, since *always has been* and *always will be* express different ideas, both verbs are necessary. (D) and (E) play with the order of the sentence and both create wordier and more awkward options than (A), the correct answer.

An 800 test taker puts the omitted pieces back into the sentence to see if the abbreviated version is correct, as in the explanations above. This is an effective strategy for dealing with ellipsis questions.

Explanation: Planet X

56. This sentence demonstrates a very common problem by omitting a necessary preposition. *Attempted* must always be followed by *to* in order for its use to be idiomatically correct, but the original sentence omits the *to*. The original sentence, without ellipsis, would read ...*several scientists attempted [prove that Planet X...] but could not prove that Planet X....* The necessary *to* cannot be implied because it doesn't exist in the paralleled phrase *could not prove*. Therefore, even though the change may seem to make the sentence wordier, the original must be changed to *attempted to but could not*. Eliminate (A) and (B). (C) is a wordier and clumsier version of (E), so eliminate (C). Finally, (D) breaks the rules of parallelism (among others); *having attempted to prove* is not parallel with *could not prove*. (E) wins.

An 800 test taker realizes that a sentence can't imply what it hasn't stated elsewhere. She makes sure that each phrase has everything it needs for its meaning to be clear.

---

5. PARTICIPLES

Participles are adjectives that are formed from verbs. Take the sentence, *Peter, distracted by his cat and wanting to do his work, decided to go to the library.* Both *distracted* and *wanting* are participles; clearly they're formed from verbs but they serve as adjectives describing Peter. You may be comforted to know that you needn't understand participles in all their glorious complexity in order to conquer the GMAT. In terms of GMAT Sentence Correction questions, all you need to know is that participles aren't verbs and therefore can't stand in for verbs. The incorrect use of participles often creates sentence fragments in the GMAT and the incorrect use of verbs when participles are required often obscures the intended meaning of the sentence.

SENTENCE CORRECTION PRACTICE SET 21

57. During and immediately after the California gold rush, the way for a merchant to generate the most profit was to move a limited amount of scarce goods to San Francisco as quickly as possible, rather than <u>to carry larger loads more slowly, determining</u> the design of the clipper ship.

   (A) to carry larger loads more slowly, determining

   (B) to carry larger loads more slowly, a situation that determined

   (C) carry larger loads more slowly, which determined

   (D) slowly carry larger loads which determined

   (E) carrying larger loads more slowly, and this was a situation in determining

58. Residents of affected coastal cities continue to lobby for funds and request supplies to aid them <u>in recovering from oil spills occurring more than a decade ago</u>.

   (A) in recovering from oil spills occurring more than a decade ago

   (B) to recover from oil spills that had occurred more than a decade ago

   (C) in recovery of oil spills that occurred more than a decade ago

   (D) in recovering from oil spills having occurred more than a decade ago

   (E) in recovering from oil spills that occurred more than a decade ago

59. After suffering the effects of several tsunamis, the residents of a Japanese city built a wall on their coast over 40 feet high and a mile long, <u>a way to protect</u> the city against another disaster.

   (A) a way to protect

   (B) in efforts to protect

   (C) protecting

   (D) to protect in one way

   (E) in order to protect

60. The regents of the University of California system have recently acted on plans to add two new <u>universities, which increases to 10 the number</u> of U.C. schools.

   (A) universities, which increases to 10 the number

   (B) universities which increase the number to 10

   (C) universities, increasing to 10 the number

   (D) universities, a plan which will have increased to 10 the number

   (E) universities to increase to 10 the number

Explanation: The Gold Rush

57. In the underlined portion of the original sentence, you've got a verb (*to carry*) and a participle (*determining*). The answer choices allow you to convert the verb into a participle (*carrying*) and the participle into a verb (*determined*). You may wonder why this matters. Well, the participle *determining* makes the final phrase of the sentence (*determining the design of the clipper ship*) into a modifier. The problem is that it's not clear what precisely this phrase modifies: Did a part of this situation (perhaps the need for speed) determine the design of the clipper ship or did the entire situation taken together? Only (B) and (E) respond to this problem so you can eliminate all the others; *which* in (C) and (D) doesn't provide the clarification that we need. (E), in addition to its clumsy phrasing, is grammatically incorrect. By replacing *to carry* with *carrying*, it breaks the parallel structure of the sentence (the best option *was to move...rather than to carry*). (B) alone survives.

Explanation: Recovery Efforts

58. There's nothing overtly wrong with the original sentence so scan the options and look for differences. Compare *in recovering from*, *to recover from*, and *in recovery of*. Considered in the context of the sentence, only the first option is fine, the second is wrong (*aid* earlier in the sentence needs to be followed by *in*), and the third is just not idiomatic. (A), (D), and (E) remain, giving you three different options with respect to *occurring*. You've got the original *occurring* in (A), of course, *having occurred* in (D), and *that have occurred* in (E). (D) is wrong because *having* should not describe an event that ended ten years ago. (E) is better than (A) because it's more active and avoids the back-to-back participles that could create some confusion in (A). (E) remains.

Explanation: City versus Ocean

59. Of the options for this sentence, only (D) is explicitly incorrect since it distorts the meaning of the sentence (*in one way* suddenly suggests that there are other ways that the city is being protected). Choices (A), (B), (C), and (E) all make the final phrase, originally *a way to protect the city against another disaster*, a modifier. The most succinct way to introduce the modifier is to use the participle *protecting*, so answer choice (C) represents the best choice. You may think that a modifier in this place is not ideal, that an option such as *and the wall protects the city...* would be better, or that the phrasing isn't very eloquent. Regardless of whether such criticisms are true, don't waste time thinking about options that you're not given.

An 800 test taker always remembers that an answer choice doesn't need to be perfect in order to be right.

Explanation: University Development

60. The final phrase (*which increases to 10 the number of U.C. schools*) describes the plan. Answer choice (D) reintroduces the object (the plan) that's being described, but the certainly awkward expression *will have increased*, as well as the general wordiness of the choice, eliminates it from consideration. If you read (B) into the sentence, the sentence becomes even more awkward. Eliminate (B). And (E) distorts the original meaning of the sentence, suggesting that the purpose of the plan was not to add two universities per se but to up the total number of universities to ten. That may be true, but it's not what the original sentence said and unnecessarily changes the sentence's meaning. Eliminate (E). Look at (A) and (C). (C) is the better choice because it's more direct, because it eliminates the unnecessary *which*, and because *increasing* makes the final phrase into a modifier as, for optimal clarity, it should be.

6. SUBORDINATION AND COORDINATION

Yes, a lesson on participles followed by one on subordination and coordination may give you the impression that you're suddenly steeped in grammatical pedantry, but you were the one who wanted the 800. Subordination and coordination are actually quite basic concepts. When you want to draw equal emphasis to two parts of a sentence, or coordinate them, you use coordinating conjunctions such as *and*, *or*, or *but*. When you want to emphasize one part over the other, you subordinate one to the other with words such as *although*, *while*, or *since*. Also, participles always mark subordinate phrases. The sentence *Gregory completed the assignment and left work* uses coordination, whereas the sentences *Since Gregory had completed the assignment, he left work* and *Having completed his assignment, Gregory left work* use subordination. The first sentence draws equal attention to both of Gregory's actions while the second and third emphasize the fact that Gregory left work; in them, completing the assignment is only important because it allows him to leave. These concepts are important on the GMAT because you'll often need to emphasize one piece of the sentence over another or give them equal emphasis. You'll be able to determine which is appropriate by focusing on the meaning of the sentence.

SENTENCE CORRECTION PRACTICE SET 22

61. Medical researchers, who have identified a genetic abnormality in parents of children with Down's syndrome, <u>which they believe, instead of the age of the mother, may be</u> the cause of this congenital birth defect.

    (A) which they believe, instead of the age of the mother, may be

    (B) which, they believe, may be more important than the age of the mother as

    (C) believe this abnormality and not the age of the mother as being

    (D) believe that this abnormality, other than how old the mother is, may be

    (E) believe that this abnormality, rather than the age of the mother, may be

62. For decades Surgeon Generals have warned that smoking increases the risk of lung disease, including lung cancer and emphysema, <u>and can complicate pregnancy, and increases the risk of low birth weight</u>.

    (A) and can complicate pregnancy, and increases the risk of low birth weight

    (B) can complicate pregnancy, and increases low birth weight risks

    (C) and can complicate pregnancy, increasing the risks of low birth weight

    (D) and can complicate pregnancy by increasing the risks of low birth weight

    (E) complicating pregnancy by increasing the risks of low birth weight

63. In the mid-fifth century, Rome was threatened by Hunnish troops <u>who, led by Attila the Hun, demonstrated his military superiority</u> over the weakened, recently conquered city.

    (A) who, led by Attila the Hun, demonstrated his military superiority

    (B) which, led by Attila the Hun, demonstrated their military superiority

    (C) that Attila the Hun led, who demonstrated his military superiority

    (D) that Attila the Hun led in demonstration of their military superiority

    (E) that were led by Attila the Hun, who demonstrated his military superiority

64. Constructed with the finest Italian marble, the floor of the church is its greatest <u>attraction and is more attractive to tourists than are its ornate stained-glass windows</u>.

    (A) attraction and is more attractive to tourists than are its ornate stained-glass windows

    (B) attraction, itself more attractive to tourists than are its ornate stained-glass windows

    (C) attraction, itself more attractive to tourists as are its ornate stained-glass windows

    (D) attraction, being more attractive to tourists than its ornate stained-glass windows are

    (E) attraction as it more is attractive to tourists than are the church's stained-glass windows

Explanation: Causes of Down's Syndrome

61. The problem with the original sentence is that it subordinates *everything*, making it a sentence fragment. It needs to complete the primary clause, the one that begins with *Medical researchers*, in order to have something to which other parts of the sentence (such as *who have identified...syndrome*) can be subordinated. If you pay attention to the meaning of the sentence, you can see that the sentence wants to emphasize the genetic abnormality more than the mother's age. Therefore, *instead of the age of the mother* can remain a subordinate clause, but *which they believe* cannot. Eliminate (A) and (B). When comparing the remaining options, you can eliminate (C) because *believe this abnormality...as being* is grammatically incorrect and certainly inferior to *believe that this abnormality...may be.* (E) is better than (D) because *rather than* is more idiomatic and precise than *other than.* (E) is the answer.

> An 800 test taker doesn't worry about knowing the names of the different pieces of grammar but focuses on understanding how they work, how to spot errors in them, and how to correct those errors.

Explanation: Surgeon General Warning

62. The original sentence has an unnecessary *and* before *can complicate*, but its larger problem is that the final item, *increases the risk of low birth weight*, should be subordinated to the previous, *can complicate pregnancy*, since the two problems are related. Choices (C), (D), and (E) all subordinate the final section by using a participle (*increasing*). (C) loses out in comparison to (D) and (E) since *increasing* is less clear than *by increasing*. (D) is better than (E). (E) wrongly subordinates *can complicate pregnancy* by replacing it with *complicating pregnancy*. The change makes no sense because, by subordinating this phrase to the previous one, (E) suggests that pregnancy complications are a type of lung disease. (D) it is.

Explanation: Attila the Hun

63. The original sentence offers a few grammatical problems to fix, but since we're in the subordination and coordination section, let's start there. As the sentence originally stands, *led by Attila the Hun* is a subordinate phrase (remember that participles, such as *led* here, create subordinate phrases). Since it is subordinated to the previous clause about the Hunnish troops and since the *who* or *which* marks the troops, rather than Attila, as the subject for the sentence, the pronouns following *troops* should refer to them. In other words, Attila only further describes the troops; the troops are the real concern of the sentence. Therefore, the original pronoun in the answer choices needs to be *which* in order to refer accurately to the troops. Eliminate (A). Further, the phrase *demonstrated his military superiority* still needs to refer to the troops. *His* is wrong because the proper pronoun for troops is *their*. Eliminate (C) and (E). (D) alters the structure of the sentence and in doing so distorts its meaning, suggesting the purpose of the attack was to showcase Attila's, rather than the troops', power. (B) remains.

Explanation: Marble and Stained Glass

64. (B)

The final segment of the sentence, *is more attractive to tourists than...* should be a subordinate phrase that modifies *the floor*. The original sentence is not overtly wrong, but since the final segment provides more information about the attractiveness of the floor, it should technically modify the clause *the floor of the church is its greatest attraction* instead of existing as a separate, redundant phrase. The original *and* suggests that the popularity of the floor and its appeal for tourists are separate ideas. Since they're related, the structure of the sentence should tie them together more clearly. Choices (B), (C), and (D) all subordinate the final phrase. Eliminate (C) because the proper idiom is *more...than* not *more...as*. Eliminate (D) because *being* is fully unnecessary. (B) it is.

An 800 test taker is aware that many Sentence Correction sentences and answer choices contain unnecessary uses of the verb *to be*, as seen in choice (D) above. She is on the lookout for such unnecessary wordiness and eliminates the choices containing it whenever possible.

---

7. THE SUBJUNCTIVE [TENSE II]

The subjunctive mood is not very common in English (though it is in other languages like Spanish and French), but it is distinctive enough to merit some attention, particularly since the GMAT tests it quite regularly. The subjunctive is used to express wishes, requests, or certain conditional (if/then) phrases. It mostly affects the verb *to be*, giving it some forms that are otherwise uncommon. It is used in expressions of desire/wish (*I wish I were you* rather than *I wish I was you*), with certain *if* sentences (*If your mother were here, she would reprimand you*), and after certain uses of *that* (*He asked that his friend* be *nominated* or *He asked that his friend* accept *the nomination*). As you can see, the subjunctive is marked by *were* and the infinitive *be* or *accept* (it is only in the final category that the subjunctive involves verbs other than *to be*). Get used to the few situations in which the subjunctive is used so that you can determine whether it is used correctly in a Sentence Correction sentence or answer choice.

SENTENCE CORRECTION PRACTICE SET 23

65. The recently reelected president of Cyprus has asked <u>that the United States would encourage Turkey, which invaded the island in 1974 and now controls their</u> northern regions, to withdraw from his country.

(A) that the United States would encourage Turkey, which invaded the island in 1974 and now controls their

(B) of the United States that it would encourage Turkey, which invaded the island in 1974 and now controls their

(C) that the United States would encourage Turkey, which invaded the island in 1974 and now controls its

(D) that the United States encourage Turkey, which invaded the island in 1974 and now controls their

(E) the United States to encourage Turkey, which invaded the island in 1974 and now controls its

66. Scientists have recently received permission to research embryonic stem cells, derived from blastocysts or early-stage embryos, <u>that they believe to be capable</u> of generating new cell growth and curing previously incurable ailments.

    (A) that they believe to be capable
    (B) that they believe are capable
    (C) that they believe will be capable
    (D) believed as capable
    (E) believed to be capable

67. State legislators fear that traffic accidents <u>would be more frequent and severe if the speed limit was increased</u> to 75 mph on rural highways.

    (A) would be more frequent and severe if the speed limit was increased
    (B) would be more frequent and severe were the speed limit to be increased up
    (C) would be more frequent and severe were the speed limit increased
    (D) would become more frequent and severe with the speed limit increased
    (E) would become more frequent and severe after the speed limit has increased

68. The architect proposed <u>that supplies for the new wing of the hospital, which hospital administrators hoped to open by the end of the year, will be</u> procured from local providers.

    (A) that supplies for the new wing of the hospital, which hospital administrators hoped to open by the end of the year, will be
    (B) that supplies for the hospital's new wing, which hospital administrators hope to be opened by the end of the year, be
    (C) that the hospital's new wing's supplies, which hospital administrators hope to be opened by year's end, might be
    (D) that supplies for the new wing of the hospital, which hospital administrators hope to be open by the end of the year, were
    (E) that supplies for the hospital's new wing, which hospital administrators hope to open by the end of the year, be

Explanation: A President's Request

65. The phrase *asked that* in choices (A), (C), and (D) requires the following verb to be in the subjunctive mood which, in situations like this (technically known as indirect speech), looks like the infinitive form of the verb. The options in the three choices are *would encourage* and *encourage*. The second is correct since *encourage* is indeed the infinitive form of the verb (*to encourage*). Eliminate (A) and (C). Answer choice (B) makes the same error. Even though it separates *asked* and *that* with some more information, (B) still presents the *asked that* construction and needs to use the subjunctive *encourage* rather than *would encourage*. (D) and (E) remain. (E) is correct because it uses *its* rather than *their* to refer to Cyprus.

An 800 test taker realizes that he doesn't need to know all of the details of the subjunctive mood in order to ace the GMAT. He familiarizes himself with the three situations in which the subjunctive is used so that he can spot them in Sentence Correction questions.

Explanation: Stem Cell Research

66. The phrase *that they believe* calls for the subjunctive mood. It needs to be completed by the verb *to be* in its infinitive form, allowing you to eliminate (B) and (C). Answer choices (D) and (E) create invalid sentence structures because they offer back-to-back modifiers without joining them with *and* or some other conjunction. Only choice (A) remains.

An 800 test taker is one of the few people who knows how to use the subjunctive correctly.

Explanation: Speeding Up the Limit

67. This sentence contains one of those *if* constructions that require the subjunctive. You'll be able to spot them by looking for if/then sentences that have *would* in the then-clause. So, if you altered the order of this sentence, it would read, *If the speed limit were increased, (then) traffic accidents would be....* The *would be* tips you off to the need for *were* rather than *was* in the if-clause. Knowing that the initial *was* needs to become *were* enables you to eliminate (A), (D), and (E). (C) defeats (B) because *increased* is far more succinct and clear than *to be increased up to*.

Explanation: Hospital Construction

68. The phrase *proposed that* creates a situation in which the subjunctive must be used. The following verb, initially *will be*, needs to become *be* in order to be correct, so you can eliminate (A) and (D) (*might be* in (C) is fine to the extent that it still uses the subjunctive). Of the remaining choices, you can eliminate (C) for misplacing a modifier. By placing *supplies* at the end of the first phrase, choice (C) illogically suggests that the administrators want the *supplies* to be opened. (E) is better than (B) because *to open* is clearer and less wordy than the passive *to be opened*. Go with (E).

An 800 test taker doesn't give up on a question just because she doesn't fully understand every component of it; she knows that educated guessing is *far* better than random guessing. Notice here that you'd be able to narrow your options down to two or three choices by applying rules other than those regarding the subjunctive.

---

8. NUMERICAL IDIOMS

No, we haven't moved into the math section; numbers are important for Sentence Correction greatness because their descriptions involve several easily confused idioms. For instance, *greater than* is appropriate when describing numbers alone but *more than* should be used when describing the numbers of objects or when making comparisons (*greater than one hundred* and *more than one hundred fish*). *Fewer* should be used to describe countable objects but *less than* when the objects are not quantifiable (*fewer hotels* and *less real estate*). Similarly, *number* should describe quantities that can be counted and *amount* should describe those that cannot (*number of people* and *amount of congestion*). Get to know these idioms well and expect to see them frequently on the GMAT.

SENTENCE CORRECTION PRACTICE SET 24

69. Local reporters investigating the labor dispute reported that only half of the workers in the plant were covered by the union health plan; <u>at least as much as a hundred and more others had not any</u> health insurance whatsoever.

   (A) at least as much as a hundred and more others had not any
   (B) at least as much as more than a hundred others had no
   (C) more than a hundred others had no
   (D) much more than a hundred others had no
   (E) more than a hundred others did not have

70. <u>The numbers of internet users has grown by more than a 10 percent increase in the past year.</u>

(A) The numbers of internet users has grown by more than a 10 percent increase in the past year.

(B) The number of internet users has grown by greater than 10 percent in the past year.

(C) The numbers of internet users have grown by more than 10 percent in the past year.

(D) The number of internet users has grown by more than 10 percent in the past year.

(E) The number of internet users grew by greater than 10 percent in the past year.

71. As a result of the Black Death, the plague that afflicted Europe in 1348–49, <u>as many as half the population died and less than half the work force remained</u> in certain cities.

(A) as many as half the population died and less than half the work force remained

(B) as much as half the population died and fewer than half the work force remained

(C) as many as half the people died and less than that remained in the work force

(D) as much as half the population died and less than half the work force remained

(E) as many as half the population and less than half the work force died or remained

72. According to the enrollment statistics published by U.S. medical schools, <u>the number of female medical students is equivalent to the number of male medical students currently enrolled in medical school</u>.

(A) the number of female medical students is equivalent to the number of male medical students currently enrolled in medical school

(B) as many female as male students are currently enrolled in medical school

(C) the number of female students is as many as that of male students currently enrolled in medical school

(D) as great as the number of female is the number of male students currently enrolled in medical school

(E) female and male students are currently enrolled in equal numbers in medical school

Explanation: Worker Health Insurance

69. There are a few problems in the sentence. First of all, *as much as a hundred* is incorrect; the idiom *as many as* should be used to describe a number of objects (*as many as 10 speakers* but *as much as the debt of…*). Eliminate (A) and (B). (D) changes the phrasing but is still wrong because *much more* distorts the meaning of the original sentence. Finally, (C) is better than (E) because *had no health insurance whatsoever* makes more sense and is more idiomatic than *did not have health insurance whatsoever*. Notice that both (C) and (E) also simplify the structure of the original *at least as much as a hundred and more others* by replacing it with *more than a hundred others*. The change is acceptable because it does not alter the meaning of the original, excessively wordy expression. If there were more than a hundred people, then it's unnecessary to also say that there were at least one hundred people; that's obvious. (C) it is.

An 800 test taker makes sure that the terms describing numbers or quantities are idiomatic.

Explanation: The Internet Explosion

70. First of all, *numbers* in the original sentence should be changed to the singular *number*. The only time that the plural *numbers* should be used is when one wants to discuss actual numbers, as in *the numbers 4 and 12*. Eliminate (A) and (C). Your remaining options ask you to choose between *greater than 10 percent* and *more than 10 percent*. As we said earlier, *greater than* is correct only when it is used to describe numbers alone (*greater than 10*). Since this sentence measures a percent rather than solely a number, the correct option is *more than*. Only (D) remains.

An 800 test taker is careful when dealing with percents. While *10* is clearly a countable quantity, *10 percent* is not and requires different terms to describe it.

---

71. First of all, *population* is not a quantity that can be counted, so *as many as* needs to be changed to *as much as*. Eliminate (A) and (E). Answer choice (C) survives this particular comparison because it changes the subject from *population* to the countable *people* and therefore uses *as many as* correctly. As for the second quantity in the underlined portion, *work force* is, like *population*, not countable and therefore *less than* rather than *fewer than* is correct. Eliminate (B). (C) is wrong because *less than that remained* distorts the meaning of the sentence and is unclear in its own right. What exactly is *that*? Half of those who died? Who survived? (D) remains.

An 800 test taker reads the entire answer choice before eliminating it; an error in one choice might not be an error in another if changes in the rest of the choice have redeemed it.

---

72. The initial sentence is certainly wordy, but look for specific problems that you can fix. Let's start with the terms describing *the number*. You're given several options: *the number…is equivalent to*, *as many female as male students*, *the number…is as many as*, *as great as the number…*, and the students are enrolled *in equal numbers*. Options (C) and (D) are grammatically incorrect because each uses the wrong idiom to describe the number. None of the remaining choices is grammatically incorrect, so focus on their expression. Answer choice (B) is clearly the most succinct option, and since it is still faithful to the original meaning of the sentence, it is the correct choice as well.

CHAPTER ELEVEN

Putting It All Together

You've now made your way through the eight standard and eight less standard—but still very important—categories of Sentence Correction errors. The 40 practice questions in this chapter will give you the opportunity to apply all of the lessons you've learned. You will be given four questions at a time, and explanations for each will follow.

By this point you've surely noticed that a lot of the grammar we've covered overlaps—that participles can be modifiers, which may be involved in parallelism, itself dependent on the correct use of pronouns, etc. These concepts will not be tested separately on the GMAT. As you've seen in the previous practice questions, nearly every Sentence Correction question tests more than one error. The same will be true of the following questions and, since they're not grouped by category, they offer a good chance for you to draw upon everything that you've learned thus far. In the explanations, we'll draw attention to some of the key concepts that each sentence tests.

Good luck!

SENTENCE CORRECTION PRACTICE SET 1

1. Any theory of grammar should answer three basic questions: what constitutes knowledge of grammar, how it is acquired, and how it is put to use.

   (A) how it is acquired, and how it is put to use
   (B) how is knowledge of grammar acquired, and how put to use
   (C) how it was acquired and put to use
   (D) its acquisition and putting to use
   (E) how its knowledge is acquired, and how it is put to use

2. In the conflict between the Israelis and the Palestinians, the refusal of each side to acknowledge each other as a legitimate national movement is closer to the heart of the problem than is any other issue.

   (A) the refusal of each side to acknowledge each other as a legitimate national movement is closer to the heart of the problem than
   (B) that the refusal of each side to acknowledge another as a legitimate national movement is closer to the heart of the problem as
   (C) the refusal of each side to acknowledge another as a legitimate national movement is closer to the heart of the problem than
   (D) that the refusal of each side to acknowledge another as a legitimate national movement is closer to the heart of the problem than
   (E) the refusal of each side to acknowledge each other as a legitimate national movement is closer to the heart of the problem as

3. The shipbuilding industry in eighteenth-century England created a need that pine and flax from Russia be made into masts and sails.

   (A) that pine and flax from Russia be made into masts and sails
   (B) for pine and flax from Russia that are made into masts and sails
   (C) that there be a production of masts and sails out of pine and flax from Russia
   (D) that masts and sails are made out of pine and flax from Russia
   (E) for pine and flax from Russia to be made into masts and sails

4. Agencies studying discrimination in housing have experimentally proved that minority clients are often discouraged as prospective buyers of residential real estate and <u>the antidiscrimination legislation of recent decades were only mitigating, rather than abolishing, inequity in housing practices</u>.

(A) the antidiscrimination legislation of recent decades were only mitigating, rather than abolishing, inequity in housing practices

(B) in recent decades, the antidiscrimination legislation only mitigated, rather than abolishing, inequity in housing practices

(C) that antidiscrimination legislation of recent decades has only mitigated, rather than abolished, inequity in housing practices

(D) that, in recent decades, antidiscrimination legislation has only mitigated, rather than abolishing, housing practices' inequity

(E) that recent decades' antidiscrimination legislation only were mitigating, rather than abolishing, housing practices' inequity

Explanation: Theories of Grammar

(Parallelism, Pronouns, Imperfect Options)

1. The three basic questions asked of any theory of grammar need to have parallel structures in the sentence. The original option is not perfect but it is parallel: each question begins with an interrogative pronoun (*what* or *how*) and contains a verb in the present tense. The fact that the first verb is active and the other two are passive makes the parallel less than ideal but not technically wrong. Choices (C) and (D) are not parallel; each breaks away from the structure of the first question, *what constitutes knowledge.* (B) is parallel at first, albeit wordy, but breaks the pattern with the odd *and how put to use.* (E) is incorrect because it adds *its* without clarifying what the pronoun refers to. Even if we can assume that *its* refers to grammar, the use of the pronoun in this instance makes little sense. (A) remains.

Explanation: Israeli and Palestinian Conflict

(Idioms, Meaning)

2. Scanning for differences among the choices, you can see that (A) and (E) contain *acknowledge each other* while the others use *acknowledge another. Another* in this instance is incorrect because it is unclear: Does it refer to a third party that neither acknowledges? If it does refer to the other national movement, then it uses the wrong idiom; *the other* or *each other* are the only viable options. Eliminate (B), (C), and (D). Choice (E) misuses the idiom *closer…than* by altering it to *closer…as.* The original sentence, (A), presents the best option.

Explanation: Eighteenth-Century Shipbuilding

(Idioms, Subordination)

3. The beginnings of the answer choices tip you off to the fact that you need to decide whether the correct idiom is *created a need that* or *created a need for.* The second is the correct option, so you can eliminate (A), (C), and (D). Of the remaining options, (B) is incorrect because it wrongly subordinates *that are made into masts and sails.* The subordination changes the meaning of the original sentence. While the sentence originally emphasizes the need for masts and sails, option (B) emphasizes the fact that pine and flax were needed from Russia; the purpose of the pine and flax becomes less important. (E) it is.

Explanation: Housing Discrimination

(Parallelism, Expression)

4. When you're dealing with long sentences and large underlined portions like this, it's even more important to isolate specific problems to help you weed out choices. The sentence describes the agencies as proving two things: one, that minority clients are discouraged, and two, that past legislation hasn't made the problem any better. The two things that are proven need to be in grammatically parallel forms and, since the first isn't underlined, the second will have to borrow the original structure. You can eliminate (A) and (B) for failing to do so right from the beginning. The underlined section needs to begin with *that* in order to recall the initial *proved that* and make it clear where this information fits into the sentence. Next, *mitigated* and *abolished* need to be in the same tense since they're in parallel positions, so eliminate (D). Finally, *only were mitigating* in (E) is not idiomatic word order, plus *were mitigating* is wordier than *mitigated*. (C) is the best choice.

SENTENCE CORRECTION PRACTICE SET 2

5. <u>By observing the techniques of medicine men, such as physical manipulation and the application of herbs, one has the capacity to learn things</u> about the human body not normally taken into consideration by practitioners of Western medicine.

    (A) By observing the techniques of medicine men, such as physical manipulation and the application of herbs, one has the capacity to learn things

    (B) By observing the techniques of medicine men, such as physical manipulation and the application of herbs, one can learn things

    (C) If you observe the techniques of medicine men, such as physical manipulation and the application of herbs, one can learn things

    (D) Observing the techniques of medicine men, such as physical manipulation and the application of herbs, things can be learned

    (E) Observing the techniques of medicine men, such as physical manipulation and the application of herbs, the capacity is given to one to learn things

6. Scientists have created a new substance that is <u>so transparent as to be</u> almost invisible.

    (A) so transparent as to be

    (B) so transparent it has been

    (C) so transparent that it was

    (D) transparent enough that it is

    (E) transparent enough so as to be

7. <u>Like most religions, the teachings of Sikhism are codified in</u> a book.

    (A) Like most religions, the teachings of Sikhism are codified in

    (B) Like most other religions, the teachings of Sikhism are codified in

    (C) Sikhism's teachings, like those of most other religions, are codified in

    (D) For their codification, like the teachings of most religions, Sikhism has

    (E) Like those of most religions, Sikhism has codified its teachings in

8. Blood banks can only make a donation useful to a hospital <u>by testing them quickly for a variety of illnesses and, before they expire, distributing them</u>.

    (A) by testing them quickly for a variety of illnesses and, before they expire, distributing them

    (B) by testing it quickly for a variety of illness and distributing it before expiration

    (C) by quickly testing it for a variety of illnesses and distributing it before it expires

    (D) by quickly testing it for a variety of illnesses and by, before they expire, distributing them

    (E) by quickly testing it for a variety of illnesses and to distribute it before it expires

Explanation: Medicine Men

(Expression, Passive Voice)

5. Start with grammatical issues before moving to expression. First of all, you can eliminate (D) and (E) because the original *by* in *by observing* is necessary in order for the end of the sentence to make sense. *Observing* on its own makes it seem as though the act of observation is in progress rather than being a potential practice. Also, you can eliminate (C) for its pronoun errors: the choice begins with *if you observe* but later adds *one can learn.* *You* and *one* are not interchangeable; they describe different subjects and therefore can't be used interchangeably. The sentence could use *you* in both instances (though that would still likely be incorrect since *you* is too informal and imprecise for the GMAT) or *one*, but it can't use both. (A) and (B) remain at this point. (B) is the correct answer because *one can learn* is far more direct than *one has the capacity to learn.*

Explanation: The Transparent Invention

(Idioms, Expression, Imperfect Options)

6. While the standard idiom is *so…that*, *so…as* can also be used in certain situations but *so…it* is never correct. Eliminate (B). Eliminate (C) for a verb tense error: The sentence begins in the present tense (*is…transparent*) and has no reason to switch from *is* to the past tense *was* at the end. (D) and (E) are not idiomatic; *transparent enough* has to be followed by *to be* in this situation and *transparent enough so as to be* combines incompatible idioms. The sentence could read *transparent enough to be* or *so transparent as to be* but (E) wrongly offers a mixture of the two options. Even though the original sentence is rather clumsy, (A) is still the best option of the ones you're given.

Explanation: Sikhism

(Comparisons, Pronouns)

7. Since this sentence creates a comparison, apply what you know about comparisons to it: comparisons need to involve like objects, so religions need to be compared to religions and teachings to teachings. Only answer choice (C) compares like objects by comparing *Sikhism's teachings* to *those [teachings] of other religions*.

> An 800 test taker will be rewarded with some quick and easy points for her knowledge of typically difficult concepts like modification or comparisons.

Explanation: Blood Banks

(Pronouns, Expression)

8. First of all, the subject for the underlined portion is *a donation*. Since the subject is singular, the pronouns that refer to it need to be singular as well. Eliminate (A) and (D) for using *they* and/or *them* rather than *it*. Compare (B), (C), and (E). Eliminate (E) because *testing* and *to distribute* are not parallel. Since both are in parallel situations, each describing what the blood banks need to do, they need to have the same structure. Finally, (C) is better than (B) because *quickly testing it* is more direct than *testing it quickly* and because *before expiration* at the end of (B) is less clear than *before it expires*. Go with (C).

SENTENCE CORRECTION PRACTICE SET 3

9. Certain gerontologists have reported that the more older people continue to challenge their brains with reading, writing, and other thought-provoking exercises, their cognitive functions are less likely to diminish.

   (A) their cognitive functions are less likely to diminish
   (B) the less likely are their cognitive functions to be diminished
   (C) the less are they likely to have diminished cognitive function
   (D) the less likely their cognitive functions will diminish
   (E) they are less likely to have diminished cognitive function

10. Archaeologists believe that the Dead Sea Scrolls, discovered in Khirbet Qumran between 1947 and 1967 and estimated at almost 2000 years old, provided rare insight into first century C. E. religious communities.

    (A) and estimated at almost 2000 years old, provided rare insight
    (B) and estimated at almost 2000 years old, provide rare insight
    (C) and estimated to be almost 2000 years old, to provide rare insight
    (D) and estimated to be almost 2000 years old, provide rare insight
    (E) and they estimate them to be almost 2000 years old, providing rare insight

11. Recent indications of weakness in the economy have led consumers to be more conservative with their purchases; so depressed have sales figures been as a result that the government has launched several initiatives to actively encourage consumer spending.

    (A) so depressed have sales figures been as a result that
    (B) the sales figures have been so depressed as a result that
    (C) as a result, so depressed has the sales been that
    (D) the resulting sales figures having been so depressed that
    (E) the sales figures have been so depressed that, as a result,

12. Proponents of the theory of spontaneous generation argued that simple living organisms sprang to life not through a recognizable reproductive process but came to life independently from non-living matter.

    (A) sprang to life not through a recognizable reproductive process but came to life
    (B) did not spring to life through a recognizable reproductive process and came to life
    (C) did not spring to life through a recognizable reproductive process but came to life
    (D) sprang to life not through a recognizable reproductive process but
    (E) did not spring to life through a recognizable system of reproduction but had come to life

Explanation: Keeping Cognitive Capacities

(Idioms, Parallelism)

9. The beginnings of the five choices present you with three options, forcing you to decide whether *the less* or *they/their* is correct. The non-underlined portion makes the decision for you; since it contains the phrase *the more*, the correct answer needs to parallel that structure in a parallel location and begin with *the less*. Eliminate (A) and (E). Comparing the remaining choices, you see that you have *the less are they likely* and *the less likely their*. The second phrasing is grammatically correct and parallel while the first, by separating *less* and *likely*, is unidiomatic. That leaves you with (D).

Explanation: Dead Sea Scrolls

(Subjunctive, Verb Tense, Subordination)

10. The phrase *estimated at* is unidiomatic, so even if you're not sure how to fix it, you can eliminate (A) and (B). The remaining choices provide only one option, *estimated to be*, so think no more on the issue and look for another problem. *To provide* in (C) is wrong; try reading it into the sentence to see that this verb tense does not work in context. (D) and (E) present significantly different options. (E) switches the subordinate and declarative phrases of (D) and the original sentence but it's wrong because the original *estimated to be* is in a subordinate phrase and is parallel with *discovered in*. The phrase has to remain subordinate based on its position in the sentence. Also, by making *provided* into *providing*, (E) subordinates the final phrase and deeply distorts the meaning of the original sentence. (D) survives.

Explanation: The Flagging Economy

(Idioms, Modifier)

11. There's nothing strictly wrong with the original sentence; it uses the *so...that* idiom correctly, the verb tenses are fine, and it makes sense. Scan the answer choices for better options. You can eliminate (C) because its subject *sales* and verb *has been* do not agree. (D) creates a sentence fragment since it makes every phrase after the semicolon subordinate (remember that a semicolon is only used correctly when the pieces on both sides of it could function as grammatically correct and complete sentences on their own). Finally, *as a result* functions as a modifier that refers to the sales slump. Choices (B) and (E) misplace the modifier and unnecessarily distort the original meaning of the sentence. That leaves (A).

Explanation: Spontaneous Generation

(Verb Tense)

12. The two things compared here are two processes by which "organisms" might have come to life. To keep them parallel, we must say it "sprang to life not [through one process], but [through an alternate process]..." And since the two verbs mean the same thing, it is needlessly wordy to say both "sprang" and "came to life." (B) uses the wrong conjunction, since the two processes are contrasted. (C) is parallel, but doesn't correct the wordiness. (E) is even wordier and shifts tense inappropriately. Choice (D) is concise and parallel. It is correct.

SENTENCE CORRECTION PRACTICE SET 4

13. The first decision to be made by a person <u>being considered for employment at Reven-Tech is if to submit</u> to a drug test.

    (A) being considered for employment at Reven-Tech is if to submit
    (B) considered for employment at Reven-Tech is if he or she should submit
    (C) being considered for employment at Reven-Tech is whether submission
    (D) considered for employment at Reven-Tech is whether, when submitted
    (E) considered for employment at Reven-Tech is whether to submit

14. The doctor observed the butterfly rash on her patient's arm and the patient's evident fatigue, <u>which was consistent with the symptoms</u> of Lupus.

    (A) which was consistent with the symptoms
    (B) which were consistent with the symptoms
    (C) that were consistent with those
    (D) which symptoms were consistent with symptoms
    (E) symptoms which were consistent with those of

15. A report released by the American Diabetes Association maintains that <u>much of the increase in cases of type II diabetes can be attributed</u> to the poor eating and exercise habits of young Americans.

    (A) much of the increase in cases of type II diabetes can be attributed
    (B) many of the increase in cases of type II diabetes are attributable
    (C) they can attribute much of the increase in cases of type II diabetes to
    (D) doctors attribute much of the increase in cases of type II diabetes to
    (E) many of the cases of increased type II diabetes can be attributed

16. Although some parents believe that the local all-girls school should begin to admit boys, others claim <u>that girls would participate actively in class only if they had all-girls classes</u>.

    (A) that girls would participate actively in class only if they had all-girls classes

    (B) that girls will only participate actively in a class if it is all-girls

    (C) that girls will only participate actively in an all-girls class

    (D) that girls would participate actively only in a class that were all-girls

    (E) that girls in all-girls classes will participate actively in that situation only

Explanation: Wary Reven-Tech

(Expression, Idioms)

13. We're told that this highly suspicious company requires its potential employees to have drug tests and the first decision that the answer choices ask you to make is whether *being considered* or *considered* is the better option. The *being* is unnecessary so eliminate (A) and (C). Next, should the underlined portion contain *if* or *whether*? Since the sentence is describing options rather than a hypothetical situation, *whether* is correct. Eliminate (B). Finally, (D) makes no sense in context. (E) is correct.

Explanation: Observed Symptoms

(Pronouns)

14. The largest problem in the original sentence is *which* because, as the sentence originally stands, it's not clear what *which* refers to (the observation or the symptoms). It more likely refers to the symptoms, but *symptoms* haven't even been discussed yet at this point in the sentence. Thus, for a few reasons, *which* on its own is an unclear pronoun. Eliminate (A), (B), and (C). Notice that *that* in (C) makes the situation no better. *Which symptoms* in (D) is not a common idiom and the rest of the choice is too wordy, so (E) it is.

Explanation: Increase in Diabetes

(Numbers, Passive Voice, Imperfect Options)

15. First of all, *much* is better than *many* because an increase isn't countable and therefore requires *much*. Eliminate (B). Notice that you can't yet eliminate (E) because it changes the subject of *many* to *cases*. Since you can count *cases*, *many* is correct. Next, the original sentence contains the passive expression *can be attributed*. (C) makes the expression active but adds the entirely unclear pronoun *they*. (D) does the same by adding *doctors*, but the addition alters the meaning of the original sentence; the original sentence doesn't suggest that doctors are the intended subject or that they're actually attributing diabetes to such causes. Therefore, keep the passive expression (it's not always wrong) in order to preserve the meaning of the sentence. Finally, eliminate (E) because *cases of increased type II diabetes* is not a phrase that uses an idiomatic word order. (A) wins.

An 800 test taker knows that the passive voice is correct when it is impossible or inappropriate to name the subject who performs an action.

Explanation: All-Girls Schools

(Expression, Verb Tense)

16. The initial sentence is a mess in terms of word order and clarity. Break down the different options. First of all, *would participate* is the incorrect tense; the verbs up to this point in this sentence have been in the simple present tense and there's no reason to switch into the conditional *would*. Eliminate (A) and (D). Next, *in an all-girls class* is far more succinct than *in a class if it is all-girls* so take out (B). Finally, (C) is the best of your remaining options because it is less repetitive and is more consistent with the meaning of the original sentence than (E). Go with (C).

SENTENCE CORRECTION PRACTICE SET 5

17. <u>With the assistance of informants, cases can often be made against otherwise elusive criminals.</u>

   (A) With the assistance of informants, cases can often be made against otherwise elusive criminals.

   (B) Cases can often be made against otherwise elusive criminals with the aid of informants.

   (C) With the assistance of informants, we can often make cases against otherwise elusive criminals.

   (D) Otherwise elusive criminals can often have cases made against them with the assistance of informants.

   (E) With the assistance of informants, litigators can often make cases against otherwise elusive criminals.

KAPLAN

18. A new initiative requires that cable companies report <u>to their new customers all the costs, including taxes, that they will be expected to pay</u>.

    (A) to their new customers all the costs, including taxes, that they will be expected to pay

    (B) to their new customers all the costs, including taxes, that the customers will be expected to pay

    (C) to its new customers all the costs, including taxes, that they will have to pay

    (D) to the companies' new customers all the costs, including taxes, that the companies have paid

    (E) to their new customers all the costs, including taxes, that its customers will be expected to pay

19. Imperceptible to the eye or the ear, <u>carbon monoxide is formed from</u> materials containing carbon, or carbonaceous materials, are only partially combusted.

    (A) carbon monoxide is formed from

    (B) carbon monoxide is formed by

    (C) the formation of carbon monoxide is when

    (D) carbon monoxide is formed when

    (E) carbon monoxide forms when its

20. Galileo's theory that <u>ours was indeed a solar system, in which Earth and other planets revolve around the sun, reinforced those of Copernicus</u>.

    (A) ours was indeed a solar system, in which Earth and other planets revolve around the sun, reinforced those of Copernicus

    (B) ours was indeed a solar system, in which Earth and other planets revolve around the sun, reinforced that of Copernicus

    (C) our solar system was indeed solar for Earth and the other planets revolve around the sun, reinforced Copernicus'

    (D) our system was indeed solar, in which Earth and other planets revolved around the sun, reinforced those of Copernicus

    (E) Earth and the other planets revolve around the sun in our solar system reinforces that of Copernicus

Explanation: Criminal Informants

(Modifiers)

17. The original phrase, *With the assistance of informants*, is a modifier. Based on the structure of the original sentence, it appears to modify *cases* but it doesn't really make sense for a case—an inanimate, abstract thing—to be assisted by people. What is more logical is that the people who are building the case are assisted by the informants. Since those people are not mentioned in the original sentence, the modifier *dangles* and needs something concrete to modify. Scanning through your options, you'll see that only (C) and (E) give you concrete subjects. (C) is out because *we* isn't logical; there's no indication that *we* are making cases. (E) is your best option.

> An 800 test taker knows that dangling modifiers create a situation in which, by adding a modifier, she'll have to change the meaning of the sentence in order to make it correct.

Explanation: Cable Companies Exposed

(Pronouns)

18. With two pronouns underlined, this sentence is likely to test your knowledge of proper pronoun usage. The pronoun *their* should refer to *cable companies*. Both items are plural and the referent of the pronoun is clear so all's well so far. Eliminate (C). Next, you have *they* in the final phrase of the sentence. Now, at this point, you've been given a lot of plural nouns, including *companies*, *costs*, *taxes*, and *customers*. While it's logical that *customers* is the intended referent of *they*, the sentence itself allows for some ambiguity (technically speaking, the companies could be the ones expected to pay these costs). Where a pronoun is ambiguous, a pronoun is used incorrectly. Eliminate (A), and take out (E) as well since *its* certainly doesn't help matters any: What singular subject could *its* logically and usefully refer to? Of your remaining options, you can remove (D) from consideration because changing the verb to *have paid* unnecessarily distorts the meaning of the original sentence. (B) survives.

Explanation: Carbon Monoxide Poisoning

(Modifiers, Meaning)

19. As we saw in number 17, this sentence begins with a modifier. Unlike the modifier in that sentence, this one is used correctly because it does indeed modify *carbon monoxide*. Eliminate (C) for creating an error where there was none. Next, you need to decide whether *from*, *by*, or *when* should end the underlined section. When you originally read the sentence, you probably noticed that something was very wrong. Since you can't change the end of the sentence, you need to alter the underlined portion in order to make the sentence grammatically correct. Only *when* does that (try reading them in), so eliminate (A) and (B). Finally, (D) is better than (E) because in this case the passive *is formed* is more accurate than *forms* and because the *its* in (E) is unnecessary. Go with (D).

Explanation: Galileo and Copernicus

(Ellipsis)

20. The sentence creates a parallel between Galileo's theory and Copernicus's theory, as you can see when you simplify the sentence's structure: *Galileo's theory...reinforced those of Copernicus*. The original sentence is right to try to compare theory to theory, but *those* is the incorrect pronoun; since *theory* is singular, the pronoun that refers to it needs to be *that*. Eliminate (A) and (D). Next, *reinforced* needs to be in the past tense like *was* earlier in the sentence. Eliminate (E). Finally, (C) presents a less clear and less direct alternative to (B), leaving (B) as the right answer.

SENTENCE CORRECTION PRACTICE SET 6

21. A result of the recent election is <u>realizing that in this increasingly urban area, there is now more worry about crime</u> than health care.

  (A) realizing that in this increasingly urban area, there is now more worry about crime

  (B) the realization that in this increasingly urban area, they now worry more about crime

  (C) the realization that in this increasingly urban area, voters now worry more about crime

  (D) a realizing that in this increasingly urban area, there is now more concern about crime

  (E) the realization that in this increasingly urban area, concerns about crime are greater

22. <u>Having lost his sight to sustained eyestrain</u>, John Milton nevertheless composed Paradise Lost, considered by many to be the greatest English epic.

   (A) Having lost his sight to sustained eyestrain
   (B) With his sight lost to sustained eyestrain
   (C) Blinded by sustained eyestrain
   (D) Having been blinded by excessive eyestrain
   (E) Blinded with sustained eyestrain

23. One benefit of learning to speak a language while learning to read it <u>rather than separately</u> is that the student can more effectively apply his or her knowledge in social settings.

   (A) rather than separately
   (B) rather than independently
   (C) instead of separately
   (D) instead of as separate processes
   (E) rather than in a separate process

24. Since 1954, when the Supreme Court ruled that segregation was unconstitutional, the Supreme Court <u>heard cases in which lawyers debated what constituted segregation</u>.

   (A) heard cases in which lawyers debated what constituted segregation
   (B) had heard cases in which lawyers debated what constituted segregation
   (C) has heard cases in which lawyers debated what constituted segregation
   (D) has heard cases in which lawyers debated what has constituted segregation
   (E) was hearing cases in which lawyers debated what constituted segregation

Explanation: Crime Trumps Health Care

(Participle, Passive Voice)

21. First of all, *realizing* in the original sentence is wrong because it doesn't really describe *a result*. Instead, the participle defines a process. Even though the phrasing may sound strange, *the realization* is correct because, as a noun, *realization* can logically describe a result. Eliminate (A) and (D). (B) introduces its own unique error with the entirely vague *they*. Since we don't know what *they* refers to, the pronoun is incorrect. (C) and (E) remain. (E) sounds fine when read on its own, but if you read it into the sentence you'll see the problem: *concerns about crime are greater than [those about] health care*. Without *those about*, the sentence misuses ellipsis. (C) it is.

Explanation: Milton's Blindness

(Expression)

22. None of the choices is overtly wrong in terms of grammar, so focus on expression. *Having lost his sight*, *with his sight lost*, and *having been blinded* are far wordier than *blinded*. Since *blinded* accurately captures the same idea, you can eliminate (A), (B), and (D). (E) uses the wrong preposition; *with* suggests that eyestrain constitutes blindness, that it is the same thing as blindness rather than a cause of it. (C) is the answer.

> An 800 test taker is systematic even when dealing with expression. He has clear and explicit reasons for eliminating each choice, knowing that the one that "sounds" best may just contain a common and therefore difficult error.

Explanation: The Benefits of Speaking

(Ellipsis, Parallelism)

23. The problem with the original sentence is *separately*. *Separately* is an adverb but in this context it's not clear exactly which verb it's modifying. (B) and (C) share the same problem. (D) and (E) both bring out the parallelism in the sentence, which you can see if you rewrite the sentence: "One benefit of learning to speak a language while learning to read it rather than as/in a separate process is...." You'll notice that (D) changes *process* to the plural *processes* and undermines the parallelism; the underlined portion should refer to only one process, that of learning to speak a language, in order to create a parallel alternative to *while learning to read it*. (E) wins.

Explanation: Segregation Examined

(Verb Tense)

24. *Since 1954* means that you're dealing with a process that began in the past and is still in progress. Therefore, *has heard* is better than *heard*, *had heard*, or *was hearing* because the perfect tense (*has heard*) describes a situation that began in the past and continues into the present. Eliminate (A), (B), and (E). (D) is wrong because changing *constituted* into the perfect *has constituted* unnecessarily changes the meaning of the sentence. Go with (C).

SENTENCE CORRECTION PRACTICE SET 7

25. Economic analysts predict that <u>there is going to be considerable alterations to the interest rate</u> in the coming months.

  (A) there is going to be considerable alterations to the interest rate

  (B) the interest rate are going to alter considerably

  (C) there are going to be considerable alterations to the interest rate

  (D) considerable alterations to the interest rate will occur

  (E) the interest rate will change considerably

26. Yellowstone National Park officials have begun to fine those campers who fail to lock their cars at <u>night, exposing their cars and other campers with</u> scavenging bears.

  (A) night, exposing their cars and other campers with

  (B) night and expose their cars and other campers toward

  (C) night, and expose their cars and others campers with

  (D) night and who expose their cars and other campers to

  (E) night, by exposing their cars and other campers to

27. <u>Except for one class in history and one in biology, all the student's graduation requirements have been fulfilled.</u>

  (A) Except for one class in history and one in biology, all the student's graduation requirements have been fulfilled.

  (B) Except for needing to take one class in history and one in biology, the student has fulfilled all of his requirements for graduation.

  (C) The student has fulfilled all his graduation requirements except for one class in history and one in biology.

  (D) Except for one history class and one biology class, the student has fulfilled all of his graduation requirements.

  (E) Aside from the history class and biology class that he needs to take, the student's graduation requirements have all been fulfilled.

28. The audience for the new opera, an inventive rendition of Wagner's Tristan and Isolde, <u>was clearly enthralled by the show for the attendees</u> paused for some moments before applauding vigorously at its conclusion.

   (A) was clearly enthralled by the show for the attendees
   (B) were clearly enthralled by the show for they
   (C) were clearly enthralled by the show as they
   (D) was clearly enthralled by the show for they
   (E) was clearly enthralled by the show as is clear since its attendees

Explanation: Fluctuating Interest Rates

(Subject/Verb Agreement, Expression)

25. Subject/verb agreement can be harder to see when you're dealing with phrases like *there are* or *there has*, which introduce the subject only *after* the verb. In this sentence, *alterations* is the subject of *there is* but, since the subject is plural, the verb needs to be the plural *are*. Eliminate (A). You can eliminate (B) as well since the singular *interest rate* does not agree with the plural *are*. The other options are grammatically fine but vary with respect to expression. (C) is much wordier than the other options and, since both (C) and (D) are passive and less direct variations of (E), (E) stands as the best, clearest, and most articulate option.

Explanation: Scavenging Bears

(Idioms, Meaning)

26. First of all, the correct idiom is *exposing...to*. Eliminate (A), (B), and (C). (E) deeply distorts the original meaning of the sentence. It illogically suggests that the campers fail to lock their cars *by* exposing the cars and campers to danger, that the exposure creates the unlocked cars. If that makes no sense to you, that's okay because it makes no sense. Eliminate (E). (D) uses the correct idiom and creates a clear parallel structure between *who fail* and *who expose*. (D) it is.

Explanation: Graduation Requirements

(Modifiers, Expression, Imperfect Options)

27. One of the reasons this question is difficult is because *except for* and *aside from* do not create modifiers; the phrases they begin don't describe an unnamed subject or object. Once you realize that, you can see that what really differentiates the answer choices is expression, not grammar. Scanning for differences, you can see that *have been fulfilled* is a passive and wordier alternative to *has fulfilled*. Eliminate (A) and (E). Next, *graduation requirements* is superior to *requirements for graduation* so eliminate (B). Finally, the meaning of (C) is less clear than that of (D) because of the confusing word order of (C). Therefore, (D) wins.

An 800 test taker knows that many sentences are challenging primarily because they contain unfamiliar syntax or sentence structure. He pauses to understand the sentence before looking for familiar errors.

Explanation: Wagner Revitalized

(Subject/Verb Agreement, Pronouns)

28. *Audience* is what's called a collective noun because, like *jury* or *family* it describes a group of people that functions as a singular subject; one says *the family is* rather than *the family are.* Therefore, the singular *was* is the correct verb for *audience* and you can eliminate (B) and (C). Next, you have to decide among *for the attendees, for they,* and *as is clear since its attendees.* (D) has a pronoun error since *they* has no clear referent. The singular *audience* wouldn't work as the referent, and the sentence doesn't provide us with any other options. *Its attendees* in (E) is fine, however wordy, but that wordiness when combined with the clumsy phrase *as is clear since* makes (A) the best option.

SENTENCE CORRECTION PRACTICE SET 8

29. The basic needs of the average cat are simple and largely inexpensive: food, water, affection, and shelter, <u>and occasional visits to the veterinarian</u>.

   (A) and occasional visits to the veterinarian

   (B) with occasional veterinarian visits

   (C) with occasional visits to the veterinarian

   (D) yet occasionally visiting the veterinarian

   (E) but some occasional visits to the veterinarian are needed

30. Deforestation significantly alters the population of an area by creating a habitat <u>in which few species and vegetation can survive</u>.

   (A) in which few species and vegetation can survive

   (B) in which few species and little vegetation can survive

   (C) where little species and vegetation can survive

   (D) in which fewer species than vegetation can survive

   (E) where little species and few vegetation can survive

31. Proponents of the Equal Rights Amendment argue for its necessity <u>if only because average salaries for women are still considerably lower than it is</u> for men with comparable jobs and work experience.

    (A) if only because average salaries for women are still considerably lower than it is

    (B) if only because average salaries for women are still considerably lower than those

    (C) because average salaries for women are only considerably lower than those

    (D) if only as a result of the fact that salaries for women are still considerably lower than those

    (E) if only because women's average salaries are still considerably lower than it is

32. That pollution harms the environment is self-evident; <u>that immediate government action to combat it is merited by the situation</u> is a matter of debate.

    (A) that immediate government action to combat it is merited by the situation

    (B) if the situation merits immediate action by the government is a matter of debate

    (C) whether to combat the situation is merited by immediate government action

    (D) that the situation merits immediate government action to combat it

    (E) whether the government should immediately combat it is merited by the situation

Explanation: Cat Care

(Parallelism, Meaning)

29. To deal with the sentence successfully you first need to consider its meaning. The sentence lists five items, four of which support the claim that cats' needs are "simple and largely inexpensive." You know that the fifth item, the trips to the vet, aren't part of this list and shouldn't be parallel with it because, first, the *and* before shelter suggests that the initial list ends with *shelter* and, second, trips to the vet are not inexpensive. Therefore, the final item needs to be expressed as an exception. Eliminate (A). At this point, the primary problem is one of expression. *Veterinarian visits*, while shorter, is less clear and idiomatic than *visits to the veterinarian*. Out with (B). As for (D), we have a dangling modifier: who is occasionally visiting the vet? Eliminate. Finally, (E) is a passive and much wordier option than (C). (C) it is.

Explanation: Deforestation

(Numerical Idioms)

30. Whenever you see *few* underlined, look to see if it's used correctly. Remember that *few* is the correct adjective for things that can be counted. Species can be counted, so *few* is right in the first instance. Nevertheless, *few* is made to perform double duty, describing both species and, through ellipsis, vegetation. Vegetation cannot be counted so *few* is the wrong adjective for it, meaning you'll need a separate adjective for vegetation. Eliminate (A), and (C) and (E) as well, because *little* is an incorrect adjective for *species*, suggesting as it does more about size than number. The new comparative structure of (D) sidesteps the "few/less" issue, but in doing so it unnecessarily alters the meaning of the sentence. Eliminate it and (B) remains. (By the way, *in which* is slightly better than *where* because it's more formal, but there's nothing inherently wrong with *where*. Some differences aren't all that important.)

Explanation: The ERA

(Parallelism, Pronouns)

31. The sentence compares salaries to salaries, but it takes a shortcut toward the end and refers back to *salaries* as *it*. *Salaries* are plural and *it* is singular, so (A) and (E) are out of consideration. Of the remaining options, (C) stands out as significantly different, but by replacing *if only* with *because* and by moving *only* so that it describes *lower*, (C) actually contradicts the meaning of the original sentence. Finally, *because* in (B) is far more succinct than *as a result of the fact that* in (D). So, (B) it is.

Explanation: Environmental Activism

(Meaning, Passive Voice)

32. First of all, you can eliminate (B) because the sentence describes alternatives and would therefore need *whether* rather than *if*. Next, (C) wrongly relocates *is merited by* and (E) changes the meaning of the original sentence. (C) suggests that government action, not pollution, is the problem and (E) just doesn't make sense. Finally, (A) and (D) are in many ways quite similar but the passive voice in (A) leaves (D) as the more active and clear option.

SENTENCE CORRECTION PRACTICE SET 9

33. The increase in the number and scope of investigations into monopolistic business practices, in addition to the expansion of definitions of such practices, <u>have resulted in more antimonopoly litigation presently than ever before</u>.

   (A) have resulted in more antimonopoly litigation presently than ever before

   (B) has resulted in greater antimonopoly litigation presently than previously

   (C) has resulted in more antimonopoly litigation at present than was seen ever before

   (D) have resulted in more antimonopoly litigation at present than ever before

   (E) has resulted in more antimonopoly litigation at present than ever before

34. Carthaginians are still commonly credited <u>as the ones who salted</u> Roman fields during the Punic Wars despite the existence of credible evidence to the contrary.

   (A) as the ones who salted

   (B) as the salters of

   (C) for salting

   (D) with having salted

   (E) with the salting of

35. One idea for Social Security reform was to disallow payments for those with a certain level of income; although the idea was rejected, citizens can choose to refuse social security payments <u>for private sources of income, whether derived by pension funds or personal savings</u>, if they want.

   (A) for private sources of income, whether derived by pension funds or personal savings

   (B) in favor of private sources of income, whether derived from pension funds or personal savings

   (C) for private sources of income, whether derived from pension funds or personal savings

   (D) and use private sources of income, derived either by pension funds or personal savings

   (E) rather than private sources of income, whether derived from pension funds or personal savings

36. <u>Standard police procedure requires that an officer interview witnesses separately rather than together.</u>

   (A) Standard police procedure requires that an officer interview witnesses separately rather than together.

   (B) A requirement, according to standard police procedure, is that an officer interview witness separately rather than interviewing them together.

   (C) Standard police procedure requires an officer to interview witnesses separately rather than to interview them together.

   (D) It is required in standard police procedure that an officer interviews witnesses separately, not together.

   (E) Standard police procedure requires that an officer interviews witnesses separately rather than together.

Explanation: Monopolies

(Subject/Verb Agreement, Modifier)

33. The answer choices indicate that you need to choose between *have* and *has*. Since the subject of the sentence is the singular *increase*, *has* is correct and you can eliminate (A) and (D). Beware: Even though the sentence discusses the expanded definition *in addition to* the increase, *in addition to* does not make the subject plural. *Only and* can create a compound, or plural, subject in these situations because it unites two subjects into one plural subject. Next, *more* is correct and *greater* is not since the sentence doesn't discuss numbers. Eliminate (B). Finally, *at present* is, however wordy, the correct alternative to *presently*. *Presently*, as with *hopefully*, is an adverb, meaning that it needs to modify a verb (*I will perform the task presently*). Since litigation is a noun, it requires an adjective, and *at present* fits the bill. (E) it is.

Explanation: The Punic Wars

(Idioms, Imperfect Options)

34. The correct idiom is *credited with* so you can eliminate (A), (B), and (C). Next, *with the salting of* in (E) is more passive than *with having salted*, so (D) is the better choice.

An 800 test taker suspects that, whenever the answer choices provide a verb followed by different prepositions, idioms are being tested. She tries to determine which preposition is appropriate by focusing on the idiom.

Explanation: Social Security Reform

(Idioms)

35. First off, the correct idiom for *refuse* is *for* (*He refused one for the other*). No, this isn't a common idiom, nor is it a particularly eloquent one, and that's why this question is hard. Eliminate (B), (D), and (E). Choices (A) and (C) ask you to choose between *derived by* and *derived from*. *Derived from* is the correct idiom. (C) is right. Unfortunately, idioms just need to be memorized since they follow no general rules, but you'll have an intuitive sense of most of them. You'll have the best shot of choosing the correct idiom if you isolate it or consider it in terms of a simple sentence, as we did with *He refused one for the other* above.

Explanation: Police Procedures

(Ellipsis, Subjunctive)

36. You're given *interview* and *interviews* as options here. *Interview* is correct because *requires that* earlier in the sentence is one of those "verb + that" formulas that need to be completed by a verb in the subjunctive (here, *interview*). Eliminate (D) and (E). Next, you need to decide whether *interview witnesses separately rather than together* uses ellipsis correctly. It does because *interview* works as an implied verb and *together* properly parallels the other adverb *separately*. Think of it this way: *Standard police procedure requires that an officer interview witnesses separately rather than that an officer interview witnesses together.* You'll notice that everything that the sentence needs to imply has already been stated. That, plus the fact that the structure of the remaining pieces is parallel, means that ellipsis is used correctly. (A) is your most succinct choice.

SENTENCE CORRECTION PRACTICE SET 10

37. <u>Charles Dickens viewed inadequate sanitation, as many Victorian authors, as</u> a pressing and dangerous problem in London.

   (A) Charles Dickens viewed inadequate sanitation, as many Victorian authors, as

   (B) Charles Dickens, like many Victorian authors, viewed inadequate sanitation as

   (C) Many Victorian authors, like Charles Dickens, viewed inadequate sanitation as

   (D) Inadequate sanitation was viewed by Charles Dickens, like many Victorian authors, as

   (E) Charles Dickens was like many Victorian authors in that he viewed inadequate sanitation as

38. One critic wrote that, if the best-selling guide to finding a husband is right, <u>the idea of the necessity of honesty and trust in a relationship</u> is fundamentally wrong.

   (A) the idea of the necessity of honesty and trust in a relationship

   (B) the idea that honesty and trust are necessary in a relationship

   (C) honesty and trust are not necessary in a relationship

   (D) the idea that honesty and trust is necessary to a relationship

   (E) the necessity of honest and trust to a relationship

39. The average income for a person with a bachelor of arts degree is several thousand dollars per year higher <u>than somebody with a high school diploma only</u>.

   (A) than somebody with a high school diploma only

   (B) than that for somebody with only a high school diploma

   (C) than for somebody with a high school diploma only

   (D) than it is for somebody with a high school diploma only

   (E) that that of somebody having only a high school diploma

40. <u>Some airline companies prefer to spend extra money on leather seats for their aircraft, sometimes twice as expensive as the others, because they last two times as long.</u>

    (A) Some airline companies prefer to spend extra money on leather seats for their aircraft, sometimes twice as expensive as the others, because they last two times as long.

    (B) Some airline companies prefer to spend extra money, sometimes twice as expensive as the others, on leather seats for their aircraft because they last twice as long.

    (C) Some airline companies prefer to spend extra money on leather seats, sometimes twice as expensive as the others, on leather seats for their aircraft, being twice as long lasting.

    (D) Leather seats lasting twice as long as the others, some airline companies prefer spending two times the extra money on them.

    (E) Some airline companies prefer to spend extra money on leather seats, sometimes twice as expensive as the others, for their aircraft because they last twice as long.

Explanation: Dickens and the Victorians

(Modifiers, Expression)

37. *Like many Victorian authors* modifies *Charles Dickens* so it needs to be placed as close as possible to his name. Eliminate (A). You can eliminate (C) as well for transposing the modifier and what it modifies. The change makes *Many Victorian authors* rather than *Charles Dickens* the subject of the sentence and therefore changes its meaning unnecessarily. The remaining options are grammatically acceptable, so focus on expression. *Viewed* is better than the passive *was viewed by*. Eliminate (D). (E) is wordier for several reasons than (B). (B) it is.

Explanation: Husband Hunting

(Passive Voice)

38. The original sentence shows you what happens when the passive voice runs amuck. *The idea of the necessity of honesty and trust* is just ugly and unclear. Since (B), (C), and (D), present you with active alternatives, eliminate (A) and (E). Next, eliminate (D) because the subject is plural (*honesty* and *trust* is a compound, plural subject) so the verb needs to be *are*. Finally, try reading (C) into the sentence and you'll see that it makes no sense. (B) wins again.

Explanation: A Degree of Value

(Ellipsis, Expression)

39. As it stands, this sentence cuts out too much when it uses ellipsis in *than somebody*. It needs to refer back to the average salary (either directly or with the pronoun *that*) and to repeat the verb *is or* the preposition *for* in order to adequately recall the first part of the sentence. Eliminate (A) and (C). Eliminate (D) for using the vague pronoun *it* rather than the correct *that*. Finally, eliminate (E) either because *of* should be *for* in order to parallel *for a person* or because *having* is awkward. (B) is correct.

Explanation: Money for Leather

(Modifier)

40. The fact that everything is underlined in this sentence means that you have a lot of issues to consider. Start with something concrete. You know that *sometimes twice as expensive as the others* modifies *leather seats* so make sure that the two are placed next to each other in the sentence. Eliminate (A) and (B). Next, *because they last twice as long* is better and clearer than *being twice as long lasting*. Eliminate (C). Finally, *two times the extra money* in (D) makes no sense, or at least it distorts the meaning of the original sentence, suggesting that companies are spending twice the increase in cost rather than twice the cost of the other seats. (E) remains.

> An 800 test taker knows how to locate familiar concepts even in the most complicated of sentences. She starts with what she knows best, eliminates the choices that she knows to be wrong, and then focuses on less familiar concepts.

section four

PROBLEM SOLVING— STRAIGHT MATH

CHAPTER TWELVE

The Straight Math Challenge

As a general introduction to the straight math in this book, one thing needs to be made very clear up front: This is not a math text.

The questions in this book have been designed to present the toughest math the GMAT has to throw at you. Therefore, the discussion will presume you know, or will remember, the basics of arithmetic, algebra, and geometry. This section will focus on *how* the GMAT tests your knowledge and skills. In fact, the focus will be on the questions that earn the top math scores.

If you find your high school math knowledge is a little rusty, avail yourself of a resource to review that material. In fact, working through the straight math sections of this book will give you a good idea of what, if anything, you need to review.

With that caveat out of the way, let's start the ride.

CHAPTER THIRTEEN

Arithmetic

Here in the arithmetic section, two key Kaplan math strategies will be introduced—backsolving and picking numbers. Then we'll see how they can help to rack up points on the most difficult arithmetic questions.

The two general topics we'll concern ourselves with are number properties and roots and exponents. Roots and exponents are just plain tough. Number properties questions are also tough because they test information no one ever uses, such as prime numbers, odd and even numbers, etc. It may seem like math trivia from eighth grade, but the GMAT considers it very important.

BACKSOLVING

Backsolving is the process of trying out the answer choices—solving backwards, as it were, from the choices. You take an answer choice and temporarily assume it's the correct answer. Then you plug it in to the question to see if it is in fact correct—if it works. If the choice doesn't work, you eliminate it and try another. (And if it does work, then—surprise!—you pick it and go on to the next question.)

Now depending on the types of answer choices, there are two orders to try them. In a case like Question 1 below, where the answer choices have variables in them, we start from the last choice and work back to the first. This is because we don't know the actual values of the choices.

But for questions where the answer choices have concrete values, we start with the middle value. This way, if the choice is wrong, we may be able to tell whether it is too large or too small. Knowing that will tell us which of the remaining choices to try next.

For example, if the middle choice is "3" and it's too small, then we try one of the two larger choices. Conversely, if "3" is too large, we try one of the two smaller choices.

Don't worry if this seems vague right now. You'll get more than enough practice and examples of backsolving throughout this book.

Question 1

1. Which of the following must be an integer if x is a positive integer and $\frac{4}{x} + \frac{5}{x} + \frac{6}{x}$ is an integer?

    (A) $\frac{x}{5}$

    (B) $\frac{5}{x}$

    (C) $\frac{x}{30}$

    (D) $\frac{30}{x}$

    (E) $\frac{x}{120}$

Explanation: Question 1

1. $\frac{4}{x} + \frac{5}{x} + \frac{6}{x} = \frac{15}{x}$. In order for $\frac{15}{x}$ to be an integer, x must be a factor of 15, that is 1, 3, 5, or 15. Since these are all possible values of x, the answer choice that produces an integer for all of these values is correct. (A): $\frac{1}{5}$ is not an integer—eliminate; (B): $\frac{5}{3}$ is not an integer—eliminate; (C): $\frac{1}{30}$ is not an integer—eliminate; (D): $\frac{30}{x}$ produces an integer for all the factors of 15, so it is the correct answer. Another way to look at this would be to realize that if $\frac{15}{x}$ is an integer, then any multiple of $\frac{15}{x}$ must also be an integer. Answer choice (D) is $2 \times \frac{15}{x} = \frac{30}{x}$, and so must be an integer (just try dividing it by the possible values for x to check if you aren't sure). Notice that we began with choice (A) on a "which of the following" question. Were we rewarded for doing so? No! Always start with (D) or (E) on "which of the following" questions; they really are more likely to be the right answers on the GMAT.

An 800 test taker knows to "backsolve" from the answer choices. When the choices have variables in them, start with the last choice and work backwards. When the choices have concrete values, start with the middle value, so you can more quickly narrow down the answer choices.

PICKING NUMBERS

Now, before examining Question 2, it's time to introduce the other of the two most important math strategies, picking numbers.

Often the quickest way to solve a math problem is to give yourself a number or numbers to work with when they aren't provided to you. Rather than struggle with the math, just assume that a certain undefined value has a specific value.

What numbers should you pick? Well, pick easy, useful numbers. Why not use 1, 2, 3, 4, or 5 here? Of course, you could pick 13,459, 13,460, 13,461, 13,462, and 13,463. The math will still work out. But you will have driven yourself nuts and impressed no one.

Question 2

This question is a "Roman Numeral" question. This format allows for more than one correct answer—sort of. We say "sort of" because there's still only one correct answer. It's just that the correct answer may list more than one correct statement.

For example, Question 2 asks "which of the following must be true?" Then three different statements are given. It could be that only one of the statements is true; or it could be that only two of the statements are true; or it could be that all three statements are true. You have to pass judgment on each of the three statements, deciding whether it must be true or not. Then you pick the answer choice that lists exactly the true statements.

The good news is that eliminating choices on these questions is easy. If you determine that, for example, Statement I *is* correct, then you can immediately eliminate every choice that *doesn't* list Statement I. And if you determine that Statement I *isn't* correct, then you immediately eliminate every choice that *does* list Statement I.

If you aren't used to this question format, don't worry. You'll get the hang of it. It's actually much easier than the math that's being tested.

2. The average (arithmetic mean) of five consecutive integers is an odd number. Which of the following MUST be true?

 I. The largest of the integers is even.

 II. The sum of the integers is odd.

 III. The difference between the largest and smallest of the integers is an even number.

(A) I only
(B) II only
(C) III only
(D) I and II
(E) II and III

Explanation: Question 2

2. Pick five consecutive integers that are easy to work with and use them to check the validity of the statements. (When testing statements concerning odd and even numbers, in general, what is true for any odd number is true for all odd numbers, and what is true for any even number is true for all even numbers.) The average of an odd number of consecutive integers is the middle number. Since the average is odd, pick a group with an odd middle number. For example pick 1, 2, 3, 4, and 5. The largest of the integers is 5, which is odd, so Statement I is not true—eliminate choices (A) and (D) because they include it. The sum of the integers is 15, so II is true—eliminate choice (C) for not including it. The difference of 5 − 1 is 4, which is even, so Statement III is also true. So choice (E), II and III, is correct.

> An 800 test taker knows to "pick numbers"—useful numbers—to make working with variables and unknowns in a problem easier.

NUMBER PROPERTIES

Questions concerning number properties are some of the hardest non-word problem math questions.

By "number properties" we are referring to ideas like: is a number odd or even? Positive or negative? Greater or smaller than another number? As was mentioned earlier, these make for difficult questions because we don't tend to think in these terms when we do everyday math. You don't have to realize that 0 is an even number, but neither positive nor negative, in order to know that your bank account is empty.

Let's look at some tough number property questions.

Questions 3–4

3. If x, y, and z are positive integers such that $0 < x < y < z$ and x is even, y is odd, and z is prime, which of the following is a possible value of $x + y + z$?

   (A) 4
   (B) 5
   (C) 11
   (D) 15
   (E) 18

4. If a and b are integers such that $a + b = 5$, which of the following must be true?

   I. The product of a and b is odd.

   II. If a is odd, b is even.

   III. If a is negative, b is positive.

   (A) I only
   (B) II only
   (C) I and II only
   (D) II and III only
   (E) I, II, and III

Explanations: Questions 3–4

3. Work with z first, since as a prime number there are fewer possibilities for its value. Except for 2, all prime numbers are odd. z is greater than two other positive integers (x and y), so z must be at least 3. Since z cannot be 2, it must have an odd value. So $x + y + z$ is the sum of one even and two odd numbers. The sum of two odd numbers is even, so this is actually the sum of two even integers, which will be even. Therefore the sum of x, y, and z must be even and you can eliminate choices (B), (C), and (D). The smallest of the three integers, x, is even, so its lowest possible value is 2. Therefore the smallest values for y and z are 3 and 5, respectively. So the smallest possible sum of x, y, and z is $2 + 3 + 5 = 10$. Eliminate choice (A) as too small, and choice (E) remains as the correct answer.

4. Try out different values for a and b such that $a + b = 5$. If $a = 4$ and $b = 1$, the product is 4×1, or 4, which is even, so Statement I is not true. Eliminating any answer choice that contains Statement I leaves only choices (B) and (D). Since choices (B) and (D) both contain Statement II, Statement II must be correct, so let's look at Statement III. If $a + b = 5$, and a is negative, then if b is either negative or zero, $a + b$ is negative. Thus, if a is negative, then b is positive, making (D) the correct answer.

Questions 5–6

5. If the sum of five consecutive positive integers is a, then the sum of the next five consecutive integers in terms of a is

    (A) $a + 1$
    (B) $a + 5$
    (C) $a + 25$
    (D) $2a$
    (E) $5a$

6. If P represents the product of the first 15 positive integers, then P is NOT a multiple of

    (A) 99
    (B) 84
    (C) 72
    (D) 65
    (E) 57

Explanations: Questions 5–6

5. If the sum of the first five consecutive integers in a set is a, then each of the next five consecutive integers will be five greater than the corresponding value of each integer in the original set. Since there are five integers in the new set, its value is $a + 5(5) = a + 25$. (C) is correct. You can easily prove this to yourself by picking numbers.

6. If P is a product of the first 15 integers, then all of its factors will be combinations of these integers. P will not be a multiple of any number that has any different prime factor than P. The prime factors of P will be all the prime factors less than 15, that is 2, 3, 5, 7, 11, and 13. If any of the other answer choices have prime factors greater than this, they will not be factors of P.

Look at the answer choices, trying to find one that has a prime factor greater than 15. Start with choice (E) in questions in which you have to check the answer choices one by one. 57 factors to 19 3 3. Since 19 is prime and greater than 15, choice (E) is your answer. Once you've found an answer, don't waste time verifying the other choices.

Question 8 below is a number properties question with a bit of exponents mixed in. This is not uncommon. In the next section, you'll see some roots and exponents questions with a touch of number properties.

Questions 7–8

7. If $F < 0$, which of the following represents the largest value?

(A) $\dfrac{2F - 5}{2}$

(B) $\dfrac{4F - 1}{4}$

(C) $\dfrac{6F - 2}{6}$

(D) $\dfrac{7F - 5}{7}$

(E) $F - 1$

8. If $-\dfrac{1}{2} \le x \le -\dfrac{1}{3}$ and $-\dfrac{1}{4} \le y \le -\dfrac{1}{5}$, what is the minimum value of xy^2 ?

(A) $-\dfrac{1}{75}$

(B) $-\dfrac{1}{50}$

(C) $-\dfrac{1}{48}$

(D) $-\dfrac{1}{32}$

(E) $-\dfrac{1}{16}$

Explanations: Questions 7–8

7. Notice that in each of the fractional answer choices, the coefficient of F in the numerator is the same as the denominator. The fraction in each answer choice can be broken down into 2 new fractions, so rewrite each answer choice and compare their values:

(A): $\dfrac{2F-5}{2} = \dfrac{2F}{2} - \dfrac{5}{2} = F - \dfrac{5}{2}$

(B): $\dfrac{4F-1}{4} = \dfrac{4F}{4} - \dfrac{1}{4} = F - \dfrac{1}{4}$

(C): $\dfrac{6F-2}{6} = \dfrac{6F}{6} - \dfrac{2}{6} = F - \dfrac{1}{3}$

(D): $\dfrac{7F-5}{7} = \dfrac{7F}{7} - \dfrac{5}{7} = F - \dfrac{5}{7}$

(E): $F - 1$

In each answer choice a number is subtracted from F. Since the value of F is the same in each answer choice, just compare the numbers. The smaller the number you're subtracting, the larger the value of the entire expression, so choice (B) has the largest value. If you were confident of your ability with negative numbers and fractions, you could have picked some simple negative number for F, plugged it into the answer choices, and seen which was the largest.

An 800 test taker puts answer choices in a form that makes them easier to work with.

---

8. Since x is negative and y^2 is positive (the square of any number, except zero, is positive), xy^2 is negative, since a positive times a negative is negative. The minimum value of xy^2 occurs when xy^2 is as negative as possible, that is, farthest from zero. Take the values of x and y that have the largest absolute values:

$x = -\dfrac{1}{2}$ and $y = -\dfrac{1}{4}$. Then $xy^2 = \left(-\dfrac{1}{2}\right)\left(-\dfrac{1}{4}\right)^2 = \left(-\dfrac{1}{2}\right)\left(\dfrac{1}{16}\right) = -\dfrac{1}{32}$, making (D) correct.

ROOTS AND EXPONENTS

Along with the questions about number properties, those testing roots and exponents are the hardest straightforward arithmetic questions on the GMAT. If you aren't comfortable working with square roots, or don't remember the rules concerning adding and multiplying exponents, you will need to review this material before taking a crack at an 800 score.

The following questions should give you a pretty good (or gruesome) idea of your current skill level.

Questions 9–10

9. $3^5 + \dfrac{1}{3^5} =$

(A) 1

(B) 3

(C) $\dfrac{3^6 - 1}{3}$

(D) $\dfrac{3^{10} + 1}{3^5}$

(E) $\dfrac{3^{25}}{3^5 + 1}$

10. $\dfrac{3\sqrt{3}}{\sqrt{2}} \times \dfrac{4\sqrt{3}}{3} =$

(A) 3

(B) $6\sqrt{2}$

(C) 12

(D) $12\sqrt{2}$

(E) 36

Explanations: Questions 9–10

9. Remember that you can only add fractions with the same denominator.

Convert 3^5 to a fraction with a denominator of 3^5. Then the numbers can be added.

$$3^5 + \frac{1}{3^5} = \frac{3^5}{1} \times \left(\frac{3^5}{3^5} \right) + \frac{1}{3^5}$$

$$= \frac{3^{10}}{3^5} + \frac{1}{3^5} = \frac{3^{10} + 1}{3^5}$$

(D) it is.

10. $\dfrac{3\sqrt{3}}{\sqrt{2}} \times \dfrac{4\sqrt{3}}{3} = \dfrac{3\sqrt{3} \times 4\sqrt{3}}{\sqrt{2} \times 3}$

$$= \frac{4 \times \sqrt{3} \times \sqrt{3}}{\sqrt{2}}$$

$$= \frac{4 \times 3}{\sqrt{2}}$$

$$= \frac{12}{\sqrt{2}}$$

This isn't one of the answer choices because having a radical alone in the denominator is not considered "proper format." Rewrite the expression by multiplying both the numerator and denominator by $\sqrt{2}$ to get rid of the radical in the denominator: $\dfrac{12}{\sqrt{2}} \times \dfrac{\sqrt{2}}{\sqrt{2}} = \dfrac{12\sqrt{2}}{2} = 6\sqrt{2}$, or (B).

An 800 test taker "rewrites" his answer to match the form used in the answer choices.

Questions 11–12

11. $\dfrac{\sqrt{1{,}919}}{\sqrt{0.1919}} =$

   (A) 0.0001
   (B) 0.01
   (C) 100
   (D) 1,000
   (E) 10,000

12. $\dfrac{1}{3^8} + \dfrac{1}{3^9} + \dfrac{1}{3^9} + \dfrac{1}{3^9} =$

   (A) $\dfrac{1}{3^6}$

   (B) $\dfrac{2}{3^8}$

   (C) $\dfrac{4}{3^8}$

   (D) $\dfrac{1}{3^{36}}$

   (E) $\dfrac{4}{3^{36}}$

Explanations: Questions 11–12

11. You are not expected to know the square root of numbers like 1,919, so look for a way to attack this problem other than straight arithmetic.

The numbers look so alike, you should be able to do some canceling to simplify things.

$1{,}919 = 10{,}000 \times 0.1919$, so

$$\frac{\sqrt{1{,}919}}{\sqrt{0.1919}} = \frac{\sqrt{10{,}000 \times 0.1919}}{\sqrt{0.1919}} = \frac{\sqrt{10{,}000} \times \sqrt{0.19190}}{\sqrt{0.1919}} = \sqrt{10{,}000} = 100. \text{ (C) wins.}$$

12. Remember that you can only add fractions with the same denominator.

Rearrange $\dfrac{1}{3^8}$ so that it can be added to $\dfrac{1}{3^9}$. That is, try and turn $\dfrac{1}{3^8}$ into a fraction with 3^9 in the denominator.

Multiply $\dfrac{1}{3^8}$ by $\dfrac{3}{3}$ to get $\dfrac{1}{3^8} \times \dfrac{3}{3} = \dfrac{3}{3^8 \times 3} = \dfrac{3}{3^9}$. So $\dfrac{1}{3^8} + \dfrac{1}{3^9} + \dfrac{1}{3^9} + \dfrac{1}{3^9} = \dfrac{3}{3^9} + \dfrac{1}{3^9} + \dfrac{1}{3^9} + \dfrac{1}{3^9} = \dfrac{6}{3^9}$.
Canceling out a factor of 3 gives $\dfrac{6}{3^9} = \dfrac{3 \times 2}{3 \times 3^8} = \dfrac{2}{3^8}$, or (B).

Now try the following questions. **Tip:** consider the answer choices to Question 14 extra carefully.

Questions 13–14

13. The integers r and s are distinct, $r \neq 0$, and $s \neq 0$. If $r^2 s^2 = -rs$, which of the following must be true?

   I. $r = -1$

   II. $s = 1$

   III. $r - s = 0$

   (A) None
   (B) I only
   (C) II only
   (D) III only
   (E) I, II, and III

14. Which of the following represents the greatest value?

   (A) $\dfrac{\sqrt{2}}{\sqrt{3}} + \dfrac{\sqrt{3}}{\sqrt{4}} + \dfrac{\sqrt{4}}{\sqrt{5}} + \dfrac{\sqrt{5}}{\sqrt{6}}$

   (B) $\dfrac{2}{3} + \dfrac{3}{4} + \dfrac{4}{5} + \dfrac{5}{6}$

   (C) $\dfrac{2^2}{3^2} + \dfrac{3^2}{4^2} + \dfrac{4^2}{5^2} + \dfrac{5^2}{6^2}$

   (D) $1 - \dfrac{1}{3} + \dfrac{4}{5} - \dfrac{3}{4}$

   (E) $1 - \dfrac{3}{4} + \dfrac{4}{5} + \dfrac{1}{3}$

Explanations: Questions 13–14

13. You are told that $r^2s^2 = -rs$. Now $r^2s^2 = (rs)^2$, so you know that the square of rs is equal to $-rs$. This can only be true if $rs = 0$ or $rs = -1$. Since you are told that neither r nor s equals 0, $rs = -1$. Now check the statements one at a time, eliminating answer choices as you go.

Statement I: Since $rs = -1$, either $r = 1$ and $s = -1$, or $r = -1$ and $s = 1$. Since it could be either possibility, Statement I need not be true and you can eliminate choices (B) and (E).

Statement II: s can equal 1 or -1, so Statement II need not be true and you can eliminate choice (C) also.

Statement III: Since either $r = 1$ and $s = -1$, or $r = -1$ and $s = 1$, $r - s = 0$ will never be true. Eliminate choice (D), and (A) remains.

14. The numbers in the answer choices are all pretty difficult to deal with. This tells you one thing: that there must be an easier way of comparing the answer choices than actually working out the values of these expressions.

Compare the choices in pairs. As soon as you determine which of the pair is the smaller, eliminate it.

Remember, when positive fractions between 0 and 1 are squared, they get smaller.

Choice (C) is each of choice (B)'s fractions squared. So, eliminate (C).

Choice (B) is each of choice (A)'s fractions squared. So, eliminate (B).

Looking at (D) and (E), they have $1, \frac{4}{5}$ and $-\frac{3}{4}$ in common, so eliminate these numbers from both choices. Looking at the two together, you can eliminate choice (D) because it is smaller.

Now, compare (A) and (E). $\frac{\sqrt{2}}{\sqrt{3}} + \frac{\sqrt{3}}{\sqrt{4}}$ is considerably greater than $1 - \frac{3}{4}$, which is just $\frac{1}{4}$. Also $\frac{\sqrt{4}}{\sqrt{5}}$ is greater than $\frac{4}{5}$ and $\frac{\sqrt{5}}{\sqrt{6}}$ is greater than $\frac{1}{3}$. Therefore, choose (A).

CHAPTER FOURTEEN

Algebra

The algebra tested on the GMAT is of the straightforward high school variety: evaluate an expression, solve an equation or inequality, etc. But that doesn't mean you should take it lightly. If you're out of practice, be sure to review. The questions here offer a good opportunity for you to gauge your skills.

Let's pick up where we left off; the first question in the following practice set deals with a square root. The twist is the inequality.

ALGEBRA PRACTICE SET 1

1. If $8 < \sqrt{(n + 6)(n + 1)} < 9$ then n could equal

    (A) 5

    (B) 6

    (C) 7

    (D) 8

    (E) 9

2. In the formula $a = b^2c$, if b is multiplied by 2 and c is multiplied by 3, then a must be multiplied by

    (A) 4

    (B) 6

    (C) 9

    (D) 12

    (E) 18

3. $(R^c)(R^d)(R^e) = R^{-12}$. If $R > 0$, and c, d, and e are each different negative integers, what is the smallest that c could be?

    (A) −12

    (B) −10

    (C) −9

    (D) −6

    (E) −1

Explanation: Question 1

1. You need to solve an inequality, so treat it like an equation, doing the same thing to both sides while remembering two things: that multiplying an inequality by a negative number reverses the inequality, and that you will solve for a range of values rather than a single value.

Simplify the inequality.

Get rid of the radical sign by squaring all the elements in the inequality $8 < \sqrt{(n + 6)(n + 1)} < 9$. (The direction of the signs won't change because all the elements are greater than 0.)

So $8^2 < (n + 6)(n + 1) < 9^2$, that is, $64 < (n + 6)(n + 1) < 81$. Now try backsolving; the answer choice for which this relationship is true will be correct.

Choice (C): $(n + 6)(n + 1) = (7 + 6)(7 + 1) = 104$. This is greater than 81—discard and move onto a smaller answer choice.

Choice (B): $(n + 6)(n + 1) = (6 + 6)(6 + 1) = 84$. This is greater than 81, so the correct answer choice must be smaller still, which leaves choice (A).

Explanation: Question 2

2. Picking numbers makes this problem manageable. Since the formula expresses a in terms of b and c, pick values for b and c and plug them into the equation to get the corresponding value of a. If $b = 1$ and $c = 1$, then $a = (1^2)(1) = 1$. Now change b and c according to the instructions and plug into the equation again to see how this changes a. Multiplying b by 2 gives you 2, and multiplying c by 3 gives you 3, so now you have $a = (2^2)(3) = (4)(3) = 12$. Since the original value of a was 1, it must be multiplied by 12. (D) is correct.

Explanation: Question 3

3. The key is to know that $R^c R^d R^e = R^{c + d + e}$. So $R^{c + d + e} = R^{-12}$, and since both sides of the equation have base R, you can set the exponents equal: $c + d + e = -12$. Since you're looking for the smallest value of c, solve this equation for c: $c = -12 - d - e$. The more you subtract from -12, the smaller you make c, so you want the largest possible values of d and e. (Remember that both d and e represent different negative integers, so d cannot equal e.) The two largest negative integers are -1 and -2, so the smallest possible $c = -12 - (-1) - (-2) = -9$. (C) it is.

ALGEBRAIC EXPRESSIONS

Evaluating an algebraic expression means finding its value when the value of a variable or variables is specified. For example, the value of the expression $x^2 + 2x + 5$ when $x = 3$ is $3^2 + 2(3) + 5 = 9 + 6 + 5 = 20$. Not only does the GMAT have questions that will ask you to do just this, but many other GMAT questions will require you to do this as one step in finding the answer.

ALGEBRA PRACTICE SET 2

4. If $s \neq -2$, then $\dfrac{2s^2 - 8}{s + 2} =$

    (A) $s - 4$

    (B) $s + 4$

    (C) $s^2 + 4$

    (D) $s^2 - 4$

    (E) $2s - 4$

5. If $x = 3$ and $y = 4$, then $\dfrac{xy}{\frac{1}{x} + \frac{1}{y}} =$

    (A) $\dfrac{7}{12}$

    (B) $\dfrac{12}{7}$

    (C) 12

    (D) $\dfrac{144}{7}$

    (E) 84

Explanation: Question 4

4. When you see this fraction, you should be thinking, "I need to get rid of the $s + 2$ in the denominator." Try factoring out $s + 2$ from the numerator, so you can cancel it with the denominator and get a simpler expression. First, factor out a 2 from both terms in the numerator: $\frac{2s^2 - 8}{s + 2} = \frac{2(s^2 - 4)}{s + 2}$.

Now the $s^2 - 4$ is in the form of one of the common quadratics: $a^2 - b^2 = (a + b)(a - b)$ so the expression equals $\frac{2(s + 2)(s - 2)}{(s + 2)}$.

Cancel $s + 2$ from the numerator and denominator. This gives you $2(s - 2) = 2s - 4$.

(E) is correct.

Explanation: Question 5

5. Plug the values for x and y into the expression, and find its value.

$$\frac{xy}{\frac{1}{x} + \frac{1}{y}} = \frac{3 \times 4}{\frac{1}{3} + \frac{1}{4}} = \frac{12}{\frac{1}{3} + \frac{1}{4}}$$

Now find a common denominator for the fractions in the denominator:

$$\frac{12}{\frac{1}{3} + \frac{1}{4}} = \frac{12}{\frac{4}{12} + \frac{3}{12}}$$

$$= \frac{12}{\left(\frac{7}{12}\right)}$$

To divide by a fraction, invert and multiply. So $\frac{12}{\left(\frac{7}{12}\right)}$ equals $12 \times \frac{12}{7}$ which equals $\frac{144}{7}$.

Choice (D) is correct.

ALGEBRA PRACTICE SET 3

6. For all a and b, $a(a - b) + b(a - b) =$

    (A) $a^2 - 2ab + b^2$

    (B) $a^2 - 2ab - b^2$

    (C) $2a^2 + 2ab + b^2$

    (D) $a^2 + 2ab + b^2$

    (E) $a^2 - b^2$

7. If $abc \neq 0$, then $\dfrac{ab + bc + ac}{\dfrac{1}{a} + \dfrac{1}{b} + \dfrac{1}{c}} =$

    (A) $a + b + c$

    (B) abc

    (C) $\dfrac{1}{a + b + c}$

    (D) $\dfrac{1}{ab} + \dfrac{1}{ac} + \dfrac{1}{bc}$

    (E) $ab + ac + bc$

Explanation: Question 6

6. None of the answer choices has parentheses, so you must get rid of them in the expression given in the stem. So, multiply out the parentheses and combine like terms:

$$a(a - b) + b(a - b) = a \times a - a \times b + b \times a - b \times b$$

$$= a^2 - ab + ab - b^2$$

$$= a^2 - b^2$$

(E) is correct.

Explanation: Question 7

7. You have to start simplifying this complex fraction by combining the three fractions in the denominator into one. Use abc as the common denominator.

$$\frac{1}{a} + \frac{1}{b} + \frac{1}{c} = \frac{bc}{abc} + \frac{ac}{abc} + \frac{ab}{abc}$$

$$= \frac{ac + ab + bc}{abc}$$

The whole expression now becomes:

$$\frac{ab + bc + ac}{\dfrac{ab + bc + ac}{abc}}$$

To divide by a fraction you invert and multiply, so:

$$\frac{ab + bc + ac}{\dfrac{ab + bc + ac}{abc}} = (ab + bc + ac)\frac{abc}{ab + bc + ac} = abc$$

(B) wins.

ALGEBRAIC EQUATIONS

Equations are what everyone always remembers about algebra. The GMAT will make you solve them. No surprise there.

For simple equations, use mathematical operations (add, multiply, etc.) to isolate the variable; that is, to get the variable by itself on one side of the equal sign. The quantity on the other side of the equal sign is your solution, the value of the variable.

For more complicated equation questions, the GMAT will ask you to solve for a variable "in terms of" another variable. In this case, get the first variable alone on one side of the equation. On the other side you will have an expression that contains the variable you are solving "in terms of."

Let's run through a lengthy sample of the "usual suspects":

ALGEBRA PRACTICE SET 4

8. If $8 < x < 9$, and $x^2 = (10 - y)(10 + y)$, which of the following is a possible value for y?

   (A) −7
   (B) −6
   (C) 3
   (D) 4
   (E) 5

9. If $(-1) \times x = 1$, which of the following is an integer?

   I. $\dfrac{x}{2 + x}$

   II. $\dfrac{x - 2}{3}$

   III. $\dfrac{x + 1}{4}$

   (A) None
   (B) I only
   (C) I and II only
   (D) II and III only
   (E) I, II, and III

Explanation: Question 8

8. This problem is best solved by working backwards from the answer choices. If $8 < x < 9$, then $64 < x^2 < 81$. Multiplying through the expression given for x^2, you get $x^2 = 10^2 - y^2$ or $x^2 = 100 - y^2$. Each answer choice gives a possible value for y, so try plugging each of these values into the equation, starting with choice (E), until you get a value for x^2 such that $64 < x^2 < 81$.

(E) $x^2 = 100 - 5^2 = 100 - 25 = 75$; $64 < 75 < 81$, so this choice is correct. Let's check the other answer choices just for the sake of the discussion.

(D) $x^2 = 100 - 4^2 = 100 - 16 = 84$—eliminate.

(C) $x^2 = 100 - 3^2 = 100 - 9 = 91$—eliminate.

(B) $x^2 = 100 - (-6)^2 = 100 - 36 = 64$—eliminate.

(A) $x^2 = 100 - (-7)^2 = 100 = 49 = 51$—eliminate.

An 800 test taker knows to backsolve when working with algebraic equations.

Explanation: Question 9

9. Solve the given equation for x and then plug that value for x into each of the three Roman Numeral statements to determine which produce an integer. Dividing both sides of the equation by -1, you find that $x = -1$. So I is $\dfrac{-1}{2 + (-1)} = \dfrac{-1}{1} = -1$, which is an integer; II is $\dfrac{(-1) - 2}{3} = -1$, again an integer; III is $\dfrac{(-1) + 1}{4} = \dfrac{0}{4} = 0$, an integer. So I, II, and III are all integers. (E) it is.

ALGEBRA PRACTICE SET 5

10. If $x > 2$ and $y = \dfrac{x}{x-2}$, which of the following is equal to $\dfrac{1}{y}$?

    (A) $2 - \dfrac{1}{x}$

    (B) $1 - \dfrac{2}{x}$

    (C) $\dfrac{2}{x-1}$

    (D) $\dfrac{-2}{x-1}$

    (E) $\dfrac{2x}{x-1}$

11. If q is equal to one-half of the sum of 6, 7, 5, and q, then $q =$

    (A) 9

    (B) 12

    (C) 18

    (D) 27

    (E) 36

Explanation: Question 10

10. $\dfrac{1}{y}$ is the reciprocal of y, and since $y = \dfrac{x}{x-2}$, $\dfrac{1}{y}$ is equal to the reciprocal of $\dfrac{x}{x-2}$. To get the reciprocal, just flip the fraction so that the numerator becomes the denominator and vice versa:

The reciprocal of $\dfrac{x}{x-2}$ is $\dfrac{x-2}{x}$. This doesn't match any of the answer choices, so try writing it in a different form: $\dfrac{x-2}{x} = \dfrac{x}{x} - \dfrac{2}{x} = 1 - \dfrac{2}{x}$. (B) is correct.

An 800 test taker knows that the solution must sometimes be written in a different form to match the answer choice.

Explanation: Question 11

11. "The sum of 6, 7, 5, and q" is $6 + 7 + 5 + q$, or $18 + q$. One-half of this sum is $\dfrac{18+q}{2}$ and we are told that this is also equal to q.

So $q = \dfrac{18+q}{2}$

   $2q = 18 + q$

   $q = 18$

(C) wins.

ALGEBRA PRACTICE SET 6

12. If $x > 1$ and $\dfrac{a}{b} = 1 - \dfrac{1}{x}$, then $\dfrac{b}{a} =$

(A) x

(B) $x - 1$

(C) $\dfrac{x-1}{x}$

(D) $\dfrac{x}{x-1}$

(E) $\dfrac{1}{x} - 1$

13. If $d = \dfrac{c-b}{a-b}$, then $b =$

(A) $\dfrac{c-d}{a-d}$

(B) $\dfrac{c+d}{a+d}$

(C) $\dfrac{ca-d}{ca+d}$

(D) $\dfrac{c-ad}{1-d}$

(E) $\dfrac{c+ad}{d-1}$

Explanation: Question 12

12. Since $\dfrac{b}{a}$ is the reciprocal of $\dfrac{a}{b}$, $\dfrac{b}{a}$ is the reciprcal of $1 - \dfrac{1}{x}$.

Combine the terms in $1 - \dfrac{1}{x}$ and then find the reciprocal: $1 - \dfrac{1}{x} = \dfrac{x}{x} - \dfrac{1}{x} = \dfrac{x-1}{x}$.

The reciprocal of this expression is $\dfrac{x}{x-1}$.

Therefore $\dfrac{b}{a} = \dfrac{x}{x-1}$.

(D) is correct.

Explanation: Question 13

13. To answer this, you'll have to solve for b; so you have to get it all alone on one side of the equation.

Solve for b: $d = \dfrac{c-b}{a-b}$

Multiply both sides by $a - b$: $d(a - b) = c - b$

Clear parentheses: $ad - bd = c - b$

Isolate all b terms on one side of the equation: $b - bd = c - ad$

Factor out b: $b(1 - d) = c - ad$

Divide both sides by $(1 - d)$: $b = \dfrac{c - ad}{1 - d}$

(D) is correct.

ALGEBRA PRACTICE SET 7

14. If $-2 \leq x \leq 2$ and $3 \leq y \leq 8$, which of the following represents the range of all possible values of $y - x$?

   (A) $5 \leq y - x \leq 6$
   (B) $1 \leq y - x \leq 5$
   (C) $1 \leq y - x \leq 6$
   (D) $5 \leq y - x \leq 10$
   (E) $1 \leq y - x \leq 10$

15. If $a = 2b$, $\frac{1}{2}b = c$, and $4c = 3d$, what is the value of $\frac{d}{a}$?

   (A) $\frac{1}{3}$

   (B) $\frac{3}{4}$

   (C) 1

   (D) $\frac{4}{3}$

   (E) 3

Explanation: Question 14

14. The range of possible values is given by the largest possible value minus the smallest possible value. The greatest value of $y - x$ will occur when y is as large as possible and x is as small as possible. That is, $y - x \leq 8 - (-2) = 10$. The smallest value of $y - x$ will occur when y is as small as possible and x is as large as possible. That is, $y - x \geq 3 - 2 = 1$. So $1 \leq y - x \leq 10$. (E) it is.

Explanation: Question 15

15. To find the ratio of d to a, you need to get a and d together in a single equation. The way to do this is to substitute for the variables b and c in order to eliminate them. Working from the information that $a = 2b$, we get $\dfrac{a}{2} = b$. We can substitute this into the equation $\dfrac{1}{2}b = c$ to get $\dfrac{1}{2} \times \dfrac{a}{2} = c$, or $\dfrac{a}{4} = c$. Since $4c = 3d$, we can substitute for c to get $4\left(\dfrac{a}{4}\right) = 3d$, or $a = 3d$. So $1 = 3 \times \dfrac{d}{a}$ and $\dfrac{d}{a} = \dfrac{1}{3}$. (A) is correct.

CHAPTER FIFTEEN

Geometry

As with the other math topics, GMAT geometry draws from your high school days. It's a sampling of angles, triangles, rectangles, circles, and the (x, y) coordinate plane. This is true for both the straight math problems and—as you'll soon see—the word problems.

The defining feature of GMAT geometry problems, to the extent they can be said to have one, is that they tend to combine different topics in the same question. That is, you will rarely get a question testing only a triangle or only a rectangle. More common is a question that tests your ability with both.

TRIANGLES, RECTANGLES, CIRCLES

Triangles, rectangles, and circles are the GMAT "Gang of Three" when it comes to geometry. These figures are the most commonly tested. And as you're about to see, they are most commonly tested together.

GEOMETRY PRACTICE SET 1

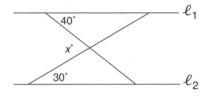

1. In the figure above, if $\ell_1 \parallel \ell_2$, what is the value of x ?

    (A) 70
    (B) 100
    (C) 110
    (D) 140
    (E) 150

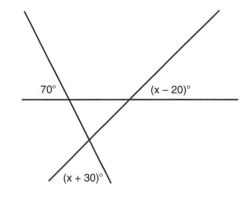

2. In the figure above, $x =$

    (A) 30
    (B) 50
    (C) 60
    (D) 80
    (E) It cannot be determined from the information given

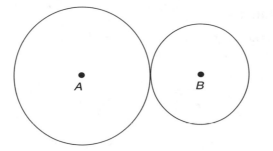

3. In the figure above, circles A and B are tangent. The circumference of circle A is 6π and the circumference of circle B is 4π. If point P lies on circle A and point Q lies on circle B, what is the greatest possible distance between points P and Q?

    (A) 5
    (B) $5\sqrt{2}$
    (C) 10
    (D) 5π
    (E) 10π

Explanation: Question 1

1. Fill information into the diagram as you go along. The transversals form two pairs of alternate interior angles, as below.

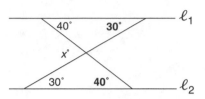

The interior angles of a triangle sum to 180°, so the angle supplementary to x is $180° - 30° - 40° = 110°$.

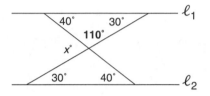

If the angle marked x is supplementary to an angle of 110°, then $x = 180 - 110 = 70$.
(A) is correct.

Explanation: Question 2

2. Vertical angles are equal. Therefore, each of the angle measures given is also the measure of its vertical angle, and each vertical angle happens to be an interior angle of the triangle. The sum of the interior angles of a triangle is 180°. So the three angles together measure 180°, and $70 + (x - 20) + (x + 30) = 180$. So $70 + 2x + 10 = 180$, $2x + 80 = 180$; $2x = 100$, $x = 50$. (B) wins.

Explanation: Question 3

3. The diagram below shows that P and Q are as far apart as possible when separated by a diameter of both circles

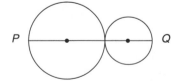

The circumference of circle A is 6π, so the diameter of A is 6 ($2\pi \times$ radius $= \pi \times$ diameter $=$ circumference). Circle B's circumference is 4π, so its diameter is 4. Therefore, the greatest possible distance between point P and point Q is $6 + 4$, or 10. (C) it is.

GEOMETRY PRACTICE SET 2

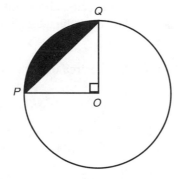

4. In circle O above, if △POQ is a right triangle and radius OP = 2, what is the area of the shaded region?

    (A) 4π − 2
    (B) 4π − 4
    (C) 2π − 2
    (D) 2π − 4
    (E) π − 2

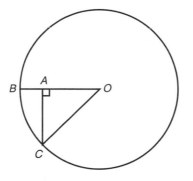

5. If the area of the circle with center O above is 100π and AC has a length of 6, what is the length of AB ?

    (A) 2
    (B) 3
    (C) 4
    (D) 5
    (E) 6

Explanation: Question 4

4. The area of the shaded region is the area of sector OPQ minus the area of $\triangle POQ$. Since $\angle POQ$ is 90°, sector OPQ is a quarter-circle. The circle's radius, OP, is 2, so its area is $\pi 2^2 = 4\pi$. Therefore, the quarter-circle's area is π.

$\triangle POQ$'s area is $\frac{1}{2}(b \times h) = \frac{1}{2}(2 \times 2) = 2$. So the area of the shaded region is $\pi - 2$. (E) is correct.

Explanation: Question 5

5. Since we know the area of the circle, we can find the length of radii OB and OC. We can't find AB directly, but if we can find the length of OA, then AB is just the difference between OB and OA.

The circle's area, πr^2, is 100π, so its radius is $\sqrt{100}$ or 10. So OC is 10 and, as we've been told, AC is 6. $\triangle AOC$ is a right triangle so we can use the Pythagorean theorem to find OA. Ideally, you should recognize that $\triangle AOC$ is a 3-4-5 right triangle; OC is twice 5, AC is twice 3, so OA must be twice 4, or 8. (If you didn't see this: $(OA)^2 + 6^2 = 10^2$, $(OA)^2 + 36 = 100$, $(OA)^2 = 64$, $OA = 8$.) AB is the difference between the radius OB and segment OA, so its length is $10 - 8$, or 2. (A) wins.

An 800 test taker "sees" lengths and regions that need to be measured as parts of larger lengths and areas with already known measurements.

GEOMETRY PRACTICE SET 3

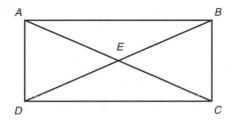

6. In the figure above, *ABCD* is a rectangle. If the area of Δ*AEB* is 8, what is the area of Δ*ACD*?

    (A) 8
    (B) 12
    (C) 16
    (D) 24
    (E) 32

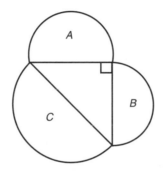

7. In the figure above, if semicircles *A* and *B* each have area 4π, what is the area of semicircle *C*?

    (A) 4π
    (B) 4π√2
    (C) 6π
    (D) 8π
    (E) 16

Explanation: Question 6

6. $\triangle CDE$ has the same area as $\triangle AEB$; they're congruent triangles. But we want the area of $\triangle ACD$, which means that we need to know $\triangle ADE$'s area as well. So we want to find a relationship between $\triangle ADE$'s area and $\triangle CDE$'s area.

Let's make AD the base of $\triangle ADE$. Its height, a line drawn perpendicularly from E (the rectangle's midpoint, where its diagonals meet) to AD is just one-half the length of side DC. So the area of $\triangle ADE$ is $\frac{1}{2} \times AD \times \frac{DC}{2} = \frac{1}{4} \times AD \times DC$.

Applying similar reasoning, let DC be the base of $\triangle CDE$. Its height is then a line drawn perpendicularly from E to DC which is one-half the length of side AD. So $\triangle CDE$'s area is: $\frac{1}{2} \times DC \times \frac{AD}{2} = \frac{1}{4} \times DC \times AD$.

The two triangles are equal in area; each has an area of 8. Therefore, the area of $\triangle ACD$ is $8 + 8 = 16$. (C) is correct.

Explanation: Question 7

7. The areas of semicircles A and B are equal, so their diameters are equal. Therefore, $\triangle ABC$ is an isosceles right triangle, and the ratio of each leg to the hypotenuse (the diameter of semicircle C) is $1:1:\sqrt{2}$.

Method I: Move step-by-step from the area given for semicircles A and B to the radius of semicircle C, and find its area with that. The area of a small semicircle is $\frac{1}{2} \times \pi r^2 = 4\pi$; $\pi r^2 = 8\pi$; $r^2 = 8$; $r = \sqrt{8}$. Each leg of the triangle is a diameter, so its length is twice the radius or $2\sqrt{8}$. Therefore, the hypoenuse of the triangle, h, is found with the Pythagorean theorem:

$$(2\sqrt{8})^2 + (2\sqrt{8})^2 = h^2$$
$$32 + 32 = h^2$$
$$64 = h^2$$
$$8 = h,$$

which is also the diameter of semicircle C. The radius is half of 8, or 4. The area of semicircle C is $\frac{1}{2} \times \pi 4^2 = 8\pi$.

Method II: Use the ratios more directly. Since the diameters of circles A, B, and C are in the ratio $1:1:\sqrt{2}$, the ratio of their areas will be $1^2:1^2:(\sqrt{2})^2$ or $1:1:2$. C must have twice the area of A, or 8π. (D) is correct.

An 800 test taker uses the diagrams to record, and derive, important information.

KAPLAN

GEOMETRY PRACTICE SET 4

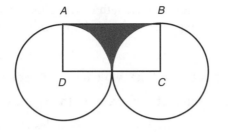

8. In the figure above, *ABCD* is a rectangle and *DA* and *CB* are radii of the circles shown. If *AB* = 4, what is the perimeter of the shaded region?

   (A) $2\pi + 4$
   (B) $4\pi + 4$
   (C) $4\pi + 8$
   (D) $8\pi + 8$
   (E) $8\pi + 16$

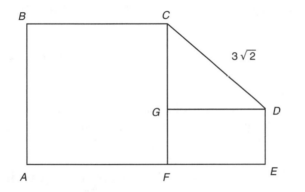

9. In the figure above, the area of square *ABCF* is 25 and $\triangle CDG$ is an isosceles right triangle. What is the area of rectangle *DEFG*?

   (A) 15
   (B) 12
   (C) 9
   (D) $6\sqrt{2}$
   (E) 6

Explanation: Question 8

8. The perimeter of the shaded region is the length of AB, plus the length of the two arcs which are part of the perimeter of the shaded region. We already know $AB = 4$, so we have only to find the length of the two arcs.

Since $ABCD$ is a rectangle, $DA = CB$ and the two circles have equal radii. DC consists of a radius of the circle on the left and a radius of the circle on the right, so $DC = 2r$. But $DC = AB = 4$. Therefore, $2r = 4$, $r = 2$. The sectors are both quarter-circles (the central angle is a right angle). The arc length of a quarter-circle is $\frac{1}{4}$ of the circumference of the whole circle, or $\frac{1}{4} \times 2\pi r$. So, the perimeter of each quarter-circle is $\frac{1}{4} \times 2 \times \pi \times 2 = \pi$. The perimeter of the shaded region is $4 + 2 \times \pi$, or $4 + 2\pi$. That makes (A) the winner.

Explanation: Question 9

9. You have to find the area of rectangle $DEFG$ which is embedded in a diagram with two other shapes. The area of rectangle $DEFG = \text{length} \times \text{width} = GD \times GF$.

Remember in multiple figure problems that the solution usually lies in the features that the shapes share.

The length of GF is equal to $CF - CG$, so we need to find CF and CG in order to find GF.

We're also told that triangle CDG is an isosceles right triangle. You can use the Pythagorean theorem or the known ratios of the sides of an isosceles triangle to find the length of leg GD, which is what we'll call the length of the rectangle. Also, $GD = CG$, and CG is one of the two lengths you need to find in order to find the width, GF.

We're told that the area of the square $ABCF$ is 25. The area of a square is the length of one side squared. So each side is equal to $\sqrt{25} = 5$. CF, then, equals 5.

The leg length to leg length to hypotenuse length ratio of an isosceles right triangle is $1{:}1{:}\sqrt{2}$. We know that here the hypotenuse is $3\sqrt{2}$. So the legs CG and GD each have a length of 3. Now let's go back and try to figure out what GF equals. $GF = CF - CG$. So $GF = 5 - 3$ or 2.

Now we know that the width GF of rectangle $DEFG$ is 2. The length, GD, is 3. So the area is 3×2 or 6, choice (E).

COORDINATE GEOMETRY

As you may recall from high school, coordinate geometry deals with two-dimensional planes. The planes are defined by an *x*-axis (which runs horizontally) and a *y*-axis (which runs vertically).

A location on the plane is expressed in (*x*, *y*) coordinates.

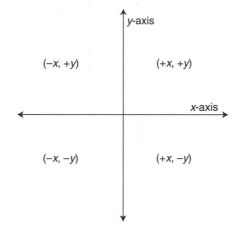

Now try a few questions. Bear in mind that you can always draw a quick coordinate plane if it helps you (and the question doesn't provide one).

GEOMETRY PRACTICE SET 5

10. In the *xy*-plane, at what point does the graph of the equation $x + 3y = 9$ cross the *y*-axis?

(A) (−3, 0)
(B) (0, −3)
(C) (0, 3)
(D) (0, 9)
(E) (9, 0)

11. Point *Q* is on the same line as (0, 0) and (3, 9). Which of the following could be point *Q* ?

(A) (0, 1)
(B) (1, 3)
(C) (2, 4)
(D) (−3, 9)
(E) (−6, −2)

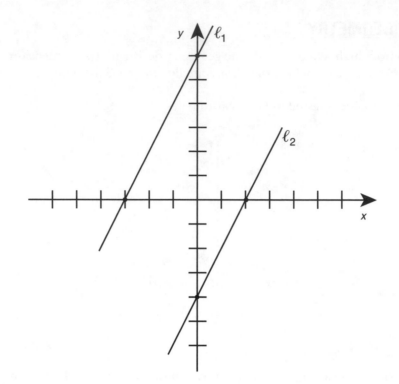

12. The equation of line ℓ_1 is $y = 2x + 6$. Line ℓ_2 is parallel to line ℓ_1. Which of the following is the equation of line ℓ_2?

    (A) $y = -4x + 2$

    (B) $y = -2x + 4$

    (C) $y = 2x - 4$

    (D) $y = 2x + 4$

    (E) $y = 4x + 2$

Explanation: Question 10

10. Since every point on the y-axis has an x-coordinate of 0, when a line crosses the y-axis, its x-coordinate is 0 (that already eliminates choices (1) and (5)). We can substitute $x = 0$ into the equation to find the y-coordinate of the line when it crosses the y-axis. $x + 3y = 9, 0 + 3y = 9; 3y = 9, y = 3$. So the line crosses the y-axis at $(0, 3)$, making (C) correct.

Explanation: Question 11

11. You can directly figure out the equation for the line through $(0,0)$ and $(3,9)$. The slope of a line is $\frac{y_2 - y_1}{x_2 - x_1}$, so the slope of this line is $\frac{9-0}{3-0} = \frac{9}{3} = 3$. The equation for a line is $y = mx + b$ where m is the slope and b is the y-coordinate at which the line crosses the y-axis. This line crosses the y-axis at $(0,0)$, so $b = 0$. Therefore, the equation for the line is $y = 3x$. Among the points given, only $(1, 3)$ fits that equation, making (B) the right answer.

If you forgot the formula for a line, you could have done the same thing informally by noticing that, starting from the origin, the y-coordinate increases by 3 for every 1 the x-coordinate increases (and conversely, the y-coordinate must decrease by 3 for every 1 the x-coordinate decreases). Only one of the points can be reached from the origin $(0, 0)$ this way.

Explanation: Question 12

12. Since parallel lines on the coordinate plane have the same slope, the correct answer must have the same slope as $y = 2x + 6$.

The answer choices are in $y = mx + b$ form, where m is the slope and b is the y-intercept. Find the slope and the y-intercept of ℓ_2.

$y = 2x + 6$ is in the $y = mx + b$ form, so the slope is the coefficient of the x term, or 2. This means we can eliminate choices (A), (B), and (E)—none of them has slope +2. Since line ℓ_2 crosses the y-axis at the point $(0, -4)$, the y-intercept is -4, and the equation of the line must be $y = 2x - 4$. (C) is correct.

An 800 test taker sometimes uses scratch paper to sketch the coordinate plane when it isn't provided, in order to make the work easier.

Finally, a little taste of the geometry of solids. If you're disappointed to get only one tough solids question here, don't worry. You'll find more in the Word Problems section, as that is where the GMAT test makers like to put them.

GEOMETRY PRACTICE SET 6

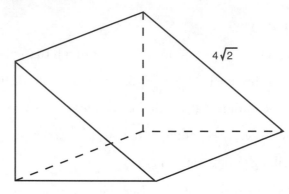

13. If the solid above is half of a cube, then the volume of the solid is

   (A) 16
   (B) 32
   (C) 42
   (D) 64
   (E) $64\sqrt{2}$

Explanation: Question 13

13. This requires some intuition. The solid is half of a cube; you can imagine an identical solid lying on the top of this one to form the complete cube. Then it becomes clear that the line segment with length $4\sqrt{2}$ is the diagonal of a square face. The diagonal is the hypotenuse of a right isosceles triangle with the two edges of the cube as legs; you can find the length of an edge by using the sides ratio for such triangles. In right isosceles triangles, the hypotenuse is $\sqrt{2}$ times either of the legs. Since the hypotenuse has length $4\sqrt{2}$, the legs (which are also the edges of the cube) have length 4. So the cube's volume is $4^3 = 64$. *But be careful, that's not the answer to the question!* The volume of the SOLID is half the cube's volume, or 32. (B) it is.

That wraps up our tour of the difficult "straight math" Problem Solving questions. Next, you'll tackle what are, for most people, the toughest of the tough—word problems.

PROBLEM SOLVING— WORD PROBLEMS

CHAPTER SIXTEEN

The Word Problems Challenge

WORD PROBLEMS

Perhaps most people's least favorite math questions are word problems. Much of that visceral fear is, believe it or not, media driven. Whenever a movie or TV show wants an example of an impossible intellectual task, they drag out the word problem. Comedians do the same. Somehow or other, way back in the mists of pre-history, the word problem became the epitome of Insoluble Math.

But this long-held fear of word problems is completely misplaced. In fact, on the GMAT the math required to solve word problems is usually easier than the math tested by the straightforward math problems. The test maker relies on the words to add in the extra difficulty. As long as you read through the problem carefully, you can translate the English into math—easy math—and rack up the points. Misunderstanding what the question says is the cause of many errors on word problems.

But don't worry about that. This section will offer some strategies you can use to your advantage.

Word Problem Strategies

Here's the general approach to any word problem:

1. Read through the whole question. Do this to get a sense of what's going on. You want to know the basic situation described, the type of information you've been given, and—most important of all—what exactly you are being asked.

2. Identify the different variables or unknowns and label them. For example, if the problem discusses Charlie's and Veronica's warts, you may wish to use "c" to represent Charlie's warts and "v" to represent Veronica's warts. Notice that we didn't use "x" and "y." If we had, we might later forget whether x represented Charlie's warts or Veronica's.

3. Translate the problem into math. This usually entails rewriting the English sentences into equations or statements. The sentence "Veronica has four fewer warts than Charlie has" would become: $v = c - 4$. Notice that the math terms are not in the same order as the English terms in the sentence. When you translate, you are translating the ideas. The idea here is "four fewer warts than Charlie." That means $c - 4$, not $4 - c$!

4. Tackle the math. Solve the equations. Determine the value that the question is asking you for.

5. Check your work, if you have time.

The Translation Table

It's a good idea to familiarize yourself with the mathematical meanings of some of the most common words used in word problems. Knowing these equivalencies can provide you with a specific, concrete starting point, especially when a word problem seems incomprehensible.

The table below can be a lifesaver—the sort of thing you might want to tattoo on your inside forearm. But that would be wrong.

English	"Mathish"
equals is, was, will be has costs adds up to is the same as	=
times of multiplied by product of twice, double, triple, half	×
per out of divided by each ratio of __ to __	÷
and plus added to sum combined total	+
minus subtracted from less than decreased by difference between	−
what how much how many a number	x, n, (variable)

Remember: If you are completely baffled by a word problem, look for some of the words in the left-hand column. Then work from their math equivalent and try to construct an equation.

CHAPTER SEVENTEEN

Arithmetic and Algebra Word Problems

The majority of word problems you'll encounter on the GMAT will test either arithmetic or algebra, and very often both. That is to say, you will be given tasks concerning fractions, ratios, percents, averages, etc. Since you will often be solving for an unknown, you'll often have to use some algebra even on the arithmetic questions.

To further muddy the waters, word problems will often concern two or more math topics or techniques. They purport to represent "real world" situations, after all, and the real world doesn't come packaged in tidy little topics. In the real world, problems involve all sorts of math tasks.

The trick, of course, is to unpack the English to get at the specific math being tested, and then to answer the *question asked*. Since many word problems contain more than one step, you may have to solve for more than one value. Picking the answer choice with the value that is asked for, rather than another value, is then a simple but often messed up last step.

Let's examine some of the most common arithmetic and algebra question types.

FRACTIONS, RATIOS, AND PROPORTIONS

Perhaps the most straightforward word problems—if you're willing to admit that any word problems can be straightforward—are those involving basic math concepts. By far the most common of these test the related concepts of fractions, ratios, and proportions. Look at these two:

Questions 1–2

1. At College X, the faculty-to-student ratio is 1:9. If two-thirds of the students are female and one-quarter of the faculty is female, what fraction of the combined students and faculty are female?

    (A) $\frac{11}{24}$

    (B) $\frac{5}{8}$

    (C) $\frac{25}{56}$

    (D) $\frac{11}{12}$

    (E) It cannot be determined from the information given.

2. An empty metal box weighs 10 percent of its total weight when filled with varnish. If the weight of a partly filled box is one-half that of a completely filled box, what fraction of the box is filled?

    (A) $\frac{3}{5}$

    (B) $\frac{5}{9}$

    (C) $\frac{1}{2}$

    (D) $\frac{4}{9}$

    (E) $\frac{2}{5}$

Don't worry about the fact that the second question includes percents and fractions. That is common; a percent is a fraction with 100 as the denominator. As previously mentioned, the boundaries between types of questions—especially in word problems—aren't very clear-cut. Because they are so common, percent questions will be covered separately in this chapter.

Both of the previous examples are susceptible to the powerful Kaplan strategy of **picking numbers**. For example, in the second question, assume a full box of varnish weighs a nice, round 100 lbs. Then attack the problem. While this sort of shortcut may be frowned on by math purists, the GMAT doesn't give a rat's behind how you get to the answer. Do it the way that is fastest for you.

A final reminder: Pick *useful* numbers. *Intelligent* numbers. You don't get extra credit for making the job tougher. When you're working with percents, use 100. For other questions, pick numbers that are easy to work with.

Questions 1–2: Answers and Explanations

Explanation: Faculty:Student Ratio

1. Pick a number for the smallest given quantity described in the question—the number of female faculty: if there's 1 female member of the faculty, then the total number of faculty is 4 times 1, or 4. There are 9 times as many students, or 36 students. $\frac{2}{3}$ of 36 students are female, so there are 24 female students. Therefore, the total number of females is 1 + 24, or 25, and the total number of students and faculty is 36 + 4, or 40. That makes the fraction $\frac{25}{40}$, or $\frac{5}{8}$. (B) is correct.

Explanation: A Box of Varnish

2. Pick numbers. Since you are dealing with percents, pick 100, so say the box weighs 100 pounds when full. In this case, the weight of the metal box is 10 percent, or $\frac{1}{10}$, of 100 pounds, which is 10 pounds. That leaves 90 pounds of varnish to fill the box. The weight of the partly filled box is half of 100 pounds, or 50 pounds. Since the box itself weighs 10 pounds, 40 pounds of varnish are in the partly filled box. Since the box has the capacity to hold 90 pounds of varnish, the box is $\frac{4}{9}$ full. (D) is correct.

Now, how much fun would it have been to work with 47 female faculty members? Or a full box of varnish that weighs 217.18 kg? Not very. . . Of course, you could solve the problems using these bizarre numbers, but that's a strategy for the Mental Hospital Admission Test, not the GMAT.

An 800 test taker often decides to "pick numbers" when working with word problems. This works best when the numbers picked are smart numbers. For percents, use 100. For other situations, use small integers.

Now let's tackle a few more fraction and ratio questions.

Questions 3–4

3. A piece of string is marked in segments of one-fourth the length of the string and also in segments of one-third the length of the string. If the string is then cut at each mark, which of the following expresses all the different lengths of the bits of string, in fractions of the original length?

    (A) $\frac{1}{12}$ and $\frac{1}{4}$ only

    (B) $\frac{1}{4}$ and $\frac{1}{3}$ only

    (C) $\frac{1}{6}$, $\frac{1}{4}$, and $\frac{1}{3}$

    (D) $\frac{1}{12}$, $\frac{1}{6}$, and $\frac{1}{4}$

    (E) $\frac{1}{12}$, $\frac{1}{6}$, and $\frac{1}{3}$

4. An assortment of candies consists of x chocolates and y buttercreams. If 2 chocolates are added and 3 buttercreams are removed, what fraction of the remaining candies, in terms of x and y, are chocolates?

    (A) $\frac{x+2}{y}$

    (B) $\frac{x}{y-1+2}$

    (C) $\frac{x-1}{x+y+2}$

    (D) $\frac{x+2}{x+y-1}$

    (E) $\frac{x+3}{x+y}$

When working with a word problem, it is often helpful to make a diagram. This is especially true with geometry word problems that don't come with one. (We'll tackle geometry problems a little later.) It can also be useful when dealing with non-geometry word problems. For example:

Questions 3–4: Answers and Explanations

Explanation: String Theory

3. This is one of those word problems that you should translate into a diagram. You have a piece of string marked into fourths and thirds. To make things easy, assume that the string is 1 foot long. Whatever the actual length, the relative lengths of the pieces will be the same. 1 foot is also convenient, as it equals 12 inches, and 12 is the least common denominator of the fractions in the problem. Making cuts every one-fourth the length of the string means making cuts every 3 inches. A cut every third the length of the string means a cut every 4 inches.

Draw the diagram:

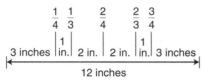

We see that some of the segments are 3 inches long, some are 2, and some are 1, or $\frac{1}{4}$, $\frac{1}{6}$, and $\frac{1}{12}$ of the whole. (D) is therefore correct.

> An 800 test taker doesn't hesitate to make a diagram whenever it is helpful for conceptualizing the problem.

Explanation: Candies

4. You are asked to find what fraction of all the candies will be chocolates after the total has been adjusted. This fraction is simply the number of chocolates over the total number of candies after the change has been made.

Find the number of chocolates and buttercreams by translating the stem. Then divide the number of chocolates by the total number of chocolates and buttercreams. Alternatively, since all the answer choices contain variables, you could try picking numbers.

You initially had x chocolates, but now have two more, or $x + 2$. The original number of buttercreams was y, and 3 were removed, so the number of buttercreams is $y - 3$.

So the fraction of candies which are chocolates =

$$\frac{\text{Number of chocolates}}{\text{Number of candies}} = \frac{x + 2}{x + 2 + y - 3} = \frac{x + 2}{x + y - 1}$$

Picking Numbers

If translating this problem was difficult—many people have trouble sorting out parts and totals—you should have tried plugging in numbers. For instance, say there are initially 5 chocolates and 5 buttercreams—10 candies total. After the 2 chocolates are added and the 3 buttercreams are removed, there are 7 chocolates and 9 candies total. Plugging in 5 and 5 for x and y in the answer choices, only choice (D) works out to $\frac{7}{9}$.

Again we see that picking numbers can be a useful strategy for word problems.

Questions 5–6

5. A batch of cookies was divided among three tins: $\frac{2}{3}$ of all the cookies were placed in either the blue tin or the green tin, and the rest were placed in the red tin. If $\frac{1}{4}$ of all the cookies were placed in the blue tin, what fraction of the cookies that were placed in the other tins were placed in the green tin?

    (A) $\frac{15}{2}$

    (B) $\frac{9}{4}$

    (C) $\frac{5}{9}$

    (D) $\frac{7}{5}$

    (E) $\frac{9}{7}$

6. In a certain school, the ratio of boys to girls is 3 to 7. If there are 150 boys and girls in the school, how many boys are there?

    (A) 45
    (B) 75
    (C) 90
    (D) 105
    (E) 129

Questions 5–6: Answers and Explanations

Explanation: Cookies

5. Pay attention to what you're asked for—it can be written as follows:

$$\frac{\text{Number of cookies in green tin}}{\text{Number of cookies in green tin} + \text{Number of cookies in red tin}}$$

You are told that $\frac{1}{4}$ of the cookies are in the blue tin and, since $\frac{2}{3}$ of the cookies were placed in either the blue or the green tin, $\frac{1}{3}$ must go in the red tin. Also notice that actual numbers for the cookies are not given; you only have fractions to work with.

You already know the fraction of the cookies that go in the red tin and blue tin, so work out the fraction of cookies that go in the green tin.

The fractions of the total cookies in each tin must add up to 1, so the fraction of all the cookies in the green tin is given by the equation $\frac{1}{3} + \frac{1}{4} + (\text{fraction in green tin}) = 1$. That is, fraction in green tin =

$$1 - \frac{1}{3} - \frac{1}{4} = \frac{12}{12} - \frac{4}{12} - \frac{3}{12} = \frac{5}{12}$$

So,

$$\frac{\text{Number of cookies in green tin}}{\text{Number of cookies in green tin} + \text{Number of cookies in red tin}} =$$

$$\frac{\frac{5}{12}}{\frac{5}{12} + \frac{1}{3}} = \frac{\frac{5}{12}}{\frac{5}{12} + \frac{4}{12}} = \frac{\frac{5}{12}}{\frac{9}{12}} = \frac{5}{9}.$$

(C) is correct.

Explanation: Boys and Girls

6. It is probably simpler to solve this problem conventionally, but harder ratio problems are often best attacked through backsolving.

Run through the answer choices starting with (C); using the correct answer choice, the ratio of boys to girls will be 3 to 7.

Choice (C): If there are 90 boys, there are 150 – 90 = 60 girls. So the ratio of boys to girls is 90 to 60, or 3 to 2. Since the actual ratio of boys to girls is 3 to 7, there must be more girls than boys. Try an answer choice with fewer boys.

Choice (B): If there are 75 boys, there are 150 − 75 = 75 girls. This time the ratio of boys to girls is 75 to 75, or 1 to 1. That is, there is an equal number of boys and girls. Since there must be more girls than boys, there are still are too many boys. Therefore the correct answer must be choice (A).

OK, admittedly that last question wasn't quite as tough as the others. It is included, though, to illustrate that backsolving works for word problems as well as for regular math.

An 800 test taker often decides to "backsolve" in word problems. Start with the middle value, so you can quickly narrow down the answer choices. If the middle value is too large, try one of the two smaller values; if the middle value is too small, try one of the two larger values.

PERCENTS

Percents show up frequently in GMAT word problems. And that just makes sense, really. Word problems rely on "real life" scenarios (well, *somebody's* real life, if not yours). Percents are common in everyday life—money, taxes, etc. Thus, they make excellent material for the bitter gnomes that devise word problems.

Let's look at a representative pair.

Questions 7–8

7. In 1966, the operative mortality rate in open heart surgery at a certain hospital was 8.1 per 100 cases. By 1974, the operative mortality rate had declined to 4.8 per 100 cases. If the rate declined by 20 percent from 1973 to 1974, by approximately what percent did it decline from 1966 to 1973?

   (A) 6%
   (B) 21%
   (C) 26%
   (D) 41%
   (E) 49%

8. Ms. DeLong needs to buy camping equipment. If she travels to state *A* to make the purchase, she will have to pay the prevailing sales tax of 8 percent. If she has the store ship the purchase to her home in state *B*, she won't have to pay tax but she'll have to pay a fixed shipping fee of $3.20. What is the least amount of money she can spend on the camping equipment so that the purchase with shipping will not be more expensive than the purchase with sales tax?

   (A) $25.60
   (B) $29.44
   (C) $40.00
   (D) $256.00
   (E) $400.00

Questions 7–8: Answers and Explanations

Explanation: Open Heart Surgery

7. To determine the percent decrease in the rate from 1966 to 1973 you need to find the rate for 1973. You know the actual rate for 1974, and since you also know the percent decrease from 1973 to 1974, you can find the 1973 rate. The rate dropped 20% from 1973 to 1974, so the 1974 rate represents 100% − 20% = 80% of the 1973 rate. Let the 1973 rate be represented by x, and plug into the percent formula: Percent × Whole = Part, so $.8x = 4.8$, $x = \dfrac{48}{8} = 6$. So the rate decreased by 8.1 − 6 = 2.1 from 1966 to 1973.

Percent decrease $= \dfrac{\text{Part decrease}}{\text{Whole}} \times 100\%$, so $\dfrac{2.1}{8.1} \times 100\%$ is approximately $\dfrac{1}{4} \times 100\%$, or 25%. Choice (C) is closest, and it is the correct answer.

Explanation: Ms. DeLong, Cheapo

8. If the purchase is shipped, the fee is $3.20. Let x dollars be the purchase amount. The sales tax is $0.08x$ dollars. We need to find the lowest purchase price before tax so that having the purchase shipped will not be more expensive than paying the tax. In other words, we need to find the lowest purchase price so that the $3.20 shipping cost will be less than or equal to the sales tax. So $3.20 \le 0.08x$. Dividing both sides of this inequality by 0.08, we have $\dfrac{3.20}{0.08} \le x$. Now $\dfrac{3.20}{0.08} = \dfrac{3.20 \times 100}{0.08 \times 100} = \dfrac{320}{8} = 40$. So $40 \le x$. That is, $x \ge 40$. The lowest purchase price possible so that having the purchase shipped won't be more expensive than having to pay tax is $40. Choice (C) is correct.

As you can see, word problems tend to involve more than one technique or type of math. Here, the use of a little algebra made the solution easier and quicker.

Let's look at some other tough percent word problems.

Questions 9–10

9. At a certain store, each item that normally costs $20.00 or less is on sale for 80 percent of its normal price, and each item that normally costs more than $20.00 is on sale for 75 percent of its normal price. If a customer purchases c items, each of which normally costs $15.00, and d items, each of which normally costs $24.00, what is the average (arithmetic mean) amount, in dollars, that she pays for each item?

   (A) $\dfrac{c + d}{30}$

   (B) $\dfrac{12}{c} + \dfrac{18}{d}$

   (C) $\dfrac{12c + 18d}{2}$

   (D) $\dfrac{12c + 18d}{c + d}$

   (E) $\dfrac{30}{c + d}$

10. In State X, 15 percent of the construction workers are unionized, while in State Y, 20 percent of the construction workers are unionized. If State Y has 20 percent more construction workers than State X, then the number of unionized construction workers in State Y is what percent of the number of unionized construction workers in State X?

    (A) $133\frac{1}{3}\%$

    (B) 145%

    (C) 160%

    (D) 175%

    (E) 180%

Questions 9–10: Answers and Explanations

Explanation: Discount Shopping

9. This is a complicated word problem; translate it one step at a time. Items that are less than or equal to $20.00 are discounted by 80%, items that are over $20.00 are discounted by 75%. The customer purchases c items costing $15.00 and d items costing $24.00, that is, c items discounted by 80% and d items discounted by 75%. The average price then is

$$\frac{\text{Total discounted cost of articles purchased}}{\text{Number of articles purchased}}$$

Find the average of the discounted prices of all the articles.

80% of $15.00 = $12.00; total amount spent on these c items: 12c$

75% of $24.00 = $18.00; the total amount spent on these d items: 18d$

$$\text{Average} = \frac{\text{Total discounted cost of articles purchased}}{\text{Number of articles purchased}}$$

$$= \frac{12c + 18d}{c + d}, \text{ or (D)}.$$

As you are probably starting to realize, one of the keys to not fouling up a word problem is to read carefully. Often, similar terms will be employed and you must keep them straight.

Explanation: Construction Workers

10. Read carefully, making sure to distinguish between construction workers and unionized construction workers.

In percent problems without any real numbers, plug in 100.

Say State X has 100 construction workers. Then the number of unionized construction workers in State X is 15% of 100 = 15.

State Y has 20% more construction workers than State X, so state Y has 120 construction workers. 20% of these 120 are unionized, that is $0.2 \times 120 = 24$.

So, "24 is what percent of 15?" requires finding the percent that 24 is of 15, that is, $\frac{24}{15} \times 100\% = 160\%$. (C) is the answer.

An 800 test taker reads carefully and notices distinctions in terms.

Questions 11–12

11. Last week Vartan spent 15 percent of his wages on recreation. This week, his wages are 10 percent less than last week's wages and he spent 30 percent of his wages on recreation. The amount he spends on recreation this week is what percent of the amount he spent on recreation last week?

    (A) 100%
    (B) 160%
    (C) 180%
    (D) 200%
    (E) 220%

12. If Sharon's weekly salary increased by 16 percent, she would earn $406 per week. If instead, her weekly salary were to increase by 10 percent, how much would she earn per week?

    (A) $374
    (B) $382
    (C) $385
    (D) $392
    (E) $399

Questions 11–12: Answers and Explanations

Explanation: Vartan's Recreation

11. Translate piece by piece, to extract the useful information from the stem: Vartan spent 15% of his wages on recreation last week; this week he earned 10% less but spent 30%.

Use the picking numbers strategy when you have only percents in the stem and answer choices.

Suppose that Vartan's wages last week were $100. 15% of $100 = $15, so last week he spent $15 on recreation. This week his wages are 10% less than $100, or $100 − $10, which is $90. 30% of $90 = 0.3 × $90 = $27. To find what percent $27 is of $15, divide $27 by $15 and multiply by 100%: $\frac{27}{15} \times 100\% = 180\%$, or (C).

Explanation: Sharon's Salary

12. Translate the stem: If her salary increased by 16%, she would earn $406. That is, $406 = 116% of her current salary.

Work out her current salary using the information. 116% of Current Salary = $406, then use this to calculate what her salary would be after it is increased by 10%.

Use a variable, say S, to represent her current salary. Then 116% of S = $406, or 1.16S= 406, so $S = \frac{406}{1.16} = 350$. Increasing her current salary by 10 percent means adding on 10 percent of 350 to 350. 10 percent of 350 is 0.1 × 350 = 35, and $350 + $35 = $385. (C) wins.

Questions 13–14

13. In a certain warehouse, 60 percent of the packages weigh less than 75 pounds, and a total of 48 packages weigh less than 25 pounds. If 80 percent of the packages weigh at least 25 pounds, how many of the packages weigh at least 25 pounds but less than 75 pounds?

   (A) 8
   (B) 64
   (C) 96
   (D) 102
   (E) 144

14. According to a recent survey, 26 percent of the 2,000 workers at Company X were discontented with their jobs. Of this group of discontented employees 20 percent had worked at the Company for at least ten years. If 40 percent of all the workers have worked at Company X for at least ten years, how many people who had worked at least ten years did not respond that they were discontented with their jobs?

   (A) 104
   (B) 208
   (C) 520
   (D) 640
   (E) 696

Questions 13–14: Answers and Explanations

Explanation: Warehouse Packages

13. Here's the information you're given: 60% of the packages weigh less than 75 pounds; 48 weigh less than 25 pounds; 80% weigh at least 25 pounds. You are asked for the number of packages that weigh at least 25 pounds and less than 75 pounds.

The number of packages that weigh that weigh at least 25 pounds and less than 75 pounds = (Number of packages that weigh less than 75 pounds) – (Number of packages that weigh less than 25 pounds). You have information about both of these quantities: there are 48 packages that weigh less than 25 pounds, and 60% of the packages weigh less than 75 pounds. If you knew the total number of packages you could determine the number the question requires and find the answer.

The fact that 80% of the packages weigh at least 25 pounds means that 100% – 80%, or 20% weigh less than 25 pounds. You're told that 48 packages weigh less than 25 pounds, so use a variable such as p for the total number of packages and set up an equation. 20% of p is 48, $0.2p = 48$, so $p = 240$. The total number of packages weighing less than 75 pounds is 60% of 240 $= 0.6 \times 240 = 144$, and the number of packages under 25 pounds is 48. So the number of packages weighing at least 25 pounds but less than 75 pounds is $144 - 48 = 96$, or (C).

Explanation: Discontented Workers

14. 26% of 2,000 workers, or 520 workers, are discontent. 20% or $\frac{1}{5}$ of these have worked at Company X for at least 10 years; that's $\frac{1}{5} \times 520$, or 104 who are long-term discontented workers. The total number of workers who have worked at the company for at least 10 years is 40% of 2,000, or 800. That means $800 - 104$, or 696 long-term workers did not respond that they were discontent with their jobs. (E) is correct.

If these next questions spin your head around like a gyroscope, consider employing a strategy like backsolving or picking numbers.

Questions 15–16

15. A room contains 160 people, 15 percent of whom are women. A group of people, 30 percent of whom are women, leaves the room. Of the people remaining in the room, 10 percent are women. How many people left the room?

   (A) 10
   (B) 20
   (C) 40
   (D) 60
   (E) 80

16. At car dealership X, the total profit from sales increased by 10 percent over the previous year, while the number of cars sold decreased by 10 percent over the previous year. Approximately what was the average percent increase in profit per car over the previous year?

   (A) 18%
   (B) 20%
   (C) 22%
   (D) 23%
   (E) 25%

Questions 15–16: Answers and Explanations

Explanation: People in a Room

15. Notice that the number of people who left the room involves a given percentage of women (30 percent). You can work with the given information to set up an equation: The number of women originally in the room minus the number of women who left equals the number of women remaining in the room. To find the number of women originally in the room, take 15 percent of 160: 15% of $160 = \left(\frac{15}{100}\right)(160) = \left(\frac{15}{10}\right)(16) = (3)(8) = 24$. Use your own variable, like x, to represent the number of people who left the room. In that case, 30% of x, or $\frac{3}{10}(x)$, represents the number of women who left the room. Since there were originally 160 people in the room and x people left, there are $(160 - x)$ people remaining in the room. 10 percent of them are women, and 10% of $(160 - x)$ is $\left(\frac{1}{10}\right)(160 - x)$. Now you can set up your equation to solve for x: $24 - \frac{3}{10}(x) = \left(\frac{1}{10}\right)(160 - x)$; $24 - \frac{3x}{10} = 16 - \frac{x}{10}$; $\frac{2x}{10} = 8$; $x = 40$. (C) it is.

Backsolving is also a good strategy to use on this question. Since the answer choices are listed in ascending order, start with choice (C); depending upon whether the result you get is higher or lower than you want, you can eliminate two of the answer choices as too big or too small. Choice (C) is 40, so if 40 people left the room, $160 - 40 = 120$ would remain. 30% of the 40 people who left are women—10% of 40 is 4, so 3 $\times$ 10% or 30% of 40 = 3 $\times$ 4 or 12—so 12 women left. Of the original 160 people in the room 15% were women—10% of 160 is 16 and 5% of 160 is half this or 8, so 15% of 160 is 16 + 8 = 24. So there were originally 24 women in the room. Since 12 women left, $24 - 12 = 12$ remain. So of the remaining 120 people, 12 are women. 10% of 120 is indeed 12, so choice (C), 40, is the correct answer.

Explanation: Car Dealership

16. Pick numbers for the original number of cars sold and the original profit per car. If the car dealership sold 10 cars at a $10 profit per car it originally made $100 profit total. The next year it sold 10% fewer cars, or 9 cars. The profit, however, increased by 10%, or equaled $100 + (10% of $100) = $110. The profit per car increased from $10 to $\frac{\$110}{9}$. You'll need to express the $10 in terms of ninths to find the amount of increase: $\frac{\$110}{9} - \frac{\$90}{9} = \frac{\$20}{9}$. The percent increase in profit per car is the amount of increase, divided by the original profit per car: $\frac{\$20}{9} \div \$10 = \frac{2}{9}$, or approximately 22%. (C) is correct.

An 800 test taker is able to quickly choose an alternative strategy when the situation demands it.

Questions 17–18

17. A magazine's survey of its subscribers finds that 20 percent are male. If 70 percent of the subscribers are married, and 10 percent of these are male, what percent of the male subscribers are not married?

    (A) 7%
    (B) 13%
    (C) 35%
    (D) 65%
    (E) 90%

18. If attendance at a school had increased by 30 percent over last year, this year's attendance would have been 10,972. Actually the attendance decreased by 35 percent from last year. What is this year's attendance?

    (A) 5,126
    (B) 5,206
    (C) 5,486
    (D) 6,136
    (E) 6,300

Questions 17–18: Answers and Explanations

Explanation: Magazine Subscribers

17. Pick a number to represent magazine subscribers. Pick 100 because it's easy to find percents of 100. 70% of the magazine subscribers are married, so there are 70 married subscribers. 10% of the married subscribers are male, so there are $10\% \times 70 = 7$ married male subscribers. 20% of all the subscribers are male, so 20 of them are males. If 7 of the 20 males are married, $20 - 7 = 13$ of them are not married. So the percent of male subscribers who are not married is given by $\dfrac{\text{Part}}{\text{Whole}} \times 100\%$, which is $\dfrac{13}{20} \times 100\% = 65\%$. (D) is the answer.

Explanation: School Attendance

18. In questions involving percent increase or percent decrease, it is often helpful to ask yourself, "What percent of the original whole is the new whole?" This is easy to calculate: just add (or subtract) the percent increase (or decrease) to (or from) 100%. Here, we know that a 30% increase over the previous year's attendance would make this year's attendance 10,972. In other words, if A represents the previous year's attendance, 100% of $A + 30\%$ of $A = 10,972$ or 130% of $A = 10,972$. We could solve for A here, and then from that find this year's actual attendance, but there is a faster way to solve this question. The actual attendance decreased 35% from the previous year's attendance, so it can be represented as (100% of A) – (35% of A), or 65% of A. Note that 65% of A is just one-half of 130% of A. Therefore, if 130% of $A = 10,972$, then 65% of $A= \dfrac{1}{2}$ of 10,972, or 5,486, making (C) the answer.

RATES

The paradigmatic word problem is probably the "rates" word problem. A rate is a ratio. It expresses the quantity of one item per unit of another. So we can solve for a rate like so:

$$\text{Rate} = \frac{\text{Units of } A}{\text{Unit of } B}$$

The rate that you'll most often encounter on the GMAT is speed. Speed is specifically the ratio of distance to time. Here's the formula:

$$\text{Rate} = \frac{\text{Distance}}{\text{Time}}$$

This can also be written as either of the following:

$$\text{Time} = \frac{\text{Distance}}{\text{Rate}}$$

$$\text{Distance} = \text{Rate} \times \text{Time}$$

All three equations say the same thing. And if we have any two of the three components (Rate, Time, and Distance), we can solve for the third.

Let's take a look at some of the tougher rate problems the GMAT may throw at you. Here are four GMAT rate problems with the characteristic GMAT flourish: you have to work with more than just one speed. Try the first two:

Questions 19–20

19. A motorist travels 90 miles at a rate of 20 miles per hour. If he returns the same distance at a rate of 40 miles per hour, what is his average speed for the entire trip, in miles per hour?

    (A) 20

    (B) $\dfrac{65}{3}$

    (C) $\dfrac{80}{3}$

    (D) 30

    (E) $\dfrac{13}{3}$

20. A riverboat leaves Mildura and travels upstream to Renmark at an average speed of 6 miles per hour. It returns by the same route at an average speed of 9 miles per hour. What is its average speed for the round trip, in miles per hour?

    (A) 7.0

    (B) 7.2

    (C) 7.5

    (D) 7.8

    (E) 8.2

Questions 19–20: Answers and Explanations

Explanation: A Motorist

19. To find the average speed for the entire trip you need to plug into the formula for average speed: Average speed $= \dfrac{\text{Total distance}}{\text{Total time}}$. The total distance is easy to find: He travels 90 miles there and 90 miles back for a total of 180 miles. Use a version of the distance formula, Time $= \dfrac{\text{Distance}}{\text{Rate}}$, to figure the time spent on each half of the trip, then add these for the total time. Leaving, he travels 90 miles at 20 miles per hour, so it takes $\dfrac{90 \text{ miles}}{20 \text{ miles per hour}} = \dfrac{9}{2}$ hours. Returning, he travels 90 miles at 40 miles per hour, so it takes $\dfrac{90 \text{ miles}}{40 \text{ miles per hour}} = \dfrac{9}{4}$ hours. So the total time $= \dfrac{9}{2} + \dfrac{9}{4} = \dfrac{18}{4} + \dfrac{9}{4} = \dfrac{27}{4}$ hours. So the average speed for the full trip $= \dfrac{180}{\frac{27}{4}} = 180 \times \dfrac{4}{27} = 20 \times \dfrac{4}{3} = \dfrac{80}{3}$. (C) is correct.

Explanation: A Riverboat

20. You cannot simply average the two speeds; each leg of the trip will take a different amount of time and you must weight the average to account for this. The average speed for the entire trip equals the total distance traveled divided by the total amount of time it took. Pick a number for the distance from Mildura to Renmark; try 18 since it is evenly divisible by both speeds. On the first leg of the trip, traveling 18 miles at 6 miles per hour will take 3 hours. On the return trip, traveling 18 miles at 9 miles per hour will take 2 hours. So the average speed for the entire trip is $\dfrac{18 + 18}{3 + 2} = \dfrac{36}{5} = 7\dfrac{1}{5}$ or 7.2 miles per hour. (B) wins.

An 800 test taker knows the formulas for determining Time, Rate, and Distance.

And here's another pair of GMAT rate problems dealing with speed:

Questions 21–22

21. Maura drives to work in 40 minutes. She takes the same route to return home. If her average speed on the trip home is half as fast as her average speed on the trip to work, how much time does she spend driving on the round trip?

    (A) 1 hour
    (B) 1 hour, 15 minutes
    (C) 1 hour, 20 minutes
    (D) 1 hour, 40 minutes
    (E) 2 hours

22. John always jogs to school at a speed of 6 kilometers per hour, and walks home along the same route at a speed of 3 kilometers per hour. If he spends exactly one hour total traveling both ways, how many kilometers is his school from his home?

    (A) 2
    (B) 3
    (C) 4
    (D) 6
    (E) 9

Questions 21–22: Answers and Explanations

Explanation: Maura's Drive

21. Consider the relationship between speed and time: Common sense tells you that increasing the speed decreases the amount of time needed to travel a particular distance, and vice versa. Since Maura's average speed returning home is half her average speed traveling to work, it will take her twice as long to drive home as it takes her to get to work. It takes her 40 minutes to get to work, so it takes her 2 × 40, or 80 minutes to return home. So the round trip takes Maura a total of 40 + 80 = 120 minutes, or 2 hours. (E) it is.

Explanation: John's Jog

22. The distance he travels jogging and walking is the same, since he is following the same route. Break John's trip into its two components: jogging and walking. The time he spent jogging to school plus the time he spent walking home equals 1 hour. The rate formula tells you that $\text{Time} = \dfrac{\text{Distance}}{\text{Rate}}$, so $\dfrac{x \text{ kilometers}}{6 \text{ kilometers per hour}}$ is the time he spent jogging and the time he spent walking is $\dfrac{x \text{ kilometers}}{3 \text{ kilometers per hour}}$, where x is the distance from school to his home. Therefore, $\dfrac{x}{6} + \dfrac{x}{3} = 1$ hour, or $\dfrac{x}{6} + \dfrac{2x}{6} = 1$, and $\dfrac{3x}{6} = 1$, that is, $x = \dfrac{6}{3} = 2$. (A) is correct.

And as if that weren't bad enough, the GMAT will also throw even tougher rate problems at you. Try your hand at two of the toughest:

Questions 23–24

23. Farmer Brown drives his tractor 40 kilometers. If he travels at r kilometers per hour for one-third of the distance and $2r$ kilometers per hour for the remainder, how many hours does the entire trip take, in terms of r?

(A) $\dfrac{24}{r}$

(B) $\dfrac{36}{r}$

(C) $\dfrac{80}{3r}$

(D) $20r$

(E) $\dfrac{r}{36}$

24. Two airplanes are 300 miles apart and flying directly toward each other. One is flying at 200 miles per hour, and the other at 160 miles per hour. How long will it take for the two planes to meet?

(A) 36 minutes

(B) 50 minutes

(C) 1 hour and 12 minutes

(D) 1 hour and 40 minutes

(E) 1 hour and 41 minutes

Questions 23–24: Answers and Explanations

Explanation: Farmer Brown's Tractor

23. The farmer travels r miles per hour for one-third of the 40 miles or $\frac{1}{3} \times 40 = \frac{40}{3}$ miles, and at $2r$ miles per hour for the other two-thirds of the 40 miles, or $\frac{2}{3} \times 40 = \frac{80}{3}$ miles. Since Distance = Rate $\times$ Time, Time = $\frac{\text{Distance}}{\text{Rate}}$. Plug the rate and distance into this formula to find the time traveled at each speed. At r miles per hour:

Time $= \dfrac{\left(\frac{40}{3}\right)}{r} = \dfrac{40}{3r}$. At $2r$ miles per hour: Time $= \dfrac{\left(\frac{80}{3}\right)}{2r} = \dfrac{80}{6r} = \dfrac{40}{3r}$. So the entire trip takes $\dfrac{40}{3r} + \dfrac{40}{3r}$

$= \dfrac{80}{3r}$ hours. (C) is correct.

Explanation: Airplanes

24. The distance formula tells you that Distance = Speed $\times$ Time, or, as is useful in this case, Time $= \dfrac{\text{Distance}}{\text{Speed}}$. It would take the same amount of time for a plane traveling 200 mph and a plane traveling 160 mph to meet as it would if one plane were standing still and the other traveling at 200 + 160 = 360 mph. It would take a plane traveling at 360 mph $\dfrac{300}{360} = \dfrac{5}{6}$ hours = 50 minutes, to travel 300 miles.

Alternatively, you could have used logic to answer the question. Consider the relative positions of the planes after one hour, since the speed of each is measured in miles per hour. One plane has traveled 200 miles, while the other has traveled 160 miles. Since they were only 300 miles apart initially, they will already have passed each other in an hour.

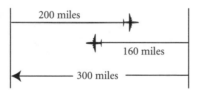

So eliminate all the answer choices that are greater than one hour. Now try $\frac{1}{2}$ hour.

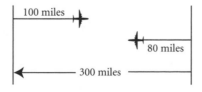

One plane has gone $\frac{1}{2}(200)$, or 100 miles, while the other has flown $\frac{1}{2}(160)$, or 80 miles. The planes are still 120 miles apart. Since it will take quite a bit more than $\frac{1}{2}$ hour for the planes to meet, choice (A), 36 minutes, is too small. Choice (B), 50 minutes, must be the correct answer choice.

And we're still not out of the Rates Woods yet. Speed is not the only rate the GMAT tests, although it is the most common. To get an idea of some of the other types of rates—rates of work or pay, for example—tackle the next four questions.

Questions 25–26

25. On each shift he works, a bus driver earns X dollars per hour for the first 8 hours worked and $1.5X$ dollars per hour for each hour over 8 hours. If the driver earns $475 for a week in which he worked 5 shifts, what is the value of X?

   (A) 9
   (B) 10
   (C) 18
   (D) 38
   (E) It cannot be determined from the information given.

26. Machine A and machine B are each used to manufacture 660 sprockets. It takes machine A 10 hours longer to produce 660 sprockets than machine B. Machine B produces 10 percent more sprockets per hour than machine A. How many sprockets per hour does machine A produce?

   (A) 6
   (B) 6.6
   (C) 60
   (D) 100
   (E) 110

Questions 25–26: Answers and Explanations

Explanation: Bus Driver

25. You're given the total amount of money the driver makes for 5 shifts, and that he makes $1\frac{1}{2}$ times as much for overtime. However, you're not given any information about how many hours he worked for the 5 shifts, either individually or in total. So you have no idea how many hours of overtime he's working. Without this information it isn't possible to solve for X. Notice that even if you were told that he worked 40 hours during the week, you still wouldn't be able to answer the question, since he could work 7 hours a day for 4 days and then 12 hours on the fifth day for 4 overtime hours, or 8 hours a day for 5 days with no overtime hours, etc. (E) is the answer.

Explanation: Sprocket Machines

26. This is a very difficult rate problem, and the best approach is backsolving. Start with the middle choice, (C). If machine A produces 60 sprockets per hour, then machine B produces 60 plus 10% of 60, or 66 sprockets per hour. According to the rate formula, the amount of work done, divided by the rate at which it is done, equals the time it takes to do the work. So it takes machine A $\frac{660}{60}$, or 11 hours, while it takes machine B $\frac{660}{66}$, or 10 hours. It doesn't take machine A 10 hours longer than machine B at these rates, so choice (C) is out. At a slower rate it will take both machines longer, so try a smaller answer choice. Choice (A) is an integer, so it will be easier to work with than (B). If machine A produces 6 sprockets per hour, then machine B produces 6 plus 10% of 6, or 6.6 sprockets per hour. At these rates, it takes machine A $\frac{660}{6}$, or 110 hours, while it takes machine B $\frac{660}{66}$, or 100 hours. Since in this case it does take machine A 10 hours longer than machine B, choice (A) is correct.

Questions 27–28

27. Working independently, Susan can perform a certain task in 6 hours and Tom can perform it in 7 hours. If Susan and Tom work together at the task for 3 hours, at which point Susan leaves, how many hours will it take Tom to complete the task alone?

    (A) $\dfrac{1}{14}$

    (B) $\dfrac{2}{5}$

    (C) $\dfrac{1}{2}$

    (D $\dfrac{29}{42}$

    (E) 1

28. When both floodgates A and B are open, a reservoir drains in $3\dfrac{1}{3}$ days. If floodgate A alone drains the reservoir in 10 days, how many days does it take floodgate B alone to drain the reservoir?

    (A) 4

    (B) 5

    (C) $6\dfrac{2}{3}$

    (D) 10

    (E) 12

Questions 27–28: Answers and Explanations

Explanation: Susan and Tom

27. Since an hour is an easy unit to work with, consider how much of the task each person working alone could complete in one hour. Susan could do the job in 6 hours, so she does $\frac{1}{6}$ of it in an hour; Tom could do the job in 7 hours, so he does $\frac{1}{7}$ of it in one hour. Working together for 3 hours they complete $3\left(\frac{1}{6}+\frac{1}{7}\right)$ or $\frac{1}{2}+\frac{3}{7}$, or $\frac{7}{14}+\frac{6}{14}=\frac{13}{14}$ of the job. That leaves $\frac{1}{14}$ of the task for Tom to complete alone.

Since $\dfrac{\text{amount of work}}{\text{rate}}=\text{time}$, it will take Tom $\frac{1}{14} \div \frac{1}{7}=\frac{7}{14}=\frac{1}{2}$ hour to finish. (C) it is.

Explanation: Floodgates

28. If floodgate A alone can drain the reservoir in 10 days, then it drains $\frac{1}{10}$ of the reservoir in 1 day. In $3\frac{1}{3}$ days, floodgate A would drain $3\frac{1}{3} \times \frac{1}{10}$, or $\frac{1}{3}$ of the reservoir. Floodgate B must drain the other $\frac{2}{3}$ of the reservoir in $3\frac{1}{3}$ days. Divide $\frac{2}{3}$ by $3\frac{1}{3}$ to find floodgate B's average daily rate. $\frac{2}{3} \div 3\frac{1}{3}=\frac{2}{3} \div \frac{10}{3}=\frac{2}{3} \times \frac{3}{10}=\frac{1}{5}$. Since floodgate B can drain $\frac{1}{5}$ of the reservoir in 1 day, it would need 5 days to drain the entire reservoir. (B) is correct.

MIXTURES

Mixture problems are another classic GMAT Word Problem type. In these questions, you'll be presented with a mixture, usually of two liquids. Then the problem either will add more of one of the liquids and ask you about the resulting mixture, or it will ask you how much more of one of the liquids needs to be added to arrive at a certain new mixture.

Try this example:

Question 29

29. A solution is 90 percent glycerin. If there are 4 gallons of the solution, how much water, in gallons, must be added to make a 75-percent glycerin solution?

   (A) 1.8
   (B) 1.4
   (C) 1.2
   (D) 1.0
   (E) 0.8

Question 29: Answer and Explanation

Explanation: Glycerin Solution

29. We have 4 gallons of 90% glycerin; we want to know how much water we must add to decrease the glycerin concentration to 75%. 4 gallons of a 90% glycerin mixture has $\frac{9}{10} \times 4$ or 3.6 gallons of glycerin. At what volume of solution will this 3.6 gallons of glycerin represent 75% of the solution? Set up an equation:

$$3.6 \text{ gallons} = 75\% \text{ of } x \text{ gallons}$$

$$3.6 = \frac{3}{4}x$$

$$x = \frac{4}{3} \times 3.6 = 4.8$$

So we will have a 75% solution when there are 4.8 gallons of liquid. Since we started with 4 gallons, we need to add 4.8 − 4 or 0.8 gallons of water. (E) is correct.

An 800 test taker knows that mixture problems often hinge on managing percents, and knows the percent formula: Part = Percent × Whole.

Now let's look at a few more mixture problems.

Questions 30–31

30. At a certain paint store "forest green" is made by mixing 4 parts blue paint with 3 parts yellow paint. "Verdant green" is made by mixing 4 parts yellow paint with 3 parts blue paint. How many liters of yellow paint must be added to 14 liters of "forest green" to change it to "verdant green"?

    (A) 2

    (B) $2\frac{1}{6}$

    (C) 3

    (D) 4

    (E) $4\frac{2}{3}$

31. A shade of paint is made by evenly mixing m gallons of white paint, costing $12.00 per gallon, with n gallons of blue paint, costing $30.00 per gallon. What is the cost, in dollars per gallon, of the resulting mixture?

    (A) $12m + 30n$

    (B) $42(12m + 30n)$

    (C) $\dfrac{12m + 30n}{42}$

    (D) $\dfrac{12m + 30n}{m + n}$

    (E) $\dfrac{42(m + n)}{12m + 30n}$

Questions 30–31: Answers and Explanations

Explanation: Forest Green Paint

30. First, use the ratio to find the amount of blue paint in the "forest green" mixture. Then figure out how much yellow paint must be in a "verdant green" mixture that contains that amount of blue paint. The difference between that amount of yellow and the amount in the original "forest green" mixture will be the amount that has to be added.

"Forest green" is 4 parts blue and 3 parts yellow, for a total of $4 + 3$ or 7 parts. Since 4 out of 7 parts, or $\frac{4}{7}$, of the "forest green" mixture is blue, the mixture must contain $\frac{4}{7} \times 14$ liters or 8 liters of blue paint. To find out how much yellow must be mixed with 8 liters of blue to get "verdant green," set up a proportion, using the 4:3 or $\frac{4}{3}$ ratio of yellow to blue:

$$\frac{4 \text{ yellow}}{3 \text{ blue}} = \frac{y \text{ yellow}}{8 \text{ blue}}$$

$$3y = 32$$

$$y = 10\frac{2}{3}$$

The "verdant green" mixture must contain $10\frac{2}{3}$ liters of yellow paint. The "forest green" already had $14 - 8$, or 6 liters of yellow, so $10\frac{2}{3} - 6$, or $4\frac{2}{3}$ liters must be added. (E) is the answer.

Explanation: Blue and White Paint

31. You could pick numbers or think algebraically. Using algebra, the total cost of the mixture is $12m + 30n$. To get the cost per gallon, divide the total cost by the total number of gallons, which is $m + n$, to get $\frac{12m + 30n}{m + n}$. If you pick numbers for m and n, pick ones that are easy to work with: try $m = 2$ and $n = 3$.

The cost of the 2 gallons of white paint at $12 per gallon is then 12×2, or $24; the cost of the 3 gallons of blue paint at $30 per gallon is 30×3, or $90. So the total cost of the paint is $24 + $90, or $114. There are 5 gallons of paint altogether, so the cost per gallon, in dollars, is $\frac{114}{5}$. Now check the answer choices to see which one(s) gives you $\frac{114}{5}$ when you plug in 2 for m and 3 for n. Choice (A): $12(2) + 30(3) = 24 + 90 = 114$. Eliminate. (Notice that all the other answer choices contain $12m + 30n$ as part of their expressions, so just plug in 114 wherever you see $12m + 30n$.) (B): $42(114)$ is much too large—eliminate. (C): $\frac{114}{42}$ is too small—eliminate.

(D): $\frac{114}{(2 + 3)} = \frac{114}{5}$ — a match! (E): $\frac{42(5)}{114}$ is approximately $\frac{200}{114}$, which is less than 2 and too small—eliminate. Since only choice (D) matches your result, it is correct.

An 800 test taker knows that mixture problems can sometimes be solved quickest by picking numbers.

Questions 32–33

32. A 50-liter solution of alcohol and water is 5 percent alcohol. If $1\frac{1}{2}$ liters of alcohol and $8\frac{1}{2}$ liters of water are added to this solution, what percent of the solution produced is alcohol?

    (A) $5\frac{1}{2}\%$

    (B) 6%

    (C) $6\frac{1}{3}\%$

    (D) $6\frac{2}{3}\%$

    (E) 7%

33. Solution X is 25 percent mercury and solution Y is 10 percent mercury. If 12 ounces of solution X are added to 13 ounces of solution Y, approximately what percent of the resulting solution will be mercury?

    (A) 12%
    (B) 17%
    (C) 21%
    (D) 23%
    (E) 37%

Questions 32–33: Answers and Explanations

Explanation: Alcohol and Water

32. To figure out what percent of the new solution is alcohol you need to know the amount of alcohol in the new solution and the total amount of the new solution. To find the amount of alcohol in the new solution, you first must find the amount of alcohol in the old solution and then add the amount of additional alcohol. 5% of the original 50-liter solution is alcohol; 10% of 50 is 5, so 5% of 50 is half this, or $2\frac{1}{2}$ liters. $1\frac{1}{2}$ liters of alcohol are added to the original solution, for a total of $2\frac{1}{2} + 1\frac{1}{2} = 4$ liters of alcohol in the new solution. The total volume of liquid in the new solution is the original 50 liters, plus the alcohol added, plus the water added: $50 + 1\frac{1}{2} + 8\frac{1}{2} = 60$ liters. Percent $= \dfrac{\text{Part}}{\text{Whole}} \times 100\%$, so $\dfrac{4}{60} \times 100\% = 6\frac{2}{3}\%$ of the new solution is alcohol. (D) wins.

Explanation: Mercury Solutions

33. Find out how much mercury there is in the resulting solution. 12 ounces of a solution of 25% mercury are mixed with 13 ounces of a solution that is 10% mercury. 12 ounces of a 25% mercury solution will contribute $\dfrac{1}{4} \times 12$, or 3 ounces of mercury to the solution. 13 ounces of a 10% mercury solution will contribute $\dfrac{1}{10} \times 13$ or $\dfrac{13}{10}$ ounces of mercury to the solution, so the resulting solution has $3 + \dfrac{13}{10} = \dfrac{30}{10} + \dfrac{13}{10} = \dfrac{43}{10} = 4.3$ ounces of mercury in a total of $12 + 13 = 25$ ounces of liquid. The solution is $\dfrac{4.3}{25}$ or $\dfrac{43}{250}$ mercury. Since $\dfrac{43}{250}$ is slightly less than $\dfrac{50}{250}$, which is $\dfrac{1}{5}$, its percent equivalent must be slightly less than 20%. Only choice (B), 17%, is close.

ALGEBRA

You may be surprised to learn that straightforward algebra accounts for relatively few GMAT Word Problems. The GMAT likes to present algebra in a pretty straightforward way—like a math text. But there are a few "usual suspects" in the Word Problems lineup.

If you are rusty with equations, variables, and all that good stuff, you may want to brush up a bit. Use the next five algebra word problems to measure yourself.

Questions 34–36

34. On four successive days, a farmer picks exactly twice as many apples each day as on the previous day. If in the course of the four days he picks a total of 12,000 apples, how many apples does he pick on the second of the four days?

(A) 800
(B) 1,000
(C) 1,600
(D) 2,000
(E) 6,000

35. If $8 < x < 9$, and $x^2 = (10 - y)(10 + y)$, which of the following is a possible value for y ?

(A) –7
(B) –6
(C) 3
(D) 4
(E) 5

36. In a scientific experiment, the hourly increase in the number of bacteria in a certain environment is given by the formula $I = p^2 - p$, where p is the current population of bacteria, in millions. The hourly decrease in the number of bacteria in this environment is given by the formula $D = 0.5p$. For what positive value of p will the hourly increase in the number of bacteria be equal to the hourly decrease in the number of bacteria?

(A) 0.25
(B) 0.5
(C) 0.75
(D) 1
(E) 1.5

Questions 34–36: Answers and Explanations

Explanation: Apples

34. Solve for the number of apples picked on the first day, then double that amount to get the number picked on the second day. Let x represent the number of apples that the farmer picks on the first day. Then on the second, third, and fourth days, the farmer picks $2x$, $4x$, and $8x$ apples, respectively. Since he picks a total of 12,000 apples, $12,000 = x + 2x + 4x + 8x$, and $12,000 = 15x$. Therefore, $x = \dfrac{12,000}{15}$, or 800 apples. But that's for the first day. On the second day, he picks twice as many: 1,600. That makes (C) correct.

Explanation: Greater Than/Less Than

35. This problem is best solved by working backwards from the answer choices. If $8 < x < 9$, then $64 < x^2 < 81$. Multiplying through the expression given for x^2, you get $x^2 = 10^2 - y^2$ or $x^2 = 100 - y^2$. Each answer choice gives a possible value for y, so try plugging each of these values into the equation, starting with choice (E), until you get a value for x^2 such that $64 < x^2 < 81$. (You should know why you're starting with choice (E) for this problem by now!)

(E) $x^2 = 100 - 5^2 = 100 - 25 = 75$; $64 < 75 < 81$, so this choice is correct. Let's check the other answer choices just for the sake of the discussion.
(D) $x^2 = 100 - 4^2 = 100 - 16 = 84$—eliminate.
(C) $x^2 = 100 - 3^2 = 100 - 9 = 91$—eliminate.
(B) $x^2 = 100 - (-6)^2 = 100 - 36 = 64$—eliminate.
(A) $x^2 = 100 - (-7)^2 = 100 - 49 = 51$—eliminate.

Explanation: Bacteria

36. Don't let all the science talk in the question stem throw you off track. You're given 2 equations, both in terms of p: the increase $I = p^2 - p$, and the decrease $D = 0.5p$. All that you're asked to do is set I equal to D to solve for p: $p^2 - p = 0.5p$. So $p^2 - p - 0.5p = 0$, $p^2 - 1.5p = 0$, $p(p - 1.5) = 0$. Therefore $p = 0$ or $p = 1.5$. Since $p > 0$, $p = 1.5$, making (E) correct.

An 800 test taker starts with choice (E) and works back to (A) when backsolving from the answer choices.

Questions 37–38

37. A travel agent offers a vacation plan which costs z dollars for the first day, and $\frac{z}{6}$ dollars for each additional day. How much does a vacation of y days cost, in dollars, where $y > 1$?

(A) $\frac{yz}{6}$

(B) $\frac{yz}{3}$

(C) $\frac{yz + 6z}{6}$

(D) $\frac{yz + 5z}{6}$

(E) $\frac{y^2z + 5yz + z^2}{3}$

38. Last year, the P members of a partnership divided D dollars profit evenly among themselves. If N people join the partnership during the year, how much more profit in the course of the year must the partnership make for the amount of profit per partner to remain the same?

(A) $\frac{NP}{D}$

(B) $\frac{ND}{P}$

(C) $\frac{N + P}{D}$

(D) $\frac{N}{PD}$

(E) $\frac{P}{ND}$

Questions 37–38: Answers and Explanations

Explanation: An Algebraic Vacation

37. Pick numbers for y and z that are easy to work with:

Since $y > 1$, try $y = 2$; to make $\dfrac{z}{6}$ an integer, try $z = 6$. In that case, the first day costs 6 dollars and the second day costs $\dfrac{6}{6}$, or 1 dollar. So the total cost for the 2 days is 7 dollars. Now see which answer choices yield 7 when $y = 2$ and $z = 6$. Remember to try all the answer choices, just in case more than one answer choice works for the numbers you picked.

(A) $\dfrac{2 \times 6}{6} = 2$, eliminate.

(B) $\dfrac{2 \times 6}{3} = 4$, eliminate.

(C) $\dfrac{2 \times 6 + 6 \times 6}{6} = 8$, eliminate.

(D) $\dfrac{2 \times 6 + 5 \times 6}{6} = 7$, possibly correct.

(E) $\dfrac{2^2 + 5 \times 2 \times 6 + 6^2}{3} = \dfrac{100}{3}$, eliminate.

Since only choice (D) works, it is the correct answer.

Explanation: Partnership Profits

38. Start by finding the amount per partner when there are only P members. There are D dollars divided equally among P members. So each got $\dfrac{D}{P}$ dollars profit. When N more people join, if each of these also make $\dfrac{D}{P}$ dollars, then the company must earn $N \times \dfrac{D}{P}$, or $\dfrac{ND}{P}$ more dollars for everyone to make the same profit. Choice (B) is correct. You could also have attacked this problem by picking numbers.

CHAPTER EIGHTEEN

Geometry Word Problems

The GMAT test makers really enjoy testing geometry inside word problems. It gives them the opportunity to combine the different areas of geometry, assigning you, the test taker, the task of working with circles *and* triangles, or triangles *and* rectangles.

Of course, as stated earlier, we can't review all of high school geometry here. This book focuses on the 800-level questions that the GMAT presents. Between the examples here and those in the geometry part of the Straight Math section, however, you'll get a very good idea of what geometry skills and information you need to have. If you're rusty, be sure to freshen up by test day.

GEOMETRY WORD PROBLEMS PRACTICE SET 1

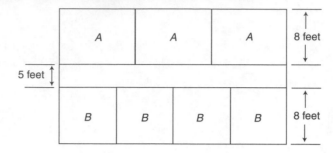

1. The figure above shows the floor plan of an office in which seven rectangular rooms are divided by a rectangular hallway. The three rooms labeled *A* have dimensions 8 feet by 12 feet, and the four rooms labeled *B* have dimensions 8 feet by 9 feet. What is the total area of the entire office in square feet (ignoring the thickness of the walls)?

   (A) 252 sq. ft.
   (B) 576 sq. ft.
   (C) 672 sq. ft.
   (D) 756 sq. ft.
   (E) 762 sq. ft.

2. A garden measuring 40 meters by 50 meters is to be surrounded by a flagstone walkway 5 meters wide. If each stone is rectangular and has the dimensions 2 meters by 1 meter, how many stones will be needed to cover the walkway?

   (A) 250
   (B) 275
   (C) 425
   (D) 450
   (E) 500

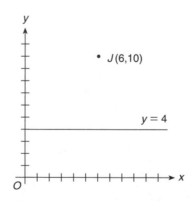

3. In the diagram above, the line $y = 4$ is the perpendicular bisector of segment *JK* (not shown). What is the distance from the origin to point *K* ?

   (A) 4
   (B) $2\sqrt{10}$
   (C) 8
   (D) $6\sqrt{2}$
   (E) $4\sqrt{34}$

Explanation: Floor Plan

1. The entire office is rectangular, so its area equals its length times its width. You can use the given information to figure out these dimensions. The vertical length is fairly easy to find: It's just the vertical length of an *A*-room, plus the vertical length of a *B*-room, plus the length of the hallway, or $8 + 8 + 5 = 21$. Now, notice that the horizontal width of the entire office is made up of 3 *A*-rooms across the top, or 4 *B*-rooms across the bottom. You're told that each *A*-room is 8 ft $\times$ 12 ft, and since the diagram shows the vertical length as 8 feet, the horizontal width of each *A*-room must be 12 feet. So the width of the entire office is equal to the sum of the widths of the 3 *A*-rooms, or $3 \times 12 = 36$ feet. So the area of the entire office is 21×36, or 756 square feet, which means (D) is correct.

Notice that this geometry word problem included a nice, clean, helpful diagram. That will not always be the case. Very often, only part of the figure will be provided. Sometimes a figure will be described solely in words.

When you don't have all the illustration you need, it's your job to provide it. Put your pencil and scrap paper to work. Draw or redraw the diagram to fit your needs.

Explanation: Garden Walkway

2. The easiest thing to do here is to draw a diagram.

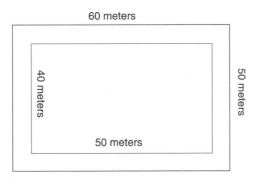

You get two rectangles: one with dimensions 40 meters by 50 meters (the lawn); one with dimensions 50 meters by 60 meters (the lawn and the walk). The area of the walk alone is the difference between the two rectangular areas, or $(50 \times 60) - (40 \times 50) = 3,000 - 2,000 = 1,000$ square meters. Since each stone has area $2 \times 1 = 2$ square meters, you would need 500 stones for the whole walk. (E) is the answer.

Explanation: Perpendicular Bisector?

3. Don't try to keep all the information in your head—add to the diagram so you can refer to it as you solve. Horizontal line $y = 4$ is the perpendicular bisector of JK, so JK must be vertical and parallel to the y-axis. Draw in segment JK, dropping straight down from point J through the x-axis. Before you can find the distance from the origin to point K, you need to know its coordinates. K is directly below J so both points are the same distance from the y-axis and their x-coordinates must be the same. So the x-coordinate of K is 6. Since the line $y = 4$ bisects JK, the vertical distance from J to the line must be the same as the vertical distance from the line to K. Vertical distance is the positive difference between the y-coordinates, so the vertical distance from J to line $y = 4$ is 10 − 4, or 6. Therefore the positive difference between the y-coordinates of line $y = 4$ and point K is also 6, so the y-coordinate of K is $4 - 6$, making -2 the y-coordinate of point K. So the coordinates of point K are $(6, -2)$. You will notice that K, the origin O, and the point where JK crosses the x-axis are the vertices of a right triangle, with its hypotenuse being the distance from the origin to point K. Use the Pythagorean theorem to find the length of the hypotenuse. Hypotenuse^2 = (length of the leg lying on the x-axis)^2 + (length of the leg parallel to the y-axis)^2 = $6^2 + 2^2 = 40$.

So the distance from the origin to $K = \sqrt{40} = 2\sqrt{10}$. (B) it is.

An 800 test taker draws useful diagrams when the word problem doesn't provide them, and adds to diagrams information that is discovered.

If you encounter a word problem dealing with solid geometry, there's a good chance it'll deal with cylinders. Let's look at a couple.

GEOMETRY WORD PROBLEMS PRACTICE SET 2

4. How many cylindrical oil drums, with a diameter of 1.5 feet and a length of 4 feet, would be needed to hold the contents of a full cylindrical fuel tank, with a diameter of 12 feet and a length of 60 feet?

   (A) 640
   (B) 720
   (C) 840
   (D) 880
   (E) 960

5. Can A and can B are both right circular cylinders. The radius of can A is twice the radius of can B, while the height of can A is half the height of can B. If it costs $4.00 to fill half of can B with a certain brand of gasoline, how much would it cost to completely fill can A with the same brand of gasoline?

   (A) $1
   (B) $2
   (C) $4
   (D) $8
   (E) $16

Explanation: Oil Drums

4. To find the number of drums needed to hold the contents of the tank, set the combined volume of all the drums equal to the volume of the tank. The combined volume of the drums is the volume per drum × the total number of drums. The volume of a cylinder is the area of the circular base × the height, and the area of the circular base is equal to π × radius squared. Since the question gives the diameter of each cylinder, you'll need to halve each diameter to find the radius, and then you can find the volume. The radius of each drum is $\frac{1.5}{2} = 0.75$ or $\frac{3}{4}$. So, the volume of each drum is $\pi\left(\frac{3}{4}\right)^2(4) = \left(\frac{9}{16}\right)(4)\pi = \frac{9\pi}{4}$. The number of drums is unknown, so use a variable such as x to represent it. So the total volume of the drums is $(x)\frac{9\pi}{4}$. The volume of the tank is $\pi(6^2)(60) = (36)(60)\pi$. So $(x)\frac{9\pi}{4} = (36)(60)\pi$; $x = (36)(60)\pi\left(\frac{4}{9\pi}\right) = (4)(60)(4) = 960$. (E) is correct.

Explanation: Gas Cans

5. The volume of a cylinder is (area of the base) × (height).

Find out the volumes of the cylinders, and work out how much greater the complete volume of can A is compared to half the volume of can B.

Volume of can B: $\pi r^2 h$.

Volume of can A: $\pi(2r)^2 \times \frac{h}{2} = \pi 4r^2 \times \frac{h}{2} = 2\pi r^2 h$, which is twice the volume of can B.

Therefore, if it takes \$4 to fill half of can B, then it will take \$8 to completely fill can B, and it will take twice \$8, or \$16, to completely fill can A. (E) wins again.

Notice that not every word problem without a diagram needs you to supply one. While a quick sketch might have helped with these questions, it certainly wasn't necessary.

Related to cylinders are circles. Circles, like triangles, are GMAT geometry favorites. You will often encounter them both in the same question.

GEOMETRY WORD PROBLEMS PRACTICE SET 3

sundial

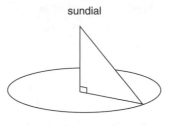

Note: Diagram not drawn to scale.

6. The above diagram represents a sundial, formed by attaching the shortest side of a right triangle to a radius of the circular base. If the length of the two longest sides of the triangle are 13 centimeters and 12 centimeters, what is the area of the circular base?

    (A) 5π
    (B) 10π
    (C) 25π
    (D) 30π
    (E) 100π

7. A circular manhole is covered by a circular cover which has a diameter of 32 inches. If the manhole has a diameter of 30 inches, how much greater than the area of the manhole is the area of the cover, in square inches?

    (A) 2π
    (B) 4π
    (C) 24π
    (D) 31π
    (E) 124π

Explanation: Sundial

6. You can find the area of the circle if you can find a value for the radius. The circle's radius is equal to the length of the shorter leg of the right triangle. You might have recognized this triangle as a 5–12–13 right triangle, so the shortest side is 5. (If you didn't recognize this special right triangle, you could have used the Pythagorean theorem to find the unknown side. The longest side is the hypotenuse, so $\text{leg}_1{}^2 + \text{leg}_2{}^2 = \text{hypotenuse}^2$, that is $\text{leg}_1{}^2 + 12^2 = 13^2$, or $\text{leg}_1{}^2 = 169 - 144 = 25$, so $\text{leg}_1 = 5$.) Since this side is equal to the radius of the circle, you are now ready to plug into the area formula: $\text{area} = \pi r^2 = \pi(5)^2 = 25\pi$. (C) is the answer.

Explanation: Manhole Cover

7. Knowing the diameter of a circle is enough to determine its area, since $a = \pi r^2$, and r, the radius, is half the diameter. The radius of the cover is $\frac{1}{2}(32) = 16$, so the cover has an area of $\pi(16)^2$, or 256π. The manhole has a radius of $\frac{1}{2}(30)$, or 15, so its area is $\pi(15)^2$, or 225π. So the area of the cover is $256\pi - 225\pi$ or 31π square inches greater than the area of the manhole. (D) it is.

Perhaps the key to the most difficult GMAT word problems is to see the figure differently. Often the figure presented can be broken down into smaller figures, or extended to create larger figures. By examining these "secondary" figures, you can derive the information you need to answer the question.

This is a skill best taught by example. And here are four of them:

GEOMETRY WORD PROBLEMS PRACTICE SET 4

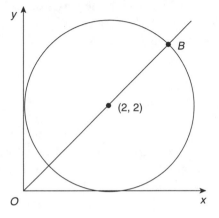

8. In the rectangular coordinate system above, the circle is tangent to the x and y axes and has center (2,2). Line segment OB connects the origin to a point on the circle that passes through the center of the circle. What is the length of OB?

    (A) $2\sqrt{2}$
    (B) $2 + \sqrt{2}$
    (C) 4
    (D) $2 + 2\sqrt{2}$
    (E) $4\sqrt{2}$

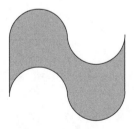

9. If each curved portion of the boundary of the figure above is formed from the circumferences of two semicircles, each with a radius of 2, and each of the parallel sides has length 4, what is the area of the shaded figure?

    (A) 16
    (B) 32
    (C) $16 - 8\pi$
    (D) $32 - 8\pi$
    (E) $32 - 4\pi$

Explanation: Line Segment *OB*

8. Look for some way to break *OB* down into familiar segments whose lengths you are able to find. Notice that the distance from the center of the circle to *B* is a radius of the circle. The radius of the circle is the distance from point (2, 2) to the point where the circle touches the *x*-axis. This distance is 2. So the radius is 2. But what about the distance from *O* to the center of the circle? Well, if you draw a perpendicular line from the center of the circle down to the *x*-axis, you form a right triangle whose hypotenuse is the distance from *O* to the center of the circle. The horizontal leg of this triangle extends from the origin to 2 on the *x*-axis, so its length is 2. The vertical leg extends from the *x*-axis to a height of 2 parallel to the *y*-axis, so its length is also 2. The triangle is an isoceles right triangle. The leg length to leg length to hypotenuse length ratio in an isosceles right triangle is $1:1:\sqrt{2}$. So the hypotenuse has a length of $2\sqrt{2}$. Therefore, the length of *OB* is $2 + 2\sqrt{2}$. Choice (D) is correct.

Explanation: A Strange Figure

9. This looks pretty tricky at first glance, but in reality is quite simple. The shaded figure looks like a rectangle which has had two semicircles removed and two added on. In other words, whatever has been cut out of the original rectangle has been added back on. In other words, what we have here is really just the area of the rectangle. What are the dimensions of this rectangle? They've told us that the width is 4 units. The area of a rectangle is length × width, so look for a way to find the length.

There are two circles along the length of the rectangle—the length is equal to four times the circle's radius.

If each radius is 2 and there are 4 of them along each horizontal side, then the length is 8 units. Since area = length × width, the area is 8 × 4 = 32 square units, answer choice (B).

An 800 test taker modifies the diagrams given to create "secondary" diagrams, which help him to discover information hidden in the original.

Two more examples of modifying a diagram. **Hint:** the first one is worth sketching so you have a diagram to modify. The second one is a suitable ending to geometry word problems.

GEOMETRY WORD PROBLEMS PRACTICE SET 5

10. If a square is formed by joining the points A (–2, 1), B (1, 5), C (5, 2), and D (2, –2), what is the area of square $ABCD$?

(A) $9\sqrt{2}$

(B) $12\sqrt{2}$

(C) 18

(D) 21

(E) 25

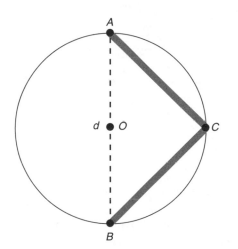

11. Points A and B are at opposite ends of a circular pond with diameter d. A bridge connects point A with point C, and another bridge connects point C with point B. The two bridges are of equal length. What is the ratio of the distance from A to B when traveling along the two bridges, to the distance when traveling along the edge of the pond?

(A) $\dfrac{2\sqrt{2}}{\pi}$

(B) $\dfrac{d\sqrt{2}}{\pi}$

(C) $\dfrac{2}{\pi}$

(D) $\dfrac{\sqrt{2}}{2\pi}$

(E) $\dfrac{2\sqrt{2}}{\pi d}$

Explanation: Area of a Square

10. First sketch the square *ABCD*. The area of any square is equal to the length of one of its sides squared. So if we can find the length of any one side of square *ABCD*, we can find the area of the square.

You can find the length of side *AB*, the hypotenuse of a right triangle with legs of 4 and 3. (In fact you can construct a right triangle just like this one for all sides of the square.)

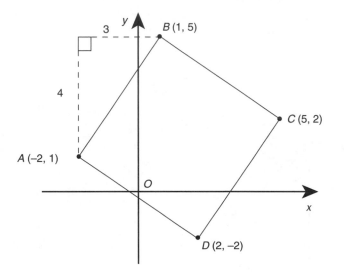

You can find the hypotenuse of this triangle using the Pythagorean theorem.

This is one of our special right triangles—it has legs in a ratio of 3:4:5, so *AB* has a length of 5. The area of the square is then 5 × 5 = 25, choice (E).

Explanation: Circular Pond

11. This is a tough problem. The best place to start is to first figure out the distance from *A* to *B* around the edge of the pond, which you can see is half of the circle's circumference. Circumference is π times diameter, so the circumference of the entire circle is π*d*, making the distance along the edge from *A* to *B* half this or $\frac{\pi d}{2}$. Finding the distance from *A* to *B* across the bridges is a bit more involved. Draw a line from point *C* to the center of the circle, *O*.

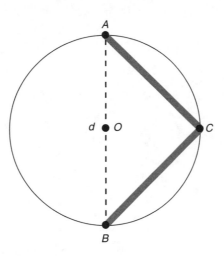

AC and *BC* are the same length. *OA*, *OC*, and *OB* are all radii of the circle so they are all the same

length. So Δ*AOC* and Δ*BOC* are congruent isosceles right triangles. (That is, their interior angles

and the length of their sides are the same.) The sides of an isosceles right triangle are in the ratio

$1: 1:\sqrt{2}$. Since the legs have a length of $\frac{d}{2}$, the hypotenuses, *AC* and *BC* have a length of $\frac{d\sqrt{2}}{2}$

and $AC + BC = \frac{d\sqrt{2}}{2} + \frac{d\sqrt{2}}{2} = d\sqrt{2}$. This is the distance from *A* to *B* when traveling along the

bridges. So the ratio of the route over the bridges to the route around the edge of the pond is

$$\frac{\sqrt{2}d}{\frac{\pi d}{2}} = \frac{\sqrt{2}d}{1} \times \frac{2}{\pi d} = \frac{2\sqrt{2}}{\pi}, \text{ or } (\Lambda).$$

CHAPTER NINETEEN

Oddball Word Problems

As with other GMAT question types, perhaps even more so, Word Problems are often oddballs. Because they deal with "real world" situations, word problems can be used to test just about every math and logic skill under the sun. You wouldn't be properly prepared for the 800-level math questions if your practice didn't include a sampling of these.

On test day, of course, you may encounter other oddballs. That's just the nature of the game. But bear in mind that just because a question seems completely new to you, it doesn't have to be difficult.

ODDBALL WORD PROBLEMS PRACTICE SET 1

1. A computer is programmed to generate two numbers according to the following scheme: The first number is to be a randomly selected integer from 0 to 99; the second number is to be an integer which is less than the square of the units digit of the first number. Which of the following pairs of numbers could NOT have been generated by this program?

   (A) 99, 10
   (B) 60, −10
   (C) 58, 63
   (D) 13, 11
   (E) 12, 3

2. A certain clock rings two notes at quarter past the hour, four notes at half past, and six notes at three-quarters past. On the hour, it rings eight notes plus an additional number of notes equal to whatever hour it is. How many notes will the clock ring between 1:00 P.M. and 5:00 P.M., including the rings at 1:00 and 5:00?

   (A) 87
   (B) 95
   (C) 102
   (D) 103
   (E) 115

3. Each of three charities in Novel Grove Estates has 8 persons serving on its board of directors. If exactly 4 persons serve on 3 boards each and each pair of charities has 5 persons in common on their boards of directors, then how many distinct persons serve on one or more boards of directors?

   (A) 8
   (B) 13
   (C) 16
   (D) 24
   (E) 27

Explanation: Computer-Generated Numbers

1. Don't get caught up in abstractly pondering the question stem's special instructions; turn to the answer choices and start testing the given pairs of numbers. Start at (D) or (E) for "which of the following" questions, since the GMAT favors these two answer choices. (E): The units' digit of 12 is 2 and $2^2 = 4$; $4 > 3$, so eliminate. (D): The units' digit of 13 is 3, and $3^2 = 9$; $9 < 11$, so this pair does not meet the conditions, making (D) correct.

That wasn't too bad, was it? The simple technique of backsolving allowed us to ignore all of the strangeness and focus on the task at hand.

So there are two lessons here. One, oddball word problems can be easy word problems. And two, the basic approach to oddball word problems is to focus on what is familiar—what you know—and employ the same strategies you use for common word problem types.

An 800 test taker doesn't panic when a strange word problem appears on the screen. She instead evaluates the question dispassionately, knowing that many "oddballs" are fairly easy and meant to distinguish the formulaic thinkers (who panic and screw up) from the creative thinkers (who rise to the challenge).

Explanation: A Very Annoying Clock

2. Even though the problem involves only simple arithmetic, don't try to do all the work in your head. Be systematic. Notice that the rings occur in an hourly pattern. You could set up a chart if that helps you see what's going on, or just take each part at a time by finding the number of rings at each interval of time and then adding up the total rings at each interval. The total rings on the hour $= (1 + 8) + (2 + 8) + (3 + 8) + (4 + 8) + (5 + 8) = 9 + 10 + 11 + 12 + 13 = 55$. The clock rings twice at a quarter past and it does this 4 times, so the total rings at a quarter past $= 2(4) = 8$. Likewise, the number of rings at half past $= 4(4) = 16$, and the number of rings at three-quarters past $= 6(4) = 24$. Adding up, $55 + 8 + 16 + 24 = 103$.

You also could have set up a chart to organize information, like the one below. Setting up the chart will take a few extra seconds, but if arranging the information visually so you can see it all at once makes the difference between a confusing problem and an intuitively clear one, by all means, draw the chart, like this:

	:00	:15	:30	:45
1 P.M.	9	2	4	6
2 P.M.	10	2	4	6
3 P.M.	11	2	4	6
4 P.M.	12	2	4	6
5 P.M.	13			
Total =	55 +	8 +	16 +	24 = 103

(D) is correct.

Explanation: How Many Directors?

3. To keep track of all the confusing information, set up a sketch like the one below and fill in the information as you go along.

Board 1: __ __ __ __ __ __ __ __

Board 2: __ __ __ __ __ __ __ __

Board 3: __ __ __ __ __ __ __ __

Since 4 persons serve on each board, fill in a letter for each person for 4 slots on each board; it doesn't matter where. This takes care of 4 of the 5 persons that are common to each pair of charities (1-2; 2-3; and 1-3):

Board A: A   B   C   D   __ __ __ __

Board B: A   B   C   D   __ __ __ __

Board C: A   B   C   D   __ __ __ __

Now you can fill in the fifth and sixth slots on each board with the fifth person common to each pair. And that means that the two positions left must be occupied by people who are members of only one board.

The results look like this:

Board A: A   B   C   D   E   F   H   K

Board B: A   B   C   D   E   G   I   L

Board C: A   B   C   D   F   G   J   M

Since each distinct letter represents a distinct person, just count up the number of distinct letters to get the number of distinct persons on the boards. The total number of people represented is the number of letters from A to M, and a quick count of the letters on the chart will show that this is 13. So a total of 13 persons serve on one or more boards, making (B) correct.

ODDBALL WORD PROBLEMS PRACTICE SET 2

As if there weren't enough real math in the world, the test makers sometimes make up their own, "phony" math. Don't let it throw you. The question will always provide the information you need.

Questions 4–5 refer to the following definition.

The "connection" between any two positive integers a and b is the ratio of the smallest common multiple of a and b to the product of a and b. For instance, the smallest common multiple of 8 and 12 is 24, and the product of 8 and 12 is 96, so the connection between 8 and 12 is $\frac{24}{96} = \frac{1}{4}$.

4. What is the connection between 12 and 21 ?

    (A) $\frac{1}{9}$

    (B) $\frac{1}{7}$

    (C) $\frac{1}{3}$

    (D) $\frac{4}{7}$

    (E) $\frac{1}{1}$

5. The positive integer y is less than 20 and the connection between y and 6 is equal to $\frac{1}{1}$. How many possible values of y are there?

    (A) 7

    (B) 8

    (C) 9

    (D) 10

    (E) 11

Explanation: Made-Up Math Terms

4. When a problem includes a special term or symbol, just follow the instructions that define it. There are two parts to a "connection": the smallest common multiple and the product. To get the smallest common multiple of 12 and 21, break each number down into its prime factors and multiply them together, counting common factors only once: $12 = 2 \times 2 \times 3$, and $21 = 3 \times 7$, giving you $2 \times 2 \times 3 \times 7$ for the least common multiple. The product of 12 and 21 is $(2 \times 2 \times 3) \times (3 \times 7)$. Therefore, the "connection" is $\dfrac{2 \times 2 \times 3 \times 7}{2 \times 2 \times 3 \times 3 \times 7}$, which reduces to $\dfrac{1}{3}$. Notice how easy it is to reduce the fraction when both the numerator and denominator are broken down into factors. (C) it is.

Explanation: Made-Up Math Terms, Part Two

5. If the connection between y and 6 is $\dfrac{1}{1}$, then the smallest common multiple of y and 6 must equal the product $6y$. The lowest common multiple of two numbers equals the product of the two numbers only when there are no common factors (other than 1). Since y is a positive integer less than 20, check all the integers from 1 to 19 to see which ones have no factors greater than 1 in common with 6: 1, 5, 7, 11, 13, 17, and 19. So there are 7 possible values for y. (A) is correct.

And how about a final pair, before leaving Problem Solving for good?

ODDBALL WORD PROBLEMS PRACTICE SET 3

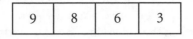

| 9 | 8 | 6 | 3 |

6. The figure above shows an example of a 4-digit identification code used by a certain bank for its customers. If the digits in the code must appear in descending numerical order, and no digit can be used more than once, what is the difference between the largest and the smallest possible codes?

    (A) 6,666
    (B) 5,555
    (C) 5,432
    (D) 4,444
    (E) 1,111

7. A machine is made up of two components, *A* and *B*. Each component either works or fails. The failure or nonfailure of one component is independent of the failure or nonfailure of the other component. The machine works if at least one of the components works. If the probability that each component works is $\frac{2}{3}$, what is the probability that the machine works?

    (A) $\frac{1}{9}$

    (B) $\frac{4}{9}$

    (C) $\frac{1}{2}$

    (D) $\frac{2}{3}$

    (E) $\frac{8}{9}$

Explanation: ID Codes

6. You need the difference between the largest and smallest possible codes. A digit cannot be repeated, and the digits must appear in descending numerical order. The largest such number will have the largest digit, 9, in the thousands' place, followed by the next largest digits, 8, 7, and 6, in the next three places, so 9,876 is the largest possible number. For the smallest, start with the smallest digit, 0, and put it in the ones' place. Work up from there—you end up with 3,210 as the smallest possible code. The difference between the largest and smallest codes is $9,876 - 3,210 = 6,666$, or (A).

Explanation: A Sometimes Working Machine

7. The fastest way to do this is to find the probability that neither component works, and subtract that from 1. Since the probability of a component working is $\frac{2}{3}$, the probability of a component not working is $1 - \frac{2}{3} = \frac{1}{3}$. Therefore, the probability that neither component works is $\frac{1}{3} \times \frac{1}{3} = \frac{1}{9}$, and the probability that the machine works is $1 - \frac{1}{9} = \frac{8}{9}$. (E) wins.

section six

DATA SUFFICIENCY

CHAPTER TWENTY

The Data Sufficiency Challenge

About a third of the points available in the math section of the GMAT appear in Data Sufficiency format. The rest of the questions are in Problem Solving format. As the name implies, Problem Solving questions ask you to solve a math problem and then look for the answer choice that matches your solution. But in Data Sufficiency you don't care about the solution to the question asked in the stem; you just need to decide whether you can answer it. As a result, most Data Sufficiency questions require little or no calculation. They're designed to be answered more quickly than Problem Solving questions, even though most people find them harder at first. It just takes a little practice to become comfortable with the format.

Data Sufficiency questions have a fixed format. The answer choices are the same for all Data Sufficiency questions. You're given a question stem followed by two statements that, taken together or separately, may or may not be sufficient to answer the question in the stem. You have to choose one of five options about the two statements.

DATA SUFFICIENCY—DIRECTIONS

Directions: In each of the problems below, a question is followed by two statements containing certain data. You are to determine whether the data provided by the statements are sufficient to answer the question. Choose the correct answer based upon the statements' data, your knowledge of mathematics, and your familiarity with everyday facts (such as the number of minutes in an hour or cents in a dollar).

A   Statement (1) by itself is sufficient to answer the question, but statement (2) by itself is not;

B   Statement (2) by itself is sufficient to answer the question, but statement (1) by itself is not;

C   Statements (1) and (2) taken together are sufficient to answer the question, even though neither statement by itself is sufficient;

D   Either statement by itself is sufficient to answer the question;

E   Statements (1) and (2) taken together are not sufficient to answer the question, requiring more data pertaining to the problem.

Note: Diagrams accompanying problems agree with information given in the questions, but may not agree with additional information given in statements (1) and (2).

All numbers used are real numbers.

Example:

$$A \qquad B \qquad C$$

What is the length of segment AC ?

(1) B is the midpoint of AC.

(2) $AB = 5$

Explanation:

Statement (1) tells you that B is the midpoint of AC, so $AB = BC$ and $AC = 2AB = 2\,BC$. Since statement (1) does not give a value for AB or BC, you cannot answer the question using statement (1) alone. Statement (2) says that $AB = 5$. Since statement (2) does not give you a value for BC, the question cannot be answered by statement (2) alone. Using both statements together you can find a value for both AB and BC; therefore you can find AC, so the answer to the problem is choice (C).

STRATEGY FOR DATA SUFFICIENCY: THE KAPLAN THREE-STEP METHOD

Example:

Team *X* won 40 basketball games. What percent of its basketball games did Team *X* win?

(1) Team *X* played the same number of basketball games as Team *Y*.

(2) Team *Y* won 45 games, representing 62.5 percent of the basketball games it played.

1. Focus on the question stem.

Decipher the question stem quickly and think about what information is needed to answer it. Do you need a formula? Do you need to set up an equation? Do you need to know the value of a variable?

The sample question involves percents. (Hint: Percent × Whole = Part.) You're given the part (the number of games team *X* won) and asked for the percent (that is, the percentage of its games that team *X* won). What do you need? The whole—the total number of games team *X* played.

2. Look at each statement separately.

Remember, while determining the sufficiency of a particular statement, you must not carry over the other statement's information.

3. Look at both statements in combination.

Proceed to step 3 only when statements (1) and (2) are both insufficient. This happens less than half the time. Note that if you reach this point on a problem, the answer must be either the third or the fifth option. When considering the two statements together, simply treat them and the stimulus as one long problem and ask yourself: Can it be solved? *Stop as soon as you know if it can be solved! Don't carry out any unnecessary calculation.*

CHAPTER TWENTY-ONE

Data Sufficiency—Straight Math

One of the most useful techniques for Data Sufficiency questions is to rephrase the information that you are given in the question. This seems obvious enough for Data Sufficiency word problems, but it is also useful for straight math questions. For example:

Is $z + z < z$?

(1) $-4z > 4z$

(2) $z^3 < z^2$

A if statement (1) BY ITSELF is sufficient to answer the question, but statement (2) by itself is not;

B if statement (2) BY ITSELF is sufficient to answer the question, but statement (1) by itself is not;

C if statements (1) and (2) TAKEN TOGETHER are sufficient to answer the question, even though NEITHER statement BY ITSELF is sufficient;

D if EITHER statement BY ITSELF is sufficient to answer the question;

E if statements (1) and (2) TAKEN TOGETHER are NOT sufficient to answer the question, requiring more data pertaining to the problem.

Here's how to approach this question: The stem asks: Is $z + z < z$? If you subtract z from both sides of the inequality, the stem now asks: Is $z < 0$? So you really just want to know whether z is negative.

Statement (1): *Sufficient.* This states that $-4z > 4z$. Adding $4z$ to both sides, we have $0 > 8z$, or $8z < 0$. Dividing both sides by 8, we have $z < 0$. So z does have to be negative. Sufficient.

Statement (2): *Insufficient.* Since $z^3 < z^2$, z cannot be 0. Since $z \neq 0$, and the square of any nonzero number is positive, $z^2 > 0$. Dividing both sides of the inequality $z^3 < z^2$ by the positive quantity z^2, we have $z < 1$. So $z \neq 0$ and $z < 1$. So z could be negative and the answer to the question would be yes. But z could be a positive fraction less than 1, such as 1/2, and the answer to the question would be no. So statement (2) is insufficient. Choice (A) is correct.

Now try a couple on your own.

DATA SUFFICIENCY—STRAIGHT MATH PRACTICE SET 1

A   if statement (1) BY ITSELF is sufficient to answer the question, but statement (2) by itself is not;

B   if statement (2) BY ITSELF is sufficient to answer the question, but statement (1) by itself is not;

C   if statements (1) and (2) TAKEN TOGETHER are sufficient to answer the question, even though NEITHER statement BY ITSELF is sufficient;

D   if EITHER statement BY ITSELF is sufficient to answer the question;

E   if statements (1) and (2) TAKEN TOGETHER are NOT sufficient to answer the question, requiring more data pertaining to the problem.

1.   If x and y are positive integers, is $2x$ a multiple of y ?

   (1) $2x + 2$ is a multiple of y.

   (2) y is a multiple of x.

2.   If m and n are both two-digit numbers, and $m - n = 11x$, is x an integer?

   (1)   The tens digit and the units digit of m are the same.

   (2) $m + n$ is a multiple of 11.

Explanation: Question 1

1. Rephrased, the question becomes: "Is $\dfrac{2x}{y}$ an integer?"

Similarly, statement (1) can be rephrased as "$\dfrac{2x + 2}{y}$ is an integer," and statement (2) as "$\dfrac{y}{x}$ is an integer." There's no quick and easy way to answer the question; your best bet is to pick numbers for x and y and see what happens. But if you find yourself spending too much time here, bail out: eliminate whatever answer choices you can and guess among the rest.

Now try statement (1). Choosing 2 for both x and y makes both $\dfrac{2x + 2}{y}$ and $\dfrac{2x}{y}$ integers. But if you pick 2 for x and 3 for y, $\dfrac{2x + 2}{y}$ is an integer, while $\dfrac{2x}{y}$ is not an integer, so statement (1) doesn't lead to a clear answer, and choices (A) and (D) are wrong. With statement (2), choosing 3 for x and 6 for y makes y a multiple of x; it also makes $\dfrac{2x}{y}$ an integer. Choosing 3 for x and 9 for y also makes y a multiple of x; however, $\dfrac{2 \times 3}{9}$ is not an integer. So you can't answer the question using statement (2) alone. That means you can rule out choice (B) as well.

For many people, it won't pay to look at each statement separately and then in tandem on this problem. You can stop and guess as soon as you get at least one statement, and should do so if this is eating up a lot of your time. But we'll be thorough here and try combining the two statements. If $x = 2$ and $y = 6$, then $\dfrac{2x + 2}{y}$ and $\dfrac{y}{x}$ are both integers, but $\dfrac{2x}{y}$ is not an integer. But if $x = 2$ and $y = 2$, then $\dfrac{2x + 2}{y}$, $\dfrac{y}{x}$, and $\dfrac{2x}{y}$ are *all* integers. Once again, inconclusive. Choice (E) is correct.

Explanation: Question 2

2. Try rephrasing the given information. Here, m and n are both greater than or equal to 10, and less than or equal to 99. You're supposed to determine if their difference is a multiple of 11.

Statement (1) implies that m is a two-digit multiple of 11. At this point, just pick numbers to show that it is insufficient. If $m = 22$ and $n = 11$, then $m - n$ is a multiple of 11, but if $m = 22$ and $n = 18$, then $m - n$ is not a multiple of 11.

If $m + n$ is a multiple of 11, as statement (2) says, then m could be 10 and n could be 12, and $m - n$ will not be a multiple of 11. But m could also be 22 and n could be 11, in which case $m - n$ is a multiple of 11.

Putting the statements together, m must be a multiple of 11 from statement (1), and that means that n must be a multiple of 11 in order to make statement (2) true (try a few examples to see it). And any multiple of 11 minus a multiple of 11 is a multiple of 11 (remember, it's fine if $x = 0$). If you find the unknowns too abstract to deal with, pick numbers. Pick any two- or three-digit multiple of 11 to represent $m + n$, per statement (2). Then pick any two-digit multiple of 11 to represent m, per statement (1). The difference between those two numbers will be n. If you then subtract n from m, the difference will still be a multiple of 11. (C) is correct. And remember, there's nothing special about the number 11 here; the same thing would work with multiples of another number (try it out if you don't see it).

DATA SUFFICIENCY—STRAIGHT MATH PRACTICE SET 2

A   if statement (1) BY ITSELF is sufficient to answer the question, but statement (2) by itself is not;

B   if statement (2) BY ITSELF is sufficient to answer the question, but statement (1) by itself is not;

C   if statements (1) and (2) TAKEN TOGETHER are sufficient to answer the question, even though NEITHER statement BY ITSELF is sufficient;

D   if EITHER statement BY ITSELF is sufficient to answer the question;

E   if statements (1) and (2) TAKEN TOGETHER are NOT sufficient to answer the question, requiring more data pertaining to the problem.

3. What is the numerical value of $\frac{1}{a} + \frac{1}{b} + \frac{1}{c}$?

(1) $a + b + c = 1$

(2) $abc = 1$

4. What is the average (arithmetic mean) of 7, 11, and x ?

(1) The average (arithmetic mean) of 11 and x is 8.

(2) The average (arithmetic mean) of 7 and x is 6.

Explanation: Question 3

3. It may help to express this as a single fraction with one denominator:

$$\frac{1}{a} + \frac{1}{b} + \frac{1}{c} = \frac{bc}{abc} + \frac{ac}{abc} + \frac{ab}{abc} = \frac{bc + ac + ab}{abc}$$

You could evaluate this expression if you had values for a, b, and c, or you may be able to find the value of the expression without solving for individual variables.

Statement (1): *Insufficient.* Don't fall for look-alike answer choices—the reciprocal of $a + b + c$ is not $\frac{1}{a} + \frac{1}{b} + \frac{1}{c}$.

Statement (2): *Insufficient.* This gives you the denominator of your fraction, but nothing else.

The statements combined still do not provide enough information to evaluate the expression. It may look like you have three equations and three unknowns, but the stem contains only an expression, not an equation: It doesn't say that $\frac{1}{a} + \frac{1}{b} + \frac{1}{c}$ is equal to anything. (E) is the answer.

Explanation: Question 4

4. A value question. Rewrite the question: Average $= \frac{7 + 11 + x}{3}$. Now, if we know what x is, we can solve for the average.

Statement (1): *Sufficient.* Rewrite as $\frac{11 + x}{2} = 8$. Once we solve for x, we can plug it into our expression for the average to get the average.

Statement (2): *Sufficient.* Rewrite as $\frac{7 + x}{2} = 6$. Once we solve for x, we can plug it into our expression for the average to get the average. (D) it is.

While geometry is not all that common on Data Sufficiency questions—accounting for about 15 percent of the questions—you will see it. And when you see it, it'll look like this:

DATA SUFFICIENCY—STRAIGHT MATH PRACTICE SET 3

A   if statement (1) BY ITSELF is sufficient to answer the question, but statement (2) by itself is not;

B   if statement (2) BY ITSELF is sufficient to answer the question, but statement (1) by itself is not;

C   if statements (1) and (2) TAKEN TOGETHER are sufficient to answer the question, even though NEITHER statement BY ITSELF is sufficient;

D   if EITHER statement BY ITSELF is sufficient to answer the question;

E   if statements (1) and (2) TAKEN TOGETHER are NOT sufficient to answer the question, requiring more data pertaining to the problem.

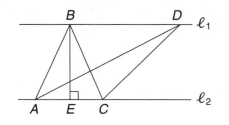

5.   In the figure above, $\ell_1 \parallel \ell_2$. What is the area of $\triangle ADC$?

(1) $AD = 9$

(2) $BE \times AC = 24$

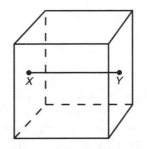

6. In the figure above, *X* and *Y* are the centers of two opposite faces of the cube. What is the length of *XY* ?

   (1) The volume of the cube is 27 cubic meters.
   (2) The surface area of the cube is 54 square meters.

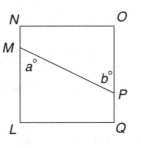

7. In the diagram above, what is the length of *MP* if *LNOQ* is a square with an area of 64 ?

   (1) $a - b = 0$
   (2) $OP = \frac{1}{2} OQ$

Explanation: Question 5

5. The area formula for a triangle is $\frac{1}{2} \times$ base $\times$ height. To find the area of a triangle, therefore, you would normally look for information about its base and height—and not necessarily within the triangle itself. Triangle ADC has base AC and height BE.

Statement (1) alone gives you no way to determine the area of the triangle, because it doesn't let us find the height perpendicular to AD. This is because AD could be nearly perpendicular to AC (nearly like BE which is perpendicular to AC) or it could be even closer to horizontal than in the diagram. Since angle DAC can vary, the height of triangle ADC perpendicular to AD can also vary, which means the area of the triangle can vary as well.

But statement (2) gives you the product of a base and height of triangle ADC. The triangle's area would be half that product, so statement (2) is sufficient to answer the question. (B) is correct.

Explanation: Question 6

6. This demands some intuition on your part. Since X and Y are the centers of the two opposite cube faces, the segment from X to Y measures the distance from one cube face to the other; that means it has the same length as an edge of the cube. So the problem reduces to finding the length of an edge of the cube.

Statement (1): *Sufficient.* It gives you the volume of the cube. For cubes, volume = e^3 where e is the cube's edge length, so if you know the volume you can find the length of the edge. (For the record, $27 = e^3$, $e = 3$, so $XY = 3$.)

Statement (2): *Sufficient.* It is only a little trickier. A cube has 6 faces of equal area. This cube's total surface area is 54 square meters, so each face has an area of $54 \div 6 = 9$ square meters. Each face is a square, and a square's area is e^2, where e is the length of a side of the square. So $e^2 = 9$, and $e = \sqrt{9} = 3$, which is also XY. (D) is the winner.

Explanation: Question 7

7. The stem asks for the length of *MP* if the square has an area of 64 (and thus sides of 8).

Statement (1): Insufficient. This states that $a - b = 0$, so $a = b$. This tells you nothing because *NL* and *OQ* are parallel (remember that when parallel lines are crossed by a transversal line, the alternate interior angles are equal). If you're not sure of the rule, try redrawing the diagram with $a = b = 60$ and $a = b = 90$ and you will see that *MP* could be different lengths.

Statement (2): Insufficient. You know that $OP = \frac{1}{2}OQ$, and therefore *P* is the midpoint of *OQ*, but this tells you nothing helpful (such as the degree measure of the angle marked $b°$, which is *b*).

Statements (1) & (2): Insufficient. Neither statement contributes any information that would allow you to determine the angle measures of *a* or *b* or the length of *MP*, so the statements together won't work either. (E) it is.

It may already have occurred to you that the technique of backsolving isn't going to be much help on Data Sufficiency. For one thing, the answer choices are fixed, and they don't give you numbers to work with. Moreover, the whole idea behind Data Sufficiency is very similar to backsolving; you're taking the information in the statements and seeing if it "solves" the question.

The good news, though, is that the other key math strategy—picking numbers—still works just fine, especially on questions testing number properties and algebra. Here are a few examples:

DATA SUFFICIENCY—STRAIGHT MATH PRACTICE SET 4

A   if statement (1) BY ITSELF is sufficient to answer the question, but statement (2) by itself is not;

B   if statement (2) BY ITSELF is sufficient to answer the question, but statement (1) by itself is not;

C   if statements (1) and (2) TAKEN TOGETHER are sufficient to answer the question, even though NEITHER statement BY ITSELF is sufficient;

D   if EITHER statement BY ITSELF is sufficient to answer the question;

E   if statements (1) and (2) TAKEN TOGETHER are NOT sufficient to answer the question, requiring more data pertaining to the problem.

8.   If z_1, z_2, z_3, ..., z_n is a series of consecutive positive integers, is the sum of all the integers in this series odd?

   (1) $\dfrac{z_1 + z_2 + z_3 + ... + z_n}{n}$ is an odd integer.

   (2) *n* is odd.

9.   If *x* and *y* are nonzero integers, what is the remainder when *x* is divided by *y* ?

   (1) When *x* is divided by 2*y*, the remainder is 4.

   (2) When *x* + *y* is divided by *y*, the remainder is 4.

Explanation: Question 8

8. A series of consecutive positive integers is just a string of regular counting numbers (like 3, 4, 5, 6 or 101, 102, 103; etc.). Whether you do it at the beginning or when looking at the statements, you'll have to experiment to see what happens when series start with odd or even numbers, and when series have an odd or an even number of terms. Of course, the way to do this is to pick simple numbers and extrapolate. (Just remember: *pick more than one set* of numbers, and pick *different kinds* of numbers.)

Here statement (2) looks much simpler, so we'll turn to it first. n is the number of terms (that's what z_n tells you), so the series has an odd number of terms, but not necessarily an odd sum. The sum of $\{2, 3, 4\}$ is odd, but the sum of $\{1, 2, 3\}$ is even. So the answer must be (A), (C), or (E).

Statement (1) says that dividing the sum of the terms by the number of terms yields an odd integer. You get a gold star for alertness if you recognized the average formula: Average = $\dfrac{\text{Sum of the terms}}{\text{Number of terms}}$. Statement (1) thus means that the average of the series is an odd integer. It also implies that the series has an odd number of terms, because the average of an even number of consecutive integers cannot be an integer. Pick simple numbers to see the pattern, and you'll notice that series in which the middle term is odd have an odd average. Since $\dfrac{z_1 + \ldots + z_n}{n}$ is odd and we have shown that n is odd, $\dfrac{z_1 + \ldots + z_n}{n} \times n$ must be odd, because an odd number times an odd number must be odd. So statement (1) is sufficient, and (A) is correct.

Explanation: Question 9

9. Picking numbers should keep you from getting lost in all the algebraic expressions. Just remember when you pick numbers to do so more than once. Otherwise, you might accidentally choose numbers that skew your results. To decide what kind of numbers to pick, think about the implications of each statement.

In statement (1), dividing x by $2y$ leaves a remainder of 4. You can't get a remainder of 4 unless the number by which you're dividing is greater than or equal to 5. Since y has to be an integer, and $2y$ has to be greater than or equal to 5, start with $y = 3$. Then $2y = 6$. A good number that you can choose for x that will give you a remainder of 4 when you divide by 6 is 10: $10 \div 6$ gives you 1 with a remainder of 4. Now check the remainder when x is divided by y: $10 \div 3$ gives you 3 with a remainder of 1. But does $x \div y$ always yield a remainder of 1 if $x \div 2y$ yields a remainder of 4? Try another set of numbers. This time, let $y = 4$. $2y$ then equals 8, so to get a remainder of 4 when $x \div 2y$; x can equal 12. Now when you check $x \div y$, you get $12 \div 4$, which leaves no remainder at all. The information in statement (1) can thus generate at least two different remainders.

Now check statement (2). This time, $x + y \div y$ leaves a remainder of 4. Again, to get a remainder of 4, the divisor must be at least 5. So when you pick numbers for statement (2), start with $y = 5$. A good number that you can choose for $x + y$ that gives a remainder of 4 when you divide by 5 is 9. If $x + y = 9$, and $y = 5$, then x must equal 4. So $x \div y = 4 \div 5$, which also leaves a remainder of 4. Again, you'll have to pick at least one more set of numbers to make sure that $x \div y$ *always* yields a remainder of 4 if $x + y \div y$ leaves a remainder of 4. This time, let $y = 6$. A good number that you can choose for $x + y$ that gives a remainder of 4 when you divide by 6 is 10. If $x + y = 10$ and $y = 6$, then x must again equal 4. So $x \div y = 4 \div 6$, which again leaves a remainder of 4. So far, statement (2) seems to lead to a consistent answer. But this problem is abstract enough and comes late enough in the section that you should probably either pick a few more sets of numbers to make sure or try to figure out mathematically why the information in the statement would always produce the same answer. In fact, statement (2) alone is sufficient, and here's why: $\frac{x+y}{y} = \frac{x}{y} + \frac{y}{y}$. Since $\frac{y}{y}$ never leaves a remainder, regardless of the value of y, the remainder when x is divided by y will always be the same as the remainder when $(x + y)$ is divided by y. (B) is correct. But all this may take you a long time to figure out; some people would have been better off guessing if they could determine that the first statement is insufficient and eliminate the wrong choices.

An 800 test taker uses the "picking numbers" strategy to attack Data Sufficiency questions.

There are now five more practice sets in this chapter. You can take the questions in pairs, as below. Or you might want to try completing all of the questions at once, flipping back afterwards to compare your reasoning to that in the explanations.

DATA SUFFICIENCY—STRAIGHT MATH PRACTICE SET 5

A   if statement (1) BY ITSELF is sufficient to answer the question, but statement (2) by itself is not;

B   if statement (2) BY ITSELF is sufficient to answer the question, but statement (1) by itself is not;

C   if statements (1) and (2) TAKEN TOGETHER are sufficient to answer the question, even though NEITHER statement BY ITSELF is sufficient;

D   if EITHER statement BY ITSELF is sufficient to answer the question;

E   if statements (1) and (2) TAKEN TOGETHER are NOT sufficient to answer the question, requiring more data pertaining to the problem.

10.   What is the value of z ?

(1) $y = 2 - 3z$

(2) $6z + 2y = 4$

11.   What is the value of x ?

(1) $\sqrt{x^4} = 9$

(2)   The average (arithmetic mean) of x^2, $6x$, and 3 is −2.

Explanation: Question 10

10. You aren't told anything about z, so go straight to the statements.

Statement (1): *Insufficient.* You have two variables and only one equation, you cannot solve for either of those variables.

Statement (2): *Insufficient.* Again, you have two variables and only one equation, you cannot solve for either of those variables.

Statements (1) & (2): *Insufficient.* Even though it looks like you have plenty to work with here—two equations and two variables—the equations are in fact identical. If you multiply both sides of the first equation by 2 you get $2y = 4 - 6z$. Adding $6z$ to both sides leaves $6z + 2y = 4$. Since you have two variables and one equation you cannot find a value for either of these variables. (E) wins.

Explanation: Question 11

11. Since no information about x is given in the question stem, go right to the statements.

Statement (1): *Insufficient.* This states that $\sqrt{x^4} = 9$, which means that $x^2 = 9$, so $x = 3$ or -3 (an all-time favorite GMAT trap).

Statement (2): *Sufficient.* This says the average of x^2, $6x$, and 3 is -2, which, according to the average formula, means that $\dfrac{x^2 + 6x + 3}{3} = -2$, so $x^2 + 6x + 3 = -6$. Thus $x^2 + 6x + 9 = 0$, so $(x + 3)(x + 3) = 0$. Thus $x = -3$, and (B) is the answer.

DATA SUFFICIENCY—STRAIGHT MATH PRACTICE SET 6

A if statement (1) BY ITSELF is sufficient to answer the question, but statement (2) by itself is not;

B if statement (2) BY ITSELF is sufficient to answer the question, but statement (1) by itself is not;

C if statements (1) and (2) TAKEN TOGETHER are sufficient to answer the question, even though NEITHER statement BY ITSELF is sufficient;

D if EITHER statement BY ITSELF is sufficient to answer the question;

E if statements (1) and (2) TAKEN TOGETHER are NOT sufficient to answer the question, requiring more data pertaining to the problem.

12. In the equation $b = ka + 3$, k is a constant. If the possible solutions are in the form (a, b), is $(2, 3)$ a solution to the equation?

   (1) $(1, 4)$ is a solution of the equation $b = ka + 2$.

   (2) $(5, 3)$ is a solution of the equation $3b = ka - 1$.

13. For all nonzero integers n, $n^* = \dfrac{n + 2}{n}$. What is the value of x?

   (1) $x^* = x$

   (2) $x^* = -2 - x$

Explanation: Question 12

12. This problem illustrates a Data Sufficiency pitfall that can trap even the most math-savvy GMAT student. If you don't remember that your goal is to determine whether the question can be answered, rather than whether it can be answered affirmatively, you can get all the math right and still pick the wrong answer.

Here's the math part of the solution. To determine whether any particular ordered pair (a, b) is a solution to the equation $b = ka + 3$, you need to find the value of k. Specifically, to find out if $(2, 3)$ is a solution, you need to know whether $3 = 2k + 3$. That's the same as asking if $0 = 2k$, or, more simply, if $k = 0$. Statements (1) and (2) say that $(1, 4)$ and $(3, 5)$, respectively, are solutions of other equations that also involve k.

Plugging the appropriate ordered pair into the equation in statement (1) gives you $k = 2$. So you can give a definite answer to the question—the answer is definitely "no."

Doing the same thing in statement (2) also gives $k = 2$, and also gives a definite negative response. (D) is the winner.

Explanation: Question 13

13. Plugging x into the expression we have that $x^* = \dfrac{x + 2}{x}$. We need to know about the possible values of x.

Statement (1): *Insufficient.* If $x^* = x$, then $\dfrac{x + 2}{x} = x$. Multiplying both sides by x gives $x + 2 = x^2$. Subtracting $x + 2$ from both sides leaves $x^2 - x - 2 = 0$. Using reverse FOIL gives you $(x - 2)(x + 1) = 0$; that is, $x = 2$ or $x = -1$.

Statement (2): *Insufficient.* If $x^* = -2 - x$ then $\dfrac{x + 2}{x} = -2 - x$. Multiplying both sides by x gives $x + 2 = -2x - x^2$. Subtracting $-2x - x^2$ from both sides leaves $x^2 + 3x + 2 = 0$. Using reverse FOIL gives you $(x + 2)(x + 1) = 0$. That is, $x = -2$ or $x = -1$.

Statements (1) and (2): *Sufficient.* Statement (1) tells you $x = 2$ or -1. Statement (2) tells you $x = -2$ or -1, so $x = -1$. (C) is correct.

DATA SUFFICIENCY—STRAIGHT MATH PRACTICE SET 7

A   if statement (1) BY ITSELF is sufficient to answer the question, but statement (2) by itself is not;

B   if statement (2) BY ITSELF is sufficient to answer the question, but statement (1) by itself is not;

C   if statements (1) and (2) TAKEN TOGETHER are sufficient to answer the question, even though NEITHER statement BY ITSELF is sufficient;

D   if EITHER statement BY ITSELF is sufficient to answer the question;

E   if statements (1) and (2) TAKEN TOGETHER are NOT sufficient to answer the question, requiring more data pertaining to the problem.

14.   What is the value of $a - b$?

(1) $a^2 - b^2 = 9$

(2) $a^2 - 2ab + b^2 = 1$

15.   If $\sqrt{x}$ is a positive integer, is $\sqrt{x}$ a prime number?

(1) x is divisible by exactly 3 positive integers.

(2)   All positive factors of x are odd.

Explanation: Question 14

14. Again, the stem just asks a question.

The expression $a^2 - b^2$ should immediately make you think of factoring. $a^2 - b^2$, the difference of two squares, can be factored into $(a + b)(a - b)$. If you knew the value of $a + b$, you could use the equation $(a + b)(a - b) = 9$ to find the value of $a - b$. As is, however, statement (1) is insufficient.

In statement (2), $a^2 - 2ab + b^2$ is the square of the binomial $a - b$, that is, it equals $(a - b)^2$, or $(a - b)(a - b)$. If $(a - b)^2 = 1$, then $a - b$ can equal ± 1. Taken by itself, then, statement (2) yields two possible values for $a - b$, so it too is insufficient to answer the question. Nor can you rule out either possibility by combining the two statements.

Many Data Sufficiency problems give you enough information to find the value of an unknown sum or difference without evaluating the individual unknowns; this one doesn't. Statement (2) allows for two possible values for $a - b$, while Statement (1) together with Statement (2) does not reduce this number of possible values to one value. (E) is right.

Explanation: Question 15

15. As with most difficult GMAT questions that involve number properties, picking numbers is your best bet here. If $\sqrt{x}$ is a positive integer, x must be a perfect square.

Start with statement (1). The first perfect square, 1, has only itself as a positive factor, so you can't pick 1 for x. The second perfect square is 4, which is divisible by exactly three positive integers: 1, 2, and 4 itself. $\sqrt{4} = 2$, which is prime. Thus, if $x = 4$, the answer to the question is "yes." But do all perfect squares that are divisible by exactly three positive integers have prime square roots? You'll have to pick more numbers to find out. The next perfect square is 9, which is divisible by exactly three positive integers (1, 3, and 9); $\sqrt{9} = 3$, which is prime. The next perfect square is 16, but it has more than three factors that are positive integers (1, 2, 4, 8, and 16), so it is inconsistent with statement (1). The next perfect square is 25, which is divisible by 1, 5, and 25; $\sqrt{25} = 5$, which is prime. Can you see the pattern yet? The square of any prime number will have exactly three factors: 1, the prime integer, and the square of the prime integer. The square of any non-prime integer will have *more* than three positive factors, because it will also be divisible by the factors of its square root. So statement (1) is sufficient.

A little thought (or the selection of appropriate numbers) will reveal that statement (2) does not always lead to a consistent conclusion. For example, 9 and 25 are perfect squares whose only positive factors are odd; $\sqrt{9}$ and $\sqrt{25}$ are also prime. However, many other odd perfect squares, such as 81, have square roots that are not prime. So statement (2) alone does not lead to a definite answer. (A) wins.

DATA SUFFICIENCY—STRAIGHT MATH PRACTICE SET 8

A   if statement (1) BY ITSELF is sufficient to answer the question, but statement (2) by itself is not;

B   if statement (2) BY ITSELF is sufficient to answer the question, but statement (1) by itself is not;

C   if statements (1) and (2) TAKEN TOGETHER are sufficient to answer the question, even though NEITHER statement BY ITSELF is sufficient;

D   if EITHER statement BY ITSELF is sufficient to answer the question;

E   if statements (1) and (2) TAKEN TOGETHER are NOT sufficient to answer the question, requiring more data pertaining to the problem.

16. If a, b, and c are distinct nonzero numbers, is
$$\frac{(a + b)^2(b - c)}{(a - b)^3(b - c)^3} \geq 0?$$

   (1) $a > b$

   (2) $b > c$

17. Is $p + q > r + s$?

   (1) $p > r + s$

   (2) $q > r + s$

Explanation: Question 16

16. Asking if the expression is greater than or equal to zero is the same as asking if the expression is non-negative. Simplify the expression:

$$\frac{(a+b)^2(b-c)}{(a-b)^3(b-c)^3} = \frac{(a+b)^2}{(a-b)^3(b-c)^2}.$$ The square of any nonzero number is positive. So you have a non-negative number, $(a+b)^2$, in the numerator, while in the denominator you have the product of a positive number, $(b-c)^2$, and a number whose sign you don't know, $(a-b)^3$. This expression will not be negative if $(a-b)^3$ is not negative, that is, if $a > b$. So you can answer the question in the stem if you know whether $a > b$ or not.

Statement (1) does tell you if $a > b$ and so is sufficient.

Statement (2) doesn't tell you anything about a and so is insufficient. (A) it is.

Explanation: Question 17

17. The stem tells you that you're dealing with a Yes/No question here.

Statement (1): *Insufficient.* This tells you that p is greater than $r + s$, but nothing about q.

Statement (2): *Insufficient.* This tells you that q is greater than $r + s$, but nothing about p.

Combining the statements tells you that p and q, on their own, are greater than $r + s$. That must mean that $p + q > r + s$, right? Wrong! This is a classic GMAT trap. Be suspicious at this "obvious" sort of an answer at the end of the test. $p + q$ could be greater than $r + s$, say if $p = q = 3$, and $r = s = 1$. But what if p and q are negative, say $p = q = -4$ and $r = s = -3$. Then $p > r + s$ and $q > r + s$, but $p + q < r + s$. Go with (E).

DATA SUFFICIENCY—STRAIGHT MATH PRACTICE SET 9

A   if statement (1) BY ITSELF is sufficient to answer the question, but statement (2) by itself is not;

B   if statement (2) BY ITSELF is sufficient to answer the question, but statement (1) by itself is not;

C   if statements (1) and (2) TAKEN TOGETHER are sufficient to answer the question, even though NEITHER statement BY ITSELF is sufficient;

D   if EITHER statement BY ITSELF is sufficient to answer the question;

E   if statements (1) and (2) TAKEN TOGETHER are NOT sufficient to answer the question, requiring more data pertaining to the problem.

18. If c and d are both positive integers, then c is what percent of d?

   (1) 75 percent of d is 30.
   (2) $c + 15 = d$

19. Sequence S consists of 24 nonzero integers. If each term in S after the second is the product of the previous two terms, how many terms in S are negative?

   (1) The third term in S is positive.
   (2) The fourth term in S is negative.

Explanation: Question 18

18. A value question. Percent $= \dfrac{\text{Part}}{\text{Whole}}$, so to find what percent c is of d you need to find values for both of these variables or the ratio of c to d.

Statement (1) tells you that 75% of d is 30, or $d = \left(\dfrac{4}{3}\right)(30)$. This allows you to solve for d, but it tells you nothing about c. Statement (1) is insufficient, so the answer is (B), (C), or (E).

Statement (2) tells you that $c + 15 = d$. If you knew the value of one of the variables, this equation would allow you to solve for the other, but as it stands you can't solve for either. All you have is one equation with two variables, which normally can't be solved. Statement (2) is insufficient, so the answer is (C) or (E).

Using both statements together, you can solve for the value of d using statement (1) and then plug it into the equation of statement (2) to solve for c, which will enable you to find what percent c is of d. Both statements together are sufficient, so the answer is (C).

Explanation: Question 19

19. This question is one of the hardest you'll ever see on the GMAT.

Statement (1): *Insufficient.* Since the third term is positive, the first two terms are either both positive or both negative.

Statement (2): *Sufficient.* Since the fourth term is negative, the second and third terms have different signs. We need to take this one a few steps to see if a pattern develops:

Term:	1	2	3	4	5	6	7	8
If term 2 is + and 3 is −	−	+	−	−	+	−	−	+
If term 2 is − and 3 is +	−	−	+	−	−	+	−	−

A 2:1 ratio develops for either case. Since the set has 24 integers, we know that there are 16 negative terms and 8 positive terms. We couldn't answer the question if the number of terms was 2 more than a multiple of 3. (B) is correct.

Since the first statement is much easier to decipher, you could have eliminated choices (A) and (D) and guessed. Since this is a question that would appear later in the section, you should avoid guessing choice (E), so guessing (B) or (C) would have been a good idea.

Even if those gave you some trouble, don't get depressed. That's as hard as Data Sufficiency gets. And you probably won't encounter a string of ten that difficult on test day.

Just like the Problem Solving questions, Data Sufficiency comes wrapped in word problems. You'll encounter those in the next chapter.

CHAPTER TWENTY-TWO

Data Sufficiency—Word Problems

As with the Data Sufficiency straight math questions, there isn't much new to introduce with Data Sufficiency word problems. The math is the same as in the Problem Solving questions. The only difference is the Data Sufficiency format.

So what we'll be doing here is looking over examples of how tough the GMAT gets with its word problems. As always, think *sufficiently*. You aren't solving problems, you are just determining whether you *can* solve the problem.

Some of the most common Data Sufficiency word problems deal with some of the main arithmetic topics—ratios, percents, averages, etc. Let's look at some of them.

DATA SUFFICIENCY—WORD PROBLEMS PRACTICE SET 1

A   if statement (1) BY ITSELF is sufficient to answer the question, but statement (2) by itself is not;

B   if statement (2) BY ITSELF is sufficient to answer the question, but statement (1) by itself is not;

C   if statements (1) and (2) TAKEN TOGETHER are sufficient to answer the question, even though NEITHER statement BY ITSELF is sufficient;

D   if EITHER statement BY ITSELF is sufficient to answer the question;

E   if statements (1) and (2) TAKEN TOGETHER are NOT sufficient to answer the question, requiring more data pertaining to the problem.

1. What is the rate, in cubic meters per minute, at which water is flowing into a particular rectangular swimming pool?

    (1) The volume of the swimming pool is 420 cubic meters.

    (2) The surface level of the water is rising at the rate of 0.5 meters per minute.

2. The average (arithmetic mean) monthly balance in Company X's petty cash account on any given date is the average of the closing balances posted on the last business day of each of the past 12 months. On March 6, 1990, the average monthly balance was $692.02. What was the average monthly balance as of June 23, 1990?

    (1) As of June 23, 1990, the total of all the closing balances posted on the last business day of each of the last 12 months was $45.64 less than it had been on March 6, 1990.

    (2) The closing balances posted on the last business days of March, April, and May 1990 were $145.90, $3,000.00, and $725.25, respectively.

3. A box office sold a total of 400 tickets to a certain performance. If b tickets were sold at the benefactor rate, g were sold at the group rate, and the remaining r at the normal rate, how many tickets were sold at the group rate?

    (1) $r = 180$

    (2) The ratio of b to g to r is 4 to 7 to 9.

Explanation: Question 1

1. There are a lot of ways to calculate this rate, so go to the statements.

Statement (1): This tells you the pool's volume, but nothing about the water flowing into it.

Statement (2): This tells you how fast the surface of the water is rising, but the rate of water coming into the pool could vary depending on the dimensions of the pool.

Statements (1) and (2): You now know the volume, and how fast the water is rising, but you still need more information. For instance, say the pool is very shallow, 1 meter deep, with the rectangular base having an area of 420 square meters. Then if the water is rising at 0.5 meters per minute, 210 cubic meters of water are entering the pool every minute. But imagine a small, deep pool with the rectangular base having an area of 10 square meters and a depth of 42 meters. Then if the water is rising at 0.5 meters a minute the rate is much lower, 5 cubic meters per minute. Since there are many different rates, the statements are insufficient even when combined. Choice (E) is correct.

Explanation: Question 2

2. The first sentence of the question stem defines the term "average monthly balance" (AMB) as it is used in this problem. But you don't need the *individual* closing balances for the last business days of June 1989 through May 1990 to find the AMB as of June 23, 1990. The arithmetic mean of any group of terms (numbers) is equal to its sum, divided by the number of terms. In this problem, the number of terms used to calculate an AMB is defined as 12 months; if you knew the sum of the closing balances for any 12-month period, dividing it by 12 would give you the AMB for that period. The question stem gives you the AMB as of March 6, 1990; multiplying $692.02 by 12 would give you the sum of the closing balances posted on the last business day of each month from March 1989 through February 1990. Since you want to find the AMB as of June 23, 1990, the problematic months are March, April, and May 1990 (which are covered by the AMB for June 23, 1990, but not by the AMB for March 6, 1990), and March, April, and May 1989 (which are covered by the AMB for March 6, 1990, but not by the AMB for June 23, 1990). If you knew the total of the closing balances for March–May 1989, and the total of the closing balances for March–May 1990, you could subtract the first total from 12($692.02) and add the second total in order to find the sum of the closing balances posted from June 1989, through May 1990.

Statement (1) finesses the situation by stating the difference between the sums for the two 12-month periods. We know that the sum of the closing balances posted on the last business day of each month from March 1989 through February 1990 was 12($692.02). Then statement (1) says that the sum of the closing balances for June 23, 1990 was $45.64 less than 12($692.02), or 12($692.02) − $45.64. So the average monthly balance posted for June 23, 1990 can be found by simply dividing this quantity by 12.

Statement (2) does not include the closing balances posted on the last business days of March–May 1989, so it alone is insufficient to answer the question. (A) is correct.

Explanation: Question 3

3. This type of question, like all those on this topical test, appears frequently on the GMAT. You have three variables and want to know the value of one of them. You can do this by getting three distinct equations. You can derive one useful equation from the stem: $b + g + r = 400$. Since you know the total number of tickets sold, to find the number of tickets sold at the group rate you need to know either the percent or fraction of the total that are group tickets, or how many tickets were sold at the other two rates.

Statement (1) tells you that 180 tickets were sold at the normal rate, but this only tells you that the remaining 220 are sold at the benefactor rate or the group rate. But we don't know anything about how many of each type of ticket were sold. Statement (1) is insufficient.

Statement (2) tells you that the ratio of benefactor to group to normal tickets sold is 4 to 7 to 9. This allows you to find the fraction of tickets that were sold at the group rate (the fraction of tickets sold at the group rate is $\dfrac{7}{4 + 7 + 9} = \dfrac{7}{20}$ of the total, but don't calculate this on test day). Since you know the total number of tickets sold (400) and what fraction of the whole the part is $\left(\dfrac{7}{20}\right)$, you can solve for the value of the part by just multiplying them. Statement (2) is sufficient, and (B) is correct.

You could also have approached this algebraically. Any time you have as many distinct linear equations as variables, you can solve for the value of any variable. The question stem gives you one equation, $b + g + r = 400$. Statement (2) gives you not just one, but two additional distinct equations you need: the ratio of benefactor to group is 4:7, and the ratio of group to normal is 7:9. You can write this mathematically as $b = \dfrac{4}{7}g$ and $g = \dfrac{7}{9}r$. Now you have three distinct equations.

DATA SUFFICIENCY—WORD PROBLEMS PRACTICE SET 2

A   if statement (1) BY ITSELF is sufficient to answer the question, but statement (2) by itself is not;

B   if statement (2) BY ITSELF is sufficient to answer the question, but statement (1) by itself is not;

C   if statements (1) and (2) TAKEN TOGETHER are sufficient to answer the question, even though NEITHER statement BY ITSELF is sufficient;

D   if EITHER statement BY ITSELF is sufficient to answer the question;

E   if statements (1) and (2) TAKEN TOGETHER are NOT sufficient to answer the question, requiring more data pertaining to the problem.

4. In a convenience store in a certain year, the average (arithmetic mean) monthly sales of soda X was n dollars, where $n > 0$. Was this less than, greater than, or equal to the average (arithmetic mean) monthly sales of soda Y, in dollars?

(1) The average (arithmetic mean) monthly sales of soda Y from January to August were n dollars.

(2) The average (arithmetic mean) monthly sales of soda Y from May to December were $2n$ dollars.

5. Mr. Odusote owns two kinds of stock shares: r shares of stock X and r shares of stock Y. Stock X yields an annual dividend of 2%, while stock Y yields an annual dividend of 6%. If Mr. Odusote were to sell all of his shares of stock X and use that money to purchase shares of stock Y, by what percent would his annual dividend increase?

(1) Each share of stock X costs twice as much as each share of stock Y.

(2) Each share of stock Y costs $45.

Explanation: Question 4

4. There are a lot of things that can give you this information; just bear in mind that if the average monthly sales of soda X was n, and since there are 12 months in a year, then $\frac{\text{Total sales of } X}{12} = n$, or Total sales of $X = 12n$.

Statement (1): *Insufficient.* This tells you that the average monthly sales of Y for the first 8 months of the year was n. So the Total sales of Y for the first 8 months of the year was $8n$. However you do not know whether the Total sales of Y for the last 4 months was less than, greater than, or equal to $12n - 8n = 4n$, so you cannot tell whether the average sales of soda Y for the remainder of the year were less than, greater than, or equal to the sales for soda X, and so you cannot determine the relationship between the average sales for the entire year.

Statement (2): *Sufficient.* This tells you that the average monthly sales of Y for the last 8 months of the year were $2n$. That is, in the final 8 months of the year total sales of soda Y was $8 \times 2n = 16n$. This is greater than the entire sales of soda X for the whole year, which we found from the stem. Since you can't make sales of less than zero, no matter how many sales were made of soda Y in the first 4 months of the year, the monthly average for soda Y must be greater than the monthly average for soda X. (B) it is.

Explanation: Question 5

5. A dividend is the money per share given out by the company to the owners of its shares. The dividends for stocks X and Y are 2% and 6%, respectively, so the monetary values of Mr. Odusote's dividends are $(2\%)(x)(r)$ and $(6\%)(y)(r)$. x and y equal the value of one share of stock X and one share of stock Y, respectively. To find the percent increase in the dividend when he sells X and buys Y, you must know the cost of a share of stock X and stock Y, or their relative costs.

Statement (1): *Sufficient.* $x = 2y$. Since stock X costs twice as much per share, he can buy twice as many shares of stock Y, so the new number of shares he owns is $3r$, and the new value of his dividend is $(6\%)(y)(3r)$, or $(18\%)(y)(r)$. The old value was $(2\%)(x)(r) + (6\%)(y)(r)$, which can be expressed as $(2\%)(2y)(r) + (6\%)(y)(r)$, or $(10\%)(y)(r)$. The percent increase in his dividend is just the value of the new dividend (the part) divided by the old dividend (the whole), minus 100%. When you divide the new by the old, y and r cancel out, so all you are left with is numbers for the percent increase. There's no need to do any more math.

Statement (2): *Insufficient.* We know what stock Y costs per share, but not what stock X costs. So there's no way we can make a comparison. (A) is the winner.

DATA SUFFICIENCY—WORD PROBLEMS PRACTICE SET 3

A   if statement (1) BY ITSELF is sufficient to answer the question, but statement (2) by itself is not;

B   if statement (2) BY ITSELF is sufficient to answer the question, but statement (1) by itself is not;

C   if statements (1) and (2) TAKEN TOGETHER are sufficient to answer the question, even though NEITHER statement BY ITSELF is sufficient;

D   if EITHER statement BY ITSELF is sufficient to answer the question;

E   if statements (1) and (2) TAKEN TOGETHER are NOT sufficient to answer the question, requiring more data pertaining to the problem.

6. A certain parking lot contains only cars and vans. If the parking lot has 120 spaces, how many of them are empty?

(1) The ratio of the number of empty spaces to vans to cars in the parking lot is 3:1:8.

(2) The number of spaces occupied by cars is two thirds of the total number of spaces.

7. A man sold only red and blue balloons in only small and large sizes. If he sold a total of 108 balloons, how many were small red balloons?

(1) He sold 35 large balloons.

(2) He sold 25 small blue balloons.

Explanation: Question 6

6. From the stem you know that the cars plus the vans plus the empty spaces equals 120, or $c + v + e = 120$.

Statement (1): You're given the ratio of $e{:}v{:}c$, and since this includes all of the parts that make up the whole, you can relate the parts to the whole. And since you know the whole—the total number of parking spaces—you can find each part, including e.

Statement (2): $c = \left(\dfrac{2}{3}\right) 120$. You can calculate the value of c but it won't help you to find v or e. (A) it is.

Explanation: Question 7

7. There are only four options here: small red, small blue, large red, and large blue.

Statement (1): *Insufficient.* But we do know that $108 - 35 =$ the number of small balloons.

Statement (2): *Insufficient.* We are given no information about small red balloons.

Now look at the statements together. Statement (1) gives the total number of small balloons. Then we can subtract the number of small blue balloons given in statement (2) from that total number of small balloons to get the number of small red balloons. Choice (C) is correct.

That last question brought in the topic of sets, which are involved in the more difficult Data Sufficiency questions. The next few are examples.

DATA SUFFICIENCY—WORD PROBLEMS PRACTICE SET 4

A   if statement (1) BY ITSELF is sufficient to answer the question, but statement (2) by itself is not;

B   if statement (2) BY ITSELF is sufficient to answer the question, but statement (1) by itself is not;

C   if statements (1) and (2) TAKEN TOGETHER are sufficient to answer the question, even though NEITHER statement BY ITSELF is sufficient;

D   if EITHER statement BY ITSELF is sufficient to answer the question;

E   if statements (1) and (2) TAKEN TOGETHER are NOT sufficient to answer the question, requiring more data pertaining to the problem.

8. Twelve jurors must be picked from a pool of n potential jurors. If m of the potential jurors are rejected by the defense counsel and the prosecuting attorney, how many different possible juries could be picked from the remaining potential jurors?

    (1) If one less potential juror had been rejected, it would be possible to create 13 different juries.

    (2) $n = m + 12$

9. Steve took 5 history exams during a semester. Each score was one of the integers 1 through 100 inclusive. What was Steve's median score for these 5 exams?

    (1) Steve's scores on the first 4 exams were 76, 87, 73, and 96, respectively, and Steve's average (arithmetic mean) score on the last 3 exams was 89.

    (2) Steve's score on the first 3 exams were 76, 87, and 73, respectively, and Steve's average (arithmetic mean) on all 5 exams was 86.

Explanation: Question 8

8. We can get at least one equation out of the stem. The number of people who are available to be selected for the jury is $n - m$.

Start with the easier statement. According to statement (2), $n = m + 12$. Therefore, $n - m$, the number of remaining potential jurors, must equal 12. Obviously, only one 12-member jury can be formed from a pool of 12 people, so statement (2) alone is sufficient, and the answer must be either (B) or (D).

At first, statement (1) looks considerably more complicated. However, the GMAT writers would expect you to know that there can be only one size group from which a given number of different 12-member juries could be formed. Therefore, if you had enough time or knew an appropriate formula, you could figure out the value of $n - m + 1$, the hypothetical number of remaining potential jurors given in statement (1). Once you knew the value of $n - m + 1$, you could easily determine the value of $n - m$. And given enough time or the appropriate formula, you could figure out how many different 12-member juries could be formed from a remaining pool of that size. So statement (1) alone is also sufficient, and (D) is correct. Incidentally, although the actual numbers used in this problem are fairly easy to work with, the logic used in the above explanation would enable you to work just as easily with much larger sizes of groups and subgroups.

Explanation: Question 9

9. You're told in the question stem that the 5 exam scores are integers between 1 and 100, inclusive. You must be able to arrange the exam scores in numerical order to answer the question.

Statement (1): This statement provides the first four exam scores and the average of the last three scores. Combining this information, you can find the score for exam 5.

Statement (2): This statement provides the first three exam scores and an average of all five scores. From this, you can find the sum of the scores, for exams 4 and 5. The sum of the scores for exam 4 and exam 5 is 194. Since the exam scores must be between 1 and 100 inclusive, there are a limited number of possible scores

100	94
99	95
98	96
97	97

Each of these pairs of scores would result in the same median, 87. (D) is correct.

DATA SUFFICIENCY—WORD PROBLEMS PRACTICE SET 5

A if statement (1) BY ITSELF is sufficient to answer the question, but statement (2) by itself is not;

B if statement (2) BY ITSELF is sufficient to answer the question, but statement (1) by itself is not;

C if statements (1) and (2) TAKEN TOGETHER are sufficient to answer the question, even though NEITHER statement BY ITSELF is sufficient;

D if EITHER statement BY ITSELF is sufficient to answer the question;

E if statements (1) and (2) TAKEN TOGETHER are NOT sufficient to answer the question, requiring more data pertaining to the problem.

10. Customers can use a manufacturer's coupon and a store coupon to obtain a discount when buying soap powder in a certain store. In one week, 65 percent of customers used the store coupon when purchasing the soap powder, and 35 percent used the manufacturer's coupon. What percent of customers used both the manufacturer's coupon and the store coupon when purchasing the soap powder?

(1) 15 percent of customers used neither coupon when purchasing the soap powder.

(2) 50 percent of customers used the store coupon but not the manufacturer's coupon when purchasing the soap powder.

11. Alan and Betty live in a multi-story apartment building. How many stories does the building have?

(1) There are 3 stories between those on which Alan and Betty live.

(2) There are 9 stories above Alan's floor and 9 stories below Betty's floor.

Explanation: Question 10

10. Don't get confused about what is going on here. There are four types of customers we are dealing with here: those that used no coupon, those that used only the store coupon, those that used only the manufacturer's coupon, and those that used both coupons. Whenever you are dealing with overlapping sets like this, it usually helps to quickly draw a chart, so you can see what is going on:

	Store Coupon Used	Store Coupon Not Used	
Manufacturer's Coupon Used			35%
Manufacturer's Coupon Not Used			65%
	65%	35%	100%

You are looking for the number of customers who used both coupons. Well, if you are able to fill in any of the blank inner squares, you will be able to calculate the value of the square that represents customers who used both coupons, and thus would have sufficiency.

Statement (1) provides that information. Put the 15% that used neither coupon in your chart:

	Store Coupon Used	Store Coupon Not Used	
Manufacturer's Coupon Used			35%
Manufacturer's Coupon Not Used		15%	65%
	65%	35%	100%

If 15% used neither coupon, then 35% – 15% = 20% used the manufacturer's coupon only:

	Store Coupon Used	Store Coupon Not Used	
Manufacturer's Coupon Used		20%	35%
Manufacturer's Coupon Not Used		15%	65%
	65%	35%	100%

So 35% – 20% = 15% used both coupons.

	Store Coupon Used	Store Coupon Not Used	
Manufacturer's Coupon Used	15%	20%	35%
Manufacturer's Coupon Not Used		15%	65%
	65%	35%	100%

(Note that you didn't actually have to do all this calculation: merely knowing that you could is enough to find sufficiency.)

Statement (2): If 65% of customers used the store coupon, and 50% used only the store coupon, then 65% – 50%, or 15%, must be the percent of customers who used both coupons. You could easily prove this by filling in the appropriate blanks in your chart. (D) is correct.

Explanation: Question 11

11. The stem doesn't give us anything we can use, so go right to the statements.

The best way to express the information in statement (1) is to draw a simple diagram. It doesn't even have to be vertical; just use A and B to represent Alan's and Betty's floors, and dashes to represent the other floors. If you express statement (1) as __?__ A __ __ __ B __?__ , you must remember that we aren't told whether A is above B or vice versa. And we certainly aren't told how many floors are on either side of them, so the statement is insufficient.

Statement (2) can be succinctly symbolized as __9__ B and A __9__ . But now we don't know how far apart A and B are, so we can't tell how many floors the building has.

Putting both statements together, it is very tempting to get __9__ B __ __ __ A __9__ . But notice this implies Betty is below Alan, and we are never told that. If Betty is above Alan, then the number of floors below Alan is 5 (9 – 3 – 1) and then number of floors above Betty is also 5. So we could have __5__ A __ __ __ B __5__ . That obviously makes the building shorter, so we don't know how many stories it has. (E) is correct.

An 800 test taker makes sketches or diagrams to focus the information given in the question.

And of course, Data Sufficiency word problems test geometry. (You just knew that would be the case, didn't you?) Here you go; you know the drill.

DATA SUFFICIENCY—WORD PROBLEMS PRACTICE SET 6

A   if statement (1) BY ITSELF is sufficient to answer the question, but statement (2) by itself is not;

B   if statement (2) BY ITSELF is sufficient to answer the question, but statement (1) by itself is not;

C   if statements (1) and (2) TAKEN TOGETHER are sufficient to answer the question, even though NEITHER statement BY ITSELF is sufficient;

D   if EITHER statement BY ITSELF is sufficient to answer the question;

E   if statements (1) and (2) TAKEN TOGETHER are NOT sufficient to answer the question, requiring more data pertaining to the problem.

12. If 25 percent of the surface area of right circular cylinder X is shaded and 40 percent of the surface area of right circular cylinder Y is shaded, what is the area of the shaded portion of right circular cylinder X?

    (1) The area of the shaded portion of the surface area of cylinder X is 75 percent of the area of the shaded portion of the surface area of cylinder Y.

    (2) The surface area of cylinder Y is 10.

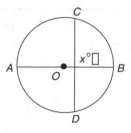

O is the center of the circle.

14. Is the circumference of the circle with center O greater than $2(AB + CD)$?

    (1) $CD = \frac{1}{2} AB$

    (2) $x = 90$

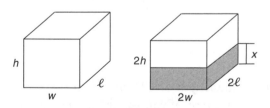

13. Tank A and Tank B are hollow rectangular solids. Tank A is empty and Tank B is filled with water to a depth of x feet. If water is transferred from Tank B to Tank A until either Tank A is completely filled or Tank B is completely empty, will there be any water left in Tank B?

    (1) The area of the base of Tank A is 8 square feet.

    (2) The volume of water in Tank B is 64 cubic feet.

Explanation: Question 12

12. 25% of the surface area of cylinder X is shaded and 40% of the surface area of cylinder Y is shaded. The stem says nothing about the actual surface areas of the two cylinders, so look for this information.

Statement (1): The surface area of the shaded portion of X = 75% of the surface area of the shaded portion of Y. So $(25\%)(x) = (75\%)(40\%)(y)$, where x is the surface area of cylinder X, and y is the surface area of cylinder Y. Now you know exactly how big x is in relation to y, but you don't know the actual size of either cylinder.

Statement (2): Now you know exactly how big y is, but this statement alone doesn't tell you anything about how big x is.

Statements (1) and (2): Now you know both the relative sizes of the surface areas and the actual surface area of Y, so you can find 25% of x, which is the area of the shaded portion of X. (C) it is.

Explanation: Question 13

13. The question is really asking "Will there be any water left in Tank B?" which is the same thing as asking "Is the volume of Tank A less than the volume of water in Tank B?" The volume of a rectangular solid is length $\times$ width $\times$ height, so the volume of Tank A is $\ell \times w \times h$, while the volume of water in Tank B is $2\ell \times 2w \times x$. So the question becomes "Is $2\ell \times 2w \times x > \ell \times w \times h$?" or "Is $4x > h$?"

Statement (1): This tells you that $\ell \times w = 8$, i.e., nothing about x or h.

Statement (2): This tells you that $2\ell \times 2w \times x = 64$, i.e., nothing about h.

Statements (1) and (2): Combining the statements tell you that $x = 2$ but still gives you nothing about h or any relationship between x and h. (E) wins.

Explanation: Question 14

14. The circumference of a circle is equal to πd, and AB is a diameter of the circle. So $2(AB + CD) = 2(d + CD) = 2d + 2CD$. So the question is asking "Is $\pi d > 2d + 2CD$?" Since $\pi \approx$ 3.14, you can write this as "Is $3.14d > 2d + 2CD$?" or "Is $1.14d > 2CD$?" or "Is $0.57d > CD$?" Look for information that will give you the relative lengths of the diameter and CD.

Statement (1): *Sufficient.* Since AB is a diameter, this tells you that $CD = 0.5d$. So $0.57d > CD$ and you can answer "yes" to the question in the stem.

Statement (2): *Insufficient.* This tells you nothing about the length of CD, since you can make it very small or nearly the same length as the diameter, as you can see if you sketch both possibilities:

(A) is correct.

And let's close out our tour of killer Data Sufficiency questions with a mixed set of four. Enjoy!

DATA SUFFICIENCY—WORD PROBLEMS PRACTICE SET 7

A   if statement (1) BY ITSELF is sufficient to answer the question, but statement (2) by itself is not;

B   if statement (2) BY ITSELF is sufficient to answer the question, but statement (1) by itself is not;

C   if statements (1) and (2) TAKEN TOGETHER are sufficient to answer the question, even though NEITHER statement BY ITSELF is sufficient;

D   if EITHER statement BY ITSELF is sufficient to answer the question;

E   if statements (1) and (2) TAKEN TOGETHER are NOT sufficient to answer the question, requiring more data pertaining to the problem.

15. Three children, Alice, Brian, and Chris, have a total of $1.20 between them. Does Chris have the most money?

(1) Alice has 35 cents.
(2) Chris has 40 cents.

16. A certain calculator is able to display at most 10 digits, so that any number with a total of more than 10 digits before and after the decimal point cannot be displayed accurately. If x and y are positive integers less than 1,000, can the result of dividing x by y be displayed accurately on the calculator?

(1) $105 < x < 108$
(2) $3 < y < 6$

17. White and black blocks are stacked in a vertical column so that no two blocks of the same color are adjacent. If there are 247 blocks in the stack, how many white blocks are in the stack?

(1) The top block in the stack is white.
(2) There are 5 white blocks in the 10 blocks at the bottom of the stack.

18. How many times was a fair coin tossed?

(1) If the coin had been tossed 4 times fewer, the probability of getting heads on every toss would have been $\frac{1}{8}$.

(2) When a coin is tossed this number of times, the number of different possible sequences of heads and tails is 128.

Explanation: Question 15

15. The stem tells you that $A + B + C = 120$. You could find the value of C if you had a value for $A + B$, or if you had another two different equations containing A, B, or C such that all three equations are different. Notice that you don't need to solve for C, however, you merely need to find out if it's the largest amount. You may not need three equations to find this information.

Statement (1): If $A = 35$, then $35 + B + C = 120$ or $B + C = 85$. You do not have enough information to tell how big C is, only that it is anywhere from 0 to 85 cents.

Statement (2): If $C = 40$, then $A + B + 40 = 120$, or $A + B = 80$. If $B > A$ then B must be greater than $80 \div 2 = 40$, so $B > C$. Similarly if $A > B$ then A must be greater than 40 and also greater than C. And if $A = B$ then $A = B = 40$, so all three children have 40 cents. So either A or B has the most money, or all three children have the same amount of money. The answer to the question in the stem is "no." (B) wins.

Explanation: Question 16

16. The stem tells you that the numbers displayed will be accurate only if they contain no more than 10 digits. So you can't display anything larger than 9,999,999,999. Smaller numbers with large decimal parts or repeating decimals (e.g., $\frac{1}{3}$) will not be displayed. Since both x and y are less than 1,000, $x \div y$ will fit on the calculator only if the result has sufficiently few decimal places.

Statement (1): This statement tells you that $x = 106$ or 107. Therefore $x \div y$ could fit if $y = 1$, but since neither 106 nor 107 is a multiple of 3, $x \div y$ would not fit if $y = 3$.

Statement (2): This statement tells you that $y = 4$ or 5. Any integer divided by 4 has a maximum of two digits after the decimal (if x is divisible by 4, the decimal part is 0, if $x \div 4$ has a remainder of 1, the decimal part is 0.25, if $x \div 4$ has a remainder of 2, the decimal part is .5, and if $x \div 4$ has a remainder of 3, the decimal part is 0.75). Similarly, any integer divided by 5 divides evenly or has a decimal part of 0.2, 0.4, 0.6, or 0.8. Since x is at most 3 digits long before division (x is a positive integer less than 1,000), and after division it can only have a decimal part at most 2 digits long, $x \div y$ will fit on the calculator. (B) it is.

Explanation: Question 17

17. Think about a stack of three blocks. If no two blocks of the same color are adjacent, then the top and bottom block must be the same color. The same is true of any such stack that contains an odd number of blocks, including the stack of 247 described in this problem. If you start counting at either end of the stack, any even number of blocks will contain equal numbers of white and black blocks. But since the top and bottom blocks are the same color, there must be one more block of that color than there are blocks of the other color. In a 247-block stack, there would be 124 blocks of the color that starts and ends the stack and only 123 blocks of the other color.

Statement (1) tells you the color of the end block, so you know that there must be 124 white blocks in the stack.

Statement (2) alone is not helpful, because the 5 white blocks in the first 10 could be either the odd- or even-numbered blocks. (A) is correct.

Explanation: Question 18

18. The question stem gives no information about how many times the coin was tossed, so go right to the statements.

Statement (1) says that if the coin had been tossed 4 times fewer, the probability of getting heads on each toss would have been $\frac{1}{8}$. Whenever a coin is tossed, the probability of getting heads is $\frac{1}{2}$. If a coin is tossed n times, the probability of heads each time is $\left(\frac{1}{2}\right)^n$. Here, if t is the number of times the coin was tossed, then $\left(\frac{1}{2}\right)^{t-4} = \frac{1}{8}$, from which the value of t can be found. Statement (1) is sufficient. Eliminate choices (B), (C), and (E).

Although you don't need to find t, let's just mention that $t = 7$.

Now look at statement (2). Each time a coin is tossed, there are 2 possible outcomes, heads or tails. If a coin is tossed t times where t is a positive integer, the number of possible sequences is $2 \times 2 \times 2... \times 2$, where there are t factors of 2. In other words, there are 2^t possible sequences. Since there are 128 possible sequences here, $2^t = 128$, and this equation can be solved for t. Statement (2) is sufficient. Choice (D) is correct.

An 800 test taker thinks sufficiently, working only to determine if a Data Sufficiency question can be answered—not to actually answer it.

What if there was a guide that guaranteed you a higher score?

With Kaplan it's guaranteed.